The contributors to this volume address questions central to the development and survival of democratic rule. Brought together under the auspices of a Nobel Symposium on democracy, leading experts in the field examine historical experiences, social and cultural problems, economic development, constitutional issues, the impact of globalization, and the prospects for promoting democratic government. The coverage of the book is global, and the approach is multidisciplinary, providing a unique perspective from leading historians, political scientists, economists, and sociologists. The chapters thus provide an excellent survey of different facets of, and approaches to, democracy, including such fundamental issues as the nature of democratic citizenship, and its prevalence around the world; the relationship between economic development and the progress of democracy; and the influence of international interdependence on sovereignty and democratic accountability.

Democracy's victory and crisis

Democracy's victory and crisis
Nobel Symposium No. 93

Edited by
Axel Hadenius
Uppsala University

CAMBRIDGE
UNIVERSITY PRESS

University Printing House, Cambridge CB2 8BS, United Kingdom

Cambridge University Press is part of the University of Cambridge.

It furthers the University's mission by disseminating knowledge in the pursuit of
education, learning and research at the highest international levels of excellence.

www.cambridge.org
Information on this title: www.cambridge.org/9780521573115

© Cambridge University Press 1997

This publication is in copyright. Subject to statutory exception
and to the provisions of relevant collective licensing agreements,
no reproduction of any part may take place without the written
permission of Cambridge University Press.

First published 1997

A catalogue record for this publication is available from the British Library

Library of Congress Cataloguing in Publication data
Nobel Symposium (93rd: 1994: Uppsala, Sweden)
   Democracy's victory and crisis: Nobel symposium no. 93 / edited
by Axel Hadenius   p.   cm.
    Includes index.
    ISBN 0 521 57311 4 (hbk.). – ISBN 0 521 57583 4 (pbk.).
    1. Democracy – Congresses.   2. Economic development – Congresses.
   3. World politics – 1989 – Congresses.   I. Hadenius, Axel, 1945– .
   II. Addi, Lahouari, 1949– . III. Title.
JC421. N63   1997
321.8 – dc20   96–16178 CIP

ISBN 978-0-521-57311-5 Hardback
ISBN 978-0-521-57583-6 Paperback

Cambridge University Press has no responsibility for the persistence or accuracy of
URLs for external or third-party internet websites referred to in this publication,
and does not guarantee that any content on such websites is, or will remain, accurate
or appropriate.

Contents

List of contributors	*page* ix	
Acknowledgments	x	
1	Victory and crisis: introduction	1
	AXEL HADENIUS	

Part 1 Historical perspectives

2	The new democracies in crisis in interwar Europe	15
	FRITZ STERN	

Part 2 Social and cultural aspects

3	Democracy in America at century's end	27
	ROBERT D. PUTNAM	
4	On sources of social and political conflicts in follower democracies	71
	ATUL KOHLI	
5	Micro-aspects of democratic theory: what makes for the deliberative competence of citizens	81
	CLAUS OFFE	
6	Political Islam and democracy: the case of Algeria	105
	LAHOUARI ADDI	

Part 3 Constitutional questions

7	Ways of constitution-making	123
	JON ELSTER	

viii *Contents*

8   Back to democratic basics: who really practices majority rule?   143
AREND LIJPHART

Part 4 Democracy and development

9   Democracy and development   163
ADAM PRZEWORSKI AND FERNANDO LIMONGI

10   Freedom and economic growth: a virtuous cycle?   195
SURJIT S. BHALLA

11   Democratization and administration   242
GÖRAN HYDÉN

Part 5 Democracy and globalization

12   Globalization, sovereignty, and democracy   263
JAGDISH BHAGWATI

13   Dangerous liaisons: the interface of globalization and democracy   282
CLAUDE AKE

14   Exploring the problematic triumph of liberal democracy and concluding with a modest proposal for improving its international impact   297
PHILIPPE C. SCHMITTER

Part 6 Promoting democracy

15   Promoting democracy in the 1990s: actors, instruments, and issues   311
LARRY DIAMOND

16   Can established democracies nurture democracy abroad? Lessons from Africa   371
JOEL D. BARKAN

17   Some thoughts on the victory and future of democracy   404
JUAN J. LINZ

Index   427

Contributors

LAHOUARI ADDI University of Oran (Algiers) and L'Institut d'Etudes Politiques de Lyon

CLAUDE AKE (deceased) formerly of Centre for Advanced Social Sciences, Port Harcourt, Nigeria

JOEL D. BARKAN University of Iowa

JAGDISH BHAGWATI Columbia University

SURJIT S. BHALLA Deutsche Bank AG, New York

LARRY DIAMOND Hoover Institution, Stanford University

JON ELSTER University of Chicago and University of Oslo

AXEL HADENIUS Uppsala University

GÖRAN HYDÉN University of Florida at Gainesville

ATUL KOHLI Princeton University

AREND LIJPHART University of California, San Diego

FERNANDO LIMONGI University of Sao Paulo

JUAN J. LINZ Yale University

CLAUS OFFE Humboldt-Universität zu Berlin

ADAM PRZEWORSKI New York University

ROBERT D. PUTNAM Harvard University

PHILIPPE C. SCHMITTER Stanford University

FRITZ STERN Columbia University

Acknowledgments

This volume is the result of a Nobel Symposium on democracy's victory and crisis, held at Uppsala University in August 27–30, 1994 (Nobel Symposium No. 93). It was arranged by an Organization Committee composed of Partha Dasgupta, Cambridge University, Jon Elster, University of Chicago and University of Oslo, Axel Hadenius (Coordinator), Uppsala University, Daniel Tarschys, University of Stockholm, and Carl Tham, SIDA. Besides this group, the following persons took part in the Symposium: Bruce Ackerman, Yale University, Lahouari Addi, Princeton University, Claude Ake, Center for Advanced Social Sciences, Nigeria, Peter Anyang' Nyong'o, African Association of Political Science, Kenneth Arrow, Stanford University, Joel D. Barkan, University of Iowa, Jagdish Bhagwati, Columbia University, Surjit S. Bhalla, Deutsche Bank AG, New York, Larry Diamond, Hoover Institution, Stanford, Carol Gould, Stevens Institute of Technology, Sverker Gustavsson, Uppsala University, Göran Hydén, University of Florida, Terry Lynn Karl, Stanford University, Atul Kohli, Princeton University, Leif Lewin, Uppsala University, Arend Lijphart, University of California, Folke Lindahl, Michigan State University, Juan J. Linz, Yale University, Seymour M. Lipset, George Mason University, Claus Offe, Humboldt-Universität zu Berlin, Carole Pateman, University of California, Adam Przeworski, New York University, Robert D. Putnam, Harvard University, Giovanni Sartori, Columbia University, Philippe C. Schmitter, Stanford University, Amartya Sen, Harvard University, Lilia Shevtsóva, Russian Academy of Science, Bengt Sāve-Sōderbergh, IDEA, Georg Sörensen, Aarhus University, Fritz Stern, Columbia University, Laurence Whitehead, Oxford University, Öyvind Österud, University of Oslo.

Indispensable assistance in all kinds of arrangements making the Symposium possible, was rendered by Maria Edin. Important support was also provided by Alexander Davidson, Laila Grandin, Per Nordlund, Per Strand, Ela Stasiewicz, Gudrun Tuoremaa, and Sten Widmalm.

The Symposium was sponsored by the Nobel Foundation through its Nobel Symposium Fund. Some additional funding was offered by SIDA.

A. H.

1 Victory and crisis: introduction

Axel Hadenius

In recent decades, unmistakable advances have been made in the area of political democracy. During the second half of the 1970s, decisive changes in a democratic direction took place in Spain and in other Mediterranean countries. Authoritarian rule has not, since then, been represented on the political map of Western Europe. Similar developments, though less farreaching, have occurred in Latin America. The dictatorial regimes (usually of a military type), which had dominated the continent for so long, were to a large extent swept away during the 1980s. In Eastern Europe, the existing wall of authoritarianism crumbled even faster. Within the course of little more than a year, starting in 1989, Communist one-party regimes have fallen from the Baltic in the north to the Adriatic in the south. And immediately following this, fundamental political changes took place in the Soviet Union, homeland of the Communist system.

Through the inspiration of these events – but also due to internal problems – a wave of political change was released in Africa, primarily in the sub-Saharan region. One-party and military regimes had long been the dominant pattern there. Yet today, after more than five years of political complications, not a single one-party state remains in this region. Many military governments have also had to leave the scene, but not all, as the striking example of Nigeria shows. Some new military regimes have, furthermore, appeared recently. And several countries are torn by civil war and political anarchy. Notwithstanding this somewhat fragmented picture one must conclude – not the least in view of events in South Africa – that the principles of pluralism and political equality have made significant gains on the African continent in recent years.

The region least affected by the new political tendencies is the Middle East and North Africa. The failed political opening in Algeria seems to have paralyzed leaders in most of these countries. Several Asian states also display a pronounced aversion to political reform. China and Indonesia may be cited as examples. On the other hand, however,

2   *Axel Hadenius*

several countries in this region have introduced significant democratic improvements.

The principles of democratic government, accordingly, have been triumphing. Almost half the states in the world (perhaps some 40 percent) may be classified today as democratic in the main, inasmuch as they uphold basic political rights. Compared with the conditions of only a decade ago, this amounts to genuine progress. If we go back another ten or fifteen years, moreover, the difference is remarkable. Yet it is important, in spite of the advance of democracy on the map, to draw attention to the crisis in terms of content afflicting democratic government. In many countries which have gone through political reform, democratic institutions are for the most part a surface phenomenon inasmuch as political life is still dominated by clientilistic structures and by rule by political bosses in conjunction with a notably low rate of political participation. The institutions of local and civic democracy, which since the time of Tocqueville have been regarded as the foundation of a democratic state, are often conspicuous by their absence. In addition, the economic and social crises from which many countries suffer are continuing or even worsening. Such well-known administrative abuses as corruption, meanwhile, continue as usual. Besides, we see in many instances signs of growing ethnic and religious polarization – a development that can only undermine the spirit of tolerance and compromise on which democratic government depends. In other words, many of the circumstances which have contributed to the fall of democracy in the past seem still to prevail in many places.

And what is more, the exercise of democracy in the old-established democracies can hardly be judged as inspiring. Elections and opinion surveys convey a clear message in this regard. Popular contempt of political representatives and institutions is growing; extremist parties and anti-political populists are gaining in support. New political giants by the name of Le Pen and Berlusconi bear witness of that. The party systems of Western Europe and other established democracies, which for so long had remained stable, seem now to be breaking up. An exceptionally clear illustration of this may be seen in the upheavals produced by recent elections in Canada, Italy, and Japan. In a similar way, radical constitutional changes – Italy, for instance, has switched from proportional to majority elections, while New Zealand has done just the opposite – reveal a popular resentment of long-established institutional forms. There was earlier talk of a political crisis resulting from excessive demands on the system by the citizens. (This implied, interestingly enough, a kind of overbelief in democracy's ability to perform.) We face the opposite situation today. Faith in the capacity of

Victory and crisis: introduction

democratic institutions is weak, it seems, and citizens are turning their back on politics. Scholars speak of a moral crisis of democracy (Maier 1994).

In many ways, the situation seems similar to that prevailing in the early 1930s, when Herbert Tingsten, the prominent Swedish political scientist, wrote his book *Demokratins seger och kris – Democracy's Victory and Crisis* – which has given its name to the Nobel Symposium on Democracy held in Uppsala in August 1994. Tingsten's study thoroughly documents the democratic progress that had previously been achieved, and presents as well – in a most illuminating manner – the advancing anti-democratic movements of the time. Naturally, however, the situation of sixty years ago differs from the one prevailing today in significant respects. Stable democracies are today much more numerous, and they are also, of course, generally of a better vintage. In contrast to the case in the early 1930s, moreover, no programmatic anti-democratic ideologies (with a broad appeal, at any rate) can be found on the political market today. Today's crisis of democracy seems rather to manifest itself in a widespread suspicion of political ideologies of the grander nature.

Another difference from the past has to do with changes on the international level. Globalization and growing interdependence create new conditions for the right of national self-determination. These tendencies may contribute to support, as well as limiting, democratic development.

It was for the purpose of exploring these questions – some old and familiar, others of a more modern character – that the Nobel Foundation took the initiative for a symposium on the problems of democracy. This volume contains a selection of the papers presented there.

The democratic practices prevailing today are in many ways stamped, of course, by the contingencies of historical background. The political institutions of a given country – and the norms associated with them – are often conditioned to a decisive degree by the circumstances which earlier had prevailed. Douglass North (1990: 94) terms this "path dependency." The idea is that we are bound, when creating new institutions, by the social setting we inherit. By scrutinizing the historical background, then, we can deepen our understanding of the present state of affairs. Yet we are not, of course, bound by our history altogether; by means of political action, we can sometimes steer developments down other paths. Even in such a process of political engineering, however, the weight of history is normally of significance. The rational actor learns from earlier examples, and analyzes carefully which previous

4   *Axel Hadenius*

"new paths" led to success, and which issued rather in failure.[1] In this way, then, past experiences furnish a source of critique and of diffusion.

Fritz Stern opens this volume with a chapter that can be read to advantage from both a determinist and an activist perspective. He examines the failure of democracy between the wars, in the Weimar Republic in particular, and stresses the difficulty of establishing democratic institutions in the midst of severe economic hardship (a predicament afflicting many parts of the world today). Popular frustration over mounting economic and social difficulties turns to suspicion of, indifference towards, or even hatred for the new political order. Most fateful of all, however, is the lack of a basic system of norms – a democratic culture – in support of the new institutions. These norms include the willingness to compromise, respect for other opinions, and reconciliation in the face of past conflicts. Such a political culture did not develop in Weimar Germany, and thus the institutions of democracy fell to the ground.

A classical subject of debate within political and social science concerns how to create that foundation for democracy which consists of a political culture marked by solidarity, mutual understanding, and tolerance for contrary opinions. It was long believed that such a spirit of unity and brotherhood was possible only in restricted political units based on small communities. According to Ibn Khaldun, for instance, genuine popular solidarity – and a civic spirit based thereupon – could only be created in traditional, tribally-based social formations. Rousseau took a similar view, although the special object of his affection was the city-state. Yet it has subsequently proved possible to establish essentially democratic systems of government within the much larger and more heterogeneous units embraced by the nation-states. The first to make this observation, and to perceive the implications thereof, was Tocqueville. He lay great stress, in his study of the young American democracy, on the role of the unique political culture – the system of popular norms – in maintaining democracy. The mores of solidarity, tolerance, and devotion to public affairs were linked, as he saw it, to the prevailing organizational and institutional structures: the vital system of local self-rule and the developed network of voluntary associations, in which traditions of democratic cooperation had been developed over a long period of time. He experienced the United States in this respect as the opposite of his native France, a country marked by great political centralization and a weak civil society. Tocqueville's theoretical perspective emphasizes, on the one hand, the connection between the level of social self-organization and the development of political norms, and, on the other hand, the link between both of these elements and the institutional structure of the state; these state structures may at some times further

Victory and crisis: introduction

and at other times frustrate the development of an active, democracy-generating civil society.[2]

Proceeding from the work of Tocqueville, Robert Putnam asks how the social networks of American society – and the norms associated with them – have fared during the century and a half since the Frenchman's visit. His answer is that, in recent years, traditional organizational activities of virtually all kinds have markedly declined. The rate of political participation has also fallen steadily. The confidence in which citizens hold politicians (and indeed each other) has diminished as well. Putnam relates the linkage between these phenomena – which constitutes the core of his analysis – to a series of changes in modern ways of life. He further assumes that certain institutional changes may have contributed to eroding traditional contact networks.

While institutions receive glancing attention in Putnam's look at American society, they are the central object of study in Atul Kohli's analysis of the problems faced by democracy in developing countries. In the new democracies, Kohli contends, political leaders have an incentive to weaken institutions that can restrain their exercise of power. By undermining such institutions, these leaders can establish more personalist and patrimonial systems of rule. The result is an increased tendency towards centralization and elitism in political life – a tendency which is especially pronounced in the many countries in which state intervention in social affairs has been marked. Political organizing thus becomes a question of mobilization from above, often on the basis of populist and polarizing appeals. The result is a weak civil society, and an exacerbation of suspicion and conflict between different population groups.

Claus Offe, for his part, asks how "deliberative competence" can be promoted among citizens. His objective is a political culture of fellowship and civic virtue. Offe affirms a left-liberal, republican tradition, which he contrasts to a libertarian approach. He urges that we strive to create such associational and institutional conditions as may be assumed to foster "good" citizens, and argues that this need not involve falling into the paternalist trap. He stresses, however, that such associations must meet two critical conditions: they must be open to all citizens, and they must be democratic in their internal arrangements. Offe deems it likely that, if these conditions are fulfilled, popular participation in organizational life will cultivate a democratic citizenship competence.

The prospects for developing a democratic system of norms is also a main theme of Lahouari Addi's chapter on political Islam. This militant movement has emerged as the most effective rival today to the principles of liberal democracy. The Islamists, Addi stresses, oppose the idea of

6   *Axel Hadenius*

popular sovereignty. As they see it, political power should be exercised through the interpretation and application of divine law. For the same reason, they are disinclined to accept the free expression of oppositional political views. Islamists thus oppose the political principles of equality and pluralism – they do not embrace, that is, the notion of political power as a vacant seat. At bottom, many Islamists fear (not without reason) that political democracy would result in a relaxation of traditional social and religious rules. Addi argues, however, that democratization cannot take place in Muslim countries against the will of political Islam. For this movement is based in deeply rooted popular notions, and its strength today derives from the organized expression it furnishes for the great frustration – born of economic and social causes – characterizing large parts of the Muslim world. It will not help matters, moreover, to try to hinder this movement until it has changed its basic ideological stance in the direction of liberal democracy. For in that case we will have to wait long – needlessly long. If, on the other hand, free and open elections are held, the principles of popular sovereignty and pluralism will – through practice – win ever more adherents in the population. Thus deprived of the fertile soil that now nourishes it, Islamism, in its present form, will lose its legitimacy, and be replaced by democratically minded political currents.

A likewise time-honored question is that concerning the effects of constitutional structures on democracy's manner of functioning. A great deal has certainly been written in this area,[3] yet Jon Elster calls our attention, in his contribution to this volume, to an aspect of this question which has largely escaped the attention of scholars: the constitution-making process itself. Constitutions are best framed, according to Elster, in the course of calm and rational discussions that focus on the long-term consequences for political life. Unfortunately, however, constitutions are typically written in the midst of turbulent events, and immediate partisan interests are usually those weighing most heavily. No simple way out of this paradox presents itself, in Elster's view.

Arend Lijphart takes up, in his chapter, a question once put by John Stuart Mill, namely how best to achieve governments broadly representative of the electorate (a quality that strengthens democracy, it is thought). Lijphart assumes, as did Mill, that this goal is best realized with the method of proportional representation. He tests this proposition by investigating the extent to which, in twenty-one countries during the postwar period, minimal winning cabinets (in contrast to oversized cabinets) have been formed. After reviewing several associated methodological problems, Lijphart finds that the hypothesis stated enjoys strong support. He concludes his chapter, however, with a dis-

Victory and crisis: introduction 7

cussion of a question that remains open: how best to specify, in empirical terms, the central theoretical issue – the problem of power-sharing.

Few would seem to dispute today that democracy is the best form of government seen from the standpoint of principle, and that the political rights it embodies find their justification above all in the worth they possess in themselves. But this does not mean that the democratic system is always the most efficient one, as far as certain practical purposes are concerned. Indeed, for a long time the view was widely held that democracy is less suited than authoritarian methods of rule for the promotion of economic development. The poor nations are faced with a trade-off, it was thought: they must make a cruel choice between democracy and rapid economic expansion. As Adam Przeworski and Fernando Limongi show in their chapter, this approach was based on the view that economic progress depends first and foremost on investments, and that these can only be generated to a sufficient degree when the political regime – in the manner of dictatorships – is isolated from popular pressures (and thus from demands for consumption). In later years, however, this theory has come under increasing question. Proponents of the opposite thesis have claimed that, in fact, democracy increases the rationality of economic decision making. This is partly because politicians and bureaucrats in a democracy are exposed to greater public inspection and control, and partly because the general flow of information in society is less restricted. Some scholars claim further that democracies are better able to offer predictable and stable conditions for entrepreneurs than are their authoritarian counterparts. Which side in this debate is right, if either? The results of two studies investigating this question are presented in this book. These studies are differently structured, and reach contrasting conclusions as well. In the one, Przeworski looks at 139 countries in the period between 1950 and 1990. He classifies states dichotomously – as democratic and non-democratic – on the basis of electoral criteria solely. His finding is that no palpable relation may be observed between democracy, on the one hand, and economic success or failure, on the other.

This conclusion – the most common one in recent empirical investigations of this subject – contrasts with the results presented by Surjit Bhalla. Bhalla's model assumes that both political and economic freedom generate growth. He measures political freedom (democracy) on a scale including both political liberties (judged largely on the basis of electoral criteria) and civil liberties (freedom of assembly, expression, and the like). For ascertaining the degree of economic freedom, he applies several indices of economic openness. Upon examining the experiences of more than ninety countries from 1973 to 1992, Bhalla

8   *Axel Hadenius*

finds that the results "are strongly in favor of the proposition that political and civil liberties, and economic freedom, help improve economic performance." Both Przeworski and Bhalla, in other words, find the trade-off theory mentioned above to be wanting. Only Bhalla, however, furnishes support for the proposition that, rather than a cruel choice between democracy and growth, a pleasant companionship between the two may be observed instead.

Göran Hydén's chapter addresses the influence of institutional structures on democratic development. It explores the structure of the state administration, focusing especially on conditions in Africa. In the states created after national independence, popular educational levels were low, and the system of parties and organizations was underdeveloped. The result was a strikingly elitist pattern of decision-making, and a pronounced societal dependence on the state. This tendency was further stimulated by the belief – very strong at the time – in the capacity of the state to serve as the engine of economic development. The result was a large and unwieldy state apparatus characterized by centralized forms of decision-making. On account of its corruption, mismanagement, and general inefficiency, this apparatus sooner hindered than promoted economic development, and it furnished, furthermore, a poor soil for democratic progress. The African state exhibited institutional patterns of a patrimonialist nature: political offices were used to advance personal and particularist interests, and the debate, openness, and popular participation that encourage democracy were conspicuous by their absence. It became, as Hydén puts it, a non-policy government focused on distributing spoils and maintaining the power of the ruling elite. The regime changes of recent years in the direction of increased political pluralism have not altered these conditions in any palpable way. Patrimonialism and centralism – which tend to go hand in hand – prevail still, with the consequence that political life is marked by a closed and arbitrary rule, and by a striking lack of legitimacy in the eyes of the public. In order to change this state of affairs, the author argues, it is necessary to establish a new form of aid administration. International assistance must be channeled through funds – controlled by representatives for donors and local organizations – independent of regimes in the recipient countries. Establishing such units outside the control of the state is requisite to the creation of an administrative order in which officials are held responsible and rules are followed and which is open and decentralized. Only such an administrative order can encourage managerial professionalism and rationality, and democratic development as well.

As mentioned earlier, globalization put the problems of democracy

Victory and crisis: introduction

in a new light. What is, indeed, meant by democracy in an international context? Are the principles of democracy relevant to the political interchange of states, and if so, how? In his contribution to this collection, Philippe Schmitter presents the major viewpoints in this debate. On the one hand, liberal internationalism emphasizes – as it has since the days of Kant – that democracy is a question of the internal arrangements of individual states. The intercourse of states should be regulated by international legal rules (for trade, etc.) and through the usual diplomatic channels. We find the opposite approach in what nowadays usually goes by the name of federalism. This is a constitutional program for establishing democratically legitimate supranational structures of decision making, which, in typical federal fashion, are to embody some sort of compromise between the one-person-one-vote and the one-state-one-vote principles. (Kelsen is one of the prominent theoreticians here.) Between these two extremes, finally, we find a more pragmatic position which we can call functionalism. This calls for the creation of particular legal arrangements, and supranational organs associated therewith, in certain special areas; especially those of an apolitical and professional nature.

Liberal internationalism finds an exponent in Jagdish Bhagwati. He argues that globalization (in the form of deepened economic integration) promotes development and enhances welfare, and thus improves the prospects for maintaining and extending democracy. Claude Ake, by contrast, is critical of the classical liberal outlook. The global market under international law, which liberal theorists champion, exacerbates imbalances in international power relations. It leads, in particular, to a yet further marginalization of economically weaker countries. Ake does not, however, view this as an argument for a supranational democratic federalism. For as he sees it, democracy is first and foremost suited for application at the level of the nation-state. The problem, however, is that popular influence at that level is weak already – a dilemma which is only sharpened by technical and economic globalization.

A closely related question (and also one bearing on international affairs) concerns whether or not it is possible for "the outside world" to promote democracy in individual countries, and if so by what means. Two of the chapters in the last section of the book address themselves to this question. Larry Diamond reviews the actors – government authorities, public organizations, private foundations – engaged in supporting democracy internationally, and inspects the considerable variety of political instruments and strategies employed. He maintains that pressures from without can in fact produce results, if the requisite will and resolution are present. Unfortunately, however, leading international

10   *Axel Hadenius*

actors sometimes lack this will – especially when they have other interests than just democracy to defend. International efforts in support of democracy often suffer, moreover, from a striking lack of coordination. Diamond proposes therefore that new international institutions be created for the purpose of coordinating such efforts.

Joel Barkan begins his chapter with a look at efforts by different countries to promote democracy. He detects, in particular, some distinct differences between the United States and Europe regarding the choice of target area. Drawing on studies done in this field, and his own experiences besides – as democracy and governance advisor for the United States Agency for International Development (USAID) in Africa – he offers some recommendations for achieving better results. He stresses, like Diamond, the importance of will: external actors must give high priority in their aid and foreign policies to furthering democracy, and they must pursue this objective with clarity, consistency, and in a coordinated manner. In addition, however, he emphasizes the critical importance of corresponding efforts within the receiving countries: if the efforts from without are to have any impact, they must be matched by developments from within. He therefore calls for a long-term strategy aimed at building up institutions and organizations capable of laying the foundations for a democratic culture. For as Barkan points out, the best efforts of outside donors are unlikely to have any impact over the long term if they are not linked to, and followed up by, a domestic democratic dynamic. Success or failure in this matter is, ultimately, a home-grown phenomenon. Or otherwise expressed: a democracy cannot be established without democratically minded citizens.

This insight underscores a message conveyed by John Stuart Mill, namely that democratic institutions depend for their performance upon the readiness of the people to fight for them when they are endangered. If too little valued, the popular mood of government is unlikely to take hold, and if it does, it will in all probability result in a failure (Mill 1991: 83). That in turn reminds us, in a broader sense, of a lesson which indeed has been learned many times before – that the victory of democracy cannot be achieved unless its essential fundaments are in place.

Some of these essential conditions of democracy are notified by Juan Linz in the final chapter of the volume, which at the same time addresses the general theme of the Nobel Symposium. Linz gives a survey of both the achievements and the current problems of democracy in various continents, and provides a broad account of the critical prerequisites of democratic government. One of his points, which links up with Kohli's argument, is that the newly established democracies have to function under different conditions than the old ones. Due to the media development, which has reached out to virtually all parts of the globe (especially the broadcast media), people are nowadays much more well informed, and thus more rational as voters, but also less inclined to be enrolled in party activities, because of the generally weakened linkages between parties and social groups. This will affect the operation of the parties as well as the general political climate. The vertical democratic cleavage, between voters and representatives, will be more accentuated to the extent that politicians will be held accountable more firmly than before, whereas the horizontal cleavage, between parties and groups, will be relaxed. On the other hand, more scope will be provided for political entrepreneurs, not least for political outsiders, as political life will be more marked by populism and plebiscitarian appeals. In many of his works, Linz has called attention to the role of the political leadership for the functioning of democratic government. Also in this chapter, he discusses a number of conditions signifying the quality of the "political class," but he also makes the point that this quality is in turn determined by the quality of the electorate (e.g., the popular "demand" for bad leadership) – a question which could be traced back to the issues of deliberative competence and good citizenship, which are addressed in particular in this volume by Offe.

In Linz's judgment it is important to recognize the unique contributions to a better society that political democracy (and only this mode of government) has proved capable of making: the peaceful solution of conflicts, the introduction of a fundamental principle of equality among citizens, the whole range of civil liberties, limits to the execution of power, etc. But even if these qualities are sometimes far from being fully materialized – as popular rule has in many places been marked by serious imperfections – there is no reason to regard these forms of governments mainly as failures. As Linz remarks, even bad democracies are better than authoritarian rule or political chaos since they contain a potential for gradual, peaceful improvements.

Despite the many shortcomings signifying the practice of political democracy, there may be light in the tunnel. Democratic government seems to evolve in a process of learning by doing: by people experiencing and being accustomed to the special institutions and the norms of behaviour associated with the principles of popular rule. In other words: it is by addressing and working out the crises of democracy that we may eventually lay the ground for the victory of this form of government.

NOTES

1 Ostrom (1990) gives many illuminating examples of this.
2 Larry Siedentop provides an excellent synopsis in *Tocqueville* (1994).
3 For a contemporary overview, see Sartori (1994).

12   *Axel Hadenius*

REFERENCES

Maier, Charles S. 1994. "The moral crisis of democracy," *Foreign Affairs* 73 no. 4: 48–64.
Mill, John Stuart. 1991. *Considerations on Representative Government*. Buffalo, N.Y.: Prometheus Books.
North, Douglass C. 1990. *Institutions, Institutional Change and Economic Performance*. Cambridge: Cambridge University Press.
Ostrom, Elinor. 1990. *Governing the Commons. The Evolution of Institutions for Collective Action*. Cambridge: Cambridge University Press.
Sartori, Giovanni. 1994. *Comparative Constitutional Engineering. An Inquiry into Structures, Incentives and Outcomes*. London: Macmillan.
Siedentop, Larry. 1994. *Tocqueville*. Oxford: Oxford University Press.

Part 1

Historical perspectives

2 The new democracies in crisis in interwar Europe

Fritz Stern

I feel out of place here: I do not believe that historians should be much given to theory or to the propounding of lessons. Moreover, a specialist in German history may not be the best person to talk of democracy though perhaps pronounced failure and recent success in that country do allow for some general remarks on a vast subject.

In 1913, the eleventh edition of the *Encyclopaedia Britannica*, the most respected compendium of its kind, had a one-column entry under "democracy," dealing principally with democracy in ancient times. In 1929, the Oxford philosopher A. D. Lindsay began his splendid book *The Essentials of Democracy* thus: "We are at the present time passing through a certain disillusionment about democracy" – a British understatement on the eve of the disastrous defeats of democracy (Lindsay 1951: 7).

I would suggest it was the Great War that saw the elevation of democracy into a universal ideal. Representative governments and liberal constitutions had existed before and indeed had been ideals in much of Europe in the nineteenth century. And democratic doctrine and practices had existed before, though it is doubtful that prewar Britain could have been called a democracy. But during the war there developed an Anglo-American assumption that democracy was not just the only legitimate form of government but alone held out the promise of peace, freedom, and human dignity. Rhetoric burdened reality, and as Lindsay pointed out: "We have suffered in the past from making democracy into a dogma, in the sense of thinking of it as something magical, exempt from the ordinary laws which govern human nature" (Lindsay 1951: 74).

The dogmas of the Wilsonian era envisioned popular sovereignty linked to national self-determination, universal suffrage, the intermediary role of political parties, the alternation between government and opposition, majority rule and minority rights. The expectations included the rule of law and equality before the law – with some notions of a greater measure of equality in other realms as well. The unspoken

16   *Fritz Stern*

assumption of the time was that democracy represented liberalism legitimated by mass or popular participation in government. What seemed to have been forgotten was that democratic rule could also threaten or pervert liberal values and practices – a danger that John Stuart Mill and Tocqueville had understood so clearly.

Democracy as an ideal was made popular during the Great War: President Wilson and American Progressives (as well as some English liberals) had a genuine faith that the triumph of democracy would redeem the horrors and sacrifices of the war and would ensure a lasting peace. It gave the Allies then an ideological justification for the unprecedented slaughter. Especially after the fateful year 1917, after America's entry into the war and the Russian revolutions, the much-touted ideal of democracy gave the Allies the means of distinguishing their cause from that of imperial autocracies and Prussian militarism. At the same time on the other side of the trenches, German writers and politicians denounced democracy as bourgeois hypocrisy and insisted that their own system of politics was morally and pragmatically superior. Thomas Mann's *Confessions of an Unpolitical Man* is but the best-known example of this sense.

We should note an enduring paradox: President Wilson and American Progressives believed that the United States had a mission – to promote democracy everywhere – yet they also believed in American exceptionalism. The latter hardly justified the faith in the exportability of democracy. Moreover, they gave inadequate thought to the securing of democratic practices and the establishment of political cultures that are democratic. These same American Progressives were very much aware of the deficiencies of American democracy, understood the economic inequalities that disfigured their own country, and fought the power of massive and uncontrolled wealth.

During the Great War the powers of the state vastly increased: as conscriptor of men and labor, as operator of the economy, as censor and educator. This rapid extension of state authority enhanced the need for all governments to assure their legitimacy, but even the governments that already had some democratic characteristics were transmuted during the war into virtual dictatorships that aimed at the regimentation of thought as well. Even in the United States, the government's crusade for democracy put its own freedoms in jeopardy. One example must suffice. In September 1918, the *New York World* warned against the government's attempt "to undertake the Prussianization of American public opinion" (Knock 1992: 160). In the end, that same public opinion, and electoral politics generally, subverted hopes for a wise or Wilsonian peace: in the United States prominent Republicans, including

Crisis in interwar Europe

Theodore Roosevelt, demanded not an armistice but "unconditional surrender," the Republicans trounced Wilson in the Congressional elections of 1918, and ultimately rejected the League of Nations. In Britain Lloyd George, having incited public opinion against "the Huns," demanded a harsh and exacting peace at Versailles.

The project "to make the world safe for democracy" presupposed a functioning international order, the guardian of which was to be the League of Nations. But France's fears of Germany, and nationalist passions in both Allied and defeated countries, did not allow for a peace that would "end all wars" or make the world safe for democracy. On the other hand, the collapse of the old autocracies did indeed enable democratic regimes to begin to form, and the hope for national self-determination made democracy possible *and* necessary – precisely because within each new, nominally democratic state were found ethnic or religious minorities that needed democratic protections.

Democratic regimes were established in Germany, in truncated Austria, in the new states of Europe, but a kind of economic, political, and cultural illiteracy prevailed: there was an unsufficient understanding of the preconditions for democracy and of the connections between economic and social conditions and democratic politics. These are questions that philosophers and political theorists since Aristotle have wrestled with – and others in this Symposium are far more qualified to talk about them than I. Let me simply add that, for example, Tocqueville's analysis of the links between autonomous social groups and democratic government in the United States was not part of public discussion at the time. The great concerns that we have heard expressed in the last few years about the problems of transition to democracy, about civil society, were almost entirely absent in Europe in the years after 1918.

The most important "transition" of that earlier period was in defeated Germany, and the Weimar Republic is the most spectacular case of the failure of democracy. There certainly existed some conditions favoring the establishment of democracy in Germany: there had been a parliamentary presence in German life, even if the imperial Reichstag lacked ultimate power; there had been political parties and a relatively free press; there had been the rule of law and rising literacy – literacy may be a necessary but it is not a sufficient condition of political participation. But there was also powerful opposition to democracy: the war and especially Germany's unexpected defeat had sharpened existing social and economic conflicts; well before the war, Max Weber, a critic of German politics, pointed to the fatality of having an economically declining class (the Junkers) insist on political preeminence, while the economically strong middle class was as yet too immature for political

18   *Fritz Stern*

power (Weber 1921: 24–25). In 1918, with the collapse of the old imperial order, the Social Democrats – more accurately, the leaders of the Majority Socialists – acted not as revolutionaries but as patriotic executors of a bankrupt system. Nor was there a revolutionary reckoning with the horrendous failure of Germany's chauvinist leaders. The German "revolutionaries" – revolutionaries *faute de mieux* – were too timid (they thought too patriotic) to expose the true causes of Germany's defeat, in a war that the imperial regime had a heavy responsibility in precipitating. Their reluctance to reveal the incriminating truths was ill-rewarded by Germany's former elites who now felt themselves to be dispossessed and threatened: they blamed the Social Democrats for the defeat and for the country's subsequent "enslavement" under the Versailles Treaty. The lies about "the stab-in-the-back" and "the November criminals" were decisive weapons in the hands of Weimar's enemies.

And still, a democratic majority adopted a progressive, democratic constitution – albeit one that was hard to implement in a bitterly divided country. Dominant groups in German society – the bureaucracy, the much-shrunk and therefore compact army, the judiciary, the churches and the universities – were basically opposed to Weimar. Yet in subsequent years some hopes were realized: conditions for the working classes improved, as did the positions of women and Jews. But the socialists' hope for a program of modest nationalization in order to diminish the power of concentrated wealth was not realized. I remind you in risibly compressed form of what is generally known about Weimar: a multiparty system representing deep social and ideological divisions necessitated a succession of weak coalition governments and induced a sense of instability. Germany's military defeat was followed by further traumas – the "humiliation" of Versailles, hyperinflation, the Great Depression – all of them intensified by the prevailing falsifications and incomprehension.

In 1920, the so-called Weimar Coalition or the three democratic parties lost their parliamentary majority – never to regain it. But the non- or anti-democrats had no viable alternative to offer: the monarchy was discredited and the yearning for an authoritarian regime or a strong man had no chance of fulfillment. Until 1930 the Allied occupation of the Rhineland imposed constraints, but the evacuation of the Rhineland in 1930 – five years before the date fixed by Versailles – coincided with the onset of the Great Depression and the consequent rise of Hitler.

Hitler remains the most terrifying example of the fragility of democracy. Hitler's appeal and gradual amassment of 37 percent of the votes in a free election (July 1932) exemplified what promises, vilifications,

Crisis in interwar Europe   19

and simplifications people will succumb to. The National Socialists
promised national renewal, communal racial cohesiveness, strong leadership, and many Germans, including members of the elites, were
attracted by these promises – despite (perhaps even to some extent
because) of the articulated brutality and the threatened violence at home
and abroad (Stern 1987: 147–191).

The retreat from democracy had begun earlier; the collapse of
Weimar was merely the most spectacular case of the subversion of
democracy by seemingly democratic means, and Hitler the object lesson
of the power of anti-democratic rhetoric and programs in a hypernation-
alistic period. But let me briefly mention two other cases. In the interwar
years, Czechoslovakia was always held up to be the great democratic
exception. Much of its strength could be attributed to its founder,
T. G. Masaryk, a philosopher-statesman who provided a moral authority for the new state and yet knew of the dangers to democracy. In
1930, he wrote

democracy is for me discussion, and therefore compromise. I was always against
political absolutism and its infallibility, and still nurse the hope that . . . we shall
overcome the absolutist habits in which we were brought up. Democracy is the
loyal recognition of civil personalities and the insurance of their cooperation . . .
Democracy must not turn to demogogy or be confused with anarchy. Democracy is the rule of the people, but there can be no government without obedience
and discipline. (Szporluk 1981)

Masaryk understood the ambiguities of democracy in his country.
Czechoslovakia had grave difficulties: its German minority demanded
special protection; the Slovaks thought themselves disadvantaged; the
resultant multiparty system did not function well. And still Czech
democracy held – in part and in the Czech lands because of a strong
civil society and a sound economy, because of Masaryk himself: he
inspired trust – an essential component of democracy, as the English
political philosopher John Dunn has emphasized, which is hard to
acquire and easy to lose (Dunn 1988: 73–93).

The counter-example to Czechoslovakia is Poland – perhaps more
maligned than it deserves, even as the Czech Republic may have been
praised more than it actually merited. The case of the newly reconstituted state of Poland makes me recall Walter Bagehot's wise comments
in 1874 apropos the uncertainties surrounding the establishment of
France's Third Republic:

Parliamentary government is not a thing which always succeeds in the world;
on the contrary, the lesson of experience is that it often fails, and seldom
answers, and this is because the necessary combination of elements is rare and
complex. First, parliamentary government required that a nation should have

20   *Fritz Stern*

nerve to endure incessant discussion and frequent change of rulers. (Bagehot 1965: 449–450)

For nerve we could speak of a psychological stamina for ambiguity and uncertainty, and it is not clear that Poles had it between the wars. The reconstituted Poland included large minorities, so the polity was divided. The country was 80 percent rural, and 64 percent Roman Catholic. By 1926, it had thirty-three ethnic parties, and twenty-six Polish parties; thirty-one of these parties were represented in parliament. In that year, Marshal Pilsudski, a man originally of the left, overthrew the fourteenth cabinet to hold office since the founding of the state and hoped to be a unifier of the nation; instead, he found himself opposed by all parties. For the first four years, Pilsudski's regime was an authoritarian version of democratic or pseudo-democratic rule; in some ways he anticipated de Gaulle's Fifth Republic. (De Gaulle acknowledged him as a predecessor.) After 1930 Pilsudski established a virtual dictatorship (Rothschild 1974: chapter 2).

Poland may have been the most striking "transition" to authoritarianism but the retreat from democracy was general. All over central Europe, some form of authoritarianism emerged, often with support of the armed forces, the one cohesive group that given its own ethos despised parliamentary bickering and considered itself the proper guardian of nation and state. These authoritarian regimes wrapped themselves in nationalist pretensions – and usually were intolerant of ethnic minorities.

Meanwhile, two alluring alternatives to democracy emerged and thus divided Europe: Bolshevism and Fascism. Both perverted elements of democratic hopes. Bolshevism claimed that it represented radical egalitarianism, social justice, an alternative to militarism and imperialism; it promised the creation of the "new Soviet man." Fascism appealed to nationalism and promised a cohesive community, real authority – in Italy and Germany it brought about total political mobilization that created the illusion of political participation and community at a time of actual political impotence and atomization. Both regimes destroyed every vestige of liberal democracy and of individual rights.

In style, too, the two totalitarian regimes were the antitheses of "bourgeois" capitalist democracy – which often seemed so enfeebled, so mired in scandals, so petty. (The one great exception, of course, was Franklin Roosevelt's New Deal: the recovery of democracy from the brink of catastrophe.) Leninism boasted simplicity cum radical transformation (mass education, electrification, collectivization), "a future that worked." In a sense the whole of the Soviet Union – at least as seen from afar – was a Potemkin village. The very appeal of Bolshevism,

Crisis in interwar Europe 21

the existence of Communist parties in other countries, strengthened the appeal of Fascism, with its aggressiveness and assertiveness, its promise of ordered modernization, and its exaltation of national unity. Both regimes, with their claim to be enemies of capitalist greed and individualism, were profoundly anti-democratic – in rhetoric and in murderous reality. Both were anti-liberal, of course. Both regimes brought to life Dostoevsky's parable about the Grand Inquisitor and the power of Miracle, Mystery, and Authority.

Even aside from the two great totalitarian temptations and the authoritarian regimes that still controlled so much of Europe we should remember that democratic thought held sway in other ways during the interwar years. Writers on the left and the right decried democracy as a bourgeois sham, as divisive and unrepresentative, as promoting egoism, individualism, moral decline, and the rule of mediocrity. Some of these were real enemies of democracy; one would think of Carl Schmitt as a celebrated example, whose thought is having a disturbing revival in Germany today – and some were sympathetic critics of democracy, such as Joseph Schumpeter.

One dramatic instance of anti-democratic thought, and an anti-democratic triumph in an old democratic country, was France in 1940. The destruction of the Third Republic was the revenge taken by those I would call the "prosperous disinherited," the people whose power had been threatened or limited, whose values they believed had been violated during the Third Republic. Vichy was not simply the consequence of military defeat but a consciously designed alternative to France's democratic republic.

We need to take account of the defects of democracy: they are real enough. Democrats need to recall the strictures of democratic leaders like de Gaulle some decades ago or Richard von Weizsäcker's critical thoughts of today (Weizsäcker 1992). Anti-democrats out of material interest and out of conviction exploit these weaknesses. A fearless, incisive critic-defender of democracy, Reinhold Niebuhr, once wrote: "The moral attitudes of dominant and privileged groups are characterized by universal self-deception and hypocrisy" (Niebuhr 1960: 117). At the very beginning of the Cold War, James B. Conant wrote in 1956, "to the normal benign chaos of a democracy will be added an almost hysterical chaos, the result of fear" (Hershberg 1993: 275). The Cold War itself extolled and weakened democracy: its virtue was deemed secure by mere reference to its totalitarian opponent (which had adopted democratic nomenclature), but the struggle itself weakened democracy, as seen in America: by the construction of a huge apparatus of surveillance and security, by intermittent threats to basic civil rights,

22   *Fritz Stern*

by what came to be called the imperial presidency. Also the huge cost of the war delayed renewal and reform, even if in some cases – the extension of civil rights and their protection – acceptance might have been made easier by virtue of our own rhetoric.

Let me conclude with a brief reference to the most inspiriting events of the last decades: the self-liberation of the East European countries and the end of Soviet tyranny. (I regret that my friend Bronislaw Geremek, admirable historian and political actor, could not address our Symposium on this topic.) These revolts in Eastern Europe had multiple causes, of course: the hatred of continued oppression, the hatred of the foreign agent of oppression, the desire for more humane material and spiritual conditions, the desire for freedom, and "a hunger to live in the truth." But it may well have been easier to topple what Václav Havel called those post-totalitarian regimes than to create functioning democracies in their place. If Conant could talk of "benign chaos" affecting an old democracy, whose people were accustomed to it, how much harder must it be for the new states whose peoples must acquire "the nerve" for democratic uncertainties. But I believe we can learn from both the insouciance and the indifference of the interwar period: the established democracies today have been far more cognizant of the real problems of political transition than they were then – cognizant, if insufficiently forthcoming.

And still, we need to recognize the deficiencies and difficulties in our own democracies. Our earlier presumption of moral superiority has lost its resonance. Nations are beset by scandals, by the decline in merit and prestige of the political class, by deficits of many kinds. I know that others in this Symposium will address these deficiencies and perhaps suggest ways of dealing with them. Democracies require certain common assumptions, not least of these the experience and expectation of political minorities becoming majorities, of opposition turning to government. Elections are not enough. To invoke Lindsay again: if these assumptions do not exist, then "voting is only a process of counting heads to save the trouble of breaking them" (Lindsay 1951: 46).

REFERENCES

Bagehot, Walter. 1965. *Bagehot's Historical Essays*, ed. Norman St. John-Stevas. Garden City, NY: Anchor Books.
Dunn, John. 1988. "Trust and political agency," in Diego Gambett, ed., *Trust Making and Breaking Cooperative Relations*. Oxford: Basil Blackwell.
Hershberg, James. 1993. *James B. Conant: Harvard to Hiroshima and the Making of The Nuclear Age*. New York: Alfred A. Knopf.

Knock, Thomas J. 1992. *To End All Wars: Woodrow Wilson and the Quest for a New World Order*. New York: Oxford University Press.

Lindsay, A. D. 1951. *The Essentials of Democracy*. Oxford University Press.

Niebuhr, Reinhold. 1960. *Moral Man and Immoral Society*. New York: Scribner's.

Rothschild, Joseph. 1974. *East Central Europe between the Two World Wars*. Seattle: University of Washington Press.

Stern, Fritz. 1987. "National socialism as temptation," in *Dreams and Delusions: The Drama of German History*. New York: Alfred A. Knopf.

Szporluk, Roman. 1981. *The Political Thought of Thomas G. Masaryk*. New York: Columbia University Press.

Weber, Max. 1921. *Gesammelte Politische Schriften*. Munich: Drei Masken Verlag.

Weizsäcker, Richard von. 1992. *Im Gespräch mit Günter Hoffmann und Werner A. Perger*. Frankfurt am Main: Eichborn.

Part 2

Social and cultural aspects

3 Democracy in America at century's end

Robert D. Putnam

Abstract

Alexis de Tocqueville attributed the success of democracy in America to an unusual national propensity for civic engagement. Recent empirical research in a wide range of contexts has confirmed that the norms and networks of civic engagement (now rebaptized "social capital") can improve education, diminish poverty, inhibit crime, boost economic performance, foster better government, and even reduce mortality rates. Conversely, deficiencies in social capital contribute to a wide range of social, economic, and political ills.

Unfortunately, new evidence also suggests that civic engagement of many sorts has unexpectedly plummeted in the United States over the last generation. The initial installment of a larger inquiry into social capital formation in America, the present paper documents these trends and explores their origins and their implications for contemporary democracy.[1]

Beyond the familiar falloff in electoral turnout, many other forms of political participation have also declined significantly over the last two decades, at the same time that political alienation and distrust in public institutions has climbed. Moreover, participation has fallen (often sharply) in many types of civic associations, from religious groups to labor unions, from women's clubs to fraternal clubs, and from neighborhood gatherings to bowling leagues. Virtually all segments of society have been afflicted by this lessening in social connectedness, and this trend, in turn, is strongly correlated with declining social trust. In sum, many forms of American social capital have badly eroded in the last quarter century.

What can explain this turn of events? Several explanations are possible, including the movement of women into the paid labor force, rising geographic mobility, and technological

28   *Robert D. Putnam*

change that is "privatizing" Americans' leisure-time. Whatever the complex causes of this weakening of social connectedness, however, it seems a likely contributor to many of the social and political ills now afflicting America, and perhaps to those besetting other advanced democracies, as well. Citizens and policymakers alike need to discover new ways to reinvest in social capital.

Americans of all ages, all stations in life, and all types of disposition are forever forming associations. There are not only commercial and industrial associations in which all take part, but others of a thousand different types – religious, moral, serious, futile, very general and very limited, immensely large and very minute . . . Thus the most democratic country in the world now is that in which men have in our time carried to the highest perfection the art of pursuing in common the objects of common desires and have applied this new technique to the greatest number of purposes . . . Nothing, in my view, deserves more attention than the intellectual and moral associations in America.

(Tocqueville 1969: 513–517)

Introduction: networks, norms, and public affairs

When Alexis de Tocqueville visited the United States in the 1830s, it was the Americans' propensity for civic association that most impressed him as the key to their unprecedented ability to make democracy work. Recently, American social scientists of a neo-Tocquevillean bent have unearthed a wide range of empirical evidence that the theoretical premise of his argument is no less accurate today – that the quality of public life and the performance of social institutions (and not only in America) are powerfully influenced by norms and networks of civic engagement.

In the field of *education*, for instance, researchers have discovered that successful schools are distinguished not so much by the content of their curriculum or the quality of their teachers, important as those factors may be, as by their embeddedness in a broader fabric of supportive families and communities. The success of private schools, James S. Coleman found, is attributable less to what happens in the classroom or to the endowments of individual students than to the greater engagement of parents and community members in school activities (Coleman and

Hoffer 1987). James Comer, an educational psychologist seeking to revitalize American public schools in disadvantaged communities, has shown the power of strategies that involve parents and community members in the educational process (Comer 1980; see also Wilensky and Kline 1988).[2]

Scholars and practitioners concerned about *urban poverty and joblessness* have similarly focused on the role of community networks and norms. William Julius Wilson's seminal work on the social isolation that characterizes the urban "underclass" has spawned a virtual industry of sociological studies of "neighborhood effects" (Wilson 1987).[3] Although the empirical verdict is not yet complete, one careful study by Anne Case and Lawrence Katz of the prospects of youths in Boston illustrates the phenomenon that has attracted so much attention. *Controlling for all relevant individual characteristics* (such as race, gender, education, parental education, family structure, religious involvement, and so on), youths who attend church or perhaps even whose *neighbors* attend church are more likely to have a job, less likely to use drugs, and less likely to be involved in criminal activity (Case and Katz 1991). In other words, church-going (the most common form of civic engagement in America, as we shall see later) may have important "externalities," in the sense that it influences the behavior and life prospects of "bystanders" whether or not they themselves are so engaged. Similarly, research on the varying economic attainments of different ethnic groups in the United States has demonstrated the importance of social bonds within each group (Light 1972; Borjas 1992; Portes and Sensenbrenner 1993). These results are consistent with research in a wide range of settings which demonstrates the vital importance of social networks for job placement and many other economic outcomes (Granovetter 1985; Powell and Smith-Droerr 1994; O'Regan and Quigley 1991).

Meanwhile, a seemingly unrelated body of research on the sociology of *economic development* has also focused attention on the role of social networks. Some of this work is situated in the developing countries (see, e.g., Esman and Uphoff 1984: esp. 15–42, 99–180; Hirschman 1984: esp. 42–77), and some of it elucidates the peculiarly successful "network capitalism" of East Asia (see, e.g., Papanek 1988; Evans 1990; Hamilton, Zeile, and Kim 1989; see also Hamilton and Biggart 1988; Greenhalgh 1988). Even in less exotic Western economies, however, researchers have discovered highly efficient, highly flexible "industrial districts," based on networks of collaboration among workers and small entrepreneurs. Far from being paleo-industrial anachronisms, these dense interpersonal and interorganizational networks undergird ultra-

30   Robert D. Putnam

modern industries, from the high tech of Silicon Valley to the high fashion of Benetton (see, e.g., Piore and Sabel 1983 and 1984; Brusco 1990; Saxenian 1990).

The control of *crime and illicit drugs* is another arena of great practical concern in which recent research emphasizes the importance of community norms and networks. The so-called "community policing" movement that has played a prominent role in recent reforms across the United States rests on empirical evidence that informal social control is much more effective than formal law enforcement in reducing criminality and violence.[4] Similarly, several recent studies suggest the efficacy of community coalitions in reducing drug and alcohol abuse. Although some have questioned the policy implications of this work, arguing that it is impossible to create viable community organizations where they do not "naturally" exist, there is little dispute that, where neighborhood social bonds exist, they provide a powerful deterrent and defense against the interrelated plagues of drugs and crime.[5]

The norms and networks of civic engagement also powerfully affect the *performance of representative government*. That, at least, was the central conclusion of my own twenty-year, quasi-experimental study of subnational governments in different regions of Italy (Putnam 1993a). Although all these regional governments seemed identical on paper, their levels of effectiveness varied dramatically. Systematic inquiry showed that government quality was determined by long-standing traditions of civic engagement (or its absence). Voter turnout, newspaper readership, membership in choral societies and football clubs – these were the hallmarks of a successful region. In fact, historical analysis suggested that these networks of organized reciprocity and civic solidarity, far from being an epiphenomenon of socioeconomic modernization, were a precondition for it.

Social epidemiologists have shown that social ties have consequences even for *physical morbidity and mortality*. People with comparatively few social and community ties face substantially greater risks of physical and mental illness and mortality, *controlling for* socioeconomic status and for physiological risk factors. One study, for example, found that *controlling for sex, age, race, socioeconomic status, physical health status, and personal hygiene*, social connectedness lowered mortality risk by more than half (Berkman and Breslow 1983: esp. chapters 4 and 5; see also Cohen and Syme 1985; and, e.g., Williams *et al.* 1992 and the sources cited therein). Joining, in short, is good for your health.

No doubt the mechanisms through which civic engagement and social connectedness produce all these miraculous results – better schools, faster growth, lower crime, more effective government, and even longer lives – are multiple and complex. Moreover, the findings that I have so briskly surveyed require further confirmation and perhaps qualification before they can be scientifically certified as "truth." Nevertheless, the parallels across hundreds of empirical studies in a dozen disparate disciplines and subfields are striking. Social scientists in several disciplines have recently suggested a common framework for understanding these phenomena, a framework that rests on the concept of *social capital*.[6] By analogy with notions of physical capital and human capital – tools and training that enhance individual productivity – "social capital" refers to features of social organization, such as networks, norms, and social trust, that facilitate coordination and cooperation for mutual benefit.

For a variety of reasons, life is easier in a community blessed with a substantial stock of social capital. In the first place, networks of civic engagement foster sturdy norms of generalized reciprocity and encourage the emergence of social trust. Such networks facilitate coordination and communication, amplify reputations, and thus allow dilemmas of collective action to be resolved. When economic and political negotiation is embedded in dense networks of social interaction, incentives for opportunism are reduced.[7] At the same time, networks of civic engagement embody past success at collaboration, which can serve as a cultural template for future collaboration. Finally, dense networks of interaction probably broaden the participants' sense of self, developing the "I" into the "we," or (in the language of rational choice theories) enhancing the participants' "taste" for collective benefits.

I do not intend here to survey (still less, to contribute to) the development of the theory of social capital.[8] Instead, the central premise of that rapidly growing body of work – that social connections and civic engagement pervasively influence our public life, as well as our private prospects – forms the starting point for an empirical survey of trends in social capital in the contemporary United States.

Trends in US civic engagement

Since Tocqueville's classic inquiry, America has played a central role in systematic studies of the links between democracy and civil society, in part because trends in American life are often regarded as harbingers of social modernization and in part because America has been traditionally considered unusually "civic," a reputation that (as we shall later see) is not entirely unjustified. For those reasons, too, I concentrate here entirely on the American case, although the developments I portray may in some measure characterize many contemporary societies. Another preliminary caution: although informal norms and networks constitute

32 *Robert D. Putnam*

highly important forms of social capital, I rely mostly (though not entirely) on measures of civic engagement in formal organizational and institutional contexts. The reason is simply methodological: for accurate, quantitative assessments of *change*, we need data that have been regularly collected over a span of years, if not decades, and such data are for the most part confined to formal contexts.[9] Nevertheless, I want to stress that formal organizational involvement is only one facet of social capital and civic engagement.

Political participation

We begin with familiar evidence on changing patterns of political participation, not least because it is immediately relevant to issues of democracy in the narrow sense. Figure 3.1 traces the well-known decline in turnout in American national elections over the last three decades. (A longer perspective would show that the post-1960 decline was essentially a resumption of a downward trend in electoral participation that has persisted throughout this century.) From a relative high point in the early 1960s, voter turnout had by 1990 declined by nearly a quarter; tens of millions of Americans had forsaken their parents' habitual readiness to engage in the simplest act of citizenship. (The presidential election of 1992, with its unusually strong third-party candidacy, witnessed a partial rebound, but the durability of this recent uptick remains highly questionable.) Broadly similar trends also characterize participation in state and local elections.

It is not just the voting booth that has been increasingly deserted by Americans. Drawing on a series of identical questions posed by the Roper organization to national samples ten times each year over the last two decades, Figure 3.2 reveals that since 1973 the number of Americans who report that "in the past year" they have "attended a public meeting on town or school affairs" has fallen by more than a third (from 22% in 1973 to 13% in 1993).[10] Similar (or even greater) relative declines are evident in responses to questions about "writ[ing] to your congress-man or senator," "attend[ing] a political rally or speech," "serv[ing] on a committee of some local organization," and "work[ing] for a political party." Even as a spectator sport civic engagement has become rarer over the last several decades, for as Figure 3.3 shows, daily newspaper readership fell by nearly a quarter between 1970 and 1993.[11] By almost every measure, Americans' direct engagement in politics and government has fallen steadily and sharply over the last generation, despite the fact that average levels of education – the best individual-level predictor of political participation – have risen sharply throughout

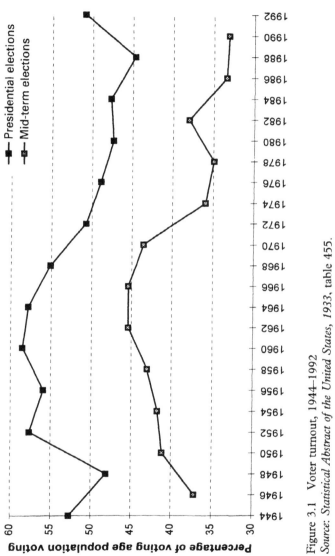

Figure 3.1 Voter turnout, 1944–1992
Source: *Statistical Abstract of the United States, 1933*, table 455.

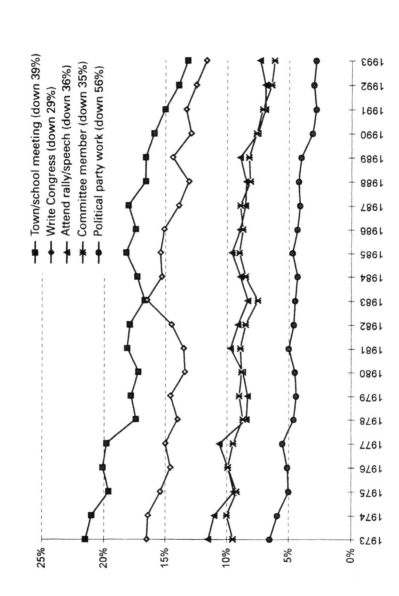

Figure 3.2 Trends in civic engagement among US adults, 1973–1993
Sources: Roper Reports, monthly surveys, nos. 73–79 through 93–97. See also Rosenstone and Hansen (1993).

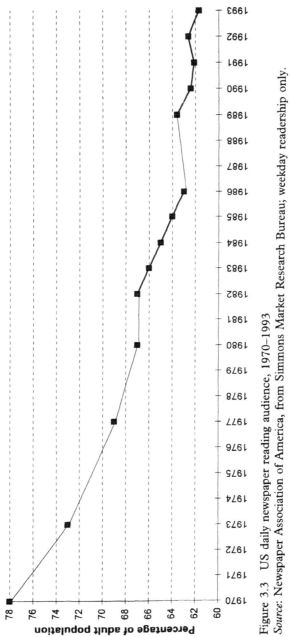

Figure 3.3 US daily newspaper reading audience, 1970–1993
Source: Newspaper Association of America, from Simmons Market Research Bureau; weekday readership only.

36   *Robert D. Putnam*

this period. *Every year* over the last decade or two, millions of citizens more have withdrawn from the affairs of their communities.[12]

Not coincidentally, Americans have also disengaged psychologically from politics and government over this era. Figure 3.4 synthesizes representative evidence from two long-term data series.

    (i) Distrust in government   "How much do you trust the government in Washington to do what is right – all of the time, most of the time, some of the time, or almost never?" Figure 3.4 shows that the number of Americans who choose one of the two less trusting alternatives has risen from 30% in 1966 to 75% in 1992. (Longer data series show that trust in government peaked in 1964 and has continued to decline even after 1992.)

    (ii) Social alienation   The Harris Alienation Index is based on the average level of agreement with five statements posed to national samples of Americans every year since 1966:

- The people running the country do not really care what happens to you.
- Most people with power try to take advantage of people like yourself.
- You are left out of things going on around you.
- What you think does not count very much anymore.
- The rich get richer and the poor get poorer.

Every item on this list has won more and more assent from Americans in recent years. By any measure, political alienation and disengagement have soared over the last three decades.[13]

Secondary associations

The trends that we have just reviewed are, of course, well known, and, taken alone, they would seem amenable to a strictly political explanation. Perhaps, for example, the long litany of political tragedies and scandals since the 1960s (assassinations, Vietnam, Watergate, Irangate, etc.) has triggered an understandable disgust for politics and government among Americans, and that in turn has motivated their withdrawal. I do not doubt that this common interpretation has some merit, but its limitations become plain when we examine trends in civic engagement of a wider sort.

Our survey of organizational membership among Americans can usefully begin with a glance at the aggregate results from the General Social

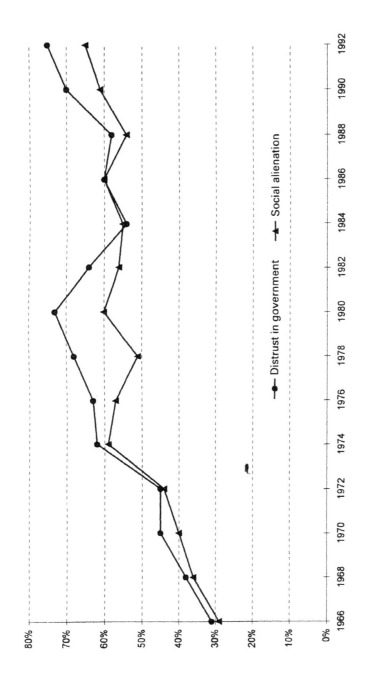

Figure 3.4 Social alienation and distrust in government, 1966–1992
Sources: Distrust in government: National Election Studies; alienation index: Harris Poll.

38   Robert D. Putnam

Table 3.1 *Group membership among American adults, 1974–1994 (by gender)*

Type of group	Male	Female	Total sample
Church-affiliated groups	30%	41%	36%
Sports groups	26%	14%	20%
Professional or academic societies	17%	13%	15%
Labor unions	21%	8%	14%
School service groups	10%	17%	14%
Fraternal groups	14%	6%	10%
Service clubs	11%	9%	10%
Youth groups	10%	10%	10%
Hobby or garden clubs	9%	10%	9%
Literary, art, discussion, or study groups	7%	11%	9%
Veterans' groups	12%	3%	7%
School fraternities or sororities	5%	4%	5%
Political clubs	4%	4%	4%
Farm organizations	6%	3%	4%
Nationality groups	4%	3%	3%
Member of *any* group	75%	67%	70%
Mean number of groups	1.95	1.65	1.78
Approximate sample size	8,391	10,936	19,327

Source: GSS, 1974–1994.

Survey (GSS), a scientifically-conducted national sample survey that has been repeated fourteen times over the last two decades. Table 3.1 aggregates results from a detailed question about associational membership that has appeared in each survey. The total number of memberships reported in this data (70 percent of all respondents report at least one such affiliation) is substantially higher than in many other surveys, and that fact reflects the exhaustiveness of the GSS probes for various group memberships. Table 3.1 shows that church-related groups constitute the most common type of membership, especially among women, but also among men. Other relatively common types of organizational memberships among women include school service groups (mostly parent–teacher associations), sports groups, professional societies, and literary societies. Among men, sports clubs, labor unions, professional societies, fraternal groups, veterans' groups, and service clubs are all relatively frequent. In the analysis that follows, we deploy the best available evidence on trends in membership in virtually all these types of organization, using both actual membership figures (where they are available) and survey data.[14]

Democracy in America at century's end | 39

Religious affiliation is by far the most common associational membership among Americans. Indeed, by many measures America continues to be (even more than in Tocqueville's time) an astonishingly "churched" society. For example, the United States has more houses of worship per capita than in any other nation on Earth (*US News* 1994).[15] Against a backdrop of widespread expectations that modernization and secularization would cause organized religion to wither away, most sociologists of American religion have emphasized that religious affiliation is probably more prevalent in contemporary America than in 1776 and that religious beliefs and practices have been relatively stable over the last half century. On the other hand, it is also true that membership in most "mainline" denominations has hemorrhaged over the several decades, with those losses partially offset by a rapid expansion in evangelical and fundamentalist congregations (Roof and McKinney 1987). Moreover, religious sentiment in America seems to be becoming somewhat more self-defined. As the leading student of American religious behavior has said, "We are becoming less theologically and institutionally grounded and more inclined toward making up our own faiths as we go along (Robert Wuthnow, as quoted in *U.S. News* 1994)." How have these complex cross-currents played out over the last three or four decades in terms of Americans' engagement with organized religion?

Figure 3.5 traces the net balance in formal religious observance over the last forty-four years, drawing on two independent measures: (1) a question about church attendance "in the last seven days" posed repeatedly in Gallup polls throughout this period and (2) a question about habitual attendance at religious services regularly posed by the National Opinion Research Corporation (NORC) since 1967. Both series show that church attendance dropped significantly during the 1960s, though they give somewhat divergent results thereafter. The Gallup polls indicate that reported weekly church-going declined from roughly 48 percent in the late 1950s to roughly 41 percent in the early 1970s. Thereafter, Gallup reports, church attendance has been rock-steady at 40–42 percent.[16] On the other hand, according to the NORC polls the proportion of Americans who say that they "attend religious services" at least "nearly every week" has continued to fall from 41 percent in 1972 to 34 percent in 1993, suggesting that the erosion in church attendance has continued into the 1990s (*The Public Perspective* 1994: 91).

Religious engagement, of course, means more than attendance at weekly worship services, for many Americans are intensely involved in a wide variety of other church-related groups, such as Sunday schools,

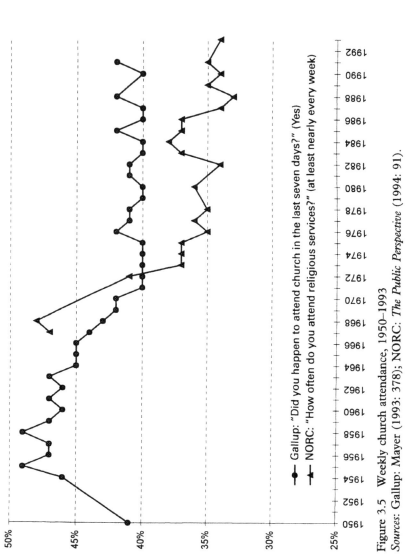

Figure 3.5 Weekly church attendance, 1950–1993
Sources: Gallup: Mayer (1993: 378); NORC: *The Public Perspective* (1994: 91).

Bible study groups, *havurot*, "singles" groups, and so on. An important recent study by Robert Wuthnow estimates that 20 percent or more of all US adults are actively involved in such "small groups." Moreover, Wuthnow argues, "During the 1980s, the small-group movement grew rapidly, especially as religious leaders began to recognize its potential as a way of revitalizing declining congregations and of achieving rapid growth in new congregations . . . In the 1990s this growth has, if anything, accelerated" (Wuthnow 1994: 44). However, Wuthnow cites no time-series data and rests this claim of growing engagement on anecdotal evidence. By contrast, data from the GSS, as charted in Figure 3.6, show a modest *decline* in membership in all "church-related groups" over the last twenty years. Further analysis (not shown here) finds this same pattern among both men and women and among all educational levels. In the face of somewhat divergent indications, then, the best summary judgment would seem to be that net participation by Americans, both in religious services and in church-related groups, has modestly declined (by perhaps a fifth) since the 1960s.

For many years, labor unions provided one of the most common organizational affiliations among American working men (and less so, working women), and Table 3.1 showed that this has remained true in recent decades. However, as Figure 3.7 documents, union membership has been falling for nearly four decades, with the steepest decline occurring between 1975 and 1985. Since the mid-1950s, when union membership peaked, the unionized portion of the non-agricultural workforce in America has dropped by more than half, falling from 32.5 percent in 1953 to 15.8 percent in 1992. By now, virtually all of the explosive growth in union membership that was associated with the New Deal has been erased, as Figure 3.7 clearly shows, and the solidarity of union halls is now mostly a fading memory of aging men.[17]

An especially important form of civic engagement in twentieth-century America has been the Parent–Teacher Association (PTA), important not merely because it is (or at least, was) one of the most common associational memberships, but also because parental involvement in the educational process represents a particularly productive form of social capital. It is, therefore, dismaying to discover that participation in parent–teacher organizations has plummeted over the last generation. Nationwide, PTA membership fell from more than 12 million in 1964 to barely 5 million in 1982 before recovering to approximately 7 million now. To interpret these changes more accurately, of course, we must adjust for demographic changes, and thus Figure 3.8 presents membership data standardized for the number of schoolchildren nationwide. These data show that the slide actually began in 1960, that it

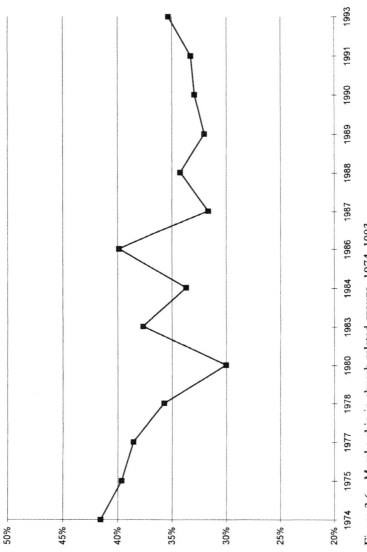

Figure 3.6 Membership in church-related groups, 1974–1993
Source: GSS.

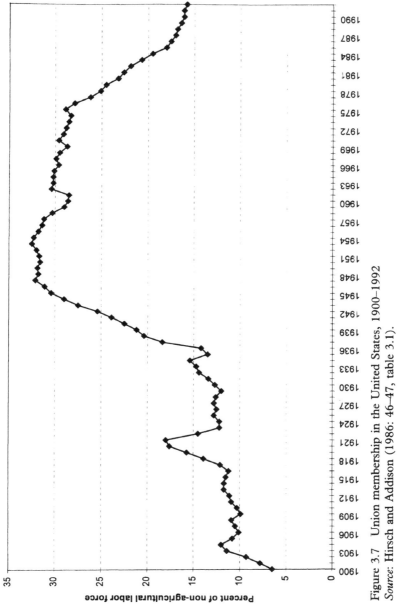

Figure 3.7 Union membership in the United States, 1900–1992
Source: Hirsch and Addison (1986: 46–47, table 3.1).

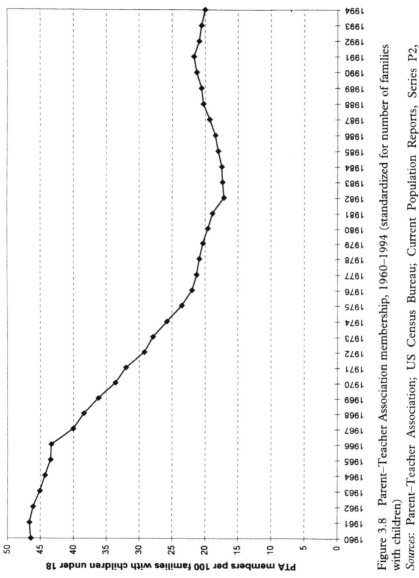

Figure 3.8 Parent–Teacher Association membership, 1960–1994 (standardized for number of families with children)
Sources: Parent–Teacher Association; US Census Bureau; Current Population Reports, Series P2, table 1 (1995).

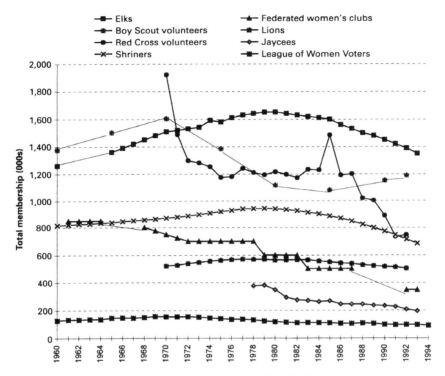

Figure 3.9 Membership trends in selected civic associations, 1960–1994
Sources: national headquarters of respective associations.

continued for more than two decades, and that the post-1982 recovery in absolute numbers is inflated by rising school enrollments. In short, the proportion of American parents organizationally engaged with their children's schools dropped by more than half during the 1960s and 1970s and has hardly recovered since then.

Next, we turn (in Figure 3.9) to evidence on membership in (and volunteering for) civic and fraternal organizations. These data (which – conservatively – are not corrected for population growth nor for the aging of "baby-boomers" into their prime "joining" years) show some striking patterns. First, membership in traditional women's groups has declined more or less steadily since the mid-1960s. For example, membership in the national Federation of Women's Clubs is down by

46   *Robert D. Putnam*

more than half (59 percent) since 1964, while membership in the League of Women Voters (LWV) is off nearly as much (42 percent) since 1969.[18]

Similar reductions are apparent in the numbers of volunteers for mainline civic organizations, such as the Boy Scouts (off by 26 percent since 1970) and the Red Cross (off by 61 percent since 1970). But what about the possibility that volunteers have simply switched their loyalties to other organizations? Survey evidence on volunteering has become available only recently and is plagued by imprecision about what counts as "volunteer work" – should taking in the newspapers for a vacationing neighbor count, for example, as it does in some national surveys? However, evidence on "regular" (as opposed to occasional or "drop-by") volunteering is available from the Labor Department's Current Population Survey (CPS) in 1974 and 1989. The CPS estimates, based on massive samples of 60,000 households and carefully constructed so as to be comparable across time, suggest that serious volunteering declined by roughly one sixth over these fifteen years, from 24 percent of adults in 1974 to 20 percent in 1989 (Hayghe 1991; see also Brudney 1990).[19] Although a decline of 4 percent may seem modest, it represents nearly 8,000,000 fewer volunteers nationwide in 1989 than in 1974. The multitudes of Red Cross aides and Boy Scout troop leaders now missing in action have apparently *not* been offset by equal multitudes of new recruits elsewhere. More episodic volunteering may have risen in counterpoint, so we cannot conclude from these data that Americans are becoming more "selfish," but the deeper ties reflected by regular volunteering appears to have diminished.

Fraternal organizations have traditionally been an important form of social engagement for American men, but Figure 3.9 presents evidence of a substantial and almost simultaneous drop in membership in many such groups during the 1980s and 1990s. Even without controlling for population growth, membership is significantly down for such groups as the Lions (off 12 percent since 1983), the Elks (off 18 percent since 1979), the Shriners (off 27 percent since 1979), and the Jaycees (off 44 percent since 1979). Other evidence shows that membership in the Masons, the oldest and largest fraternal organization in the world, has dropped steadily from a peak of 4.1 million and now hovers at around 2.5 million, down 39 percent since 1959 (*Boston Globe* 1993).[20] Note that whereas for organizations catering primarily to women (including, for example, the PTA, roughly 90 percent of whose members are female), membership generally began to plunge in the 1960s, the comparable declines in most men's organizations began ten to fifteen years later. Whatever the significance of that fact, the cumulative weight of

Democracy in America at century's end 47

the evidence we have reviewed thus far is substantial: after expanding steadily throughout most of this century, many key civic organizations in many American communities have experienced a substantial decline in membership over the last decade or two.

The most whimsical, yet discomfiting bit of evidence of social disengagement in contemporary America that I have discovered is this: more Americans are bowling today than ever before, but *league* bowling has plummeted in the last ten to fifteen years. Between 1980 and 1993 the total number of bowlers in America increased by 10 percent, while league bowling decreased by 40 percent.[21] (Lest bowling be thought a wholly trivial example, I should note that, according to the American Bowling Congress, nearly 80 million Americans bowled at some point during 1993, *nearly a third more than voted in the 1994 Congressional elections*. Even after the 1980s' plunge in league bowling, nearly 3 percent of American adults regularly bowl in leagues.) The rise of solo bowling threatens the livelihood of bowling lane proprietors because league bowlers consume three times as much beer and pizza as solo bowlers, and the money in bowling is in the beer and pizza, not the balls and shoes. The broader social significance, however, lies in the social interaction and even occasionally civic conversations over beer and pizza that solo bowlers forego. Whether or not bowling beats balloting in the eyes of most Americans, bowling teams illustrate yet another vanishing form of social capital.

At this stage in the argument, however, we must confront a serious counter-argument. Perhaps, it might be said, the traditional forms of civic organization whose decay we have thus far traced have been replaced by vibrant new organizations. For example, national environmental organizations, like the Sierra Club, and feminist groups, like the National Organization for Women, grew rapidly during the 1970s and 1980s and now count hundreds of thousands of dues-paying members. An even more dramatic example is the American Association of Retired People (AARP), which grew exponentially from 400,000 card-carrying members in 1960 to 33 million in 1993. The national administrators of these organizations are among the most feared lobbyists in Washington, in large part because of their massive mailing lists of presumably loyal members (see Schlozman and Tierney 1986 and Walker 1991).

These new mass membership organizations are plainly of great political importance. From the point of view of social connectedness, however, they are sufficiently different from classic "secondary associations" that we need to invent a new label – perhaps "tertiary associations." For the vast majority of their members, the only act of membership consists in writing a check for dues or perhaps occasionally

48   *Robert D. Putnam*

reading a newsletter.[22] Few ever attend any meetings of such organizations, and most are unlikely ever (knowingly) to encounter any other member. The bond between any two members of the Sierra Club is less like the bond between any two members of a gardening club and more like the bond between any two Red Sox fans (or perhaps any two devoted Honda owners): they root for the same team and they share some of the same interests, but *they are unaware of each other's existence.* Their ties, in short, are to common symbols, common leaders, and perhaps common ideals, but *not* to each other. The theory of social capital argues that associational membership should, for example, increase social trust, but this prediction is much less straightforward as regards membership in tertiary associations. From the point of view of social connectedness, to put the Environmental Defense Fund and a bowling league in the same category is a fundamental conceptual mistake.[23]

If the growth of tertiary organizations represents one potential (but probably not real) counter-example to my thesis, a second counter-trend is represented by the growing prominence of non-profit organizations, especially non-profit service agencies. This so-called "Third Sector" includes everything from Oxfam and the Metropolitan Museum of Art to the Ford Foundation and the Mayo Clinic.[24] In other words, although most secondary associations are non-profits, most large non-profit agencies are *not* secondary associations. To identify trends in the size of the non-profit sector with trends in social connectedness would be another fundamental conceptual mistake (see Salamon 1994; see also Salamon 1987).[25]

A third potential counter-trend is much more relevant to an assessment of social capital and civic engagement. Some able researchers, most notably Robert Wuthnow, have argued that the last few decades have witnessed a rapid expansion in "support groups" of various sorts (Wuthnow 1994). Wuthnow's fascinating study reports that fully 40 percent of all Americans claim to be "currently involved in [a] small group that meets regularly and provides support or caring for those who participate in it." Many of these groups are religiously affiliated, as we earlier discussed, but many others are not. For example, nearly 5 percent of Wuthnow's national sample claim to participate regularly in a "self-help" group, such as Alcoholics Anonymous, and nearly as many say they belong to book discussion groups and hobby clubs. Although Wuthnow's statistical evidence is drawn from a single survey and thus cannot itself substantiate claims about trends, he argues that such small groups have become a much more common feature of American communities in recent years.

Whether or not they are proliferating, the groups described by

Democracy in America at century's end

Wuthnow's respondents unquestionably represent an important form of social capital, and they need to be accounted for in any serious reckoning of trends in social connectedness. On the other hand, they do not typically play the same role as traditional civic associations. As Wuthnow emphasizes,

> the kind of community [these small groups] create is quite different from the communities in which people have lived in the past. These communities are more fluid and more concerned with the emotional states of the individual . . . The communities they create are seldom frail. People feel cared for. They help one another. They share their intimate problems . . . But in another sense small groups may not be fostering community as effectively as many of their proponents would like. Some small groups merely provide occasions for individuals to focus on themselves in the presence of others. The social contract binding members together asserts only the weakest of obligations. Come if you have time. Talk if you feel like it. Respect everyone's opinion. Never criticize. Leave quietly if you become dissatisfied . . . We can imagine that [these small groups] really substitute for families, neighborhoods, and broader community attachments that may demand lifelong commitments, when, in fact, they do not. (Wuthnow 1994: 3–6)

All of these potential counter-trends – tertiary organizations, non-profit organizations, and support groups, as well as newer forms of associationism, like neighborhood crime-watch groups and residential associations – need somehow to be weighed against the erosion of conventional civic organizations. One way of doing so at least over the last two decades is to consult the GSS, which has gathered longitudinally comparable evidence from extensive probes about various types of associational membership.

Because educational levels are closely correlated with associational membership, and because educational levels in America have risen sharply over the last several decades, it is instructive to array the changes in membership for three broad educational categories – less than high school, high school, and more than high school. Figure 3.10 presents the relevant evidence.

Within all educational categories, total associational membership declined significantly between 1974 and 1994. Among the college-educated, the average number of group memberships fell from 2.8 to 2.5; among high school graduates, the number fell from 1.8 to 1.6; and among those with less than twelve years of education, the number fell from 1.4 to 0.8. In other words, at various educational (and hence social) levels of American society, and counting *all* sorts of group memberships, the average number of associational memberships has fallen over the last two decades.

Without controls for educational levels, the decline in memberships

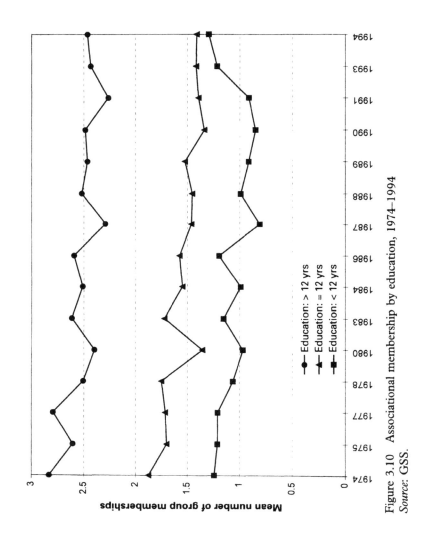

Figure 3.10 Associational membership by education, 1974–1994
Source: GSS.

Democracy in America at century's end 51

is much more modest, barely reaching statistical significance in the raw GSS data. However, to assess changes in associational engagement accurately we need to consider broader demographic trends in American society. For example, PTA membership necessarily depends on the size of the school-aged population, and thus Figure 3.8 is corrected for changes in school enrollment. Similarly, the movement of women into professions obviously increases the number of potential female members of professional organizations. When the number of lawyers doubles, we would expect bar associations to grow. A fourth example: it is well established that over the life-cycle organizational membership peaks in late middle age, so we must take into account any demographic changes that move a large fraction of the population into or out of their prime "joining" years. To adjust for these problems in any net assessment of trends in associational engagement, we need to control for such factors as education, age, and occupational status. The central result of such an analysis of the GSS data: *more Americans than ever before are in social circumstances that encourage associational involvement (higher education, middle age, and so on), but nevertheless associational membership is stagnant or declining.*

Broken down by types of group, the downward trend is most marked for church-related groups, for labor unions, for fraternal and veterans' organizations, and for school-service groups (e.g., PTAs). These patterns are, of course, quite consistent with the directly reported membership rates for these sorts of organizations, as we saw earlier. Conversely, membership in professional associations rose over these years, although no more than might have been predicted, given the sharply rising educational and occupational levels over this quarter century. Essentially the same trends are available for both men and women in the sample.

In short, the available survey evidence, taking into account – insofar as respondents themselves consider the affiliations significant – tertiary associations, non-profit organizations, various "New Age" support groups, and any other groups that might have been missed by our organizationally targeted radar scope, confirms our earlier conclusion: *American social capital in the form of civic associations has significantly eroded over the last generation.*

Other forms of social capital: good neighborliness and social trust

I noted earlier that most readily available quantitative evidence on trends in social connectedness involves formal settings, such as the voting booth, the union hall, or the PTA. One glaring exception is so widely discussed as to require little comment here: the most funda-

52   *Robert D. Putnam*

mental form of social capital is the family, and the massive evidence of the loosening of bonds within the family (both extended and nuclear) is well known. In addition to the century-long increase in divorce rates (which accelerated from the mid-1960s to the mid-1970s and then leveled off) and the more recent increase in single-parent families, the portion of one-person households has more than doubled since 1950 (Caplow, Bahr, Modell, and Chadwick 1991: 47, 106, 113). This trend is, of course, quite consistent with – and may help explain – our theme of social decapitalization.

A second aspect of informal social capital on which we happen to have some time-series data involves neighborliness. In each GSS since 1974 respondents have been asked, "How often do you spend a social evening with a neighbor?" Figure 3.11 summarizes the results: the proportion of Americans who report socializing with their neighbors more than once a year has slowly, but steadily, declined over the last two decades, from 72 percent in 1974 to 60 percent in 1994. (The same pattern is found among both men and women and at all levels of education. On the other hand, socializing with "friends who do not live in your neighborhood" appears to be on the increase, a trend that may reflect the growth of workplace-based social connections.) This evidence corresponds accurately to the personal experience of almost any American who can recall the world of the 50s and 60s. In the harried and sometimes menacing worlds in which we now live, few of us spend the time playing bridge with neighbors or chatting over the back fence that our parents did.

We are also less trusting. Since trust is so central to the theory of social capital, it would be desirable to have strong behavioral indicators of trends in social trust or misanthropy. I have as yet discovered no such behavioral measures, but one simple questionnaire-based measure of social trust has been used repeatedly in this country and abroad for thirty years and more: "Some say that most people can be trusted, while others say that you can't be too careful in dealing with people. Which do you believe?" Figure 3.12 shows a strong and reasonably steady trend in a familiar direction: the proportion of Americans saying that most people can be trusted has fallen by two-fifths between 1960, when 58 percent chose that alternative, and 1994, when only 35 percent did. The same trend is apparent in all educational groups; indeed, because social trust is also correlated with education and because educational levels have risen sharply, the overall decrease in social trust is even more apparent if we control for education.

From the point of view of civic life, this erosion in social trust may be even more significant than the decline in organizational

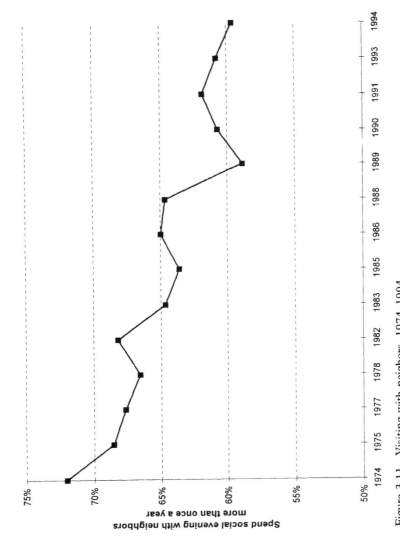

Figure 3.11 Visiting with neigbors, 1974–1994
Source: GSS.

54   Robert D. Putnam

involvement already documented. Eric Uslaner has shown that people who are trusting are more optimistic about the future, more altruistic, more likely to contribute to charity, to volunteer their time, to entertain strangers in their home, to work on community problems, to vote, and to be willing to serve on a jury. They are more tolerant of social and political minorities and more accepting of differing lifestyles, but also more critical of political correctness (Uslaner 1995). A world in which we distrust one another is a world in which social collaboration seems a bad gamble, a world in which democracy itself is less safe.

Our discussion of trends in social connectedness and civic engagement has tacitly assumed that all the forms of social capital that we have discussed are themselves coherently correlated across individuals. This is in fact true. Members of associations are more likely than non-members to participate in politics, to spend time with neighbors, to express social trust, and so on. Conversely, recent research on declining electoral turnout, for example, has argued that a decline in social connectedness is an important part of the explanation (Knack 1992; Teixeira 1992; Rosenstone and Hansen 1993). Since all these indicators of social capital are themselves highly correlated with education (and other measures of socioeconomic status), it is worth noting that the intercorrelations among the social capital measures persist even when we control for education. Figure 3.13, for example, shows that both education and associational membership are strongly and independently correlated with social trust. It is, of course, impossible to tell from these data whether membership causes trust or the reverse; it is quite likely that both are true.

This close correlation between social trust and associational membership is true not only across time and across individuals, but also across countries. Drawing on evidence from the 1990–1991 World Values Survey, we can demonstrate this fact and at the same time get a rough comparative benchmark for assessing the trends in American social capital that I have outlined in this chapter. Figure 3.14 provides the relevant evidence.[26] Much could be inferred from this chart about the correlates of social capital, but I wish here to emphasize two facts.

1. Across these thirty-five countries, social trust and civic engagement are strongly correlated; the greater the density of associational membership in a society, the more trusting its citizens. Trust and engagement are two facets of the same underlying factor – social capital.
2. By cross-national standards, just as Tocqueville argued, America still ranks relatively high on both these dimensions of social capital. Even

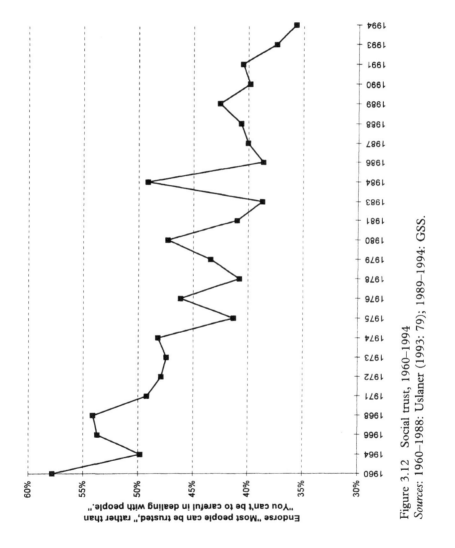

Figure 3.12 Social trust, 1960–1994
Sources: 1960–1988: Uslaner (1993: 79); 1989–1994: GSS.

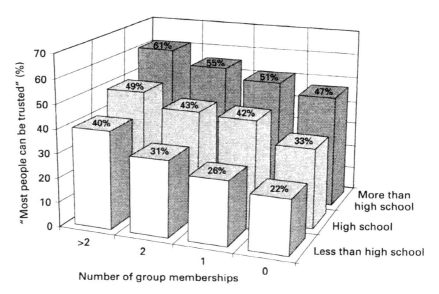

Figure 3.13 Social trust by education and group membership
Source: GSS, 1974–1991.
Which do you agree with: "Most people can be trusted" or "You can't be too careful in dealing with people"?

in the 1990s, after several decades' erosion, Americans are more trusting and more civically engaged than most other people in the world.

Why is social capital in America eroding?

Thus far I have, I hope, shown that there is good reason to suspect that something has happened in America in the last two or three decades to diminish civic engagement and social connectedness. What could that "something" be? I now want simply to lay out several possible explanations, along with some initial evidence on each, pro and con.[27]

The movement of women into the labor force

Over these same two or three decades many millions of American women have moved out of the home into paid employment. This is the primary, though not the sole, reason why the weekly working hours of the average American have increased significantly during these years (Schor 1991). It seems highly plausible that this social revolution should have reduced the time and energy available for building social capital.

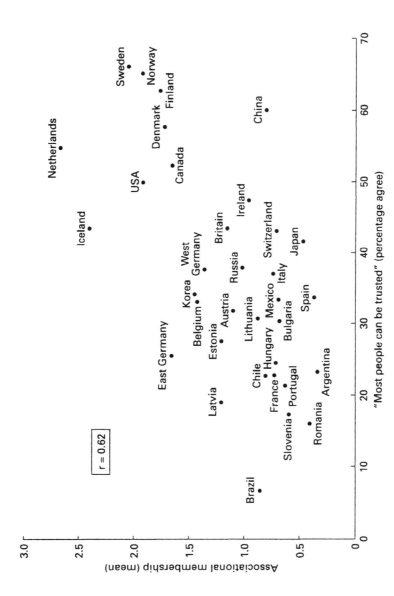

Figure 3.14 Associational membership and social trust
Source: 1990–1991 World Values Survey

58   *Robert D. Putnam*

For certain organizations, such as the PTA, the LWV, the Federation of Women's Clubs, and the Red Cross, this is almost certainly an important part of the story. Recall, too, that the sharpest decline in women's civic participation seems to have come in the 1970s and now amounts to roughly 50 percent in the typical organization. By contrast, most of the decline in men's organizations came about ten years later and now amounts to roughly 25 percent in the typical organization. On the other hand, the survey data imply that the aggregate declines for men are virtually as great as those for women. It is logically possible, of course, that the male declines might represent the knock-on effect of women's liberation, as dish-washing crowded out the lodge, but time-budget studies suggest that most husbands of working wives have assumed only a minor part of the housework. In short, something besides the women's revolution seems to lie behind the erosion of social capital.

Mobility: the "repotting" hypothesis

Numerous studies of organizational involvement have shown that residential stability and such related phenomena as homeownership are clearly associated with greater civic engagement. Mobility, like frequent repotting of plants, tends to disrupt root systems, and it takes time for an uprooted individual to put down new roots. It seems plausible that the automobile, suburbanization, and the movement to the Sun Belt might have reduced the social rootedness of the average American. Further investigation on this hypothesis is warranted, but one fundamental difficulty is already apparent: the best evidence is that residential stability and homeownership in America have modestly *risen* since 1965, and they are surely higher now than during the 1950s, when civic engagement and social connectedness by our measures was definitely higher (Fischer 1991: esp. 82–84).

Other demographic transformations

A range of additional changes have transformed the American family since the 1960s – fewer marriages, more divorces, fewer children, lower real wages, and so on. Each of these changes might account for some of the slackening of civic engagement, since married, middle-class parents are generally more socially involved than other people. Moreover, the changes in scale that have swept over the American economy in these years – illustrated by the replacement of the corner grocery by the supermarket and now perhaps of the

Democracy in America at century's end

supermarket by electronic shopping-at-home or the replacement of community-based enterprises by outposts of distant multinational firms – may perhaps have undermined the material and even physical basis for civic engagement.

The technological transformation of leisure

There is reason to believe that deep-seated technological trends are radically "privatizing" or "individualizing" our use of leisure time and thus disrupting many opportunities for social capital formation. The most obvious and probably the most powerful instrument of this revolution is television. Time-budget studies in the 1960s showed that the growth in time devoted to television literally dwarfed all other changes in the way Americans spent their days and nights (Robinson and Converse 1972). Television has made our communities (or rather what we experience as our communities) wider and shallower (Meyrowitz 1985). Rather than playing football on weekends, we watch other people play it half a continent away. Rather than confide in close friends, we watch Oprah discuss astonishingly intimate matters with total strangers on TV.

These effects of the technology of leisure are not limited to television, however. The cassette tape, the compact disk, and the Walkman have made it possible for us to receive musical entertainment in private, a development that previous cultures would have found inconceivable. The logic of this trend is clear: if I (a devotee of Romantic symphonies) attend the Boston Symphony Orchestra, I must fidget through long passages of Schoenberg before the orchestra gets to Brahms. My CD player allows me to concentrate on *precisely* the kind of entertainment that I find most appealing. The same is true for my friend who cherishes twelve-tone harmonics and finds Brahms saccharine. The result, however, is that we rarely see each other at the concert hall nowadays.

In the language of economics, electronic technology enables individual tastes to be satisfied more fully, but at the cost of the positive social externalities associated with more primitive forms of entertainment. The same logic applies to the replacement of vaudeville by the movies and now movies by the VCR. The new "virtual reality" helmets which we will soon don to be entertained in total isolation are merely the apotheosis of this trend. Technology is thus driving a wedge between our individual interests and our collective interests – or, at least, that is a hypothesis that seems worth exploring more systematically.[28]

60   *Robert D. Putnam*

What is to be done?

The last refuge of a social scientific scoundrel is to call for more research. Nevertheless, I cannot forbear from suggesting some further lines of inquiry.

- We must sort out the dimensions of social capital, which clearly is not a unidimensional concept, despite language (even in this chapter) which implies the contrary. What types of organizations and networks most effectively embody – or generate – social capital, in the sense of mutual reciprocity, the resolution of dilemmas of collective action, and the broadening of social identities? In this chapter I have emphasized the *density* of associational life. In earlier work I stressed the *structure* of networks, arguing that "horizontal" ties represented more productive social capital than vertical ties (Putnam 1993a: esp. chapter 6). Another potentially important dimension reflects the *distribution* of the networks: more diverse and encompassing networks are especially important for binding society together. That insight, or something close to it, inspired the integration and civil rights movement of the 1960s, although it later became highly controversial, as in the dispute about "neighborhood schools." Perhaps the most menacing social phenomenon in America today is the paucity of social capital that *bridges* the deepest cleavages in our society, above all, the racial divide. In addition, we need to explore more carefully the *mechanisms* that link social capital and institutional outcomes.[29]
- Another set of important issues involve macro-sociological cross-currents that might intersect with the trends described in this chapter. What will be the impact of electronic networks on social capital, for example? My hunch is that meeting in an electronic forum is *not* the equivalent of meeting in a bowling alley – or even in a saloon, come to that (Moore 1897) – but hard empirical research is needed. What about the development of social capital in the workplace? Is it growing in counterpoint to the decline of civic engagement, reflecting some social analogue of the first law of thermodynamics – social capital is neither created nor destroyed, merely redistributed? Or do the trends described in this chapter represent simply a deadweight loss? What is the significance of more episodic or informal contacts, as

Democracy in America at century's end

contrasted with the more conventional sorts of civic engagement stressed in this chapter?

- A rounded assessment of changes in American social capital over the last quarter century needs to count the *costs* as well as the *benefits* of community engagement. We must not romanticize small-town, middle-class, civic life in the America of the 1950s. In addition to the deleterious trends emphasized in this chapter, recent decades have witnessed a substantial decline in intolerance[30] and probably also in overt discrimination, and those beneficent trends may be related in complex ways to the erosion of traditional social capital. Moreover, a balanced accounting of the social capital books would need to reconcile the insights of this approach with the undoubted insights offered by Mancur Olson and others who stress that closely knit social, economic, and political organizations are prone to inefficient cartelization and to what political economists term "rent seeking" and what ordinary men and women call corruption (see Olson 1982).

- Finally, and most urgently, we need to explore creatively how public policy impinges on (or might impinge on) social capital formation. In some renowned instances public policy has destroyed highly effective social networks and norms. American slum clearance policy of the 1950s and 1960s, for example, renovated physical capital, but at a very high cost to existing social capital. The consolidation of country post offices and small school districts has promised administrative and financial efficiencies, but full-cost accounting for the effects of these policies on social capital might produce a more negative verdict. On the other hand, such past initiatives as the agricultural county agent system, community colleges, and tax deductions for charitable contributions illustrate that government has the power to encourage social capital formation. Even a recent proposal in San Luis Obispo, California, to require that all new houses have front porches illustrates the power of zoning regulations to influence where and how networks are formed.

It is one of history's ironies that at the very moment when liberal democracy has swept the battlefield, both ideologically and geopolitically, growing numbers of citizens in the West are questioning the effectiveness of our public institutions. In America, at least, there is reason

62   *Robert D. Putnam*

to suspect that this democratic disarray may be linked to a broad erosion of civic engagement that began a quarter century ago. Political philosophers nowadays are much preoccupied with "deliberative democracy," in which public policy emerges from a civic conversation. Deliberation of this sort requires that we know one another well enough to weigh one another's views. Deliberative democracy is not merely about expressing opinions, and it is undermined by anonymity and incivility. It requires that we take responsibility for our own views and that we test them in give-and-take with others who take us seriously. In this sense, "Ted from Toledo" -style talk-shows undermine deliberative democracy, while weekly conversations on bowling teams (as well as other, more elevated forms of social capital) can contribute to it. An adequate stock of social capital is an important precondition for deliberative democracy.

Tocqueville was an acutely observant social philosopher, not a statistician, but he saw quite accurately the special importance of civic engagement for democracy in America and elsewhere. A contemporary social philosopher, Michael Walzer, also relied on poetry and inspiration, not social science, when he recently asserted that

weakness is a general feature of associational life in America today. Unions, churches, interest groups, ethnic organizations, political parties and sects, societies for self-improvement and good works, local philanthropies, neighborhood clubs and cooperatives, religious sodalities, brotherhoods and sisterhoods: this American civil society is wonderfully multitudinous. Most associations are, however, precariously established, skimpily funded, and always at risk. They have less reach and holding power than once they did. I can't cite statistics; I'm not sure that anyone is collecting the right sorts of statistics; but I suspect that the number of Americans who are unorganized, inactive, and undefended is on the rise. (Walzer 1994: 187)

The prosaic statistics and scholarly literature reviewed in this chapter are meant to establish in the idiom of social science both that

- Tocqueville was right that connectedness counts, that civic engagement has real consequences for our public affairs,

and that

- Walzer is right that the American tradition of civic engagement has weakened in recent years and that many of the social and political ills afflicting America (and perhaps other advanced nations) can be attributed to this contagious disengagement from our collective life.

Evaluating this diagnosis and considering possible therapies – reweaving the social fabric – require the creative collaboration of poets, policy

Democracy in America at century's end

wonks, community activists, and thousands of ordinary citizens, along (perhaps) with a few social scientists.

NOTES

1 This article, which appeared in an abridged version in *Journal of Democracy*, vol. 6, no. 1 (January 1995), pp. 65–78, triggered a lively public debate about the state of civic life in America. The text reproduced here is only slightly revised from the version delivered in Uppsala in 1994. In light of the subsequent debate, I would now formulate some part of the argument slightly differently, but I have not attempted to do so in this setting.

2 For a larger review of the literature linking social capital and educational outcomes, see Braatz and Putnam (1996).

3 Wilson's central thesis is that the tragic chaos of American urban ghettos is attributable to the exodus of middle-class and working-class African-American families from the ghetto, coupled with larger economic trends that have deprived these communities of stable jobs. See also Wilson (1991). For a fuller account of this author's perspective, see Wilson (1987) and Wacquant and Wilson (1990). Other illustrations of the voluminous literature on neighborhood effects include Crane (1991) and Anderson (1991). Mayer and Jencks (1989) emphasize the inconclusiveness of much of the initial literature on "neighborhood effects."

4 "Community policing" refers to a public strategy that encourages more active cooperation in crime control between police officers and community members. For introductions to the research that underlies this approach, see Wilson and Kelling (1982); Skogan (1990); Sparrow, Moore, and Kennedy, (1990); Taub, Taylor, and Dunham (1984).

5 For a useful overview of this research, see Smith (1994).

6 James S. Coleman deserves primary credit for developing the "social capital" theoretical framework (1988 and 1990). See also Granovetter (1985); Loury (1987); and Putnam (1993b). To my knowledge, the first scholar to use the term "social capital" in the current sense was Jane Jacobs: "These [social] networks are a city's irreplaceable social capital. Whenever the capital is lost, from whatever cause, the income from it disappears, never to return until and unless new capital is slowly and chancily accumulated" (1961: 138).

7 For theoretical work on these points, see Raub and Weesie (1990) and Taylor and Singleton (1993).

8 For some initial reflections on this topic, see my 1993a: chapter 6.

9 For more poetical insights into many of these same themes, see Bellah *et al.* (1985) and Walzer (1994).

10 I am grateful to John Mark Hansen and to the Roper Center (Storrs, Connecticut) for generously making these data available. Each data point in Figure 3.2 aggregates ten surveys per year, so that the total sample size for each year is nearly 20,000. Thus, the trend over time for each question is statistically highly significant.

64   *Robert D. Putnam*

11 An important part of the explanation for this trend has been the rise in TV viewership, of course, but viewership of public affairs programs has actually declined in the recent decades, quite apart from the fact that coverage of public affairs is "thinner" in the electronic media than in the print media.

12 The massive study by Verba, Schlozman, Brady, and Nie (1995), comparing citizen participation in 1967 and 1990, finds that as a general rule forms of participation that require *money* (such as contributing financially to a candidate or political organization) have become more common. They also find some evidence that some other forms of participation have been stable or rising.

13 One plausible interpretation of these trends would trace them to economic distress. However, a detailed multi-variate analysis demonstrates that even the best macro-economic predictor of distrust in government (which happens to be the so-called "misery index," a simple summation of the inflation and unemployment rates) accounts for less than half of the year-to-year variance in trust. If economic conditions had been held constant between 1958 and 1994, this analysis suggests, trust in government would have dropped from 75 percent to 30 percent, whereas in fact, it dropped to 19 percent; taken together, the misery index and a straight-line time trend account for virtually all the yearly variance in trust ($R^2 = .90$). Although systematic data on political alienation in America before the advent of regular national surveys in the 1950s is sketchy, some evidence suggests that alienation had declined from the mid-1930s to the mid-1960s. See Lane (1965: esp. 893–895).

14 Several "time-budget" studies of the 1960s and 1970s provide a useful supplement to our understanding of the role of organizational activities in the daily life of Americans, although methodological difficulties make them imperfect guides to change over time. These data suggest that in that era women spent more time on organizational activities than men (3.35 hours/week, as compared to 2.72 hours/week). For both men and women, roughly half of all organizational activity involved religious groups, a proportion quite consistent with other evidence reviewed in this chapter. Beyond that, women spent most of their organizational time in "helping" and child-related organizations, like the PTA and the Red Cross, while men spent most time in fraternal organizations. Women also spent more time "visiting" than men (5.84 hours/week, as compared to 4.24 hours/week). Of course, these gender differences were attributable, at least in part, to differences in workforce participation rates. See, in particular, Robinson and Converse (1972), and the studies cited therein.

15 The sociological literature on religion in America is enormous. As entry points, see Wald (1987) and Wuthnow (1988).

16 For this and other time-series survey evidence on religiosity in the American public, see Mayer (1993). Studies that have compared survey results to local censuses of people actually in the church pews suggest that many people exaggerate the regularity of their church attendance, and there are even hints that this fibbing may have increased in recent years. See Hadaway, Marler, and Chaves (1993).

17 Any simplistically political interpretation of the collapse of American union-

Democracy in America at century's end

ism would need to confront the fact that the steepest decline began more than six years before the Reagan Administration's attack on PATCO. The membership figures in Figure 3.7 are fully consistent with GSS survey data, which show a roughly 40 percent decline in reported union membership between 1975 and 1991.

18 Data for the LWV are available over a longer time span and show an interesting pattern: a sharp slump during the Depression, a strong and sustained rise after World War II that more than tripled membership between 1945 and 1969, and then the post-1969 decline, which has already erased virtually all the postwar gains and continues still. This same historical pattern applies to those men's fraternal organizations for which comparable data are available – steady increases for the first seven decades of the century, interrupted only by the Great Depression, followed by a collapse in the 1970s and 1980s which has already wiped out most of the postwar expansion and continues apace.

19 Another widely discussed source of information on voluntarism is the biennial Gallup poll commissioned by the Independent Sector organization, as reported, for example, in *Giving and Volunteering* (1992). These surveys suggest some growth in volunteering between 1988 and 1990, followed by a decline between 1990 and 1992. For our purposes, however, these data are less useful. First, they define volunteering in the most expansive way possible; by thus counting many episodic encounters, they turn up twice as much voluntarism as the CPS surveys, for example. Second, they cover a much shorter time span and thus do not (yet) speak to the secular trends we are examining. Third, the sample size (roughly 2,500) is *much* smaller than the CPS surveys, with a much higher sampling error (±3 percent). Consequently, it is harder to interpret these data than the more reliable CPS figures. It is worth noting, finally, that roughly half of all volunteering (slightly less in the CPS figures, slightly more in the IS figures) is done through religious organizations, yet another mark of the extraordinary importance of religion in American life.

20 We are still seeking detailed data on other service clubs, including Kiwanis and Rotary. Male Kiwanis membership has dropped since 1970, although in the aggregate that trend is offset by the admission of women in 1976. As in the case of women's clubs, the available evidence on long-term trends in membership of fraternal organizations suggests a pattern of substantial and continuing growth through most of this century, interrupted only in the 1932–1945 period, until the reversals of the late 1970s.

21 Data from the American Bowling Congress.

22 Some of these organizations, of course, provide their members with commercial services, like group insurance or high-fashion T-shirts, but in this role they are indistinguishable from other mail-order firms.

23 For a valuable study of voluntary group membership that, however, fails to distinguish between what I here term secondary and tertiary associations, see Baumgartner and Walker, Jr. (1988).

24 For overviews of the extensive literature on non-profit organizations, see Powell (1987); Van Til (1988); and Dimaggio and Anheier (1990).

25 Salamon (1994: 114) writes of a global "associational revolution," not

66 *Robert D. Putnam*

merely of a growing role for non-profit agencies, and argues that "the associational revolution may prove as significant as the rise of the nation-state", but his empirical evidence does not sustain these broad claims. I share Salamon's view that associations are of great importance, and I agree that they may be proliferating in some parts of the world, although systematic evidence for a global upsurge is wholly lacking. Salamon may also be right that non-profit organizations now play a larger role in American society, but as far as secondary associations are concerned, his case rests solely on the empirical claim that a high proportion of extant national organizations have been formed recently. However, rapid organizational birth is quite consistent with even more rapid organizational death and decay, and Salamon's methodology entirely overlooks issues of organizational morbidity and mortality. From the point of view of social connectedness, I believe, the cumulative evidence of associational erosion presented in the present chapter is more relevant.

26 I am grateful to Ronald Inglehart, who directs this unique cross-national project, for sharing these highly useful data with me.

27 For subsequent work on this issue, see Putnam (1995).

28 This is in some sense merely the continuation of a trend that has concerned social philosophers for much of this century. See, for example, Dewey (1988).

29 For one useful illustration, see Uslaner (1993) on the links between social trust within the American electorate and the effectiveness of legislative processes.

30 See the evidence summarized in Mayer (1993).

REFERENCES

Anderson, Elijah. 1991. "Neighborhood effects on teenage pregnancy," in Christopher Jencks and Paul E. Peterson, eds., *The Urban Underclass.* Washington, DC: The Brookings Institution.

Baumgartner, Frank R., and Jack L. Walker, Jr. 1988. "Survey research and membership in voluntary associations," *American Journal of Political Science* 32: 908–928.

Bellah, Robert N. *et al.* 1985. *Habits of the Heart: Individualism and Commitment in American Life.* Berkeley: University of California Press.

Berkman, Lisa, and Lester Breslow. 1983. *Health and Ways of Living: The Almeda County Study.* New York: Oxford University Press.

Borjas, George J. 1992. "Ethnic capital and intergenerational mobility," *Quarterly Journal of Economics* 107: 123–150.

Boston Globe. 1993. March 31.

Braatz, Jay, and Putnam, Robert D. 1996. *Families, Communities, and Education in America: Exploring the Evidence.* University of Wisconsin.

Brudney, Jeffrey L. 1990. "The availability of volunteers," *Administration and Society* 21: 413–424.

Brusco, Sebastiano. 1990. "The idea of the industrial district: its genesis," in Frank Pyke, Giacomo Becattini, and Werner Sengenberger, eds., *Industrial*

Democracy in America at century's end 67

Districts and Inter-Firm Co-Operation in Italy. Geneva: International Institute for Labour Studies.

Caplow, Theodore, Howard M. Bahr, John Modell, and Bruce A. A. Chadwick. 1991. *Recent Social Trends in the United States: 1960–1990.* Montreal: McGill-Queen's University Press.

Case, Anne C., and Lawrence F. Katz. 1991. "The company you keep: the effects of family and neighborhood on disadvantaged youths." NBER Working Paper No. 3705. Cambridge, Mass.: National Bureau of Economic Research.

Cohen, Sheldon, and Syme, S. Leonard, eds. 1985. *Social Support and Health.* New York: Academic Press.

Coleman, James S. 1988. "Social capital in the creation of human capital," *American Journal of Sociology* (Supplement) 94: S95–S120.

1990. *The Foundations of Social Theory.* Cambridge Mass.: Harvard University Press.

Coleman, James S., and T. B. Hoffer. 1987. *Public and Private High Schools: The Impact of Communities.* New York: Basic Books.

Comer, James. 1980. *School Power.* New York: The Free Press.

Crane, Jonathan. 1991. "The effects of neighborhoods on dropping out of school and teenage childbearing," in Christopher Jencks and Paul E. Peterson, eds., *The Urban Underclass.* Washington, DC: The Brookings Institution.

Dewey, John. 1988. "The Public and its Problems," in John Dewey, *The Later Works,* vol. II, ed. Jo Ann Boydston. Carbondale: Southern Illinois Press.

Dimaggio, Paul J., and Helmut K. Anheier. 1990. "The sociology of nonprofit organizations and sectors," *Annual Review of Sociology* 16: 137–159.

Esman, Milton J., and Norman Uphoff. 1984. *Local Organizations: Intermediaries in Rural Development.* Ithaca, N.Y.: Cornell University Press.

Evans, Peter B. 1990. "The state as problem and solution: predation, embedded autonomy and structural change," in Stephan Haggard and Robert Kaufman, eds., *The Politics of Economic Adjustment.* Princeton: Princeton University Press.

Fischer, Claude S. 1991. "Ambivalent communities: how Americans understand their localities," in Alan Wolfe, ed., *America at Century's End.* Berkeley and Los Angeles: University of California Press.

Giving and Volunteering. 1992. Washington, DC: Independent Sector.

Granovetter, Mark S. 1985. "Economic action and social structure: the problem of embeddedness," *American Journal of Sociology* 91: 481–510.

Greenhalgh, Susan. 1988. "Families and networks in Taiwan's economic development," in Edwin Winckler and Susan Greenhalgh, eds., *Contending Approaches to the Political Economy of Taiwan.* Armonk, N.Y.: Sharp Cop.

Hadaway, C. Kirk, Penny Long Marler, and Mark Chaves. 1993. "What the polls don't show: a closer look at U.S. church attendance," *American Sociological Review* 58: 741–752.

Hamilton, Gary G., and Nicole Woolsey Biggart. 1988. "Market, culture, and authority: a comparative analysis of management and organization in the Far East," *American Journal of Sociology* (Supplement) 94: S52–S94.

Hamilton, Gary G., William Zeile, and Wan-Jin Kim. 1989. "Network structure

68   Robert D. Putnam

of East Asian economics," in S. R. Clegg and S. G. Redding, eds., *Capitalism in Contrasting Cultures*. Berlin: De Gruyter.

Hayghe, Howard V. 1991. "Volunteers in the U.S.: who donates the time?," *Monthly Labor Review* 114: 17–23.

Hirsch, Barry T., and John T. Addison. 1986. *The Economic Analysis of Unions*. Boston: Allen & Unwin.

Hirschman, Albert O. 1984. *Getting Ahead Collectively: Grassroots Experiences in Latin America*. New York: Pergamon Press.

Jacobs, Jane. 1961. *The Death and Life of Great American Cities*. New York: Random House.

Knack, Stephan. 1992. "Civic norms, social sanctions, and voter turnout," *Rationality and Society* 4: 133–156.

Lane, Robert E. 1965. "The politics of consensus in an age of affluence," *American Political Science Review* 59: 874–895.

Light, Ivan. 1972. *Ethnic Enterprise in America*. Berkeley: University of California Press.

Loury, Glenn C. 1987. "Why should we care about group inequality?," *Social Philosophy and Policy* 5: 249–271.

Mayer, Susan E., and Christopher Jencks. 1989. "Growing up in poor neighborhoods. How much does it matter?" *Science* 243: 1441–1445.

Mayer, William G. 1993. *The Changing American Mind*. Ann Arbor: University of Michigan Press.

Meyrowitz, Joshua. 1985. *No Sense of Place: The Impact of Electronic Media on Social Behavior*. New York: Oxford University Press.

Moore, Ernest C. 1897. "The social value of the saloon," *American Journal of Sociology* 2: 1–12.

Olson, Mancur. 1982. *The Rise and Decline of Nations: Economic Growth, Stagflation, and Social Rigidities*. New Haven: Yale University Press.

O'Regan, Katherine M., and John M. Quigley. 1991. "Labor market access and labor market outcomes for urban youth," *Regional Science and Urban Economics* 21: 277–293.

Papanek, Gustav. 1988. "The new Asian capitalism: an economic portrait," in Peter L. Berger and Hsin-Huang Hsiao, eds., *In Search of an East Asian Development Model*. New Brunswick, N.J.: Transaction Books.

Piore, Michael J., and Charles F. Sabel. 1983. "Italian small business development: lessons for U.S. industrial policy," in John Zysman and Laura Tyson, eds., *American Industry in International Competition*. Ithaca, N.Y.: Cornell University Press.

1984. *The Second Industrial Divide*. New York: Basic Books.

Portes, Alejandro, and Julia Sensenbrenner. 1993. "Embeddedness and immigration: notes on the social determinants of economic action," *American Journal of Sociology* 98: 1320–1350.

Powell, Walter W., ed. 1987. *The Nonprofit Sector: A Research Handbook*. New Haven: Yale University Press.

Powell, Walter W., and Laurel Smith-Doerr. 1994. "Networks and economic life," in Neil Smelser and Richard Swedberg, eds., *The Handbook of Economic Sociology*. Princeton: Princeton University Press.

Public Perspective, The. 1994. Vol. 5 no. 4.

Putnam, Robert D. 1993a. *Making Democracy Work: Civic Traditions in Modern Italy*. Princeton: Princeton University Press.

1993b. "The prosperous community: social capital and public life," *The American Prospect* 13: 35–42.

1995. "Tuning in, tuning out: the strange disappearance of social capital in America," *Political Science and Politics* 28: 1–20.

Raub, Werner, and Jeroen Weesie. 1990. "Reputation and efficiency in social interactions: an example of network effects," *American Journal of Sociology* 96: 626–654.

Robinson, John P., and Philip E. Converse. 1972. "Social change reflected in the use of time," in Angus Campbell and Philip E. Converse, eds., *The Human Meaning of Social Change*. New York: Russell Sage.

Roof, Wade Clark, and William McKinney. 1987. *American Mainline Religion*. New Brunswick, N.J.: Rutgers University Press.

Rosenstone, Steven J., and John Mark Hansen. 1993. *Mobilization, Participation, and Democracy in America*. New York: Macmillan.

Salamon, Lester M. 1987. "Partners in public service: the scope and theory of government-nonprofit relations," in Powell 1987.

1994. "The rise of the nonprofit sector," *Foreign Affairs* 73: 109–122.

Saxenian, AnnaLee. 1990. "Regional networks and the resurgence of Silicon Valley," *California Management Review* 33: 89–112.

Schlozman, Kay Lehman, and John T. Tierney. 1986. *Organized Interests and American Democracy*. New York: Harper and Row.

Schor, Juliet B. 1991. *The Overworked American: The Unexpected Decline of Leisure*. New York: Basic Books.

Skogan, Wesley G. 1990. *Disorder and Decline: Crime and the Spiral of Decay in American Neighborhoods*. New York: The Free Press.

Smith, Steven Rathgeb. 1994. "Social capital, community coalitions, and the role of institutions." Unpub. MS, prepared for delivery at the annual meeting of the American Political Science Association, New York City, September 1–4.

Sparrow, Malcolm, Mark H. Moore, and David M. Kennedy. 1990. *Beyond 911: A New Era for Policing*. New York: Basic Books.

Taub, Richard P., D. Garth Taylor, and Jan D. Dunham. 1984. *Paths of Neighborhood Change: Race and Crime in Urban America*. Chicago: University of Chicago Press.

Taylor, Michael, and Sara Singleton. 1993. "The communal resource: transaction costs and the solution of collective action problems," *Politics and Society* 21: 195–214.

Teixeira, Ruy A. 1992. *The Disappearing American Voter*. Washington, DC: The Brookings Institution.

Tocqueville, Alexis de. 1969. *Democracy in America*, ed. J. P. Mayer, transl. George Lawrence. Garden City, N.Y.: Anchor Books.

U.S. News. 1994. April 4.

Uslaner, Eric M. 1993. *The Decline of Comity in Congress*. Ann Arbor: University of Michigan Press.

1995. "Faith, hope, and charity: trust and collective action." Unpublished MS, University of Maryland/College Park.

70 Robert D. Putnam

Van Til, Jon. 1988. *Mapping the Third Sector: Voluntarism in a Changing Social Economy*. New York: Foundation Center.

Verba, Sidney, Kay Lehman Schlozman, Henry Brady, and Norman H. Nie. 1995. *Voice and Equality: Civic Voluntarism in American Politics*. Cambridge, Mass.: Harvard University Press.

Wacquant, Loïc J. D., and William Julius Wilson. 1990. "The cost of racial and class exclusion in the inner city," *Annals of the American Academy of Political and Social Science* 501: 8–25.

Wald, Kenneth D. 1987. *Religion and Politics in the United States*. New York: St. Martin's Press.

Walker, Jack L. 1991. *Mobilizing Interest Groups in America: Patrons, Professions, and Social Movements*. Ann Arbor: University of Michigan Press.

Walzer, Michael. 1994. "Multiculturalism and individualism," *Dissent* Spring: 185–191.

Wilensky, R., and D. M. Kline III. 1988. *Renewing Urban Schools: The Community Connection*. Denver: Education Commission of the States.

Williams, Redford B. *et al.* 1992. "Prognostic importance of social and economic resources among medically treated patients with angiographically documented coronary artery disease," *Journal of the American Medical Association* 267: 520–524.

Wilson, James Q., and George Kelling. 1982. "Broken windows: the police and neighborhood safety," *Atlantic Monthly* 252: 29–38.

Wilson, William Julius. 1987. *The Truly Disadvantaged: The Inner City, the Underclass, and Public Policy*. Chicago: University of Chicago Press.

1990. "The cost of racial and class exclusion in the inner city," *Annals of the American Academy of Political and Social Science* 501: 8–25.

1991. "Studying inner-city social dislocations: the challenge of public agenda research (1990 presidential address)," *American Sociological Review* 56: 1–14.

Wuthnow, Robert. 1988. *The Restructuring of American Religion*. Princeton: Princeton University Press.

1994. *Sharing the Journey: Support Groups and America's New Quest for Community*. New York: The Free Press.

4 On sources of social and political conflicts in follower democracies

Atul Kohli

The tone of this chapter is at least sober, if not pessimistic. I anticipate that over the short to medium term, most developing country democracies – labeled here, follower democracies – will continue to perform at fairly low levels of effectiveness, i.e., the capacity of these democracies to diagnose and solve pressing socioeconomic problems on the one hand, and to absorb social conflict on the other hand, will remain low. Many of these democracies will be characterized by considerable political and social conflict, including overt violence.

A central political tendency in follower democracies will be towards the emergence of two-track polities, with a democratic track in the sphere of society and politics, especially electoral politics, and a not-so-democratic track in the state sphere, especially in the areas of economic policy making. The political society of many poor democracies is thus likely to be characterized by "too much democracy," i.e., by a variety of political, class, and ethnic conflicts. By contrast, the state in these settings will increasingly insulate itself from social demands and conflicts and thus exhibit "not enough democracy." Before these follower democracies become institutionalized and effective political systems, it will be necessary to bridge this gap between "too much" and "not enough" democracy. Bridging this gap, in turn, is likely to require deliberate changes that will not be easy, namely, creation of new institutions that systematically devolve political and economic power.

What is it about the structure of the state and society in developing countries that will continue to militate against ready consolidation of effective democracies? If one agrees with the propositions that democracy is mainly a product of economic development[1] and/or of capitalism[2] then low levels of development and/or weak capitalism become the main explanation of problems of follower democracies. While incorporating these concerns, the argument below is somewhat different. It is rather based on a perspective that "you cannot step in the same river twice." The fact that the world today is dominated by advanced industrial democracies changes the problem of democratization for those who

72   *Atul Kohli*

arrive "late" and must now "follow"; follower democracies are not likely to replicate historical patterns and sequences, i.e., moving to stronger and stronger democracies mainly as economic development proceeds.[3]

I thus eschew "closed models" of democracy, both developmental and Marxist, in which democratization is viewed as a process of political change in self-contained units, fueled mainly by economic changes. Instead, the "model" underlying the argument below is more "open" insofar as democratization in contemporary developing countries is viewed as conditioned by global forces, both material and ideological. More specifically, I argue below that democracy to most developing countries comes as imported ideas. As these ideas are translated into institutions of follower democracies and these institutions provide new incentives for political actors to organize and mobilize, the results over the short to medium term are often disquieting. Social structural traits of follower democracies – i.e., aspects of their culture, political institutions, and state–economy links – help explain why this should be so.

The first general trait I wish to point to is well understood, but needs to be underlined mainly to orient the discussion. Western political models have spread to the non-West. A diverse set of mechanisms has helped this spread: colonialism, especially British colonialism, left behind the legacy of democracy in several colonies; in more recent decades, global spread of plebiscitarian ideals made a variety of authoritarianisms untenable; and finally, decline of Communism and global victory of capitalism has pushed democracy – a political system that is by now deeply associated as most suited to house capitalist economies – to the forefront of global political agenda. Whatever the mechanisms, cultural conditions in the developing world do not readily mesh with these imported political models. For example, if I may overgeneralize about developing countries: identities tend to be more local than national; authority in society tends to be dispersed but, within dispersed pockets, quite rigid and hierarchical; and community norms often prevail over narrow individualism.

An authoritarian state imposed on such societies often froze these social patterns, or at least enabled them to continue without profound changes. By contrast, rapid introduction of democracy has a disquieting impact on established social and cultural patterns. Again, some examples. First, as competing elites undertake political mobilization, old identities are rekindled and new identities are forged. Modern technology hastens the process: witness, for example, the rapid spread of militant Islamic teachings on cassettes or the rendering of the ancient Hindu

Conflicts in follower democracies

epic *Ramayana* on television across India. Collision of mobilized identities, in turn, is not totally surprising. Similarly, the spread of democratic politics undermines (or at least threatens) the authority of traditional elites. Threatened local elites, in turn, often join hands, sometimes turning their wrath upon the newly empowered underlings or, at other times, upon those above them, the national elite. And finally, erosion of community norms, that commercial and political individualism fosters, is perceived to be deeply disruptive. As a reaction, some groups attempt to regroup, again giving rise to a variety of "reactionary" movements. In sum, as imported political models and indigenous cultural conditions interact and adapt to each other, political turbulence ought to be expected.

A second general set of issues concerns weakness of political institutions in follower democracies. The obstacles that this condition generates for creating effective democracies are also well known (see, e.g., Huntington 1968) but some specific causes and consequences of fragile institutions need to be discussed. First, the manner in which most recent "transitions" have occurred has not been the most auspicious from the standpoint of future consolidation. Disintegration of authoritarian regimes was often relatively rapid – rapid, at least, on the scale of "political time" over which new institutions take root – and left in its wake a divided elite, a mobilized populace with heightened expectations, and weak institutional links between the elite and the masses. Consolidation, by contrast, would be helped by the presence of some consensus-generating, or, more appropriately, boundary-setting, forces in the body politic – a force that was both larger than and somewhat independent of the ruling political elite – that could tame the scope and intensity of societal power conflicts. A few historical examples will help illustrate the point.

Successful Western democracies – for example, England – evolved such consensus facilitating institutions as political parties and parliaments over a long time, though often punctuated by reversals, violent struggles, and discontinuities. Proto-democratic traditions born of a feudal past, and contending class interests within an increasingly hegemonic capitalism, generated both open political conflict and the framework that eventually bounded these conflicts within a democratic form. By contrast, democracy in most non-Western cases has been more an import than a product of an evolving indigenous class order. Here again, however, in rare cases where democracy has taken root, democratic consolidation was facilitated by the presence of society-wide consensual forces. Compare, for example, India and Nigeria: both emerged from British colonialism as poor, deeply divided societies. Democracy,

74   *Atul Kohli*

however, has fared better in India. Why? Among the numerous factors at work, India was helped by a prolonged nationalist movement. Developed over half a century preceding sovereignty, this movement generated a unifying ideology and patterns of organization that facilitated the formation of a national, hegemonic political party. While a single, hegemonic party is not to be recommended to all democratic comers, in the Indian case these national structures generated a boundary-setting force that, at least for a few decades, helped tame intra-elite and elite-mass conflicts.[4]

Democratic political traditions, a class order and national political movements are examples of consensus-generating forces that have historically helped proto-democracies consolidate into democracies. Intra-elite pacts under very special political circumstances – such as Venezuela and Colombia – and the binding role of external actors – e.g., that of the European Economic Community in such cases as Portugal – have also provided "functional equivalents" of sorts. Clearly, a variety of historical alternatives exist. Nevertheless, the general point is this: consolidation of new democracies is smoother when there exists some society-wide consensual force to facilitate peaceful resolution of intra-elite and elite-mass conflicts in the "post-transition" period.

For those hoping to encourage democracy in the developing world, there is a policy lesson here: consolidation will be easier if the transition itself was pushed forward, not primarily by external pressure, but by a national, cohesive, pro-democratic political force. Unfortunately, cohesive and consensual forces of this nature have been relatively weak in many of the new cases of "transitions." For example, let us take the case of Brazil. The "transition" there left in its wake a heterogenous political society and fairly weak political institutions. Following the "transition," therefore, populism, nepotism, and corruption, a highly divided elite, and growing elite-mass polarization reemerged very quickly as significant political trends (see, e.g., Schneider 1991). Whether a popular leader like Fernando Henrique Cardoso can reverse these trends or not remains an open question at the time of writing. And Brazil is not alone; several other new democracies have also begun to experience similar pains. A memory of the shared antipathy to authoritarianism of the past is probably the most important binding force for many of these new democracies; so far there are no credible enemies of democracy on the horizon. What will happen, however, as this memory fades over the next five to ten years, and the record of poor governmental performance again comes to dominate the democratic scene? Will "soft authoritarianism" of the East Asian variety or a variety of religious fundamentalisms provide alternate legitimacy formulae?

Conflicts in follower democracies 75

Continuing with the discussion of political institutions, such democratic institutions as parties and parliaments are obviously fragile in most countries that have recently "transited" from authoritarianism. A typical outcome follows: irrespective of the levels of civil society activism during the anti-authoritarian phase, power in many a new democracy comes to rest in the hands of a few individuals, if not a single leader. A further recurring consequence is that whenever the ruling elite are threatened, further centralization of power is a readily available alternative. Because centralization of power in individuals nearly always further emasculates fragile institutions – strong institutions do constrain the power of individuals – there is a built-in incentive in new democracies for leaders to undertake periodic deinstitutionalization. Weak institutions and personalistic rule thus become vicious and mutually re-enforcing processes. As long as a democracy remains more an affair of a few elite and less an established framework that dwarfs the leaders, only exceptional leaders are likely to resist the tendency to maintain personal power at the expense of institutional development.

An elite-dominated democracy also structures patterns of political mobilization. Leaders in these settings mobilize socioeconomic groups more as power resources in intra-elite struggles and less to satisfy group aspirations. While a fair amount of this is "normal" politics, what is not always appreciated is that mobilized but unorganized groups that are ignored by politicians once they have served their political purposes add considerable volatility to the polity. When "real groups" with "real interests," such as labor, are mobilized, there is a realistic chance that the mobilization will be accompanied by organization and that group demands can be accommodated after negotiations. By contrast, mobilization from above often attracts demagogues who utilize populist, nationalist, and ethnic appeals to bolster their position. Because it remains unorganized and really does not have concrete, even if incremental, gains for the mobilized groups as its priority, such mobilization periodically tends to generate political turmoil.

Weakness of political parties is another central and related issue in the whole gamut of institutional issues. Both the causes and the consequences of party weakness need to be better understood.[5] One hypothesis that would fit a number of countries is that strong parties – parties with well-developed political identification, programmatic goals, and organization – develop mainly as vehicles for gaining power. Conversely, leaders who acquire power because of personal appeal have little incentive to encourage the development of parties from above; on the contrary, parties as institutions often constrain the individual discretion and personalistic power of towering leaders. Thus, well-developed parties often emerge from below rather than from above, and just as often, take time and require sustained open political spaces. If this proposition is valid, significant policy implications follow: the typical resort to personalistic, concentrated executive power as a post-transition, stabilizing measure only postpones the deeper need to work out a society's power conflicts.

As to the consequences of party organization, well-organized parties can perform several important political tasks. They can help train and socialize new leaders, minimize factional conflict among existing leaders, and clarify lines of authority. Mobilization undertaken by parties, rather than by individuals, is also more likely to be accompanied by organization: not only are new participants brought into the political arena, but their political energies are simultaneously harnessed to accomplish specific goals. More important, well-organized parties tend to have long-term programs and a stable core of membership to support those programs. When such parties come to power, they help narrow the gap between the state's representative and developmental goals. The coalition that such a party brings to power is likely to favor the policies that the new government wishes to pursue.

It thus stands to reason that absence of strong parties are likely to remain a major source of political problem for new democracies. Moreover, it is conceivable, nay, likely, that follower democracies will never develop political parties along Western lines. Instead, they may have to come up with alternate institutional arrangements for tasks that were performed by parties in older democracies. Whatever the eventual institutional constellation, organizational vacuum in the near future will continue to be a root cause of the growing gap in these countries between how power is won and how power is used, or between personalization of power, on the one hand, and the inability to use that power to solve pressing problems on the other hand.

The third set of conditions that needs to be discussed concerns the political economy, especially the political problems generated by misdirected state intervention in the economy. While the issue of state intervention is generally discussed in connection with problems of "rent seeking" (see, e.g., Bates 1981), the political impact of an interventionist state at low levels of development – a characteristic that is rather widespread in follower democracies – is not fully understood. These deserve our attention. An interventionist state in the early to middle stages of economic development has difficulty establishing a separation between the public and private spheres in social life. That has several consequences. The most important from the standpoint of democratic consolidation is that an interventionist state cannot claim that distributive problems are social and not political problems. The coexistence of political equality with considerable economic inequality facilitated the establishment of proto-democracies in parts of nineteenth-century Europe. The interventionist welfare state developed only under resource-abundant, mature capitalism. In follower democracies, however, a highly interventionist state is inherent to the overall design of state-led development; it is part of the condition of being "late" in the game of development, now wishing to hasten the process, i.e., to catch up. This could change with waves of "liberalization" or with improving economic conditions, but certainly not much over the short to medium term. Moreover, once democracy is introduced to the brew, the combination of democracy, a low-income economy, substantial inequities, and state intervention tends to politicize all forms of societal cleavages – old versus new, ethnic and economic. Thus, the accumulating distributive claims on the state partly reflect the state's attempt to penetrate and reorganize socioeconomic life.

Relatedly, an interventionist developing state typically controls a substantial proportion of a poor economy. Thus, many of the society's free-floating economic resources are controlled by politicians and bureaucrats. Who should have access to those resources? Unlike situations involving the products of private endeavor, the legitimacy of claims on public resources is not easy to establish. Given the scarcities in a poor economy, moreover, the competitive energies of the many individuals and groups seeking economic improvements tend to get focused on the state. Thus, competition over the state's resources often results in intense conflict, contributing to the problems of consolidating follower democracies.

So far I have pointed to several conditions – cultural, political and of the political economy – that contribute to political turbulence in low- and middle-income democracies. Before discussing the last condition, I wish to briefly recapitulate the discussion. The cultural conditions I pointed to were the political difficulties that emerged as localized identities and authority patterns adjusted to imported political models. The more structural conditions I have discussed concerned the weakness of political institutions and the political consequences of heavy state intervention in the economy and society. All of these conditions are clearly interrelated; if one thinks of them in the context of a broad historical sweep, they are all aspects of "follower" democracies, i.e., traits of democracies that are not a product of evolving capitalism. Democracy in developing countries starts out more as an imported idea than a "natural" product of social changes. Once the imported formal system is put in place, the state and society must necessarily adapt to each

78 Atul Kohli

other. Based on political equality, democracy naturally tends to generate expansionary political pressures. Such expansionary pressures were historically tamed by evolving capitalism, with occasional help from state coercion. For most developing country democracies, however, especially those that have recently "transited," extensive recourse to state coercion to limit demands will not be acceptable and, given less-than-robust capitalism, a more decentralized approach to limit expansionary pressures will not work.

This brings me to my last point. Follower democracies will continue to experience expansionary pressures i.e., pressures towards a more equal distribution of power in society. A movement towards genuine devolution of political and economic power could accommodate such tendencies, i.e., establish a new "equilibrium" between demands and governance, and help strengthen these democracies. Any such trend, however, is likely to run up against two pervasive global tendencies, both near intellectual hegemonies. These are, first, a belief in strong, centralized states as a necessity for the welfare of nations. Ambitious national elites, specific conceptions of nationalism and the reality of the global interstate system all feed into the pervasiveness of the centralized state model. And second, for the time being, there is a widespread tendency towards more and more pro-capitalist models of development. Often dubbed "market friendly," these economic models have further centralized power in many developing countries, especially in the hands of more technocratic elites. Power devolution is thus a fairly low priority for state elites in most follower democracies. The juxtaposition of expansionary political pressures from below and centralizing state elites at the apex produces a typical outcome, namely, the evolution of these democracies towards two-track polities, with a democratic track in the sphere of society and politics, especially electoral politics, and a not-so-democratic track in the state sphere, especially in the areas of economic policy making. The political society of many follower democracies is thus increasingly characterized by "too much democracy" – i.e., by a variety of political, class, and ethnic conflicts – on the one hand and, on the other hand, the state in these settings increasingly insulates itself from social demands and conflicts and thus exhibits "not enough democracy."

Introduction of democracy to a developing country setting nearly always exacerbates political conflicts over the short to medium term. Some observers are surprised by such outcomes because, extrapolating from the Western experience, they expect democracy to be a solution to existing, rather than a source of new, power conflicts. In the West, however,

Conflicts in follower democracies

if I may over-generalize again, democracy evolved over a long time, and both suffrage and political competition expanded slowly within the framework of centralized authority structures at the apex and growing popular pressures from below. In this sense, democracy in the West was indeed a "solution" to growing power conflicts in society. By contrast, democracy to most developing countries comes as imported ideas. As these ideas are translated into democratic institutions of follower democracies and these institutions provide new incentives for political actors to organize and mobilize, the results over the short to medium terms are often disquieting.

I have attempted in this brief chapter to suggest why this should be so. While many are busy celebrating the "victory" of democracy, caution is also warranted. Many developing country democracies in the near future will continue to perform at fairly low levels of effectiveness. The surprises of the future will be well functioning and not the troubled democracies of Asia, Africa, and Latin America. The roots of conflict and turbulence in these democracies, while numerous, are traceable back to the fact that as follower democracies these societies must adapt to larger political and economic forces, often beyond their control. One common global wisdom today is that, given a democratic framework and pro-capitalist economic policies, most social conflicts in these countries will work themselves out. Given the analysis above, I am skeptical of this view. Instead, the conclusion I am attracted to is that expansionary political pressures are inherent to the design of follower democracies and will need to be accommodated. This, in turn, suggests that institutions that genuinely devolve political and economic power will remain a prerequisite for strengthening developing country democracies. Whether this takes the form of social democracy of the European variety or fairly novel forms is less important from the standpoint of creating effective democracies; what is more important is that the current tension between expansionary demands and centralizing states be reduced by creating more egalitarian political economies.

NOTES

1 The proposition is now generally associated with the works of Seymour Martin Lipset. For his original statement, see Lipset (1959). For a recent, favorable discussion of this old proposition, see Diamond and Marks (1992).
2 This proposition is obviously associated with the writings of Karl Marx. For an important restatement, see Moore (1966). A recent "revisionist" account is Rueschemeyer, Stephens, and Stephens (1992).
3 For general political sociological accounts of "development" that eschew "evolutionary" thinking, see Bendix (1977 and 1978).

80   *Atul Kohli*

4 For a discussion of the role of the Congress party in facilitating political stability in post-independence India, see Weiner (1967). For a contrasting discussion of Nigeria's post-independence political difficulties, see Diamond (1988).
5 I discuss this issue in some detail, but mainly with reference to one case, India, in Kohli (1991).

REFERENCES

Bates, Robert. 1981. *Markets and States in Tropical Africa: The Political Bases of Agricultural Policies*. Berkeley: University of California Press.
Bendix, Reinhard. 1977. *Nation-Building and Citizenship: Studies of our Changing Social Order*. Berkeley: University of California Press.
    1978. *Kings or People: Power and the Mandate to Rule*. Berkeley: University of California Press.
Diamond, Larry. 1988. *Class, Ethnicity and Democracy in Nigeria: The Failure of the First Republic*. Syracuse, N.Y.: Syracuse University Press.
Diamond, Larry and Gary Marks, eds., 1992. *Reexamining Democracy: Essays in Honour of Seymour Martin Lipset*. Newbury Park, Calif.: Sage Publications.
Huntington, Samuel P. 1968. *Political Order in Changing Societies*. New Haven: Yale University Press.
Kohli, Atul. 1991. *Democracy and Discontent: India's Growing Crisis of Governability*. New York: Cambridge University Press.
Lipset, Seymour Martin. 1959. "Some social requisites of democracy: economic development and political legitimacy," *American Political Science Review* 53 no. 1: 69–105.
Moore, Barrington, Jr. 1966. *Social Origins of Dictatorship and Democracy: Lord and Peasant in the Making of the Modern World*. Boston: Beacon Press.
Rueschemeyer, Dietrich, Evelyne Huber Stephens, and John D. Stephens. 1992. *Capitalist Development and Democracy*. Oxford: Polity Press.
Schneider, Ben Ross. 1991. "Brazil under Collor: anatomy of a crisis," *World Policy Journal* 8 no. 2: 321–350.
Weiner, Myron. 1967. *Party Building in a New Nation: The Indian National Congress*. Chicago: University of Chicago Press.

5 Micro-aspects of democratic theory: what makes for the deliberative competence of citizens?

Claus Offe

In this chapter I am concerned with the micro-foundations of democratic politics. The basic unit of the democratic political process is the citizen. The quality of policy decisions and outcomes generated by such regimes, as well as the durability of democratic regimes, will ultimately depend upon the quality of the citizens' thought and action. To be sure, modern politics is largely a matter of collective representative actors, such as parties and associations. But this fact does not seem to diminish the role of individual citizens, as representative collective actors consist of and depend upon citizens as members, voters, and supporters. As so much depends upon the citizen and his/her competence to adequately perform the citizen role, equally much will also depend on the ways in which the preferences, evaluations, and cognitive orientations that citizens bring to the political process are formed. Civic competence of the sort that is compatible with and sustains democratic institutions, both in terms of the latters' legitimacy and effectiveness, is neither naturally given nor durable once achieved. Democracies can fail to come into being for lack of appropriate dispositions among citizens, and they can self-destruct because of a decline in civic competence or the breakdown of background conditions that are conducive to it.

Becoming a "good" citizen is a demanding project, both for the individuals themselves and for all those professions (such as educators), political elites, and the designers of political institutions involved in the formation of the qualities of citizens. Along the road leading to the formation of a citizen who then plays some "authorizing" role in the conduct of government, there are a number of issues that must be settled. First, there is the question of the *reference unit* that is adopted by individual agents as guiding their political judgment. This reference unit can be more or less inclusive, ranging from strict concern with the individual himself to the concern with mankind as a whole, with the more likely intermediate reference units of the family, the locality, region, class, occupational group, or nation. Second, and after the appropriate reference unit or significant community is chosen, the *evaluative* question

82   Claus Offe

must be settled: is the citizen's concern with the *welfare* of the unit, or is it with questions of *justice*, duty, and obligations? In other words, what is the appropriate decision criterion, or mix of criteria, according to which political questions are to be approached by the citizen? Third, *knowledge* is an important component of the citizenship role. The citizen, in order to adequately perform his role, must be in possession of some knowledge about the outside world, i.e., information concerning available policy choices and their effects. The citizen must also, in addition to an adequate cognitive assessment of the world, be knowledgeable about himself: he must have made up his mind as to which of the possibly conflicting preferences he wishes to follow, thus making sure that "his" will is actually "his own" well-considered preference, the holding and enactment of which will thus not be regretted at a later point or blamed upon some manipulative effort by others. Finally, and as the political action is just a subset of collective action, and collective action just a subset of all action of individual citizens, the citizen needs to avail himself of some cognitive map that allows him to determine whether a problem or issue is actually a "political" one, i.e., one that deserves or requires a worthwhile course of *collective* action involving political representation and *state* power, rather than either individual action or associative action within civil society. All these premises (identifications, criteria, knowledge, preferences, and codes) enter into the picture before the political role of the citizen can be enacted; and that role will be performed in more or less adequate and competent ways, i.e., ways conducive to the stability and effectiveness of democratic institutions, depending upon the nature of these rather complex premises.

If that much is granted, two questions become central to democratic theory. First, what standards of competence can and must we realistically require of citizens? Second, what kind of background conditions and institutional frameworks are called for in order to generate this competence and to maintain it over time?

What I intend to do in this chapter is to review some of the answers to these two questions that are being offered in contemporary democratic theory and to explore some of the inherent dilemmas of these answers.

All modern theorizing about democracy is self-reflectively divided into three camps. These are (a) the *"libertarian"* position emphasizing rights and liberties, state neutrality, and often state minimalism, (b) substantive theories about the *common good* and the traditions and communal identities from which the obligations of individuals toward the common good derive, and (c) some hybrid *"left-liberal"* or civic republican position "in between" these two positions which argues that while (b)

Deliberative competence of citizens 83

demands "too much" it is also true that (a) offers "too little." In a shorthand characterization, the last can be described as advocating "less than the 'good', but more than the 'right'." I will limit myself largely to a confrontation of the first and the third of these positions, the "libertarian" and the "left-liberal," and their respective requirements and presuppositions concerning the role of the citizen and the criteria of the adequate and competent performance of this role.

The libertarian case

In the libertarian tradition, both markets and (democratic) politics can be described and justified as preference-aggregating machines. People are provided with the means of communicating (through money or through the vote) what they prefer most, and the aggregate result is then accepted by the theorist, and eventually by the people themselves, as the optimum of social choice. This is the core of the theory of exogenous preferences, which centers on the freedom of choice according to "given" preferences. These preferences are seen to form the ultimate independent variable of economic and political processes and are advocated as the legitimate ultimate determinants of these processes.

The classical Utilitarians believed that there is a fixed set of (in Bentham's case: fifteen) "simple pleasures" of which all observable preferences, as revealed in action, could be somehow derived. This anthropological assumption has been dropped by today's neoclassical economists who find it difficult to either descriptively or prescriptively impose any constraints upon the variability of preferences. Having lost their foundation in some construct of human nature, preferences become amorphous by content and a-rational by their origin. In analytical terms, they must be treated as "exogenous," and in normative terms they must be taken for granted and *accepted* as they "are," i.e., as they reveal themselves in behavioral terms; preferences are inherently beyond explanation and evaluation. The only thing we can know about them is that they must be respected as the legitimate expression of a person's freedom. Citizens cannot be expected to have particular preferences, nor arrive at them in a particular way, in order to qualify as democratically competent citizens.

The strength and, at the same time, the controversial nature of this liberal-utilitarian axiom, reside in its negative and polemical implication. Not only does it say that what happens in markets and politics is the aggregate outcome of individual preferences. It also claims as its normative precept that "I" know best what is good for me, whatever it may be, and nobody has the right to interfere with my freedom of choice as

84   *Claus Offe*

long as the latter is made within the limits of the law. "Any rule or command that prohibits a person from choosing some preference order is morally unacceptable . . . from the point of view of democracy" (Riker 1982: 117).[1] This is clearly meant to include preference orders which suffer from one of three potential deficiencies: they may be based on demonstrably false assumptions about the world (as in magical thinking), they may immorally disregard the well being of others (as in racist preferences), or they may be excessively short-sighted and ill-considered. It is hard to specify to what extent preferences and political choices must be "competent" in these three dimensions, i.e., must be fact-regarding ("informed"), other-regarding ("fair"), and future-regarding (adequately "far-sighted"). Consistent libertarians, at any rate, seem to be remarkably tolerant of preferences that exhibit extremely low levels in these three dimensions, perhaps with an implicit reliance on some version of learning theory that suggests that such deficiencies are self-healing.

For the bottom line of this approach is something like this. First, it takes a strongly polemical position against all kinds of paternalism and other attempts to dictate or constrain preferences. On a normative plane, the approach is *"permissive"* to an extreme degree. Second, and on the positive plane, the approach is *"agnostic"* as to the causes of those preferences that we observe as motivating the behaviour of actors; preferences originate from within the individual, and hence nobody other than the individual is causally and also morally responsible for them. Taken together, there is the dual negative proposition that we can neither prescribe nor explain preferences. Of course, the view of preferences as individually given does not preclude the possibility that preferences undergo spontaneous changes. Actors may hit upon experiences, evidences, opportunities, arguments, etc., which may lead them to change their preferences by some form of "learning." But such learning is in no way to be conditioned or enforced by agents other than the actor himself.[2]

The only thing that the liberal theorist demands from the holder of preferences is that any individual preference order be transitive (i.e., if a > b and b > c, then also a > c), and perhaps also that different preference orderings are compatible with each other, which is to say that it makes little sense to express a preference for, e.g., higher overall government expenditures *and* general cuts in taxation. Furthermore, one might demand, following Gary Becker (1976), that preference orders should be chosen in such a way as to make best use of "consumption capital." But all these demands are just designed to impose a certain discipline upon action, filtering out the unreflective modes of action that sociol-

Deliberative competence of citizens

ogists describe as affective, habitual, or traditional. In no way do they relate to the problem of interindividual compatibility of preferences or their aggregation into some general will.

If the conceivable and, by implication, admissible range of preferences is that broad, and if no self-restraint can be expected to govern their formation, the resulting situation is that of a veritable state of nature. Within the libertarian framework, all behavior is driven by preferences, all preferences must be taken as authentic, and all of them are equivalent in the sense that the observer is not entitled to pass judgment as to which preferences are "true" or in any sense more worthy than any other preferences. The last of these assumptions implies, apart from its normative agnosticism, that a society can be realistically imagined in which all preferences are in fact *recognized* as equivalent. That would obviously be a society without any trace of what sociologists and anthropologists understand by "social integration." But the full extent of the artificiality and the lack of realism of this assumption becomes apparent only if we take into account that "systems" integration is equally absent in such a society.

This can be demonstrated in the following way. Following Dworkin, preferences can be subdivided into "personal preferences" and "external preferences," the former consisting of a ranking of states that affect "me" and the latter of states that affect others as well. External preferences have a relational aspect; they rank states of the world that affect not just "me," but me in relation to how others are affected. Such external preferences can be located on a scale that extends between the polar cases of "altruism" and "sadism." On such a scale, the following types may be distinguished: most preferred are outcomes in which

(a) (all or some) others win at my expense (strong altruism or altruistic redistribution)
(b) others win regardless of the consequences to me (indifferent altruism)
(c) others *and* I win (positive-sum games)
(d) I win regardless of the consequences to others (competitive individualism, *sauve qui peut*)
(e) others lose even if I do *not* win (sadism).

It appears impossible to conceive of a society (or more precisely: a relatively durable social order) in which case (e) preferences and at least some of the case (d) preferences are admitted as equally worthy of tolerance and recognition as all of the personal preferences and the external preferences of cases (a) to (c). For such a society would suffer from symptoms of rampant disorganization – unless, that is, we have strong

86   *Claus Offe*

reasons to believe that "anti-social" preferences of the types (d) and (e) do not significantly occur in practice. A (deceptive) way out of this dilemma of wishing to insist upon the utilitarian equivalence postulate while still wishing to take into account realistic minimum requirements of a social "order" is suggested by Harsanyi (1977: 647) who proposes to exclude from the universe of preferences "all clearly anti-social preferences, such as sadism, envy, resentment, and malice." But utilitarian liberalism of the kind we are modeling here has no basis for being consistently selective among preferences, and the attempt to introduce such selectivity in an *ad hoc* fashion is more a symptom than a cure of its basic deficiency. For, as Fishkin (1988: 170) points out, "this kind of exclusion of some preferences based on our moral evaluation of their appropriateness represents a sharp departure from the utilitarian tradition which has generally avoided specifying the substantive content of preferences." Thus libertarian political philosophers seem to be stuck in the dilemma that they must either violate their neutrality postulate concerning preferences or make strongly optimistic, though weakly founded, assumptions concerning the inherent benevolence of human beings.

The objection that not all preferences are compatible with the notion of social order or orderly social life is, however, further dealt with by liberals and libertarians by referring to the rule of law and its protection of (inalienable, or at least constitutionally entrenched) rights. The law is invoked to render ineffective those preferences that are considered inimical to social order, e.g., my preference to live by way of theft on your resources rather than my own. (Note, however, that the law that constrains the range of effective preferences is itself contingent upon the aggregate effect of voter preferences, as any "positive" law may by definition undergo change through legislation.) At any rate, within the theoretically limitless universe of possible preferences and at any given point in time, the law defines a range of preferences that actors may well "*have*," but are not allowed to enact or *pursue*, thus leaving a feasible set of non-prohibited preferences. All the preferences, the realization of which is not explicitly prohibited by law, must be recognized and treated as equal in both markets and politics. No one is allowed to censor, manipulate, repress, or privilege certain preferences, unless they are opposed to the rights of particular others (as currently defined by law), as this would amount to paternalism or, still worse, tyranny.

Even this modified position is hardly tenable. This is so for the two reasons that preferences, even within this remaining permissible set, (a) are *evaluated* and (b) are (and are known to be) *caused*, both of which qualities make it difficult to relate to preferences as something being

Deliberative competence of citizens 87

"given" from within the individual, be it in analytical or normative terms. Let me elaborate on these two points.

(i) Approved vs. disapproved preferences First, it must be claimed to be a universal social fact that people take an evaluative perspective on other peoples' (as well as their own, see below) preferences. Members of social collectivities – ranging from families to nations and beyond – prefer other members to have certain preferences and more or less strongly object to the "bad tastes" of having other than the preferred ones. They develop and apply fairly precise notions on whether preferences are "virtuous," "acceptable," "unreasonable," "alien," etc. The universe of tastes that occur in a society is always embedded into a hierarchic (though normally contested) code of "good" vs. "bad" tastes. Such approval or disapproval of the preferences of others is not only (and not always) due to the negative or positive externalities that the pursuit of a particular set of preferences may (be believed to) entail. Even those preferences (some might even say: precisely those preferences) that do not conceivably lead to any violation of interests of others, such as some sexual, religious, or esthetic preferences, may be subject to disapproval. Seen from the point of view of individual actors, preferences are held, revealed, and pursued by them in the awareness that they are evaluated, approvingly or disapprovingly, by at least some (in that sense "relevant") others. Strict neutrality (of the state) may be desirable from the point of view of political theory, but it is most certainly not a fact of social life and its pervasive limits of toleration of difference. In analytically exogenizing preferences as "given" and immune from social evaluation, economists abstract from this phenomenological reality that preferences are in fact inherently the object of the social evaluation by others. Economists and political theorists who operate on the assumption that "all preferences must equally be respected" and similar heroic abstractions should at least show some awareness of the fact that this neutrality is not widely shared in any society. A society in which any legally non-prohibited preference would be equally tolerated, permitted, and considered worthy of the same measure of respect as any alternative preference (if only it does not violate the rights of others!) is (perhaps) a libertarian utopia, but not an observable reality anywhere. Arguably, it would still be a contradiction in terms, as it amounts to the notion of a "society" without social norms (or conflicting sets of social norms) which serve as evaluative criteria for the preferences actors pursue and which are known by actors as such criteria.

(ii) Causal knowledge about the origin of preferences Nor is it, secondly, plausible to insist upon the a-rational and individual nature

88   *Claus Offe*

of preferences. After all, preferences that we observe are by no means randomly distributed across historical time and social space. In fact, we can fairly reliably predict at least some of the preferences of a person if we know his or her family background, national identity, economic position, associative involvement, age group, educational background, etc. Preferences emerge from and are shaped by a formative context, or background conditions. The hardly controversial sociological fact is that preferences are, among other things, contingent upon the kind and amount of information to which a person is exposed. These contexts are not just accidental to or distorting of individually given preferences; they are necessary background conditions in the absence of which individuals can be shown to be unable to develop any preferences at all, i.e., fail to *become* individuals. This is illustrated by the fact that anomic conditions of social change, such as they are experienced, for instance, after the breakdown of state socialist regimes, leave many individuals profoundly uncertain about the question what their political preferences and interests "are." Furthermore, preferences emerge contingent upon the institutional and other opportunities provided for their realization. For instance, in the absence of museums it is hard to imagine that a person develops a preference for impressionist over romantic paintings. Thus information, opportunities, and structural settings, as well as cultural traditions, will allow us not only to explain and predict, but at least to some extent also change the shape and distribution of preferences, thus rendering implausible the "agnostic" and "exogenizing" libertarian perspective.

Left-liberal responses

Taken together, these two objections to exogenous preference theory appear to lend support to the following activist-interventionist syllogism of "preference engineering":

(1) as "all of us" approve of certain preferences of others and disapprove of other preferences, and
(2) as we know that preferences are malleable and can be changed by manipulating their causal determinants,
(3) there is nothing wrong with trying to manipulate, rather than treating and respect as "given," preferences by changing their causes, thereby optimizing the stock of existing preferences. In the words of Cass Sunstein (1991: 10): "Respect for preferences that have resulted from unjust background conditions . . . hardly appears the proper course for a liberal democracy."

Deliberative competence of citizens

Such conclusions go evidently much too far from a libertarian point of view. The libertarian, as I model the position here, is well prepared to assent to the prohibition of that segment of preferences that, if permitted, would turn out, according to the preferences and insights of constitution makers and legislators, to be inimical to social order and peaceful civil life. But the remaining feasible set should not be constrained further – neither by moral considerations, nor social norms of approval or disapproval, nor the practical application of causal knowledge about what determines preferences and how a different set of preferences within parts or all of the population might be engineered.

Although most theorists and certainly many citizens share the intuition that something must still be wrong with this theory of state neutrality, negative political freedom, moral relativism, and abstract individualism, an alternative is less well formulated and less easy to come by – unless, that is, we are willing to resurrect "given" communal traditions, religious or otherwise, as binding and attach to them a somewhat fictitious authority. The key problem of contemporary left-liberal political theorizing is to develop arguments which, while respecting individual freedom of preference formation and the pursuit of preferences in the realms of markets, politics, and private life, also provide justification for a wide range of taste-shaping and taste-discriminating interventions by democratic governments which are seen as valuable for themselves or instrumentally indispensable for the sake of maintaining and furthering such collective values as solidarity, welfare, autonomy, deliberation, and democracy itself.

The intuition that those authors start with, which I group together here under the name of "left-liberalism," is derived from the writings of Tocqueville and John Stuart Mill. It consists, in the words of Kymlicka (1989: 19), in the belief "that people not only want to act on their choices, they also want to get those choices right." But who tells them what the right choices are? As no political authority is entitled to do so, the citizen him/herself will have to be involved in a process of continuous self-evaluation and self-examination of choices. The inner split within the citizen, the separation of the examiner and the examined that is suggested by the idea of self-examination leads to a notion of a "multiple self." The person is envisaged as a unit that consists of different departments or hierarchical levels, one of them specializing in making choices according to preferences and the other in evaluating and perhaps rejecting the choices made in the name of second-order preferences concerning the "right" choices. To be precise, this ideal does *not* derive from any substantive notion about what the criteria (such as solidarity and justice) of self-evaluation should or would be,

90   *Claus Offe*

and their desirability for *"everyone else."* The ideal is rather supposed to be the fulfillment of the actor's *own* desire "to get those choices right," his interest in his autonomy. But it is hardly realistic to assume that this happy coincidence of citizens making free choices and citizens making (what they themselves desire to be able to consider as) right choices were an automatic occurrence. The potential for critical and conceivably painful self-examination must be encouraged and assisted, and conditions must be created under which this dynamic of preference-development is most likely to unfold.

What are these formative conditions and mechanisms, and can they at all be intentionally created? I now want to explore the burdens of argument that such an "activist" approach to preferences must shoulder. According to this approach, preferences are no longer treated as exogenous and given, but rather as malleable and subject to various kinds of social and political formative mechanisms through which the individuals' capacity for self-examination is enhanced. If preferences are thus to be seen as the raw material of social and political life, who is entitled to self-consciously shape and transform them, and on the grounds of which kind of justification, by what means, and within which limits? It is this set of questions to which I now turn.

A representative example of the state of the art of dealing with these thorny questions is an essay by the legal scholar and philosopher Cass Sunstein (1991). It starts with the recognition of the fact that modern societies are "modern" exactly in the sense that the claim to a monopolistic definition of "good" preferences, be it based upon religious or other doctrines, has evaporated. "A constitutional democracy should not be self-consciously concerned, in a general and comprehensive way, with the souls of its citizens" (1991: 34). As conceptions of the common good diverge and cannot be brought into a hierarchical order, modern societies are liberal by default. More seriously, not only has the authority disappeared to tell the "true" conception of the good from other conceptions of the good, but also the authority to determine whether some set of opinion and behavior on the part of a social agent should at all pass for a particular "conception of the good," or whether it is simply a manifestation of selfish, myopic, and opportunistic private interests.

There are two questions here that must be distinguished. They can be depicted on a horizontal and a vertical axis. The horizontal dimension represents the problem of the (as left-liberals would argue, perfectly) legitimate *plurality* of conceptions of the common good. The vertical dimension measures *formal qualities* of political preferences, demands, or proposals. At the one extreme of this latter scale is a type of preferences that can seriously lay claim to being a thoroughly considered and

Deliberative competence of citizens 91

deliberatively explored conception of the good, while at the other extreme we find utterances of political preferences which are just dressing up as having anything to do with concerns about the public good, while in actuality being inspired by nothing but private self-interest or the unenlightened and capricious picking of preferred courses of action. On the horizontal dimension, propositions of the following kind would be represented: "Conduct of life X is morally better than conduct of life Y." On the vertical axis, we deal with this kind of propositions: "Procedure A to arrive at preferences and choices is better than procedure B." The first dimension, as it were, concerns the *outcome* of the debate, and the second the *level* of the debate. While it is probably fair to say that *left*-liberals are "liberal" (i.e., take a non-discriminatory position, or do not pretend to be able to rank in somehow binding ways X and Y) in the first dimension, as they recognize and respect various conceptions of the good as equally worthy of respect and consideration in a pluralist society, they are still by no means neutral concerning *procedural qualities of the debate itself* (i.e., they do most emphatically rank A over B).

In contrast, "libertarians" are, in addition, non-discriminatory in the vertical dimension, too. The latter do not claim to have an analytical procedure to determine (and hence dismiss the question as irrelevant) whether a set of preferences can count as an instance of (granted, the many conceivable) seriously reasoned and autonomously formed conceptions of the good or whether it is just the outcome of thoughtless, irresponsible, and opportunistic inclinations. Libertarians, that is to say, would almost instinctively suspect efforts to introduce that vertical distinction and, by implication, to "raise the level of the debate," as just a pretext to manipulating it and leading it toward a preconceived substantive outcome, thus violating the standards of neutrality and freedom.

Left-liberals take an uneasy position on preferences in general (and political preferences in specific) that can be described, as suggested above, as "less than the 'good', but more than the 'right'." The "good," in a world of "ethical irrationalism" (Max Weber) is not only hard to define, but also full of dangerous consequences in case it is believed to be identifiable and if it subsequently gains control over public policies (cf. Goodin 1992: chapter 9). In other words, while rejecting "objective collective interests" or the "common good," substantively defined, as rather meaningless (as well as potentially dangerous) constructs that also include some of the precepts of communitarian political theorists, left-liberals still wish to insist that citizens must be called upon to elevate their preferences beyond the level of unreflective private desires before

92   *Claus Offe*

they deserve to be taken seriously as legitimate inputs of the *political* process, the right of any person to speak freely notwithstanding. "Collective decision-making ought to be different from bargaining, contracting, and other market type interactions" (Cohen 1989: 17). It is, they claim, exactly the vicissitude of the sphere of politics that not every expression of preferences can be granted equal dignity, while in *markets* every dollar carries equal weight, whether it is spent by the most careless or the most sophisticated consumer. Although we cannot, *contra* communitarian or neo-Aristotelian positions, acquire certainty about what is good in *substantive* terms, we can well be certain, *contra* the libertarians, that no political preference deserves to be taken seriously unless there is some evidence that it has been *processed and supposedly enriched through efforts such as self-examination, reflection, and deliberation* which is called for in order to make it respectable as "serious," i.e., autonomously arrived at. The object of this deliberation is a "public conception of common good" (Cohen 1989: 19), which differs from the strategic achievement of *mutual advantage* in that the latter, but not the former, may well involve exploitative disadvantages strategically imposed upon third parties within the collectivity. As we have lost solid substantive criteria of good politics, what we must insist upon all the more strictly and rigorously are those formal qualities of political communication and preference formation. Though no one has the authority to determine what the common good is, we still can insist, without violating liberal principles of freedom, that inputs into the political process pass a rigorous test of the formal qualities of being *some version* of the common good. Correspondingly, a good citizen is not defined by *what* his desires are, but *how* he has arrived at his desires and how seriously he has weighed them against other desires of his own and the desires of others – in essence: how believably he is guided by the second-order desire to pursue "right" desires.

The appeal of this intermediary position in democratic theory is significantly increased if it is complemented by arguments effectively demonstrating that either of the two contenders amounts to a veritable impossibility. Concerning liberalism, the argument (mainly derived from the debate dating back to Arrow's social choice theory) is the following (cf. Miller 1993: 78–81). Even if (and especially if) all preferences are admitted to the democratic aggregating game, there is no uniquely fair and objectively adequate rule by which these preferences could in fact be aggregated. Whether we pick majoritarian or proportional procedures, chances are that we get either less or more than the one and only "will of the people," or its collective preference. And even if there were an objective and unobjectionable aggregating rule, it

Deliberative competence of citizens

would not be strategy-proof, as it would provide both the opportunity and a strong incentive to *misreveal* preferences in order to make an option (and the associated distribution of costs) win that would lose in case everyone voted sincerely.

As a result of this exercise in social choice theory, we are left with the sobering conclusion that democracy as a pure aggregating machinery of "given" individual preferences is a logical impossibility. "Social choice theory seems to undermine the liberal view of democracy in a systematic way" (Miller 1993: 80). For it would suffer, should it ever be seriously applied, from a dual arbitrariness. First, the arbitrariness in the choice of aggregation rules (none of which is self-evidently fairer than conceivable alternatives, and none of which can be selected by democratic means for logical reasons, as the aggregation rules must be fixed before democracy, as it were, "can begin") and, second, the (strategic) arbitrariness in the individual voter's revelation of his or her preferences under these aggregation rules. As a result, if only "given" preferences are to count in politics, in fact *other* things than these preferences will actually count! Unqualified libertarian democracy is not a deficient or second-best solution – it is no solution at all.

No less compelling is the argument against "substantive" conceptions of the good and the belief in the feasibility of a democratic process that would aim at some "one best way" of solving a problem or even "the true common good" to be revealed by the vote of the people (or the decision made by its avant-garde). All modern political theory must come to terms with what Weber termed the ethical irrationality of the world, or the basic contestability of any public policy decision and the value premises from which it derives. "Epistemic" theories of the common good, or anti-relativist theories based on some substantive conception of the moral and political good, presuppose the existence of "a correct judgment about what a collective ought to do" (Coleman and Ferejohn 1986: 16), and the search for a uniquely correct judgment simply does not appear very promising in modern societies, even if the search is undertaken in the name of finding not one definition of the common good that is valid for all of mankind, but in the more modest spirit of finding one particular set of values that should govern the public and private life of one particular political community. But still, public policy decisions *must* be made, and on a wider range of issues and with more direct consequences for the life of citizens than ever. How can such decisions be defended, and how can citizens be justly expected to comply with them? What are, in other words, the sources of legitimacy of political decisions? The only conceivable answer is that these decisions follow from a serious, open, public, exchange of arguments in

94   *Claus Offe*

which not "given" and unrefined preferences, but careful and informed deliberations are the basis for a judgment supported by all or by a majority. Again, formal qualities of the debates leading to decisions provide the latter with legitimacy, not the brute exercise of individual freedom or the invocation of some authoritative doctrine or tradition.

To be sure, these are arguments not *for* the feasibility and justification of the "intermediate" democratic position that we have termed "left-liberal", but *against* its two major competitors. If we want to defend a position that defines demanding requirements as to *how* citizens should arrive at and hold their preferences in order to be recognized as worthy citizens, and how these preferences should be processed in order to count, there are obviously a number of difficult arguments that need to be made.

If we were to adopt the intermediate position, two weighty consequences seem to follow, one for policy and one for politics. As far as public *policies* are concerned, political authorities can derive a mandate from the deliberation principle that some preferences, although they are strongly held by private actors in some fields of public policy, do not deserve to be admitted to the policy-making arena, as they fall, as narrow-minded "special interest groups" as opposed to encompassing and "responsible representative collective actors", under the verdict of insufficient deliberation. Whenever policy makers hit upon preferences that they find impossible to accept as serious, well-considered, or authentic preferences resulting from autonomous choice, they may feel entitled to adopt taste-changing policies designed to eradicate "bad tastes" through education programs, media policies, the imposition of punishments and rewards, propaganda, prohibition, etc. As far as *politics* is concerned, an analogous line of thought would suggest that existing preferences must not only be aggregated through the channels of collective choice, but also refined and "laundered" in the process through appropriate mechanisms of debate, confrontation, justification, testing, publicity. For instance, in order to screen out what in today's terminology would be named "populism," the makers of the German Constitution have thought it wise to assign a special supervisory role to the (partly state-financed) political parties in forming the "will of the people."

Taken together, these two considerations would suggest an activist approach to the formation of political preferences. Far from being the ultimate determinant and independent variable of political life, they can and in fact must be shaped through public policies, and they must be selectively, if certainly not arbitrarily, admitted to the political process according to some standard of worthiness. But note that these insti-

Deliberative competence of citizens 95

tutional designs aimed at screening out "special interests" and "populist demagogues," while emphasizing the distinction (depicted by our vertical axis) between ill-considered and well-considered preferences and the greater worthiness of the latter, still do not rely on the liberal principle of *self*-examination of preferences; for the examining is done by elites and institutional arrangements and traditions, not individual and collective actors themselves. This automatically raises the question of who should be in charge of the task of taste-shaping and preference selection? These practices of intentional taste-shaping raise concerns about standards of political *liberty* as much as concerns about political *equality*, as people might ask why it is that some political preferences pass as sufficiently refined while others are, perhaps in ways that appear arbitrary, rejected as insufficiently reflective. What, then, are conceivable reasons for adopting, on the part of political elites, what I have called activist approaches to the formation of preferences, be it by either inculcating desired preferences through educational and media policies or by discriminating against holders or representative associations of undesired ones?

One justification for installing preference filters in policy and politics can either be derived from the claim that the *causal determinants* of collectively undesired preferences are unjust and hence call for improvement through compensatory educational efforts for justice-related reasons, or that the *consequences* of these causes, namely the undesired preferences (such as addiction) are themselves the causes of unjust negative externalities and hence call for correction for consequentialist reasons.

At any rate, Sunstein (1991: 5) finds the notion dubious "that a democratic government ought to respect private desires and beliefs in all or almost all contexts." In some contexts, that is, we seem to be entitled to take a discriminating position to other peoples' preferences. The cases in which good reasons seem present for doing so, as he demonstrates, are in fact numerous.

First, many preferences are mere reflections or derivations of existing opportunities and incentives, and these premises are in part put in place through legislation and other acts of government itself. After the government has licensed gambling, it also has the right to regulate access to it, for instance by age. When, as in this case, preferences are an artefact of legal rules which condition the coming-into-being of these preferences, the rules cannot be justified by reference to preference (Sunstein 1991: 8).

Second, some preferences are contingent upon unjust conditions that could have been changed by government action, but which government

96   *Claus Offe*

has so far failed to change. It makes perfect sense to claim that such preferences, e.g., the widespread preference of young people from poor minority neighborhoods to drop out from high school rather than finishing it, should not be taken as given, as "respect for preferences that have resulted from unjust background conditions [which have prevailed so far due to government inaction, we might add] and that will lead to human deprivation or misery hardly appears the proper course for a liberal democracy" (Sunstein 1991: 10).

Third, all preference phenomena of addiction, akrasia, myopia, and future discounting seem to call for the determinate overriding of preferences – not only because some of these preferences might arguably derive from unjust background conditions, but because they violate the own best long-term interests of people who pursue them. Inversely, counter-preferential policies are also mandated when not only collective "bads" are to be prevented, but also collective goods are to be generated such as would normally be insufficiently appreciated as such – as in the case of subsidies for arts and history museums and other "merit goods," including mandatory social insurance.

Fourth, legitimate reasons for making an effort to change preferences, change the background conditions, or curtail the rights to pursue them may be present if the uninhibited pursuit of such preferences will result in damage inflicted upon others, as in the widely used paradigm cases of pornography, the use of free speech for racist purposes, and violence in the media.

Finally, counter-preferential government action appears unproblematic if contributions to the production of collective goods must be authoritatively enforced because there is, as in the case of taxation and the enforcement of other laws, no spontaneously agreed-upon solution to collective goods problems.

These arguments provide reasons for why political elites can legitimately ignore or override even those preferences the pursuit of which is not contrary to the law. But the validity of the five arguments which provide a rather compelling license for governmental preference overriding or preference shaping is different from a sixth argument. So far we have been considering "welfarist" arguments, which basically say that it is demonstrably "better" for people if some of their preferences are made the object of selective or even taste-changing policies or if they are altogether banned from the policy process. Now a new type of argument is being employed, an argument which claims that, even in the absence of unjust causes or undesirable consequences of empirical preferences, only those preferences deserve to be respected which flow from a deliberative and reflective process of autonomous preference forma-

Deliberative competence of citizens 97

tion. Such autonomous preference formation is said to flow from decisions "reached with a full and vivid awareness of available opportunities, with reference to all relevant information, and without illegitimate or excessive constraints on the process of preference formation" (Sunstein 1991: 11).

This proposition, to put it mildly, is demanding a lot, namely preferential treatment in the political process of those citizens who are accomplished in the practice of autonomy and republican virtue, or who have built for themselves the reputation of such accomplishment. It also excludes a lot, namely all those whose preferences, as registered both in markets and in democratic politics, are (or at any rate can be suspected to be) of a more mundane nature, having to do with private life and the satisfaction of private desires and subjective welfare. The proposition thus seems vulnerable to the charge of a moralizing republican elitism due to the privileged role it assigns to an elite of politically virtuous republican aristocrats whose public-spirited judgments are beyond the suspicion of petty interest politics. As Sunstein states: "Consideration of autonomy will argue powerfully against taking preferences as the basis for social choice" (1991: 12). The thrust of this argument seems to be that all those preferences might be censored or ignored which do not result from a formative process in which highly reflective and autonomous *self*-censorship plays a prominent role. This appears to leave the author in need of an argument pointing out what he would prefer to enter into social choice *other* than preferences. It is as if citizens were to be divided into two classes – the many striving after the satisfaction of their preferences and the few ("more fundamentally") trying "to ensure their autonomy . . . in the process of preference formation" (Sunstein 1991: 12). Cohen anticipates this kind of objection (which he terms "sectarianism", 1989: 27ff) and tries to refute it. A political conception, in his view, would be "objectionably sectarian only if its *justification* [emphasis in original] depends on a particular view of the human good . . . [or] a conception of the proper conduct of life," but not so if it just favors the ideal of active citizenship. I read this to mean, using the above horizontal/vertical metaphor: as long as we do not fix a *point* on the horizontal axis, we may still fix a *lower limit* on the vertical axis, without being "objectionably sectarian" – the obvious implication of this phrase being that there could be such a thing as unobjectionable sectarianism.

What worries me in these formulations is the apparent transition that is being made by the author from a ("welfarist") censorship over those preferences that are *causally* constrained or less than rational in terms of their *consequences* (for the actor himself or other actors), and which

98   *Claus Offe*

for *that* reason must be either changed or ignored, to a critique of preferences due to their *origin* from conditions other than those that can be unequivocally considered as fulfilling demanding standards of "deliberation," "autonomy," and "collective self-determination." No doubt, as it is *imprudent* in terms of individual and collective welfare to pursue preferences that violate standards of welfare, government is free to ignore or even actively try to change such preferences. But is this also true regarding preferences which are quite neutral in terms of their welfare effects, but just happen to differ from those that disinterested and virtuous citizens might adopt as the outcome of a deliberative collective judgment? I doubt it.

My reasons for this doubt are twofold. First, the attempted analytical uncoupling of the "prepolitical desires" of the *bourgeois* from the "collective judgment" of the *citoyen*, as well as the proposal to make public policies contingent upon the latter alone, is *exclusive*. Perhaps for lack of inclination or resources (such as time), some people (arguably a majority) will not only fail to pass the test of the reflective making of "collective judgments"; they will not even, or so the libertarian theorist will be inclined to argue, develop an adequate understanding, taste, or ambition for that ideal – and still insist that their voices, though representing their possibly unrefined and "prepolitical" desires, be heard in politics. Conversely, they will certainly resist, invoking egalitarian democratic rights and principles, the division of the citizenry into "worthy" and "unworthy" ones. Second, apart from being anti-egalitarian, the division of the universe of human preferences into those that are "prepolitical" and those that originate from "citizens" in the fullest sense of the word is itself a somewhat arbitrary intellectual operation that does not appear to justify the serious consequences attached to it.

The underlying criterion of adequate citizenship competence lacks the precision that we would like to see if so much comes to depend on it. For instance, Sunstein declares it an indicator of citizen competence and virtue if "people seek . . . to bring about a social state that they consider to be in some sense higher than what emerges from market ordering" (1991: 15). Another criterion is the presence of "altruistic or other-regarding desires." Thirdly, people qualify as citizens if they "have wishes about their wishes" (i.e., meta-preferences). And finally, they must be capable and willing to engage in precommitments. The problem with this checklist is that it is only on the basis of additional criteria or insights that it can conceivably help us to tell the "citoyen" (or citoyen-like preferences) from the "bourgeois". For instance, it may be mandated by the most unscrupulous pursuit of "prepolitical desires," such as the desire to extract monopoly rents through the formation of

Deliberative competence of citizens   99

a cartel, to engage in elaborate precommitments in order to avert defection of the members of the cartel. Upon closer inspection, the criteria that Sunstein offers do not really help us to tell dismissable "selfish" from truly and virtuously "political" preferences – without implicitly relying on additional criteria, perhaps even of a substantive sort. And whose right it should be to establish and apply such additional criteria (such as, in the German case of conflicts concerning civil service *Berufsverbote*, or ban on public sector employment, the requirement of a "commitment to the free democratic basic order") is again an open question.

The standard response to this liberal dilemma which also Sunstein endorses is educational. On the one hand, or so we can state the dilemma, not all preferences can count equally. But on the other, nobody can claim the authority to privilege those that count (because they derive from the virtues of the citizen) over those that do not because they are selfish and "prepolitical." The solution is perfection through compulsory education, including education in the rights and obligations of citizens. Thus Sunstein advocates "a mild form of liberal perfectionism. Such a system would see the inculcation of critical and disparate attitudes towards prevailing conceptions of the good as part of the framework of liberal democracy. Liberal education is of course the principal locus of this concern" (1991: 20).

Again, the objection to this solution is twofold. On the one hand, a strong version of civic education may do "too much," i.e., turn into some form of indoctrination rather than stimulate the capacity for autonomous judgment. More relevant is probably the other objection, which, however, may apply at the same time: it may do too little, as formal schooling competes with a variety of other agents of political socialization, such as parents, peer groups, the media, the market, and representative political actors themselves, and not all of them can be trusted to adhere to the ideal of deliberative preference formation. In a society in which, as in the US, average twelve-year-olds have spent more time in front of the TV set than in the classroom, the potential of formal schooling for developing demanding citizenship competences may well be questioned. Civic education is also likely to do "too little" because, as it is limited to a relatively short and early period of the life course, its effects are likely to be superseded in adult life by other and more durable formative effects.

There seems to be a further bifurcation here within the discourse of contemporary democratic theory. The first bifurcation is that between libertarian and left-liberal perspectives, with the latter introducing the standard of reflectiveness, deliberation, and self-examination into the

100   *Claus Offe*

prerequisites of democracy, while the former takes preferences at face value. Now the second bifurcation is between those that give this distinction of "raw" vs. "deliberative" preferences an elitist, educational, and moralizing twist, while more democratic and universalist approaches remain underexplored. To be sure, an alternative to left-liberal republican elitism is not readily available. It would consist in the design and strengthening of institutions that effectively transform the privilege of civic-republican elites into a social and mental property shared by all citizens. Given this theoretical perspective, the unresolved design problem is to devise institutional arrangements which would provide both the opportunity and the encouragement "to get their choices right" and thus to fulfill their interest in autonomy not just to reflective elites with an inherited taste for deliberation, but to the citizenry as a whole.

Institutional background conditions favoring a taste for deliberation?

What the ideal deliberative procedure (Cohen 1989: 21) requires the citizens to accomplish is exceedingly demanding. They must develop certain commitments and attitudes and must then act in accordance with these mental routines of preference formation. "They share . . . a commitment to coordinating their activities within institutions that make deliberation possible . . . For them, free deliberation among equals is the basis of legitimacy." At the same time, "they have divergent aims, and do not think that some particular set of preferences, convictions or ideals is mandatory . . . The participants regard themselves as bound only by the results of their deliberation . . . Their consideration of proposals is not constrained by the authority of prior norms or requirements" (1989: 21–2). They are also expected to be able to resist the omnipresent temptation "to disguise personal or class advantage as the common advantage" (1989: 24). The preferences that they avow must be of a quite uncommon sort in that they must be autonomously formed and self-consciously based on principles, that is, neither "adaptive" nor reflexively fatalistic (in which case, termed "accommodationist" by Cohen (1989: 25), the logic would be something like "I know that it is wrong, but I also know that I cannot change a world that leaves me no other options than doing the wrong thing").

Even if it were agreed that the ideal of a deliberative democracy is the only consistent model of democracy applicable to a modern (i.e., pluralistic or inhomogeneous) society, as its two competitors, libertarian democracy and substantive definition of the common good, must fail for the reasons given above, it does not follow that the only remaining model is in fact the one that actually can be implemented. The difficulties that stand in the way of its realization may be simply too great, or the means and ways to overcome these difficulties insufficiently known or tested. To be sure, acting according to the demanding standards of deliberative political action may be intrinsically rewarding for the individual citizen who derives some "process benefit" from doing so, but it also involves costs and risks for him or her. This style of behavior has collective good qualities in that if "I" am the only one to play by the rules of this deliberative mode of political participation, while "everyone else" pursues his or her private preferences, I find myself in the worst possible position: not only will the deliberative discovery and implementation of the common good not be served, but also my private well being will suffer in the process, due to the costs of missed opportunities. Thus deliberative practices make sense only if they are widely adopted; however, if they are as demanding as we have reason to imagine they are, they are quite unlikely to be that widely adopted. If everyone thinks that everyone else is unlikely to adopt the deliberative mode of acting in politics and that, moreover, both the endurance and the sincerity of those who have (or pretend to have) adopted it is deemed questionable, this perceived unlikelihood of the deliberative mode becomes virtually self-fulfilling.

With these considerations in mind, the (enlightened) libertarian would conclude that the left-liberal deliberative democrat's plans do make a lot of sense in theory, but not so in practice, as it amounts to asking too much from the ordinary holders of preferences. What I am now interested in is the range of responses available to the left-liberal democrat who is also, at the same time, aware of the less attractive features of civic republican elitism. The burden of proof he must accept concerns the realism of both the necessary and the sufficient conditions of the deliberative mode of arriving at and "having" preferences.

The *necessary* conditions are relatively easy to prove. Citizens must consciously pursue their desire of "getting their choices right" through a continuous examination of their preferences. The *sufficient* conditions are harder to specify. They involve cultural/religious, economic, and institutional background conditions that are conducive to the activation of multilayered, complex, or multireferential preference structures. Focusing on institutions, Cohen (1989: 26) emphasizes that "a central aim in the deliberative conception is to specify the institutional preconditions for deliberative decision-making." Thus he calls for "deliberative institutions" which "would make deliberation possible." He insists that it would be an error to believe that "free deliberation could proceed in

102   *Claus Offe*

the absence of appropriate institutions," as "the institutions themselves must provide the framework for the formation of will." Similarly, it is claimed that the citizen cannot achieve adequate democratic competence by his or her own means, i.e., in the absence of supportive background conditions:

Normative individuation requires supportive context. To reestablish the foundations of normative individuality in self-knowledge, self-identification, and self-responsibility, it is imperative to strengthen the "intermediate associations" that buffer individuals against the conditioning effects of impersonal association-at-large. (Norton 1991: 155)

When writing on political life in North America in the 1830s, Alexis de Tocqueville specified the institutional factors that were conducive to the civic spirit prevailing in the North American settler society: democratic equality, strong local government, and also religious traditions transferred from the Old Continent. The author was himself aware of the ambiguities of some of these background conditions that would subvert, as he feared, rather than maintain those aristocratic virtues within a democratic setting. But today, within urban, open, highly stratified, mass media-mediated, bureaucratic modern (or "post-modern") societies we have even less of a tested answer than Tocqueville as to what structural and institutional conditions provide the most fertile ground for the habits of heart and mind that would provide for a mass base of the democratic form of government. Note that we have now come full circle. For we are now focusing upon, as it were, the macro-foundations of the micro-foundations of democracy, namely democratic citizen competence. In conclusion, I wish to discuss some of the quite ambiguous features of the associational and institutional preconditions to which a decisive role is assigned by various theorists in fostering and supporting adequate citizen competence.

On the one hand, the "good" citizen is seen to be the "embedded" citizen who has been, from his early childhood on, exposed to the formative impact of communal and associational ties and traditions that have taught him his obligations to his fellow citizens as well as the practice of taking into account, in a benevolent, cooperative, and deliberative spirit, their interests and potentially conflicting points of view. Family ties, civic associations, local political systems, religious, ethnic, and cultural communities are seen to perform this indispensable function of public-regarding and eventually "republican" political socialization.

On the other hand, this associational and communitarian approach to the problem of citizen competence encounters the dual objection of lack of realism of its premises *and* of undesirability of its consequences.

Deliberative competence of citizens

In a nutshell, the presence of the associational conditions mentioned before cannot be presupposed in "modern" (and even less so in "post-modern") societies; and even where they are found to be present, they operate in much less attractive ways than envisaged by the above assumptions concerning their enabling and competence-fostering effects.

As to the first of these two objections, the history of liberal political theory has clearly abandoned the early contractarian conceptions of an explicitly constituted political community to the more modern and individualist conception of systemic integration that operates "behind the back" of individuals, namely through the anonymous and impersonal forces of the market and the law and its enforcement. At the same time, self-consciously constituted communities capable of inculcating the republican virtues of deliberation and benevolence are no longer reckoned with. As to the second objection, associations and primordial communities, to the extent they survive the disorganizing process of individualization and rationalization, are discredited for their inherent propensity to cultivate not civic virtues, but, to the contrary, collective selfishness, particularism, or "amoral familism." They obstruct the proper course of democratic government, operate as exploitative coalitions, or can easily give rise to exclusive, xenophobic, and authoritarian forms of the exercise of political power.

Which leaves us with the difficult task to specify in theory – and study in empirical and practical terms – those seemingly rare hybrids of associative institutions that (a) do have the potential for cultivating democratic citizenship competence and that (b) are sufficiently available and viable under the structural and functional conditions and requirements of "modern" societies. The nature and viability of such supportive institutional background conditions is an open question of democratic theory, as well as, I wish to submit, its most important one. Instead of trying to answer it in any conclusive way, let me end with a conjecture about what kinds of association are plausible candidates for the role of catalysts of civic virtues in democratic participation.

Associations can be analyzed in terms of two questions. First, open vs. rigid criteria of membership: are individual citizens free to enter the association, regardless of "primordial" characteristics and their location within the matrix of societal division of labor, and correspondingly to leave them at will? Second, hierarchical vs. discursive formation of consensus: is agreement authoritatively enforced or is it defined (and continuously changed) through arguing and debate, in the course of which the leadership of the association itself is held accountable for its course of action? The rather unsurprising hypothesis that is suggested by the

104 *Claus Offe*

combination of these two variables is that those associational forms are more promising as catalysts of demanding versions of preference formation than any of their alternatives in which openness of membership and discursive forms of consensus building are combined.

NOTES

1 Bentham himself coined the term "ipsedixitism" (from *ipse dixit*) for this doctrine, cf. 1834–1843: vol. III, 293.
2 Note, however, that in politics there is not an automatic mechanism of "punishing" ill-chosen preferences and choices, as there is in markets. For instance, if I stick to a preference for inefficient modes of production, the market will put me out of operation and/or enforce upon me efforts of adaptive learning; it is not clear that such learning pressures operate in politics as well, at least not on the level of the individual voter. This is so because outcomes in politics are too distant in time from the expressed preferences to allow for much learning; also, synergetic effects may make it difficult to detect which preferences of which actors were "mistaken" in view of the outcomes.

REFERENCES

Arrow, Kenneth J. 1963. *Social Choice and Individual Values*, 2nd edn. New York: Wiley.
Becker, Gary. 1976. *The Economic Approach to Human Behavior*. Chicago: University of Chicago Press.
Bentham, Jeremy. 1834–1843. *Works*. Edinburgh.
Cohen, Joshua. 1989. "Deliberation and democratic legitimacy," in A. Hamlin and Philip Petit, eds., *The Good Polity*. Oxford. Blackwell.
Coleman, Jules L., and John Ferejohn. 1986. "Democracy and social choice," *Ethics* 97: 6–25.
Drysek, John. 1990. *Discursive Democracy*. Cambridge: Cambridge University Press.
Fishkin, James S. 1988. "Reconstructing the social contract: towards a new liberal theory." MS, Stanford.
Goodin, Robert E. 1992. *Motivating Political Morality*. Oxford: Blackwell.
Harsanyi, John C. 1977. "Morality and the theory of rational behavior," *Social Research* 44, 4: 623–656.
Kymlicka, Will. 1989. *Liberalism, Community, and Culture*. Oxford: Clarendon.
Manin, Bernard. 1987. "On legitimacy and political deliberation," *Political Theory* 15: 338–368.
Miller, David. 1993. "Deliberative democracy and social choice," in David Held, ed., *Prospects for Democracy*. Cambridge: Polity.
Norton, David L. 1991. *Democracy and Moral Development*. Berkeley: University of California Press.
Riker, William H. 1982. *Liberalism against Populism*. San Francisco: Freeman.
Sunstein, Cass. 1991: "Preferences and politics," *Philosophy and Public Affairs* 20 no. 1: 3–34.

6 Political Islam and democracy: the case of Algeria

Lahouari Addi

The majority of political scientists studying democratization in the Third World avoid Muslim countries due to the difficulty posed by Islam religion which is intricately linked to politics. Indeed, analysis of the relationship between Islam and democracy is only speculative when separated from historical experience. As a religion, Islam does not take sides for or against democracy. The importance for this discussion is the human interpretation of religion in relation to political conflicts. I will deal with the issue of Islam and democracy throughout the Algerian experience from this perspective.

The bid for democratization made by Algeria between 1989 and 1992 is of interest, for it sought to combine two features. The country was (a) trying to free itself from an authoritarian regime, while (b) remaining Muslim at the same time.[1] Following violent riots in October 1988, Algeria adopted a multiparty system, and in February 1989, a constitution institutionalizing the contest for power came into force. As a result of this constitution, some sixty political parties emerged; one of these, however, demonstrated an imposing strength at once – both for the number of its militants, and for the favorable response it met on the part of the working classes. Indeed, in June 1990, the Islamic Salvation Front (ISF) swept the local elections and won control of 55 percent of the local councils, and was in the lead following the first round of voting in the general election of December 1991. The army responded by canceling the second ballot, thus putting an end to the process of democratization, which had only lasted three years. The justification invoked by the army was that elections should not serve the purposes of a party that threatened democracy. Since that time, Algeria has sunk into violence, with around 60,000 deaths between January 1992 and January 1996. In this chapter, I shall examine why democratization failed in Algeria, and I shall explore the relationship between democracy and the political dimension of Islam by emphasizing that the Islamist movement is a contradictory product of modernity and that it meets ideological limits impeding the construction of a modern state,

106   *Lahouari Addi*

and that, nevertheless, democracy is possible in the Islamic countries because democratization of institutions and liberalization of society are two historical processes and their rhythms of evolution are different.

The influence of the army on the political system

One reason why democratization broke down in Algeria was that the army wished to avoid any sudden change of political regime, for this would have exposed its leaders – especially its field officers – to legal proceedings and squarings of accounts. One obstacle was therefore the leaders' fear of being taken to court for past mismanagement and bribery. This fear was not unfounded, for the state monopoly in foreign trade had fostered considerable embezzlement and overbilling in contracts with foreign companies. The managerial elite were seeking a smooth transition, and the victory of a single party – Islamic or otherwise – frightened them. This is an undeniable reason for the breakdown of the democratization process; indeed, it helps to explain why democratic transitions have come to a halt in many Third World countries (such as Nigeria, where elections won by a non-Islamic party were canceled). In Argentina, generals accused of ordering the torture and assassination of opponents long obstructed democratization. In Algeria, after the elections won by the ISF were canceled, and as repression has increased, this factor has assumed a greater complexity. The number of people jailed, tortured, or killed has complicated any negotiations aimed at the restoration of civil peace, for animosity between people has turned to hatred. The situation involves a powerful process of self-destruction. Either the present situation will continue, and hundreds of lives week after week will be lost; or one side will prevail militarily, costing tens of thousands of lives.

The conflict has taken such a bloody turn because the physical survival of the protagonists is at stake. The ruling elite felt physically threatened, and after an unsuccessful attempt to neutralize the Islamists by any and every means, has decided to exterminate them.

This situation can be explained by the army's attempt to manipulate the democratization process. Until February 1989, the leaders of the military clearly favored the continued monopolization of political power by the National Liberation Front (NLF). But as this system reached its limits, they came to believe that they could revitalize the NLF by offering it some opposition. For them, democratization meant an institutional reorganization of the political system for renewing the NLF elite and introducing market practices. Thus conceived, democratization would not affect the unwritten law of the Algerian political system

Political Islam and democracy: the case of Algeria 107

according to which the source of power is the army. It bears noting that the army has always appointed the president, and appointees to government positions have required its approval. Furthermore, the ministry of defense unofficially controls both the ministry of the interior (on which the police and administration depend) and the ministry of justice.

Military leaders did not fear elections, for they believed the NLF would eventually form an alliance with the ISF in the national assembly, and indeed would invite it to join in a coalition government – and that army preeminence in the political system would be respected at the same time. But the Islamists' resounding victory meant that the ISF could control the national assembly alone, and could form a government without military approval. In asserting their independence from the army, the Islamists had made clear their intention to form a government in which the ministry of defense would no longer control the justice and interior ministries. The ministry of the interior would regain its sovereignty vis-à-vis the ministry of defense, and the ministry of justice would resist the pressures of the security services. Officers would become individually vulnerable in the face of the administration they had once controlled, and which now had slipped from their hands. Not only was power – as something to be plundered, and as the basic means of domination – escaping the army's control, but the new situation would expose military leaders to legal proceedings for embezzlement and corruption.[2]

In a word, democracy is the process by which power changes hands without violence or force. Democracy is the means by which a political system works and develops in a pacific manner, while accepting changes in the political regime. Holding or gaining power by force – which is contrary to the very principle of democracy – means that the political order is not consensual, and is not the result of a majority choice. This takes us back, in a way, to T. Hobbes' methodological hypothesis of a *state of nature*, or, even better, to H. Arendt's, who took the view that, as long as force regulates the contest for power, society is still in the *prepolitical* phase.[3] The major contradiction of Algerian democratization resides in the fact that the military leaders tried to democratize the institutions while at the same time maintaining the political system at a *prepolitical* level, and while continuing to serve as the source of power themselves. In any political system, there can be but one source of power – the tyrant in an authoritarian system, and the electorate in a democracy.

Might this imply that the Islamists are attached to democracy, and to the idea that the electorate is the only source of power? This is not certain, for the Islamist movement is riven by a profound ideological

108   *Lahouari Addi*

and political contradiction: it expresses, on the one hand, the wish of the working classes to play a part politically; but it lacks, on the other, the ideological means to materialize such an aspiration.

The Islamist movement: a contradictory product of modernity

The people's protest: a modern pattern of political behavior

Generally speaking, the Islamist movement, in its anti-authoritarian and working-class dimension, is the product of the wish of the masses to enter the political fray (from which they have been excluded by the institutions of the authoritarian single-party regime). Until October 1988, political life in Algeria was dominated by official events, which the press would describe in a manner contrasting with the reality of everyday life. In addition, rumors circulated in the streets about antagonisms between various vested interests in the elite. The exaggerated attention shown the comings and goings of the president, and the loud publicity surrounding ministers' routine activities, contrasted sharply with the alleged passivity of the population (who on television were only shown cheering the rulers). The political system was centered on the ruling elite and founded on the exclusion of the masses, who were unable to make their voice heard about which national leaders should be chosen, or about which social and economic policies should be adopted.

Social protest took a religious turn because it was hard for the Algerian leaders to repress opposition expressed in religious terms. In this respect, the Islamist movement does represent the people's wish to assert their existence vis-à-vis the fossilized political system that had been born in the resistance to the colonial power. By embracing Islamism, the street disturbed the political system's peace of mind. The street had, as it were, broken into the political scene, and become the actor who insists that the state is a public affair, not a private one. In this sense, the Islamist protest is a modern phenomenon, for only modernity allows the masses to play a political role.

In medieval society, politics – which was regulated by the logic of patrimonialism – was the exclusive business of the aristocracy and the king's court. Only after the English and French Revolutions, the urban riots of the nineteenth century, and the Russian Revolution did political systems open up and integrate the working classes. Aside from the Russian Revolution (which repeated the "gagging" policies of the previous regime), these overtures resulted in citizenship in Western countries. An

Political Islam and democracy: the case of Algeria   109

expression of this is the fact that elections are regularly held for choosing representatives to public office.

From this point of view, Abbassi Medani and Ali Belhadj, the two leaders of the ISF, are closer to the European model than to traditional Islam. They are closer to Robespierre and Lenin than to Mawardi or Al Ash'ari.[4] For Muslim tradition forbids the uprising of the people, condemning it as *fitna*.[5] Obedience to an unjust prince is preferable to *fitna*, say the doctors of the law of the faith. This traditional Islamic rule excluding the masses from the political scene is violated by the Islamist protest. Islamist leaders reject the accusation of *fitna*, and justify their struggle by asserting that their opponents are impious. Although traditional Islam accepts rebellion against an impious prince, Algerian presidents – from Chadli Bendjedid to Liamin Zeroual – have all claimed to be attached to Islam, and so they cannot be impious according to Islamic law. Article 2 of the constitution, moreover, stipulates that Islam is the religion of the state. From a religious point of view, rebellion cannot be justified in Algeria. As this rebellion is not founded in religion, then, it must be explained by new Muslim aspirations reflecting the influence of modernity.

Content of the Islamist claims

If we examine further why the Islamist message meets with such a response from the working classes, we discover it is because of the social nature of the claims the message conveys. The message concerns neither the redemption of believers' souls in the beyond nor the promise of paradise for the masses. It has to do with jobs, housing, transportation, running water, health care, etc.[6] It condemns, furthermore, corruption in the civil service, and defends the constituent's dignity in the face of a harsh, arrogant and scornful bureaucracy. In a word, it demands social justice, equality, and an end to privileges. Let us look more closely at these demands.

In the medieval social model, whether European or Muslim, the prince handed out neither material nor immaterial benefits to his subjects; he simply guaranteed their safety. Princes and other lords received incomes from sinecures and various taxes, and exploited labor by means of serfdom and the corvée. The population were completely subject to those who held power (through tallage and the corvée). This reality gave birth to the myth of the prince who was just and good, and who aided the poor and the meek. According to this myth, however, the humble and weak do not demand of the prince that he be kind and hand out benefits. Rather, the prince's kindness is the result of his own initiative. In the Islamic tradition, Omar Ibn Khattab is viewed as the just prince and the model for other princes. He became a model of justice because the princes who succeeded him were not troubled by the destitution of the poor, the widows, and the orphans, who requested the prince's favors and appealed to his humane feelings and faith.

In the modern model, destitute social groups rebel because they consider that, if they fall below a certain level of poverty, they have a right to rebel against the prince. Such revolts and riots are started by people who are convinced that they have social rights, and that these must prevail. Demanding respect for social rights is a recent form of political behavior – in the spirit of the kind of modernity that sparked off the idea that it is the duty of the state to assist the needy. This concept of social rights is the foundation of the welfare state, the aim of which is to integrate the underprivileged social classes into the political system by means of social policies guaranteeing distribution of goods and services. The state thus seeks to avert riots by working on their economic and social causes. As the right to vote is not enough to ensure civil peace, the state intervenes to minimize social exclusion and the marginalization of entire sectors of the population. Thus, the relation between the prince and his subjects differs, both in form and in substance, from that between the state and its citizens.

But if the state claims the monopoly on violence in order to assure everyone's security, it will become a welfare state, insofar as the protection of life involves rescuing those in economic need. This dynamic is contained in the Hobbesian contract:

And whereas many men, by accidents inevitable, become unable to maintain themselves by their labour; they ought not to be left to the charity of private persons; but to be provided for, as far forth as the necessities of nature require, by the laws of the commonwealth. For as it is uncharitableness in any man, to neglect the impotents; so it is in the sovereign of a commonwealth, to expose them to the hazard of such uncertain charity.[7]

In this same perspective, the Declaration of the Rights of Man and the Citizen affirmed in article 21: "Public assistance is a sacred debt. Society owes subsistence to less fortunate citizens, either by finding them work or by securing the means of existence of those who are not in the condition to work."

In a word, the demand for social rights is a recognition of the modern state. Therefore, community would like the state to entirely assume its prerogatives of guarantor of security and solidarity at national community level. This indicates that the autarky of social groups as we know them (family, clans, tribal groups, etc.) has faded away to be replaced

Political Islam and democracy: the case of Algeria

by a representation of social bonds which transcends blood ties and local mechanisms of solidarity. Modernity has consisted, precisely, in destroying such old forms as villages, extended families, and tribes.

The same goes for the condemnation of corruption. Such a proscription implies the notion of a public service. Corruption is considered evil only when society has become aware that public office should not serve private ends. But in the past, public office was venal and an institutional source of wealth. In the precolonial Maghreb, a civil servant could raise revenues for his own use, a form of excise called "jah."[8] The amount collected for "jah" depended on the civil servant's rank. In one form or another, "jah" still exists, but it is viewed as abnormal by constituents. It can be observed from the top to the bottom of the state, but public opinion condemns it as corrupt. This same public opinion has forgotten that "jah" was once part of the local political culture. The Islamist message condemns corruption, forgetting its origins in the ancient "jah" practices of traditional society.

Yet the condemnation of corruption does not necessarily signify that people have assimilated all of the elements of modern political culture. For this condemnation results from an opinion held by most Algerians that a certain given amount of wealth exists, which should be equitably shared by the members of the national community. They believe there is enough of this wealth to go around, and that it would afford a decent living to each and every family, were it not for corruption and the embezzlement of public assets. Corruption is thus seen not as an abuse of power in itself, but as an immoral practice preventing the fair distribution of riches. For the Islamist militant, the economic crisis results from the bad apportioning of wealth attendant upon corruption. The relationship between the economic crisis and low productivity is not truly felt, because wealth is regarded as God's gift, or that of Nature, and not the fruit of work. This pre-Ricardian conception of material wealth leads the man in the street to believe that, if incorruptibles were appointed to positions of responsibility, the distribution would return to something equitable, that all would receive their due, and that the crisis would vanish. But who can offer such guarantees? Those who fear God, in other words the militants of the ISF!

As far as the claims to dignity, social justice, and equality are concerned, these are inconceivable in traditional society, which is divided into social groups of unequal legal status and rank. A society composed of nobles and commoners, of aristocrats and plebeians, of *Khassa* (the elite) and *'amma* (masses), of *chorfa* (religious nobility) and *jouad* (war nobility) – such a society can hardly aspire to equality. Such an aspiration would be interpreted as a will to breach the moral code. In its

112   *Lahouari Addi*

demand for equality, the Islamist message denies these structural inequalities of traditional society, and is therefore a new and paradoxical product of modernity. But although new and modern, it fails to introduce a modern political project.

This does not mean that from the view point of the average Muslim there is a differentiation between the religious and temporal aspects of the political arena. In Muslim psychology, if daily living conditions are not satisfactory, it is due to the fact that one has displeased God. Very often, popular religiosity attributes an accident or natural disaster (drought, flooding, earthquake, etc.) to the sins of leaders and other faithful. However, what we must remember is that on the one hand, the aspirations for social justice, equality, and the end of economic and social privileges are the ambitions of a modern society, but that on the other hand, the average Muslim believes that he can obtain these ambitions thanks to religion only by the believer serving God and observing the religious commandments.

The ideological limits of the Islamist movement

Islamist militants are the children of modernity, both in their political attitude toward the state and in the content of their social claims. They could not, however, be conscious actors of modernity if they came to power, because they have no institutional, political project likely to support the claims they voice as political opponents. Modernity is the transition from the prepolitical to the political age, as defined by H. Arendt. For the latter, modernity is the contest for power without the resort to violence. Once in power, however, Islamists would remain in the prepolitical age, since they have no project tending toward a contest for power without the recourse to violence. There are two reasons for this: first, they reject the notion of man's sovereignty; second, they consider power to be something substantially and for ever in the hands of God.

The notion of sovereignty

J. Bodin's discovery of the sovereignty of man is crucial to the constitution of a political landscape which does not depend on the natural or divine order. Without sovereignty, there can be no representation. Originally, Bodin referred to sovereignty as held by the prince or the state. It is useful to recall that the idea of sovereignty has evolved by many stages. Originally, sovereignty belonged to God, and the monarch had to conform to the divine will from which he derived his legitimacy. With Jean Bodin, the monarch became sovereign and affirmed his

Political Islam and democracy: the case of Algeria 113

autonomy from the church. The state subordinated divine will and made it an instrument of the monarch's power. This concept evolved, however, so that in time it was asserted that only the electorate was sovereign. This idea is expressed in constitutions in such phrases as "sovereignty is the property of the people." This means the people are endowed with a power – sovereignty – which they *pass on* and *delegate to* representatives, whom they elect at regular intervals. This is what elections are about, the basic principle of democracy.[9]

Contesting royal absolutism, the French revolutionaries of 1789 declared that sovereignty belonged to the nation and not to any individual, whoever it may be. However, the problem of absolutism would not be so easily solved, since every individual identifying himself with the nation and speaking – by the force of the arms – in the name of the Nation proclaimed himself to be the possessor of sovereignty. The dictatorial and totalitarian regimes of the twentieth century built their political ideologies on the premise that sovereignty belongs to the nation. In fact, the nation is an abstraction, an idea; so making sovereignty belong to the nation produces the same political effects as making it belong to God, to martyrs, to the army, etc. The notion of sovereignty only got rid of its idealism – the seed of dictatorship and absolutism – when it was bound directly to the electorate. It was only at that moment that the concept produced its full effects, definitely freeing the political sphere from mysticism which had until then marked the political history of mankind.

Soon after independence, in many Third World countries, the ruling elite proclaimed that sovereignty belongs to the nation, and that their legitimacy stemmed from the fact that they had liberated the nation. In affirming that sovereignty belongs to God, Islamists do not take a step back vis-à-vis the regimes they oppose. They only replace one abstraction by another. Even more than that, this substitution has received a favourable welcome by the man in the street for whom taking sovereignty from the hands of the rulers means preventing them from being unjust and limiting corruption. These two political positions – those of the military and the Islamists – referring to the negation of the political sphere, express a predetermined conception of man and social relations, negating the political sphere. The refusal of man's sovereignty is the ideological justification for the absolute domination of the governed by those in power.

But the Islamist message rejects this idea of popular sovereignty – without which there can be no democracy. Islamists do not object to the idea of elections as such, since the *choura* (consultation) responsible for designating the *imam* or *calife* incorporates the elective principle,

114   *Lahouari Addi*

even if in an embryonic form. The voter – whether enjoying this status within the framework of tax qualifications (*choura*) or on account of universal suffrage – lacks the *power* delegated by the electorate of Western democracies to those it elects to enact laws in its name. The *imam* or the *calife* is not elected, he is appointed, chosen. The process of choosing a leader does not, as with the Hobbesian contract, specify that the people should give up their natural rights to those chosen to protect them.[10] At the mosque, the contracting parties do not represent the whole society and, fundamentally, the chosen person will not have "legislative prerogative." We must understand this expression to mean only the capacity to interpret the *sharia* and not the power of making laws.[11] Understood as such, "legislative prerogative" belongs to the Ulemas for they alone have the power of "tying and untying" (*Ahl al hal oual 'aqd*).

The man in the street aspires to participate in the choice of the ruler and would not understand why the choice belongs to a restricted body of electors. Hence, Islamist movements do not oppose universal suffrage; Islamist militant expects the electorate to choose a candidate who knows the divine laws, in order that these might be better implemented. This candidate is not elected to enact laws – only to ensure the application of divine law. To a certain extent, then, the Islamist militant favors a religious political order based on the principle of elections. Is this possible in theory and in practice? The answer is negative for the following reason.

The notion of power as a vacant seat

Democracy consists, politically speaking, of a number of procedures by which the electorate at regular intervals chooses those who are to hold power. This is the golden democratic rule, and to be effective, it requires freedom of speech – in order to allow the opposition to express itself as such. But this golden rule also implies a conception of power vital to democracy: that the *seat of power is a vacant seat* (Lefort 1986: 27), and that the representatives designated to exercise power in the name of the majority occupy only temporarily a seat which, by nature, is vacant.[12] Without this conception of power as a vacant seat, there can be no democracy. Islamists do not regard the seat of power as vacant. It has always been and always will be occupied by God or by the idea men have of God. The men appointed or elected to exercise power do so with the sole aim of applying divine teachings. But an election of this sort would be empty, meaningless. Indeed, elections are not even necessary in such a context; it would suffice if some authority or other simply appointed the most literate and learned persons in religious matters and entrusted them with the responsibility of running the community. In Islamist political ideology, elections are not a necessity; however, some accept the idea since most believers call for elections in order to be able to choose their leaders. Although refusing to grant their leaders the power they do not regard men as possessing – sovereignty – most believers do not wish to be denied the opportunity of choosing their leaders.

There was once a debate among the doctors of the law concerning the official title given to the *calife*. Etymologically, the word means "substitute." His official title is *Khallifatou Allahi fi ardihi*, which means "Substitute for God on His Earth." Some doctors of the law criticized this title, arguing that the *calife* could not substitute for God; rather, he replaces the Prophet, himself sent to Earth by God. For God occupies the seat of power eternally, and is therefore the only Sovereign. The *calife* is appointed to replace the Prophet by enlightened men with a thorough knowledge of divine law. In other words, sovereignty does not belong to the people, and the latter are therefore not in a position to pass it on to their representatives. The seat of power is not vacant, and the voters/believers do not send representatives to occupy a vacant seat temporarily. In the event of being elected, those representatives placed in power by the voters/believers are expected to serve Him who holds eternal power: God. Elections are thus superfluous; for in a democracy, elections are the ebb and flow by which voters transfer sovereignty to a vacant seat. With no sovereignty, and with no vacant seat, this transfer is meaningless and without purpose.

The Koran nevertheless designates man in general as *calife* of God on Earth. Thus God makes man his representative on Earth. But there is a basic difference between affirming that man – that is to say all men – is the representative of God on Earth and proclaiming that a single man among them is. While the first case gives all men a responsibility towards God in the quest to live on Earth in conformity with divine law, the second case gives this responsibility to one man towards all men. By distinguishing himself from other men, the *calife* substitutes himself for God. While the first case has no political effect, the second has an effect of great importance, for it provokes a transfer of the allegiance owed to God on to one man. In proclaiming the *calife* the substitute of God on Earth, the political order presents itself as a divine order in which the obedience of subjects is as natural as obedience to God himself.[13]

The democratization of institutions and the liberalization of society

The Islamists' inability to build a democratic political order is essentially due to their denial of popular sovereignty, and to their belief that the seat of power is eternally occupied by the notion of God. These two elements are not, however, absolute obstacles to democratization, insofar as Islamists are themselves divided as to how opportune elections are. If the elective principle is accepted, together with that of the alternation of power, a democratic transition will have been set in motion, and as time goes by the people will less and less easily relinquish their right to elect their leaders. Through elections, the notions of popular sovereignty and of power as a vacant seat will progressively take root in the political culture of the electorate, without the latter being clearly aware of this.

One could object at this point that such considerations do not suffice to found a democracy, which consists also of public liberties, equality of the sexes, secularization of the public sphere, etc. But the latter are not the foundation of democracy; rather, they derive from it. It is thanks to political democracy – power as the object sought in a peaceful confrontation – that these notions have spread, as society liberalized on account of the struggle of elites through literature, the press, human sciences, schooling, social work, etc. The liberalization of society is not a condition of democratic transition, although it can trigger the process.

Political democracy fundamentally means popular sovereignty and power as a vacant seat. Without these two elements, power cannot be the prize sought in a free and public competition. On the other hand, such arrangements can characterize a society where a portion of the population is deprived of the right to vote, all candidates must belong to a certain faith, catechism is taught at school, blasphemy is legally punished, and a party claims to be religious on the sole condition that it acknowledges public sovereignty and does not consider power its own by right.

If democracy is limited to its political definition, it can be imagined in societies that have not been liberalized. The liberalization of society is the result of an evolution in men's political history, and it has been strengthened every time the idea of popular sovereignty has gained ground in the majority. This is why eliminating religion from the public sphere is not a condition of democracy. In many democratic countries, religious symbolism is strongly present in the public sphere. Religion is compatible with democracy when the former does not regard itself as the legitimate holder of power, for democracy is not atheistic, and it does not demand that citizens be so either. Democracy is areligious. Hobbes' political atheism is not incompatible with the citizens' faith, as long as external demonstrations of this faith, in the public sphere, do not go beyond certain limits.

Democracy consists of two aspects: the first is political and relates to

Political Islam and democracy: the case of Algeria 117

the choice of leaders by the electorate; the second concerns the liberalization of society (equality of the sexes, freedom of speech, autonomy of
the individual, religious tolerance). All Islamists reject the second aspect
of democracy, but they are divided on the first. Some believe the choice
of leaders by the electorate is compatible with Islam; others object to it
because of what it entails, i.e., popular sovereignty. The fact that Islamists are likely to accept elections paves the way for democratization in
Muslim countries. The objections of Islamists to the second aspect of
democracy do not constitute an insurmountable obstacle to democratization. The liberalization of society is the fruit of an evolution in men-
tality and political culture, and by its nature it evolves and broadens
endlessly. It developed in Western countries as the history of these
societies unfolded. To this day, judging by the hostile reactions to voluntary abortion both in the United States and in Europe, individual autonomy is not accepted by large sections of public opinion. Moreover, when
European countries legitimized elections, the liberal ideology – which is
the basis of democracy – was not as sophisticated as it is today. For an
entire century – from 1848 to 1945 – elections took place in France in
which women could not vote. The liberalization of society is a consequence of political democracy and not an essential precondition. It can
be felt in daily life through the imperceptible changes in the symbolic
representations which structure social ties while ensuring cohesion
between individuals in the national community. Weapons cannot
modify symbolic representations that are rooted in the past and in the
collective unconscious. A non-liberal or non-liberalized society can be
a democratic society in which power is gained through elections. The
best example is India, which has been a parliamentary democracy since
its independence, notwithstanding all the sociological archaisms that
characterize Indian society.

Political democracy means elections, a legal opposition, respect for
others' freedom of speech, free labor unions, and an independent
judiciary. On the basis of these principles, the masses take part in political life, and citizenship is built. Moreover, these principles will *eventually*
reshape the imaginary political world of the believer, who will no longer
feel the need to resort to religion to make himself heard.

Thus, democratization in Muslim countries will not be achieved
against the will of the Muslims, or with their physical extermination. It
will be accomplished with them, or not at all, for at least three reasons.
The first is that political Islam was born from the local political culture,
and was an outcome of the history of the national liberation movement.[14] This ideological reality is deeply rooted in society, and it would
be pointless to use violence against it: it would simply foster martyrdom

118   *Lahouari Addi*

and confer political legitimacy upon the Islamists. The second reason is that political Islam is the bearer of the popular discontent fueled by high population growth, rampant unemployment, an acute housing crisis, and deep social disintegration. The third reason is that it expresses religious concern in the face of the social upheavals of recent decades. Religion is trying to assert the permanence of its values in a changing society in which identity landmarks are blurred.[15]

It would therefore be a mistake to wait for all political parties and currents of opinion to embrace liberal ideologies before setting the democratic process into motion. Democratization simply requires that the principles of alternation and legal opposition be accepted by all concerned. If we were to await the advent of political parties which defend liberal ideological values, Third World countries in general – and Muslim countries in particular – would be running the risk of never emerging from authoritarian systems.

In conclusion, the Islamists have no future as founders of a political regime. Without realizing it, they undoubtedly nurture aspirations for modernity, and even for democracy, but they have no political model for institutionalizing such aspirations. That is why they are condemned to being strong as opponents of non-democratic regimes. In power, they would quickly contradict the aspirations of the masses who had supported them. I term *fruitful regression* the process by which Islamists would lose their popularity, allowing democrats to win over many categories of the population which formerly had favored the Islamists. Indeed, democrats could attract many voters with the ideas of *sovereignty* and *power as a vacant seat*, thus enriching local political culture and no doubt contributing to the initiation of the *social liberalization process.*

NOTES

1 In the preface to their book, O'Donnel, Schmitter, and Whitehead (1986) stress that, in view of the specificities of Islam and of the link between politics and Islam, they had decided not to include Muslim countries in their study.

2 This does not mean that power, after slipping from the army's hands, would be exercised by people interested in democracy. Any political project devised by a religious movement is anti-democratic, for it grants sovereignty to God, i.e., to those who speak in God's name and who believe themselves to be invested with a divine mission allowing them to kill off those they consider their opponents. Religious feeling implies elements of self-sacrifice and denial that brook no contradiction. When it deals with politics, furthermore, it requires all citizens to subscribe to the same political project, or even to belong to the same political party – which is the very denial of a democratic

Political Islam and democracy: the case of Algeria   119

way of life. But religious feeling is not religion, the latter having been perceived in various ways through the centuries.

3 Arendt (1970).

4 To learn more about medieval Islamic political thought, see Rosenthal (1958).

5 What is called *fitna* in Islamic tradition (upheaval against legal authorities) is also condemned in the European tradition. The first thinker who did not condemn it was Locke. One of the differences between Hobbes (1960) and Locke (1966) is that the latter legitimizes the right of resistance against an unjust Prince which does not respect the natural rights of the citizens. In affirming the legitimacy of resistance, J. Locke distinguishes himself from the thinkers of the social contract who preceded him and who did not dare go so far.

6 See Addi (1992b).

7 Hobbes, (1960: 227).

8 See Cheddadi (1980).

9 John Locke (1966) was the first to elucidate the relationship between *trustor* and *trustee*. It is not coincidental that this modern political theorist uses the notion of *trust* when referring to voters, who entrust representatives with their sovereignty. (The latter, in turn, can betray this trust by acts of tyranny or absolute power which encroach upon the people's rights.) J. J. Rousseau (1977), by contrast, does not address the issue of trust, for he regards sovereignty as the property of the people, and thus as something which cannot be delegated. Sovereignty is an attribute of the general will, and it cannot be delegated to individuals.

10 The Hobbesian contract is a myth, but the designation of the *calife* is also a myth. In reality, this designation is the result of a balance of power in the community between the competing forces.

11 See Schacht (1964).

12 I borrow this notion of power as a vacant seat from Lefort (1986).

13 In the Koran, the word calife (in the sense of Vicare or Lieutenant of God) is used nine times: two in the singular and seven in the plural. In the singular, it designates Adam (sourate II, verse 30) and David (sourate XXXVIII, verse 26) as Lieutenants of God on his Earth. But in no case whatsoever does the word have the meaning of political leadership either in the plural or in the singular.

14 See Addi (1994).

15 See Addi (1992a).

REFERENCES

Addi, L. 1992a. "Religion and modernity in Algeria," *Journal of Democracy* 3 no. 4: 75–84.

1992b. "Islamicist utopia and democracy," *The Annals of the American Academy of Political and Social Science.* November, vol. 524. Newbury Park, Calif.: Sage Periodical Press.

120   *Lahouari Addi*

1994. *L'Algérie et la démocratie*. Paris: La découverte.

Arendt, H. 1970. *On revolution*, New York: Harcourt, Brace, Jovanovitch.

Bodin, J. 1986. *Les six livres de la République*. Paris: Fayard.

Cheddadi, A. "Le pouvoir selon Ibn-Khaldoun," *Annales ESC*. Paris: Armand Colin.

Hobbes, T. 1960. *Leviathan*, ed. with an introduction by Michael Oakeshotts. Oxford: Basil Blackwell.

Lefort, Claude. 1986. *Essais sur la politique, XIXè–XXè siècles*. Paris: Esprit-Seuil.

Locke, J. 1966. *Two Treatises of Government*, a critical edn. with an introduction by Peter Laslett. Cambridge: Cambridge University Press.

O'Donnel, G., P. C. Schmitter, and L. Whitehead. 1986. *Transition from Authoritarian Rule*. Baltimore: Johns Hopkins University Press.

Rosenthal, E.I.J. 1958. *Political Thought in Medieval Islam*. Cambridge: Cambridge University Press.

Rousseau, J.J. 1977. *Du contrat social*. Paris: Le Seuil.

Schacht, J. 1964. *An Introduction to Islamic Law*. Oxford: Clarendon Press.

Part 3

Constitutional questions

7 Ways of constitution-making

Jon Elster

I Introduction

The topic of this chapter is how new constitutions are made, the mechanics of constitution-making. Surprisingly, there is no body of literature that deals with the constitution-making process in a positive, explanatory perspective. There are, to be sure, a number of studies, on which I shall draw heavily, of particular constitution-making episodes. There is a large comparative and theoretical literature on the ordinary legislative process. There is a substantial body of writings on comparative constitutional law. Much has also been written on normative issues of optimal constitutional design – presidential versus parliamentary systems, unicameralism versus bicameralism, and so on. But there is not, to my knowledge, a single book or even article that considers the process of constitution-making, in its full generality, as a distinctive object of positive analysis.[1] Here, I take a few steps towards remedying that deficiency.[2]

I shall proceed as follows. In Section **II**, I discuss various ways of defining the constitution and the relation among them. In Section **III**, I survey various modes of constitution-making, from Lycurgus to the present. In Section **IV**, I discuss the psychology of constitution-makers. I conclude in Section **V** by discussing some normative aspects of the constitution-making process.

II Defining the constitution

Constitutions can be written or unwritten. Some countries that do have a written constitution also operate through unwritten "constitutional conventions" (Marshall 1986). In the United States, for instance, the independence of the Central Bank (i.e., the Federal Reserve Board) is not explicitly stated in the constitution, as it is in some other countries. Yet *de facto* the Board enjoys considerable autonomy because of a constitutional convention by virtue of which any attempt by the executive or

124   *Jon Elster*

the legislature to interfere with its activities would incur costly political sanctions. Other countries, notably Britain, rely exclusively on constitutional conventions. In this paper I am exclusively concerned with the making of written constitutions. The emergence of unwritten conventions is subject to causal mechanisms that remain poorly understood and that are in any case very different from the (mainly) collective deliberations that are the topic of the present chapter.[3]

From now on, then, "constitution" will always refer to a written document. If we want to distinguish the constitution from other legal texts, three criteria offer themselves. First, many countries have a set of laws collectively referred to as "the constitution." Second, some laws may be deemed "constitutional" because they regulate matters that are in some sense more fundamental than others. And third, the constitution may be distinguished from ordinary legislation by more stringent amendment procedures. These characterizations, however, do not always yield the same results.

(i) New Zealand has a constitution according to the first and second criteria, but not according to the third. In that country, "only ordinary legislative efforts are required to supplement, modify or repeal the Constitution" (Eule 1987: 394).[4]

(ii) Conversely, Israel has a constitution according to the second and third criteria, but not according to the first. After 1948, there was no agreement on the need for a constitution. Whereas some "stressed the stabilizing effect of a constitution, which is particularly necessary in a dynamic and volatile population," others "stressed the dangers of a rigid constitution, and the likely calamities ensuing from a reactionary supreme court with powers of judicial review, particularly in a dynamic society" (Gutmann 1988: 292, 295). Although the latter view prevailed, the Knesset has since 1950 adopted a number of basic laws that satisfy the second and third criteria. They regulate basic matters such as the Knesset itself, Israeli lands, state president, the government, the state economy, the army, Jerusalem, capital of Israel, and the judiciary. Most of these laws contain a provision that they cannot be modified during a state of emergency, thus satisfying also the third criterion. The law on the Knesset is also entrenched in the sense of requiring an absolute majority for its amendment.

(iii) Some countries have a body of "organic laws" that, although not part of the document referred to as "the constitution," require a supermajority for their amendment. In France, the requirement is that of an absolute majority; in Hungary, two-thirds.

(iv) Some aspects of political life that we tend to think of as fundamental are not regulated by the constitution, or not by all constitutions;

Ways of constitution-making 125

nor are the laws regulating them always subject to more stringent amendment procedures. The most important example is provided by laws governing elections to parliament. Some constitutions specify the electoral system in some detail; others (Poland, the Czech Republic) only in general outlines; and some (France, Hungary) not at all. In Hungary, but not in France, electoral laws are "organic" in the sense indicated above. The status of the Central Bank is similarly omitted from most constitutions, or mentioned only in general terms. An exception is the Czech constitution, which explicitly forbids the government from instructing the bank. Even more striking is the absence from all constitutions (known to me) of constitutional provisions ensuring the independence of the state-owned media.

The main explanandum in this chapter is the adoption of a document called "the constitution." In practice, this document will also satisfy the second criterion. All constitutions regulate fundamental matters, although not only such matters nor all such matters. With the exception of New Zealand, it will also satisfy the third criterion. Because of the fundamental importance of electoral laws in regulating political life we should regard them on a par with constitutional provisions proper. This practice seems especially justified when the inclusion or non-inclusion of electoral laws in the constitution was a matter of debate in the constitution-making process.

III Modes of constitution-making

Constitutions arise in a number of different ways. At the non-democratic extreme of the spectrum, we may imagine a sovereign lawgiver laying down the constitution for all later generations. At the democratic extreme, we may imagine a constituent assembly elected by universal suffrage for the sole task of writing a new constitution. And there are all sorts of intermediate arrangements. Roughly speaking, the more democratic the substance of the constitution, the more democratic is the process by which it is adopted. We shall encounter instances in which democratic constitutions have been imposed in a non-democratic manner, but none in which a democratic procedure leads to the adoption of an autocratic constitution.

Internally imposed constitutions

Some constitutions are unilaterally imposed or octroyed by a sovereign lawmaker. If "internally imposed", the lawmaker is himself a citizen – but not necessarily the ruler – of the country for which he is legislating.

126   *Jon Elster*

If "externally imposed" (see below), he is the agent of an occupying or colonial foreign power.

Tradition – historians disagree over its veracity – has Lycurgus (7th century BC?) as the first constitution-maker. According to Plutarch's Life of Lycurgus, the greatest innovation in his constitution for Sparta was the system of political checks and balances.

> For the state, which before had no firm basis to stand upon, but leaned one while towards an absolute monarchy, when the kings had the upper hand, and another while towards a pure democracy, when the people had the better, found in [the] establishment of the senate a central weight, like ballast in a ship, which always kept things in a just equilibrium; the twenty-eight always adhered to the kings so as to resist democracy, and on the other hand supporting the people against the establishment of an absolute monarchy.

The historical existence of Solon (approx. 630–560 BC) is not in doubt, although it is not clear exactly which reforms should be imputed to him. He, too, was concerned about balance in politics. According to Aristotle,

> The mass of the people had expected him to make a complete redistribution of all property, and the upper class hoped he would restore everything to its former position or, at any rate, make but a small change. Solon, however, had resisted both classes. He might have made himself a despot by attaching himself to whichever party he chose, but he preferred to incur the enmity of both, by being the savior of his country and the ideal lawgiver. (*The Constitution of Athens* 11)

Solon also decreed that his constitution should stand unchanged for ten years.

For my next examples of constitution-making by decree I skip 2,500 years. In the wake of the democratic revolutions of 1789 and 1848, autocratic rulers more or less unilaterally laid down constitutions tailored for themselves. Examples include the Napoleonic constitutions of 1799, 1802, and 1804, the Prussian constitution of December 5, 1848, and the French constitution of 1852. Although their adoption went together with plebiscites or plebiscitary elections which showed considerable popular support for the counter-revolutionary rulers, there was no democratic participation in the constitution-making process. Recent Chinese history provides another example when,

> to give a semblance of legality to his regime, Yuan [Shikai] convened a body of 66 men from his cabinet and from various posts in the provinces, and these men produced, on May 1 1914, a "constitutional compact" to replace the provisional constitution. The compact gave Yuan as president virtually unlimited power over war, finance, foreign policy, and the rights of citizens (Spence 1990: 284).

Here, we are obviously very close to the Stalinist paper constitutions.

Ways of constitution-making 127

The making of the French constitution of 1958 offers a somewhat different case.[5] Unlike the other cases discussed so far, this constitution was pushed through against the will of the political elite. To get his way, de Gaulle relied partly on his popular support, partly and more crucially on the threat/warning potential created by the rebellious military leaders.

Externally imposed constitutions

"MacArthur's Japanese constitution"[6] from 1946 provides an example of a constitution imposed, in its smallest detail, by a foreign power. Disregarding a Japanese draft of a revised imperial constitution, Mac-Arthur instructed his legal advisors to draft a new democratic constitution for Japan. "It apparently did not occur to MacArthur, or to many other Americans, that there was any contradiction in imposing democracy on another nation, or that many Japanese might not select democracy, as understood in the United States, if given a free choice." The Japanese had no other option than to accept. "Nonetheless, it was necessary to maintain the facade of Japanese authorship, so that no one could challenge the legitimacy of the document. For the same reason, the Japanese legislative bodies created under the Meiji Constitution had to go through the motions of deliberation and ratification." Yet in the end it is not clear that the Americans got what they wanted:

In retrospect, the acceptance of the New Japanese Constitution by both the Americans and the Japanese depended heavily on the ambiguities of cross-linguistic and cross-cultural communication between both parties. Had the Japanese really understood the democratic ideas that the Americans had intended, it would have been far more difficult and painful for them to accept them. Likewise, had MacArthur and his staff understood precisely how the Japanese were interpreting American democratic principles, they might have been more reluctant to approve the final version of the Constitution. The cultural and linguistic barriers in Communication between the Americans and the Japanese were without doubt a hindrance to mutual understanding. But, ironically, the same difficulties made it possible for the two sides to agree on a document without agreeing on its fundamental meaning.

Another example of imposed constitutions is found in the political systems of the American Indians.[7] Most American tribes operate under constitutional government drafted for them and imposed on them by the US Department of the Interior in the 1930s. These Indian Reorganization Act constitutions vary little across tribes, typically providing for a chief executive (tribal chairman), a small unicameral legislature (tribal council), and a non-independent judiciary (some judicial powers were vested in the tribal council). The US government retained the right

128   *Jon Elster*

to approve any changes in constitutional form. Later developments indicate that these constitutions "work," in terms of promoting economic development, only when they coincide with the preexisting unwritten constitutions of the tribes.

Constitution-making under imposed constraints

Even when the framers have a choice between different constitutional solutions, they may be working under externally imposed constraints, affecting procedure, substance, or both. A case in which the constraints eventually made little difference is the attempt by the British cabinet to shape the drafting of the Indian constitution of 1949.[8] Among other things, the British authorities declared that any resolution passed by the constituent assembly could not be binding on parties that "had not been represented." Later, Sikhs and the Muslims that remained in India after partition tried to exploit this declaration to obtain various group rights, such as those eventually granted to the Untouchables. By threatening to boycott the assembly, Sikhs and Muslims believed that the dominant Congress Party's fear that Britain might nullify the proceedings would get them what they wanted. In the end, however, internal dissensions within the two groups undermined the credibility of the threat, and the Congress Party got its way instead.

Although the Bonn constitution of 1949 was made under the tutelage of the Western Occupying powers, the Allied powers were able to impose only a few of their demands. The most important factor that enabled the Germans to resist their requests was the new political climate created by the Prague coup of February 1948. The German framers successfully argued that ratification by referendum would give a dangerous scope for Communist propaganda. Also, they got a hearing for their claim that an excessively decentralized Germany would be an easy prey for Communist takeover. They were able to play on internal division among the Allied powers, and notably to exploit the fact that the British wanted to be relieved quickly of the costs of occupation (Golay 1958: 8, 17, 110).

More recent and somewhat different examples concern the making of the post-1989 constitutions in Bulgaria and Romania. Initial drafts of these constitutions contained several illiberal articles, especially with regard to the rights of ethnic minorities. After the Council of Europe made it clear that these provisions were incompatible with eventual membership of these countries in the organization, the necessary if (especially in Bulgaria) quite minimal changes were made. The constraints laid down by the Council of Europe were obviously much softer

Ways of constitution-making 129

than those that could be imposed by an occupying or colonial power, yet not necessarily less effective.

Constitution-making as a contract

Some constitutions take the form of a contract between the ruler and the social elite. An example is Magna Carta (1215), a contract between the English king and his barons that included among other things an impeachment procedure. According to Wiktor Osiatynski, this mode of constitution-making has a long history in Poland:

> These Polish constitutions, starting with the Pacta Conventa, the Covenants of King Henry Valois, were in fact a contract between the authorities, which had *de facto* powers, and the political nation which thought it had a moral and social mandate for sharing power. I would like to draw your attention to one thing, the fact that this tradition is the one that is most alive – for example, the decisions of the Round Table amounted to precisely such a contract. The agreement of the Round Table was a contract between the communist authorities, which held power, and the representatives of society, which agreed to contract specifying a division of powers. (in Grudzinska-Gross 1994: 20)

Minority constitution-making

Before the time of universal suffrage, delegates to constituent assemblies were usually elected by a minority of the population. The Federal Convention, for example, did not represent women, slaves, or those who did not satisfy the income and property requirements in the states that selected delegates to the Convention. The same was true of the state conventions that ratified the constitution. Women remained excluded from the constitution-making process until the twentieth century, and exclusions on economic grounds were also frequent.

These elite-made constitutions also defined the elites that could participate in the political process. Not surprisingly, the elites created by the constitutions tended to coincide with the elites which made them.[9] In that sense one may, albeit loosely, speak of constitution-making as an act of self-binding. With successive extensions of the suffrage, that characterization became increasingly inaccurate. Constitutions made by male property-owners now regulated the political behavior of all citizens. To be sure, constitutions could be (and had to be) amended to reflect the extension of the suffrage. Yet because the procedures for amending the constitution are typically more stringent than those used for adopting it in the first place, there is no reason to think that these

130   *Jon Elster*

adjustments yielded the constitution that would have been adopted by a constituent assembly that included these recently enfranchised groups.[10]

Constitution-making by elite accommodation

In the so-called "consociational" political regimes politics takes the form of elite negotiations behind closed doors. In some countries, notably Canada, this mechanism also extends to constitution-making.[11] The Canadian example shows that this form of constitution-making can operate both within a non-democratic system (as in the making of the 1867 constitution in Canada) and within a system that is based on universal suffrage (as in the making of the 1982 constitution). Whether the pedigree of the elites is democratic or not, consociational constitution-making is characterized by the fact that they reach agreement among themselves without any further popular consultations. For that reason, the Federal Convention – despite various claims by later constitution-makers to the contrary[12] – does not fall in this category.

Constitution-making by indirectly elected assemblies

The constitution-making process is prima facie less democratic when the constituent assembly is indirectly elected, as was the case in Philadelphia in 1787 and in Bonn in 1949, than when the delegates are chosen in direct elections. In the classical view of the subject, two-step elections, along with the bicameral system, age limits for representatives and restricted suffrage, belong to the "aristocratic" devices that temper the excesses of untrammeled democracy. One may well argue that these devices actually serve democracy rather than undermine it. Be this as it may, I am here only concerned with measuring the distance, as it were, that separates the framers from the people. It seems uncontroversial that indirect elections do increase that distance. They can take two forms: nomination by the elected state legislatures as in Philadelphia and Bonn or by specially elected electors as in Frankfurt in 1848 (some states used direct elections).

Constitution-making by directly elected assemblies

In the twentieth century, this is by far the most frequent mode of constitution-making, confirming the general claim that as constitutions become more democratic so do the processes by which they are shaped. Virtually all assemblies in this category share one further feature, viz. that they serve as ordinary legislatures at the same time as they are

Ways of constitution-making 131

engaged in constitution-making. The Italian constituent assembly of 1947 is an exception. Conversely, few indirectly elected assemblies serve concurrently as legislative assemblies. The main exceptions seem to be the post-1945 assemblies in India and Pakistan (Fafard and Reid 1991).

IV   The psychology of constitution-making

Human motivations enter twice into the constitution-making process. On the one hand, we need to know the motivations of the framers in order to understand the genesis of the document they produce. On the other hand, we may want to explain their choice of provisions by considering the motivations they impute to the later generations for whom they are legislating. Now, there are many ways of classifying human motivations. In the context of constitution-making, I have found the trichotomy of reason, interest, and passion to be the most useful.

Consider first the relation between reason and interests, which has been extensively discussed in the literature on constitutional choice. According to Calvin Jillson the framers at the Federal Convention were swayed by rational argument if and only if their interests were not at stake. According to Viktor Vanberg and James Buchanan, people are swayed by impartial arguments when uncertainty about the future induces them to put themselves "in everybody's place" (1989). There were several examples of this kind of reasoning at the Convention, most strikingly in an intervention by George Mason:

We ought to attend to the rights of every class of people. He had often wondered at the indifference of the superior classes of society to this dictate of humanity & policy, considering that however affluent their circumstances, or elevated their situations, might be, the course of a few years, not only might but certainly would distribute their posteriority through the lowest classes of Society. Every selfish motive therefore, every family attachment, ought to recommend such a system of policy as would provide no less carefully for the rights and happiness of the lowest than of the highest orders of Citizens. (Farrand 1966: vol. I, 49)

This veil-of-ignorance argument was also used in other contexts. Thus against Gerry's proposal to "limit the number of new states to be admitted into the Union, in such a manner, that they should never be able to outnumber the Atlantic States" (Farrand 1966: vol. II, 3), Sherman replied that "we are providing for our posterity, for our children and grand children, who would be as likely to be citizens of new Western states as of the old states" (Farrand 1966: vol. II, 3).

These arguments should not be confused with genuine appeals to impartiality, as in Mason's argument for granting new states equal status:

132   *Jon Elster*

Strong objections have been drawn from the danger to the Atlantic interests from new Western states. Ought we to sacrifice what we know to be right in itself, lest it should prove favorable to states which are not yet in existence. If the Western states are to be admitted into the Union as they arise, they must, he would repeat, be treated as equals, and subjected to no degrading discrimination. (Farrand 1966: vol. I, 578)

This argument does not rest on the long-term interests of family lines, but on a conception of intrinsic fairness.

We may further distinguish between three kinds of interests and two ways in which they may shape constitutional proceedings. The main interests involved are those of the framers, of their constituencies (political parties or territorial subunits), and of the institutions to which they belong. These interests may enter into their utility functions either as maximands or as constraints on ratification. To explain this distinction, we may note that the interests of constituencies or institutions may affect a delegate in two ways. On the one hand, he may seek to represent these interests as well as possible, whether out of duty or out of self-interest. On the other hand, he may view the interests of his constituency or institution as a constraint rather than as an end to be promoted, believing that unless those interests are minimally satisfied the constitution will not be ratified. There is no point in proposing a constitution that is a perfect embodiment of impartial ideals if one can predict with confidence that it will fail to be adopted. For that reason, even the most impartially motivated framer may have to take account of partial interests. Conversely, as I argue later, even the most partial framers may have to resort to impartial arguments.

Charles Beard argued that the American constitution expressed the personal economic interests of the framers, a view that has since been largely but not totally abandoned (Beard 1986; McGuire 1988). In the recent wave of constitution-making in Eastern Europe, some provisions may have their origin in the personal interests of some of the framers to avoid demands for restitution of property and prosecution for their collaboration with the Communist regimes. According to one observer-participant, the immunity provisions in the recent Czech constitution were largely due to the desire of the framers to avoid traffic penalties (Jan Sokol in Grudzinska-Gross 1994: 92). By and large, however, the direct self-interest of the framers is a relatively unimportant aspect of the constitution-making process.

The interests of constituencies are much more important. At the Federal Convention, the interests of the slave states and of the commercial states were crucial in shaping the final compromise, as were the interests of the small and large states in, respectively, equal and proportional representation in the Senate and in the electoral college. In modern constituent assemblies, the electoral prospects of the political parties under various constitutional arrangements are more salient. Thus in the West German constituent assembly "the Socialists . . . supported equal representation of the Laender, while the Christian Democrats voiced its preference for representation according to population. This can be explained by considerations of partisan advantage, for the Christian Democrats were predominant in the larger states while the Socialists controlled most of the smaller Laender" (Merkl 1963: 72). The result was a compromise, with the smaller states getting more than proportional but less than equal representation. In the preparation of the Spanish constitution of 1978, the most likely governmental parties pushed for a constructive motion of no confidence, whereas the smaller parties opposed it (Bonime-Blanc 1987: 77). In the making of the Polish Little Constitution, the ex-Communist party successfully pushed for a constitutionalization of proportional representation, assuming that this would enhance their electoral prospects. Similarly, parties with a popular candidate for President tend to support a strong presidency in the constitution, whereas their opponents usually want to limit the powers of the office.

As suggested above, these interest-based arguments rarely present themselves as such. Those who advocate plurality voting in single-member districts, a constructive motion of no confidence or a strong presidency usually state their argument in terms of the impartial values of efficiency and governability. Those who argue for the alternative arrangements appeal to impartial values of democracy and equality. True, it does happen that parties advocate arrangements that go counter to their electoral interests. Also, the mere fact that an impartial argument coincides with the interest of the speaker's constituency does not automatically render the former suspect. Yet evidence from many case studies overwhelmingly support the two hypotheses that (i) parties tend to favor the arrangements that favor them (and do so *because* they favor them), and (ii) that they tend to argue for these arrangements in impartial language. Whereas the first hypothesis follows immediately from the general assumptions of public choice theory, the second is more difficult to square with that framework (see also Elster 1995).

Finally the constitution may be shaped by what, for want of a better term, I shall call institutional interest. To explain what I have in mind, let me first observe that many constituent assemblies have been, at the same time, ordinary legislatures. Examples include the Assemblée Constituante and all later French constituent assemblies, and the constituent assemblies in Southern and Eastern Europe over the last two decades.

134   *Jon Elster*

Now, assemblies with this dual role obviously have a conflict of interest: they are being asked to propose a scheme that will, among other things, regulate their own place in the political system. There will be a natural tendency for the assembly to write a prominent place for the legislature into the constitution, at the expense of the executive and the judiciary. Conspicuous recent illustrations from Eastern Europe are the provisions in the Polish and Romanian constitutions that allow the legislature to overrule the decisions of the Constitutional Court. Similarly, if the constituent assembly is bicameral, it can hardly be expected to adopt a unicameral system. The making of the Little Constitution in Poland illustrates this point.

It might appear that this problem could be solved by means similar to the ones used in legislative bodies, by checks and balances. In Paris, a royal veto over the constitution might have kept the legislative tendency to self-aggrandizement in check. On reflection, however, this solution is unsatisfactory. There is no reason to expect the actual balance of power among the constitution-making actors – upper house, lower house, executive – to correspond to the normatively desirable balance of power that one might want to write into the constitution. In the Assemblée Constituante, Clermont-Tonnerre was correct when he asserted that the "three-headed hydra" – king, first chamber, and second chamber – that was to be regulated by the constitution could not itself create a constitution. But it took Robespierre – in his first great speech – to observe that a legislature-created constitution also presented its dangers, and to make the assembly adopt his solution, which was to render its members ineligible to the first ordinary legislature.

Consider next reason vs. passion in the constituent assembly. We may distinguish, quite generally, between standing passions and sudden, momentary ones. The former include ethnic or religious animosities, strong egalitarian or nationalist feelings, and other passions that do not need any special occasion to be triggered. The latter, by contrast, arise and disappear with special circumstances, such as a threat of invasion or terrorism, economic recessions, and public scandals of various kinds.

At the constitutional stage, the framers are immune to neither kind of passion, as we shall see. But let me first digress for a moment from the motives of the framers to consider the motives of the framed, if I may use that expression to designate the actors whose behavior is to be regulated by the constitution. On a traditional view, a key role of the constitution is to prevent the framed from acting on sudden, unconsidered impulses. "Constitutions are chains with which men bind themselves in their sane moments that they may not die by a suicidal hand in the day of their frenzy."[13] This restraining function is achieved partly

Ways of constitution-making 135

by built-in delays in the machinery of government, such as bicameralism and suspensive veto, partly by time-consuming amendment procedures.

Similarly, it has been argued that the constitution should protect ethnic or religious minorities from oppression by majorities that are subject to permanent passions and prejudice. As Cass Sunstein writes, "Constitutional provisions should be designed to work against precisely those aspects of a country's culture and tradition that are likely to produce most harm through that country's ordinary political processes" (Sunstein 1991: 385). A bill of rights is the most prominent instrument for ensuring that protection. Another is to reserve some seats in parliament for minority groups.

It would indeed be a good thing if constitutions could serve these two functions. They will do so, however, only if the conditions of the framers are sufficiently different from those of the framed. But consider the idea that constitutions are chains imposed by Peter when sober on Peter when drunk (Holmes 1988: 176). If constitutions are typically written in times of crises, it is not obvious that the framers will be particularly sober. The French constitution-makers of 1791, for instance, were not famous for their sobriety, and the document they produced contains few devices for restraining majorities that are swept by passion, eschewing bicameralism as well as judicial review.

Similarly, the framers will typically be subject to the same standing passions and prejudices as the framed. As observed by Adam Przeworski and Fernando Limongi "advocates of commitment . . . do not consider the political process by which such commitments are established" (Przeworski and Limongi 1993: 66). In Bulgaria, for instance, one might wish for the constitution to protect the rights of the Muslim, Turkish-speaking minority against oppression by ethnic Bulgarians. The fact, however, is that the latter exploited their control of the constitution-making process in 1990–1991 to adopt some of the most illiberal provisions in the new East European constitutions.[14]

Framers can and do, however, take rational precautions against their predictable tendency to yield to sudden attacks of *vanity*. The key variable is the choice between open and secret proceedings. If debates are open, the pride and vanity of the delegates may prevent them from backing down from a position which they have expressed in public. For this reason Mounier – the leader of the moderates in the Assemblée Constituante – wanted to keep as much as possible of the work in committees, which favored "cool reason and experience," by detaching the members from everything that could stimulate their vanity and fear of disapproval (Mounier 1989: 926). For the radical Bouche, committees tended to weaken the revolutionary fervor. He preferred the large assemblies,

136   *Jon Elster*

where "souls become strong and electrified, and where names, ranks and distinctions count for nothing" (*Archives Parlementaires* 1875–1888: vol. VIII, 307). On his proposal, it was decided that the assembly would sit in plenum each morning and meet in committee in the afternoon. Soon there were only plenary sessions.

Things worked out differently at the Federal Convention, where the sessions were closed and secret. As Madison said later, "had the members committed themselves publicly at first, they would have afterwards supposed consistency required them to maintain their ground, whereas by secret discussion no man felt himself obliged to retain his opinions any longer than he was satisfied of their propriety and truth, and was open to the force of argument" (Farrand 1966: vol. III, 479). However, he did not consider another effect of secrecy – that of pushing the debates away from rational argument and towards threat-based bargaining.

Consider next reason vs. interest in future legislatures. Impartial framers may try to affect future legislators in two ways. On the one hand, they may proceed on Hume's worst-case assumption that "every man must be supposed to be a knave," and arrange future institutions so as to channel the self-interest of legislators into socially beneficial forms. This public-choice approach was centrally represented at the Federal Convention, where the framers constantly based their arguments on the incentive effects of various schemes. Let me cite two examples from Madison. He was worried about requiring landed property for members of Congress. Looking back, he observed that "It had often happened that men who had acquired landed property on credit, got into the legislatures with a view of promoting an unjust protection against their creditors" (Farrand 1966: vol. II, 123). Another argument is less convincing. Arguing against selection of the executive by the legislature, Madison asserted that "the candidate would intrigue with the legislature, would derive his appointment from the predominant faction, and be apt to render his administration subservient to its views" (Farrand 1966: vol. II, 109). But it is not clear that a candidate's promise to favor his electors would be credible. Unless the executive can stand for reelection, we would rather expect the legislature to become subservient to its creature. The kingmaker should beware of the king.

On the other hand, the framers might want to create conditions that would encourage impartial reasoning and reduce the role of interest among future legislators. In the Assemblée Constituante this idea was central. The French founders believed that an assembly exists for the purpose of transforming preferences through rational discussion, going well beyond a simple process of aggregation. In the best-known state-

Ways of constitution-making

137

ment of this view Sieyès argued that the "voeu national," the desire of the nation, could not be determined by consulting the *cahiers* of complaints and wishes that the delegates had brought with them to Versailles (*Archives Parlementaires* 1875–1888: vol. VIII, 595). Bound mandates, similarly, could not be viewed as expressions of the national will. This view had several implications for institutional design, ranging from the choice between unicameralism and bicameralism to the choice of a quorum for the assembly and the procedures for revising the constitution.

Consider, finally, reason vs. passion in future legislatures. Sudden, passionate impulses among legislators may derive from popular fears, hatreds, or angers or from factors that are at work in the assembly itself. I shall discuss the former case in a moment. The latter case, once again, may be illustrated by the problem of vanity. In the Assemblée Constituante, many speakers asserted that one should never place an agent in a situation in which his vanity might lead him to act against the public interest. Bergasse repeatedly argued the need to accommodate the vanity or pride of the agents whose behavior will be regulated by the constitution (*Archives Parlementaires* 1875–1888: vol. IX, 115). The prosecutor, he says, should not also serve as judge, because if the functions are combined, the *amour-propre* of the magistrate might bias him towards the guilt of the accused (*Archives Parlementaires* 1875–1888: vol. VIII, 443). If the legislature accuses a minister of misconduct, he should not be judged by an ordinary court, which might make this an occasion to "humiliate the pride" of the legislative body (*Archives Parlementaires* 1875–1888: vol. IX, 111). A suspensive veto for the king will not have the intended effect of making the assembly reconsider, because its *amour-propre* will prevent it from backing down (*Archives Parlementaires* 1875–1888: vol. IX, 116).

V   The normative theory of constitution-making

At the outset I said that the positive theory of the constitution-making process does not yet exist. In conclusion, I want to point to another blank spot on the map: the normative study of constitution-making. Building on the normative analysis of constitutions and the positive theory of the constitution-making process, one might try to design an optimal structure for constituent assemblies.

The most important desideratum is probably that constitutions be written by specially convened assemblies and not by bodies that also serve as ordinary legislatures. Nor should the legislature be given a central place in the process of ratification. The place of the legislature in

138   *Jon Elster*

the political system being a central aspect of the constitution, that body should not be allowed to act as judge in its own cause. In this respect the Federal Convention and the Bonn assembly of 1948–1949 can serve as models.

Another implication of the analysis offered here is that the process ought to contain both elements of secrecy (committee discussion) and of publicity (plenary assembly discussions). With total secrecy partisan interests and logrolling come to the forefront, whereas full publicity encourages grandstanding and rhetorical overbidding. At the Federal Convention, there was too little publicity; at the Assemblée Constituante, too much. The making of the 1978 Spanish constitution may have come closer to the optimal balance.

More tentatively, I also suggest the following recommendations. (i) Elections to the constituent assembly ought to follow the proportional system rather than the majority system. Whatever the advantages of the majority system in creating ordinary legislatures, a constituent assembly ought to be broadly representative (Osiatynski 1994). (ii) The constituent assembly ought to be unicameral, not bicameral. Whatever the arguments for having bicameralism in ordinary legislatures, they do not apply to the constituent assembly. (iii) To reduce the scope for threats and attempts to influence the deliberations by mass demonstrations, the assembly should not convene in the capital of the country or in a major city; nor should armed forces be allowed to sojourn in the vicinity of the assembly. (iv) The role of experts should be kept to a minimum, because solutions tend to be more stable if dictated by political rather than technical considerations. Lawyers will tend to resist the technically flawed and deliberately ambiguous formulations that may be necessary to achieve consensus. (v) The assembly should work with a time limit, so that no group can use delaying tactics to get its way. (vi) If delays are affordable, the constitution should not come into effect until some time after it has been adopted, so as to reduce the impact of short-term partisan motives. As new constitutions usually are called for in times of crises, however, delays will rarely be affordable.

This last observation points to an inherent paradox in the constitution-making process. On the one hand, being written for the indefinite future, constitutions ought to be adopted in maximally calm and undisturbed conditions. On the other hand, the call for a new constitution usually arises in turbulent circumstances. On the one hand, the intrinsic importance of constitution-making demands procedures based on rational argument. On the other hand, the external circumstances of constitution-making invite procedures based on threat-based bargaining. I see no easy way out of this dilemma.

Ways of constitution-making

NOTES

1 The only partial exception I have come across is Bonime-Blanc (1987: chapter 8), but even that discussion is less than fully general. Being limited to transitions from authoritarianism to democracy, it does not, for instance, cover such constitution-making episodes as the Federal Convention. The essays in Goldwin and Kaufman (1988) describe individual constitution-making episodes, with no comparative or theoretical perspectives, except for the fact that the contributors were asked to address the same issues. Fafard and Reid (1991), while useful, is mainly descriptive (and to some extent prescriptive).

2 The present exposition is highly selective, and ignores a large number of relevant aspects of the constitution-making process. A fuller exposition will be available in Elster (forthcoming). See also Elster (1993 and 1994).

3 For some attempts to explain the emergence of conventions see Taylor (1976); Ullmann-Margalit (1977); Schotter (1981); Hardin (1982); Sugden (1986); Elster (1989); Coleman (1990); Ellickson (1991).

4 Eule goes on to say, however, that "even in such a system . . . there remain moral and political restraints on the legislative alteration of constitutional doctrine." In other words, satisfaction of the first criterion may to some extent automatically ensure satisfaction of the third.

5 See notably Denquin (1988). Documentation and transcripts of relevant debates are found in *Documents* (1987–1991).

6 This is the title of a book by Inoue (1991). The following quotes are taken from pp. 74, 31, and 269–70 of this work.

7 The following draws very heavily, with occasional paraphrases, on Cornell and Kalt (1993).

8 The following draws on an unpublished paper by Ethan Putterman.

9 There are, to be sure, some exceptions. The French constitution of 1791, for instance, created three distinct classes of political actors, with the *electors* being subject to more stringent economic requirements than both the *voters* who elected them and the *representatives* whom they elected. None of these classes coincided with the groups that had elected the delegates to the Assemblée Constituante.

10 There are several phenomena that need to be distinguished. (i) A constitution, when adopted, may represent the rule of the political part of the nation over the disenfranchised part. (ii) A constitution may represent the rule of one generation over later generations, independently of any changes in the suffrage. (iii) A constitution may represent the rule of one part of the political nation over another part, if it was adopted at a time when the latter did not yet have the suffrage and is too hard to change when it acquires the suffrage. (iv) A constitution may represent the rule of a minority over a majority, if the former can block amendments desired by the latter.

11 See notably Russell (1993). Documentary background is provided by Bayefsky (1989).

12 According to Bronislaw Geremek, "if the constitution is introduced by conspiracy – and such was, simplifying the matter, both the case with the American constitution and the Polish constitution of May Third – then it is a

140 *Jon Elster*

situation of imposing, from the top, a systemic order" (in Grudzinska-Gross (1994: 9). In the initial stage of the making of the French constitution of 1958, Edgard Pisani, later de Gaulle's minister of agriculture, made the following absurd claim about the American constitution: "C'est un comité secret de cinq sages qui l'a élaborée. Ces cinq personnes ont été condamnées au secret. Tous les papiers provenant de leurs travaux ont été brulés et ils se sont engagés par serment à ne jamais trahir le secret de leurs délibérations. C'est ainsi qu'a été élaborée la Constitution américaine" (*Documents* 1987–1991: vol. I, 192).

13 John Potter Stockton in debates over the Ku Klux Klan Act of 1871, as cited in Finn (1991: 5). On the general theme of self-binding see Elster (1984: chapter 2) and Holmes (1988). On the theme of constitutional self-binding, see Elster (1992). For a discussion of the putative paradoxes involved in self-binding, see Suber (1990).

14 Standing passions can be overcome, though, if the constitution is written under foreign supervision or by a small and enlightened minority within the country. As mentioned in the text, some (but not all) of the illiberal provisions in the first draft of the recent Bulgarian constitutions were eliminated after strong pressure from the Council of Europe. And it is at least arguable that the standing passion for leveling equality among the Americans was overcome by the elitist constitution of 1787.

REFERENCES

Archives Parlementaires. 1875–1888. *Archives Parlementaires. Série I: 1789–1799.* Paris.

Bayefsky, A. F., ed. 1989. *Canada's Constitution Act 1982 & Amendments: A Documentary History.* Toronto: McGraw-Hill.

Beard, C. 1986. *An Economic Interpretation of the Constitution of the United States.* Reprinted with a new Introduction by Forrest McDonald. New York: The Free Press.

Bonime-Blanc, A. 1987. *Spain's Transition to Democracy: The Politics of Constitution-Making.* Boulder and London: Westview Press.

Coleman, J. 1990. *Foundations of Social Theory.* Cambridge, Mass.: Harvard University Press.

Cornell, S., and J. P. Kalt. 1993. "Where does economic development really come from? Constitutional rule among the modern Sioux and Apaché." Harvard: Working Project on American Indian Economic Development.

Denquin, J.-M. 1988. *1958: la genèse de la Ve République.* Paris: Presses Universaires de France.

Documents. 1987–1991. *Documents pour servir à l'histoire de l'élaboration de la constitution de 4 octobre 1958,* vols. I–III. Paris: La Documentation Française.

Ellickson, R. C. 1991. *Order without Law.* Cambridge, Mass.: Harvard University Press.

Elster, J. 1984. *Ulysses and the Sirens.* Rev. edn. Cambridge: Cambridge University Press.

1989. *The Cement of Society.* Cambridge: Cambridge University Press.

Ways of constitution-making

1992. "Intertemporal choice and political theory," in G. Loewenstein and J. Elster, eds., *Choices over Time*. New York: Russell Sage Foundation.

1993. "Rebuilding the boat in the open sea: constitution-making in Eastern Europe," *Public Administration* 71: 169–217.

1994. "Argumenter et négocier dans assemblées constituantes," *Revue Française de Science Politique* 44: 187–256.

1995. "Strategic uses of argument," in K. Arrow *et al.*, eds., *Barriers to Conflict Resolution*. New York: Norton.

Forthcoming *Arguing and Bargaining in the Constitution-Making Process*.

Eule, J. N. 1987. "Temporal limits on the legislative mandate," *American Bar Foundation Research Journal*: 379–459.

Fafard, P. A., and D. R. Reid. 1991. *Constituent Assemblies: A Comparative Survey*. Kingston, Ontario: Institute of Governmental Relations, Queen's University.

Farrand, M., ed. 1966. *Records of the Federal Convention*. New Haven: Yale University Press.

Flinn, J. E. 1991. *Constitutions in China*. New York: Oxford University Press.

Golay, J. Ford. 1958. *The Founding of the Federal Republic of Germany*. Chicago: University of Chicago Press.

Goldwin, R. A., and A. Kaufman, eds. 1988. *Constitution-Makers on Constitution-Making*. Washington, DC: American Enterprise Institute for Public Policy Research.

Grudzinska-Gross, I., ed. 1994. *Constitutionalism in East Central Europe: Discussions in Warsaw, Budapest, Prague, Bratislava*. Bratislava: Czecho-Slovak Committee of the European Cultural Foundation.

Gutmann, E. 1988. "Israel: democracy without a constitution," in V. Bogdanov, ed., *Constitutions in Democratic Politics*. Aldershot: Gower.

Hardin, R. 1982. *Collective Action*. Baltimore: Johns Hopkins University Press.

Holmes, S. 1988. "Precommitment and the paradox of democracy," in J. Elster and R. Slagstad, eds., *Constitutionalism and Democracy*. Cambridge: Cambridge University Press.

Inoue, K. 1991. *MacArthur's Japanese Constitution: A Linguistic and Cultural Study of its Making*. Chicago: University of Chicago Press.

McGuire, R. A. 1988. "Constitution making: a rational choice model of the Federal Convention of 1787," *American Journal of Political Science* 32: 483–522.

Marshall, G. 1986. *Constitutional Conventions*. Oxford: Oxford University Press; first published 1984.

Merkl, P. 1963. *The Origin of the West German Republic*. New York: Oxford University Press.

Mounier, J. J. 1989. "Exposé de ma conduite dans l'Assemblée Nationale," in F. Furet and R. Halévi, eds., *Orateurs de la Révolution Française.I: les constituants*. Paris: Gallimard.

Osiatynski, W. 1994. "Poland's constitutional ordeal," *East European Constitutional Review* 3: 29–41.

Przeworski, A., and F. Limongi. 1993. "Political regimes and economic growth," *Journal of Economic Perspectives* 7: 51–69.

142　*Jon Elster*

Russell, P. 1993. *Constitutional Odyssey: Can Canadians Become a Sovereign People?*, 2nd edn. Toronto: University of Toronto Press.

Schotter, A. 1981. *The Economic Theory of Social Institutions*. Cambridge: Cambridge University Press.

Spence, J. D. 1990. *The Search for Modern China*. London: Hutchinson.

Suber, P. 1990. *The Paradox of Self-Amendment*. New York: Peter Lang.

Sugden, R. 1986. *The Economics of Rights, Co-Operation and Welfare*. Oxford: Blackwell.

Sunstein, C. 1991. "Constitutionalism, prosperity, democracy," *Constitutional Political Economy* 2: 371–394.

Taylor, M. 1976. *Anarchy and Cooperation*. Chichester: Wiley.

Ullmann-Margalit, E. 1977. *The Emergence of Norms*. Oxford: Oxford University Press.

Vanberg, V., and J. Buchanan. 1989. "Interests and theories in constitutional choice," *Journal of Theoretical Politics*. 1: 49–62.

8 Back to democratic basics: who really practices majority rule?

Arend Lijphart

Democracy's victory in the 1990s, while a major development in world history, is only a partial victory. It represents the defeat of Communism, Fascism, and other ideological anti-democratic forces, but democracy continues to face enemies of a different nature: in particular, the deep ethnic-communal divisions within countries, often aggravated by great socioeconomic inequalities, which pose a grave threat to the viability and consolidation of democracy in the many newly democratic countries.

The leitmotiv of much of my previous work has been that the challenge of deep cleavages does not represent an insuperable problem. Democracy of the "consociational" or "consensus" type – similar concepts, although I have defined them in slightly different terms (Lijphart 1977, 1984) – provides formal and informal constitutional rules that can facilitate interethnic and intercommunal accommodation. The two most important elements are broad participation in decision making by the representatives of the different ethnic-communal groups and cultural autonomy for those groups that wish to have it. The empirical evidence for this proposition is very strong. For instance, Ted Robert Gurr's recent *Minorities at Risk* (1993: esp. 290–313), a massive study of all of the world's minorities in the post-World War II era, concludes that, first of all, intercommunal conflict is by no means intractable; that, second, partition and secession do not work well, mainly because it is in practice very difficult to draw boundaries in such a clean and neat way that homogeneous countries are created; but that, thirdly, there are methods that do work, namely broad power-sharing and group autonomy.[1]

This chapter explores one aspect of the question of how broadly representative democratic governments are: to what extent do democratic governments – in the narrow sense of "governments," that is, democratic *executives* – enjoy the support of the voters and citizens in their countries? In particular, do democratic executives have sufficiently broad support to satisfy the principle of majority rule? These questions

144   *Arend Lijphart*

affect both the quality and stability of democracy. As John Stuart Mill forcefully argues in his famous *Considerations on Representative Government* (1861), majority rule is a basic qualitative requirement of democracy. He worries that when democratic majority rule is used twice – first, in the conversion of popular votes to legislative seats, and, second, as a decision rule in the legislature – it runs the risk of turning into undemocratic minority rule.

In ethnically and communally divided countries – that is, in most of the countries of the world – the breadth of representation is also important for the viability of democracy. In fact, as stated with exceptional clarity by Sir Arthur Lewis in his classic *Politics in West Africa* (1965: 66), majority rule – if it means bare-majority rule – is dysfunctional for such plural societies. The most important requirement of democracy is that citizens have the opportunity to participate, directly or indirectly, in decision making. This meaning of democracy is violated if significant minorities are excluded from the decision-making process for extended periods of time. Under such circumstances, narrow majority rule is "totally immoral, inconsistent with the primary meaning of democracy, and *destructive of any prospect of building a nation in which different peoples might live together in harmony*" (emphasis added). Lewis would therefore certainly agree with Mill that minority government is unacceptably undemocratic. And he would add that minority rule is even more dangerous than narrow majority rule for the chances that democracies will be stable and peaceful.

After discussing Mill's arguments in greater detail below, I shall explore the influence on the breadth of representation by two basic institutional features of democratic systems: the contrast between plurality and majority election systems on the one hand and proportional representation on the other, and the contrast between majoritarian and consensus institutions. I shall also take a brief look at the question of breadth of representation from a methodological perspective. What is the optimal – reliable and valid – operationalization of the first and most important characteristic of consensus democracy: broad and inclusive representation in the executive branch of government? In particular, is Mill's variable of popular cabinet support a better measure of executive power-sharing than the measure that I use in *Democracies*: the degree to which democracies are governed by oversized instead of minimal winning governments (Lijphart 1984: 46–66)?

My universe consists of the twenty-one advanced industrial democracies that have been continuously democratic since approximately the end of World War II: fifteen West European democracies plus the United States, Canada, Japan, Israel, Australia, and New Zealand.[2]

These are the twenty-one countries analyzed in my book *Democracies* (Lijphart 1984), which covers the 1945–1980 period. Here I extend the coverage by ten years to 1945–1990. The one exception is France which drastically changed its constitutional system in 1958: I shall focus exclusively on the Fifth Republic, because the Fourth Republic (1946–1958), as it recedes into the past, looks more and more like a brief and fairly insignificant interlude in French political history.

John Stuart Mill's majority-rule criterion

Majoritarians and consensualists disagree on the basic goal of democracy: the former seek to concentrate power as much as possible in the hands of the majority, whereas the latter try to include as many citizens as possible in the sharing of power. Consensualists can argue that they are not against majority rule as such but that they favor broad instead of narrow majority rule. The majoritarians counter that insistence on extraordinary majorities leads to too much minority power and/or political stalemate. In *Federalist Paper* Number 22, Alexander Hamilton (1788) presents the majoritarian argument in the following words:

What at first sight may seem a remedy, is, in reality, a poison. To give a minority a negative upon the majority (which is always the case where more than a majority is requisite to a decision), is, in its tendency, to subject the sense of the greater number to that of the lesser ... Hence, tedious delays; continual negotiation and intrigue; contemptible compromises of the public good.

Hamilton's principal worry here is minority *veto* power or what may be called *negative* minority power. Neither Hamilton and other majoritarians nor the consensualists favor *positive* minority rule, that is, the power of minorities to make decisions against the wishes of majorities. In other words, they agree on majority rule as a *minimum* requirement of democracy.

The criterion of majority rule in this sense was first clearly formulated as the most fundamental requirement of democracy by John Stuart Mill in his *Considerations on Representative Government* (1861; see also Spafford 1985). I shall henceforth refer to it as the John Stuart Mill criterion. The further innovation proposed by Mill is that proportional representation must be used to satisfy the basic majority-rule criterion – a rather surprising proposition because proportional representation is the consensualists', instead of the majoritarians', preferred electoral system.

Mill's (1861: chapter 7) argument proceeds as follows. First, he defines the objective of democracy as "giving the powers of government

146   *Arend Lijphart*

in all cases to the numerical majority." He then states that his objective is violated in representative democracy if a majoritarian method for electing representatives is used: this gives governmental power "to a majority of the majority, who may be, and often are, but a minority of the whole."

Next he proves this point by examining the logic of the most extreme case:

Suppose . . . that, in a country governed by equal and universal suffrage, there is a contested election in every constituency, and every election is carried by a small majority. The Parliament thus brought together represents little more than a bare majority of the people. This Parliament proceeds to legislate and adopts important measures by a bare majority of itself.

Although Mill does not state so explicitly himself, one of these "important measures" would be the formation of a cabinet supported by a majority of the legislators. Mill continues:

What guarantee is there that these measures accord with the wishes of a majority of the people? Nearly half the electors, having been outvoted at the hustings, have had no influence at all in the decision; and the whole of these may be, a majority of them probably are, hostile to the measures, having voted against those by whom they have been carried. Of the remaining electors, nearly half have chosen representatives who, by supposition, have voted against the measures. It is possible, therefore, and not at all improbable, that the opinion which has prevailed was agreeable only to a minority of the nation, through a majority of that portion of it whom the institutions of the country have erected into a ruling class.

Mill's final conclusion is that proportional representation is necessary in order to avoid giving the powers of government to such a minority "ruling class":

If democracy means the certain ascendancy of the majority, there are no means of insuring that but by allowing every individual figure to tell equally in the summing up. Any minority left out, either purposely or by the play of the [two-stage majoritarian] machinery, gives the power not to the majority but to a minority.

Mill's logical argument clearly proves that it is possible that plurality and other majoritarian electoral systems may lead to a violation of the John Stuart Mill criterion. But, in the passage quoted above, he also argues that this situation is not just possible but also probable or "not at all improbable." As far as proportional representation is concerned, he proves that perfect proportionality will satisfy the John Stuart Mill criterion. He does not consider less than perfectly proportional methods, but presumably even such methods are more likely to satisfy

Who really practices majority rule? 147

the criterion than majoritarian election systems. We can therefore also read his argument as an empirical hypothesis: democracies that use proportional representation are more likely to satisfy the John Stuart Mill criterion, that is, they are more likely to have true majority rule than democracies that use plurality or other majoritarian election systems. A related, more general, hypothesis is that consensus democracies are more likely to pass the minimum requirement of majority rule than "majoritarian" democracies – which are more likely to be pluralitarian or minoritarian instead of truly majoritarian.

Measuring breadth of representation

In *Democracies*, I define the contrast between majoritarian and consensus forms of democratic governments in terms of two dimensions and eight characteristics (Lijphart 1984). I shall focus here on the first dimension consisting of five closely related characteristics of executives, parties, and elections: bare-majority versus power-sharing executives, dominant executives versus executive-legislative balance of power, two-party versus multiparty systems, party systems in which the main parties differ primarily on socioeconomic issues versus systems in which the parties also differ on religious, ethnic, urban–rural, foreign policy, or other dimensions, and majoritarian and disproportional versus more proportional electoral systems.[3]

Of these five characteristics, the contrast between bare-majority and power-sharing cabinets is the most important because it appears to capture the essence of the conceptual distinction between majoritarian and consensus democracy particularly well. My operational measure was the percentage of time each of my countries was ruled by minimal winning cabinets instead of oversized cabinets – a dichotomous classification that has become standard, and that has proved to be very fruitful, in the analyses of coalition theorists from the early work of William H. Riker (1962) on.

My one practical problem was the question of how to fit minority cabinets into this dichotomy. Minority cabinets may be near-majority cabinets which govern with the steady support of one other party that gives them a parliamentary majority. But they may also be either near-majority or much smaller cabinets that govern with the support of shifting parliamentary coalitions. The former resemble minimal winning cabinets, and the latter oversized cabinets. My solution was to apportion periods of minority cabinet rule equally to the periods under minimal winning cabinets and under oversized cabinets (Lijphart 1984: 61–62).

Although this solution has not, to my knowledge, been criticized by

148   *Arend Lijphart*

other scholars, I am no longer fully satisfied with it, and I have also become dissatisfied with two other aspects of the measurement in terms of minimal winning versus oversized cabinets. One is that minimal winning cabinets can, in fact, be very broadly based cabinets. For instance, the Christian Democratic-Socialist *Grosse Koalition* cabinets in Austria from 1949 to 1966 and in Germany from 1966 to 1969 were technically minimal winning cabinets, because both parties were necessary to give the coalitions majority support in parliament, and the withdrawal of either party would have turned the cabinets into minority cabinets. Yet, all of these cabinets had the support of about 90 percent of their legislatures. On the other hand, oversized cabinets may not have a very broad base of parliamentary support. For example, most oversized cabinets in Israel, with the exception of the 1967–1970 and 1984–1990 "national unity" governments, have included one or a few quite small surplus parties and have had the support of only 55 to 60 percent of the members of parliament. The solution to this problem could be to use the percentage of a cabinet's parliamentary support as an alternative or additional measure of the degree of power-sharing.

The second problem is that the general category of minimal winning cabinets includes both one-party cabinets and minimal winning coalitions of two or more parties, but that the bargaining style of coalitions, even when these are merely minimal winning, makes them at least a bit less majoritarian in orientation than one-party, non-coalition cabinets. For instance, most German cabinets have been minimal winning cabinets with a relatively narrow support base in the Bundestag, but they have been considerably more consensual, centrist, and compromise-oriented than British bare-majority, single-party cabinets – a difference that has loomed large for British critics of their country's adversarial style of politics and that has made them advocate German-style electoral reform (see Finer 1975). This problem could be solved by including either the one-party versus coalition distinction or the number of cabinet parties in the measure of the degree of power-sharing in addition to one or both of the two measures discussed above. A further variant would be to count not the raw number of cabinet parties but their effective number so as to give greater weight to larger than to smaller parties in the cabinet – similar to the measure of the effective number of parties in the legislature (Taagepera and Shugart 1989: 77–81).

Yet another possibility is suggested by John Stuart Mill's view of the essence of democratic government: the percentage of popular or voter support on which a cabinet is based. This measure has the potential advantage of being very directly and closely linked to the basic conceptual distinction between narrow majority rule and power-sharing, and may thus have greater validity than the other measures. It is also a simple and straightforward measure. I shall compare it with the minimal winning/oversized measure later on in this chapter.

Measurement problems

Measuring the degree of popular support for cabinets does not present many serious problems in most parliamentary democracies. It is simply the total percentage of the vote in the most recent parliamentary election received by the parties included in a particular cabinet. The data are also readily available: I used the 1945–1990 cabinet data collected by Jaap Woldendorp, Hans Keman, and Ian Budge (1993) – with a few adjustments suggested in the work of Jean-Claude Colliard (1978: 311–354), Heikki Paloheimo (1984), and Kaare Strom (1990: 245–269) – and Thomas T. Mackie and Richard Rose's (1991) election data. Nevertheless, there are a number of issues with regard to operationalization and measurement that must be addressed.

1. First of all, parties that actually participate in cabinets should clearly be counted as cabinet parties, but what about parties that support a cabinet without being represented in it? Coalition experts have tended to disagree on this issue: most have counted actual participants in cabinets only, but a few have also included so-called support parties (e.g., De Swaan 1973: 143–144). In *Democracies*, I followed the majority practice of ignoring any support parties. On second thought, however, it seems to me that a better solution – instead of either completely including or completely excluding support parties – is the compromise solution of regarding them as half in and half out of the cabinet. After all, support parties are in a kind of half-way position between the governing parties that are actually in the cabinet on the one hand and opposition parties on the other. In accordance with this reasoning, I counted half of the votes for support parties toward the total popular support for a cabinet. For instance, I credited Denmark's 1955–1957 Social Democratic cabinet, which enjoyed Radical Party support, with the popular votes cast in the previous election for the Social Democrats, 41.3 percent, plus half of the 7.8 percent of the votes cast for the Radicals, for a total of 45.2 percent popular cabinet support.[4]

2. A related problem is the treatment of minority cabinets. In parliamentary systems, they can survive only if they are supported – or merely tolerated – by half of the legislators, and, in countries in which their installation requires a formal vote of investiture, slightly more than 50 percent support is needed. This problem can be solved analogously to the solution of counting support parties. Minority cabinets have the

150   *Arend Lijphart*

implicit support of enough legislators to bridge the gap between the number of legislators belonging to the cabinet parties and half of the membership of the legislature. These bridging legislators can be regarded as an implicit support party. The only practical problem that remains is that we do not know who exactly these legislators are, and hence that we do not know what their popular support is. My solution is to simply count this implicit support in terms of seats – and to assume that there is not too much of a discrepancy between seats and votes. To give one specific example, Canada's 1962–1963 Conservative minority cabinet was formed after the Conservatives won 37.3 percent of the votes and 43.8 percent of the seats; popular cabinet support was 37.3 percent plus half of the difference between 50 percent and 43.8 percent (3.1 percent): a total of 40.4 percent.

3. Three of our parliamentary or semi-parliamentary democracies have bicameral legislatures in which the two houses have equal powers and are both popularly elected: Belgium, Italy, and Switzerland.[5] Belgian and Italian cabinets are responsible to both chambers and the Swiss executive (Federal Council) is elected by a joint session of the two chambers. On which of the two parliamentary elections should the measure of popular cabinet support be based? Partly for pragmatic reasons – the easier availability of the necessary election data – my decision was to use the lower house elections. This choice can also be defended on substantive grounds: the similarity of the electoral systems (proportional representation) used for the simultaneous election of the two chambers in Belgium and Italy, and the fact that in joint sessions of the Swiss legislature the lower chamber outweighs the much smaller upper chamber by about four to one.

4. How should popular cabinet support be measured in systems with powerful and directly elected presidents? In the case of the United States, I used the votes cast for the winning presidential candidate. In semi-presidential France and Finland, cabinets require the confidence of the legislature; hence they can be treated like the cabinets in fully parliamentary systems. The only nettlesome problem concerns the 1986–1988 French cabinet mainly consisting of Gaullists and Republicans but chaired by Socialist President François Mitterrand; were the Socialists part of this cabinet? My solution was to split the difference again and to count half of the Socialist vote in the 1986 election toward the popular support of this cabinet.

5. A much more serious problem is that of insincere voting (often also referred to as tactical, strategic, or sophisticated voting). When we compare the raw percentages of popular cabinet support in plurality systems – Canada, New Zealand, the United Kingdom, and the United

States – with that in proportional representation systems, the former are deceptively high because some of the votes cast for the winning parties are votes that, in the latter, would have been cast for small parties. Some adjustment is also clearly required in order to do justice to the majoritarian systems of Australia and France where the popular support percentages are based on, respectively, the first-preference and first-ballot votes, which are influenced only marginally by insincere voting. The big difficulty is to estimate the percentage of insincere voters among those who voted for the cabinet parties. My initial rough estimate is that this percentage is somewhere between 10 and 30 percent.

There are two additional problems. One is that insincere voters may support a small party because of, rather than in spite of, its small size and low probability of entering the government, in order to "send a message" to the major well-established parties – like some of the Ross Perot supporters in the 1992 American presidential election. This difference corresponds with the distinction that Mark Franklin, Richard Niemi, and Guy Whitten (1994: 552) make between the "instrumental" form of insincere voting, based on the voters' calculation that they do not want to waste their votes on weak parties and candidates, and the "expressive" form of insincere voting based on various other considerations. They also suggest, however, that the latter occurs much more rarely than the former. The other problem is that a certain amount of insincere voting can also occur under proportional systems, especially those that use low-magnitude districts or high thresholds (Sartori 1986; Cox and Shugart 1994).

The major contrast, however, is between the different systems of proportional representation on the one hand and plurality on the other. In order to take these two problems into consideration, the adjustment percentage should be on the low end of my initial estimate of 10 to 30 percent. I opted for the lowest estimate in this range: 10 percent insincere voting – which I believe is an extremely conservative estimate. One example: the country with the lowest average popular cabinet support in the 1945–1990 period is Canada; its adjusted percentage is 41.2 percent, that is, 90 percent of its unadjusted 45.8 percent. In a further effort not to "penalize" plurality systems unduly, I used the adjusted figures only to calculate average popular cabinet support and not in the determination of the extent to which the different democracies fulfill the John Stuart Mill criterion.

6. Democratic purists might argue that popular cabinet support should be based on the votes cast for cabinet parties as a percentage not of all *voters* (casting valid votes), but of all adult *citizens* (eligible voters). For instance, when we compare the two highest average

152   *Arend Lijphart*

percentages of popular cabinet support, 77.7 percent in Switzerland and 70.6 percent in Austria, the latter is especially impressive because Austrian turnout rates have generally been above 90 percent, whereas Swiss turnout decreased gradually from just above 70 percent to below 50 percent. An adjustment for low turnout seems particularly justified in the other low-turnout country, the United States, where onerous registration requirements represent a deliberate attempt to depress voter participation.

The big difficulty is to find the appropriate adjustment. First of all, using 100 percent voter turnout as the basic yardstick is patently unrealistic. But which turnout level *is* an expectation that can realistically be attained: 90 percent, 85 percent, 80 percent? Second, does not any adjustment of this kind unfairly "advantage" countries with compulsory voting? Third, for many countries it is by no means easy to find accurate figures for the total number of eligible voters (Powell 1986; Jackman 1987). Faced with these dilemmas, my final operational decision was not to make any adjustments for different turnout levels – but without full confidence that this is the optimal decision.[6]

John Stuart Mill's Hypotheses

The first two columns of Table 8.1 show average popular cabinet support, in descending order of magnitude, as well as the percentage of time that John Stuart Mill's majority-rule criterion was fulfilled for the twenty-one democracies. For each country, the period covered is from the first to the last parliamentary election between 1945 and 1990. Both sets of percentages are averages for these periods, weighted according to the length of time (number of days) that each cabinet was in office.

Average cabinet support has a very wide range: from a low of 41.2 percent in Canada to a high of 77.7 percent – almost twice as high – in Switzerland. The range was considerably smaller within most countries. The Finnish case, with a high of more than 83 percent popular support (the first postwar cabinet) and a low of about 25 percent (several non-party cabinets relying solely on support parties and implicit parliamentary support), is exceptional. The range is similarly wide as far as the fulfillment of the John Stuart Mill criterion is concerned: two countries (Switzerland and Luxembourg) *always* and two countries (the United Kingdom and Norway) *never* satisfied it. Approximately half of the countries have an average popular cabinet support above 50 percent, and about half below 50 percent. And about half of the countries satisfied the Mill criterion more than 50 percent of the time; the other half

Who really practices majority rule? 153

Table 8.1. *Popular cabinet support, John Stuart Mill criterion, dispro-portionality, consensus democracy, and minimal winning coalitions in twenty-one democracies, 1945–1990*

	Popular cabinet support (%)	J. S. Mill criterion (%)	Index of dispro-portionality (%)	Majority / consensus democracy (factor scores)	Minimal winning cabinets (%)
Switzerland	77.7	100.0	2.4	−1.65	4.9
Austria	70.6	87.7	2.7	1.50	89.7
Luxembourg	64.0	100.0	3.1	0.08	91.7
Israel	62.6	85.2	1.7	−1.07	20.3
Netherlands	61.6	87.9	1.3	−1.69	44.7
Iceland	60.6	97.0	4.5	−0.06	82.7
Belgium	59.3	80.3	3.2	−0.55	71.3
Germany	55.9	82.1	2.3	0.68	75.3
Finland	55.3	59.9	2.9	−1.49	25.8
Italy	51.8	53.2	2.8	−0.10	30.8
Japan	50.4	32.6	5.7	0.12	86.7
Sweden	48.3	25.3	2.1	0.48	64.7
United States	48.3	70.0	5.4	1.11	100.0
Ireland	47.9	17.6	3.5	0.61	81.1
Australia	47.8	15.0	8.9	0.67	88.7
France	47.7	49.4	13.1	−0.18	44.7
Denmark	45.1	15.9	1.8	−0.78	61.1
Norway	45.0	0.0	5.0	0.42	77.0
New Zealand	41.9	18.1	10.7	1.42	100.0
United Kingdom	41.4	0.0	10.5	1.16	97.4
Canada	41.2	20.1	11.3	0.81	89.5

Source: based on data in Woldendorp, Keman, and Budge (1993) (columns 1, 2, and 5); Lijphart (1994: 160–62) (column 3), and Lijphart (1984: 216) (column 4).

less than 50 percent of the time. The two variables are highly correlated (r = .87).

Mill predicts that majoritarian countries are likely to fail his majority-rule criterion but that proportional representation countries are more likely to satisfy it. This prediction is largely borne out. Of the six democracies with majoritarian election systems (Australia, Canada, France, New Zealand, the United Kingdom, and the United States), only the United States satisfies Mill's criterion more than half of the time. Of the fourteen proportional systems (the remaining countries except semi-proportional Japan), only four – Denmark, Norway, Sweden, and Ireland – fail Mill's criterion.

154   *Arend Lijphart*

A more sensitive test regresses the percentage of time that the Mill criterion is fulfilled on the exact degree of disproportionality, using the least-squares index designed by Michael Gallagher (1991: 38–40; Lijphart 1994: 60–61, 160–162). The values of this index are shown in the third column of Table 1. The correlation coefficient is − .51, significant at the 1 percent level.[7] The regression line in Figure 8.1 shows that for each percentage increase in electoral disproportionality there is an almost 5 percent decrease in the time that Mill's majority-rule criterion is satisfied. The principal deviant cases are the four countries that are located far above the regression line (Switzerland, Luxembourg, Iceland, and France) and four countries at a considerable distance below the regression line (the three Scandinavian countries and Ireland). The latter satisfy the Mill criterion less often than expected on the basis of their relatively low levels of electoral disproportionality; the former fulfill the Mill criterion more often than expected.

The main explanation of the deviant position of Denmark, Sweden, Norway, and Ireland is their frequent minority cabinets which almost inevitably have less than 50 percent popular support; minority cabinets were in office in these four countries during respectively 77.8 percent, 70.7 percent, 46.0 percent, and 37.9 percent of the period. Of the other four countries, Switzerland's 100 percent performance can be explained in terms of its almost permanent grand coalition, while Luxembourg and Iceland had mainly minimal winning cabinets which still had ample parliamentary support. The French outlying position is partly an artifact of the way disproportionality is calculated in two-ballot systems, which tends to exaggerate the "true" degree of disproportionality. Disproportionality is also significantly correlated at the 1 percent level – in fact, somewhat more strongly correlated – with average popular cabinet support ($r = -.60$).

Moreover, the more general hypothesis that I derived from Mill concerning the relationship between majoritarian versus consensus democracy on the one hand and both popular cabinet support and the Mill criterion on the other is also significantly supported, albeit less strongly and only at the 5 percent level: the correlation coefficients are −.48 and −.43 respectively. To sum up, as Mill suggests, consensus and proportional democracies are indeed more likely to be truly majority-rule systems, and supposedly "majoritarian" democracies and electoral systems are indeed more likely to be pluralitarian and minoritarian instead of genuinely majoritarian.

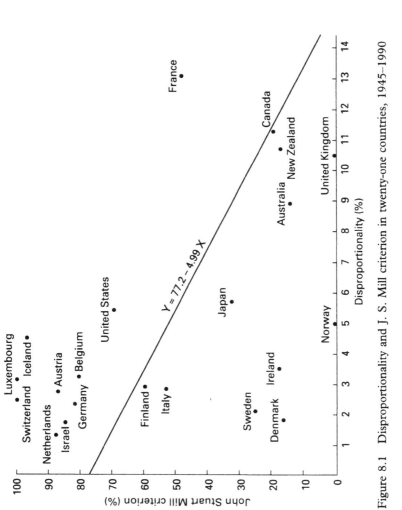

Figure 8.1 Disproportionality and J. S. Mill criterion in twenty-one countries, 1945–1990

Popular cabinet support versus minimal winning/ oversized cabinets

Finally, I should like to briefly consider the question of whether popular cabinet support may be a more accurate – more valid – measure of executive power-sharing than the contrast between minimal winning and oversized cabinets. The percentage of time that the twenty-one democracies were ruled by minimal winning cabinets between 1945 and 1990 is shown in the fifth column of Table 8.1. As discussed earlier, half of the time under minority cabinets was also credited to the period of minimal winning cabinets.[8] The two variables are correlated but with only moderate strength: $r = -.47$, significant at the 5 percent level. In Figure 8.2, three countries – Switzerland, Austria, and Luxembourg – are located far above the regression line, indicating that their percentages of average popular cabinet support are considerably higher than expected on the basis of their frequency of minimal winning cabinets.

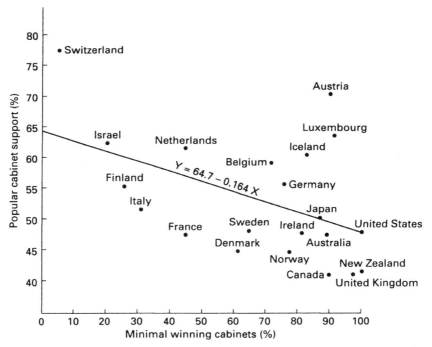

Figure 8.2 Minimal winning cabinets and popular cabinet support in twenty-one countries, 1945–1990

The explanation of the Swiss and Luxembourg cases is the same as for their deviant position in Figure 8.1. The Austrian case is an artifact of the classification of its grand coalitions in the 1949–1966 period as minimal winning (as explained earlier); Austria's "true" location should be much more to the left in Figure 8.2. There are no strongly deviant cases below the regression line, but the three Scandinavian countries again do not score impressively with regard to the breadth of popular support for their cabinets.

These results do not convince me that popular cabinet support works better than the frequency of minimal winning cabinets as a measure of power-sharing. For instance, it seems to me that Swedish, Norwegian, and Danish styles of governing are closer to the give-and-take bargaining and accommodationist styles of the power-sharing democracies than to the adversarial and confrontational spirit of the Anglo-American majority-rule democracies. After all, a classic study of the Swedish political system was appropriately entitled *The Politics of Compromise* (Rustow 1955)!

What can and should be done instead is to strengthen the measure of the frequency of minimal winning cabinets in three ways. One is to admit that, with regard to the need for bargaining and compromise, most minority cabinets are much more like oversized cabinets than like minimal winning cabinets. Therefore, it makes more sense to count them on a par with oversized cabinets instead of half-way between oversized and minimal winning cabinets. Second, as suggested above, an adjustment should be devised for broadly based but technically minimal winning cabinets (like Austria's) and for narrowly based but technically oversized cabinets (like Israel's). Third, because minimal winning *coalitions* entail a much greater need for bargaining and compromise than minimal winning *one-party cabinets*, it would make sense to make the further adjustment of adding the number of parties as an element of the measure of executive power-sharing – probably in the form of the effective number of parties in the cabinet, as I have also already discussed earlier.

This does not mean that I propose that the breadth of popular cabinet support and the fulfillment of the John Stuart Mill criterion be abandoned. My argument is that these measures should not be used as indicators of the degree of consensus versus majoritarian democracy, but rather as indicators of intrinsically important democratic values. Many attempts to measure degrees, and hence the quality, of democracy – such as in the two recent edited volumes that both have *Measuring Democracy* as part of their titles (Inkeles 1991; Beetham 1994) – are based on Dahl's (1971: 3) eight "institutional guarantees" of

158   *Arend Lijphart*

democracy, but they take such basics as universal suffrage and majority rule for granted – which means that these basics are forgotten. For instance, Switzerland usually receives a high score in spite of the fact that universal suffrage for women as well as men was not realized at the federal level until 1971.[9] Similarly, we should heed John Stuart Mill's admonition that majority rule is a minimum requirement of democracy, and we must not hesitate to judge the world's democracies by this standard.

To end on a substantive note, let me emphasize two important conclusions. One is the fact that consensus democracies and proportional representation systems are considerably more successful than majoritarian democracies and plurality election systems in achieving genuine majority rule, in accordance with John Stuart Mill's hypothesis. For the purposes of constitutional engineering, this is a strong argument in favor of the former. Second, minority cabinets may be regarded as, on balance, consensual instruments, but they suffer from the democratic deficit of usually failing Mill's majority-rule criterion.

NOTES

1 The only minor exceptions to Gurr's broad coverage is that he excludes countries with less than 1 million inhabitants and groups with less than 100,000 members or 1 percent of a country's population.
2 According to my definition of long-term democracy, India and Costa Rica should have been included in *Democracies*, too. I again exclude these two countries here, but purely on practical grounds: their cabinet data are not in the Woldendorp, Keman, and Budge (1993) data set on which I relied. My definition of democracy is not a very demanding one: I follow the basic criterion of "one person, one vote," but I obviously do not apply this standard very strictly when I include pre-1971 Switzerland, in which women did not yet have the right to vote, and the United States before the 1965 Voting Rights Act, which finally introduced universal suffrage. I also ignore the arguably just as serious violations of "one person, one vote" represented by colonial control and lengthy occupation of territories conquered by military action: the cases in point are the United Kingdom, France, the Netherlands, Belgium, the United States, and Israel.
3 The second dimension, which I shall not discuss further, may be called the federal-unitary dimension and consists of the three related characteristics of centralization–decentralization, unicameralism–bicameralism, and flexible versus rigid constitutions.
4 This solution obviously does not solve the problem that it is often difficult to determine which parties should be counted as support parties. I simply accepted the judgments of Woldendorp, Keman, and Budge (1993).
5 In Belgium and Switzerland, not all, but a large majority of the second chamber legislators are popularly elected.

Who really practices majority rule? 159

6 In addition, there were a number of minor methodological problems to be resolved, in particular, the question of how to apportion votes received by joint party lists to the separate parties; on this matter, I used the procedures outlined in my book on electoral systems (Lijphart 1994: 163–177).
7 All of my tests of significance are one-tailed.
8 I used several splitting-the-difference rules in classifying borderline cases as oversized, minimal winning, or minority cabinets. If there were support parties, and if with the support parties the cabinet would belong to one type, but without the support parties to another type, I divided the time that the cabinet was in office half to one type and the other half to the other type. If a cabinet had exactly 50 percent parliamentary support (a so-called "blocking" coalition), I counted it as half minimal winning and half minority. If the loss of the smallest party in a majority coalition would reduce its parliamentary support to exactly 50 percent, I counted it as half minimal winning and half oversized. Moreover, I counted the closely allied Liberal and National parties in Australia and the German CDU and CSU first as one party and next as two separate parties; if this led to different classifications of cabinet type, I split the difference once again.
9 In Dahl's (1971: 231–248) own classification of 114 countries according to 31 scale types, from the highest degree of democracy to complete non-democracy, Switzerland is placed in the highest, most democratic, scale type, too.

REFERENCES

Beetham, David, ed. 1994. *Defining and Measuring Democracy*. London: Sage.
Colliard, Jean-Claude. 1978. *Les régimes parlementaires contemporains*. Paris: Presses de la Fondation Nationale des Sciences Politiques.
Cox, Gary W., and Matthew Soberg Shugart. 1994. "Strategic voting under proportional representation." Unpublished paper.
Dahl, Robert A. 1971. *Polyarchy: Participation and Opposition*. New Haven: Yale University Press.
De Swaan, Abram. 1973. *Coalition Theories and Cabinet Formations: A Study of Formal Theories of Coalition Formation Applied to Nine European Parliaments after 1918*. Amsterdam: Elsevier.
Finer, S.E. 1975. *Adversary Politics and Electoral Reform*. London: Anthony Wigram.
Franklin, Mark, Richard Niemi, and Guy Whitten (1994). "The two faces of tactical voting," *British Journal of Political Science* 24 no. 4: 549–557.
Gallagher, Michael. 1991. "Proportionality, disproportionality and electoral systems," *Electoral Studies* 10 no. 1: 33–51.
Gurr, Ted Robert. 1993. *Minorities at Risk: A Global View of Ethnopolitical Conflicts*. Washington, DC: United States Institute of Peace Press.
Hamilton, Alexander, James Madison, and John Jay. 1788. *Federalist Papers*. New York: McLean.
Inkeles, Alex, ed. 1991. *On Measuring Democracy: Its Consequences and Concomitants*. New Brunswick, N.J.: Transaction Publishers.

160   Arend Lijphart

Jackman, Robert W. 1987. "Political institutions and voter turnout in the industrial democracies," *American Political Science Review* 81 no. 2: 405–423.

Lewis, W. Arthur. 1965. *Politics in West Africa*. London: George Allen and Unwin.

Lijphart, Arend. 1977. *Democracy in Plural Societies: A Comparative Exploration*. New Haven: Yale University Press.

Lijphart, Arend. 1984. *Democracies: Patterns of Majoritarian and Consensus Government in Twenty-One Democracies*. New Haven: Yale University Press.

Lijphart, Arend. 1994. *Electoral Systems and Party Systems: A Study of Twenty-Seven Democracies, 1945–1990*. Oxford: Oxford University Press.

Mackie, Thomas T., and Richard Rose. 1991. *The International Almanac of Electoral History*, 3rd edn. London: Macmillan.

Mill, John Stuart. 1861. *Considerations on Representative Government*. London: Parker and Bourn.

Paloheimo, Heikki. 1984. *Governments in Democratic Capitalist States, 1950–1983: A Data Handbook*. Turku: University of Turku, Department of Sociology and Political Science.

Powell, G. Bingham, Jr. 1986. "American voter turnout in comparative perspective," *American Political Science Review* 80 no. 1: 17–43.

Riker, William H. 1962. *The Theory of Political Coalitions*. New Haven: Yale University Press.

Rustow, Dankwart. 1955. *The Politics of Compromise: A Study of Parties and Cabinet Government in Sweden*. Princeton: Princeton University Press.

Sartori, Giovanni. 1986. "The influence of electoral systems: faulty laws or faulty method?," in Bernard Grofman and Arend Lijphart, eds., *Electoral Laws and their Political Consequences*. New York: Agathon Press.

Spafford, Duff. 1985. "Mill's majority principle," *Canadian Journal of Political Science* 18 no. 3: 599–608.

Strom, Kaare. 1990. *Minority Government and Majority Rule*. Cambridge: Cambridge University Press.

Taagepera, Rein, and Matthew Soberg Shugart. 1989. *Seats and Votes: The Effects and Determinants of Electoral Systems*. New Haven: Yale University Press.

Woldendorp, Jaap, Hans Keman, and Ian Budge. 1993. "Political data 1945–1990: party government in 20 democracies," *European Journal of Political Research* 24 no. 1: 1–119.

Part 4

Democracy and development

9 Democracy and development

Adam Przeworski and Fernando Limongi

Introduction

Does democracy in the political realm foster, hinder, or does it have no effect on economic growth? We answer this question on the basis of a statistical analysis of 139 countries between 1950 or the year of independence or the first year when the economic data are available, and 1990 or the last year for which the data are available.

The chapter is short on theory and long on methods: the methodological issues entailed are complex, involving economics, econometrics, and a fair dose of metaphysics. The first section is a brief review of arguments about the effect of political regimes on economic growth. The second section is devoted to the central methodological issue. The results are presented in the third section, followed by Conclusions. Mainly technical, but also some substantive, issues are relegated to appendices.

Democracy, dictatorship, and economic growth

We summarize theoretical arguments only briefly, since we recently reviewed them in some detail (Przeworski and Limongi 1993; see also Bhalla [in this volume]). In a nutshell, arguments in favor of dictatorship add up to the claim that they are more effective at mobilizing resources for investment; arguments in favor of democracy maintain that they allocate better such resources.

The principal argument that there exists a trade-off between democracy and development was developed in the late 1950s and early 1960s, perhaps first by Galenson (1959) and de Schweinitz (1959), and it was made influential by Huntington (1968). This argument runs as follows. People whose livelihood hovers around subsistence cannot afford to make intertemporal trade-offs. They need to consume now. Democracy makes this pressure toward immediate consumption effective. When workers can organize, they are able to demand higher wages, which

164 *Adam Przeworski and Fernando Limongi*

reduces profits and, thus, investment. When citizens can vote for competing parties, they are able to demand social services, which again diverts resources from investment. Since at the time physical investment was seen as the – almost exclusive – engine of growth, the conclusion was that democracies, at least in poor countries, stagnate or decay economically. More recent versions of this argument, entailed in analyses of the East Asian miracles, add a model of interest group politics, claiming that governments must be insulated from particularistic pressures for unproductive uses of resources and that they must be capable of forcing firms to invest and export (Haggard 1990). Dictatorship can repress the demands for immediate consumption, either by ordering the state firms to invest or forcing private firms to do so, as President Park did in South Korea (Westphal 1990).

Arguments in favor of democracy add up to the assertion that democracies allocate better whatever resources they mobilize. These arguments come in three varieties.

The obvious question left open by the claims in favor of dictatorships is why would dictators invest rather than steal or squander the resources they extract: why Park and not Mobutu (Evans 1989)?[1] Recently there has been a rush of analyses in the light of which different forms of dictatorship are injurious for economic growth because they either undersupply or oversupply government productive services.[2] Under "Autocracy," a regime in which rulers appropriate privately a part of the fiscal residuum, growth suffers because the state is too small. Under "Bureaucracy," a regime in which rulers benefit from providing government services, growth suffers because the state is too large. The general conclusion of these analyses is that unless there exist effective mechanisms to make government accountable to citizens, rulers will extract a large share of resources but they will either consume them privately or squander them publicly. Grossman and Noh (1990) have shown that self-interested rulers have incentives to allocate resources efficiently if this will cause them to stay in power and if, in turn, their expected tenure in office is highly sensitive to misallocation of resources. Hence, efficient allocation is not just a matter of government objectives but also of mechanisms of accountability, and in a widespread view (Dahl 1971), democracy offers such mechanisms, forcing rulers to extract just the amount of resources that are optimal for growth and to use them productively. Yet this model of democracy is flimsy at best: democracy enforces accountability only under very demanding institutional and political conditions (Ferejohn 1986; Powell 1990; Stokes 1994).

Secondly, it has become recently fashionable to claim that democracy

Democracy and development

protects property rights. The effect of secure property rights, in turn, is to reduce uncertainty and to encourage investment. This argument is based on an implicit, and false, assumption that the only threat to property originates from the state, rather than from those who do not have it. Indeed, the belief that the dispossessed would use their political rights to confiscate property led political thinkers on the right and the left, from Macaulay to Marx, during the first part of the nineteenth century to expect that private property and democracy would be incompatible: a conclusion one gets from the median voter model, at least if there are no deadweight losses. True, Przeworski and Wallerstein (1988) have shown that, concerned about investment and thus future consumption and employment, powerful unions would moderate their wage claims. But political rights can be and have been used for redistributing incomes: they are a threat to property. Moreover, it is striking that, to our best knowledge, no one has elaborated this argument and no one has mustered systematic evidence to support it.[3] It remains purely ideological.

A more subtle argument in the same vein is that democracy (Olson 1991), or more precisely constitutionalism (Elster 1994), permits rulers to precommit themselves not to pursue their self-interest, thus generating confidence that stimulates a productive use of endowments. Yet, to continue our debate with Elster,[4] short of pure time inconsistencies of the Kydland–Prescott variety, there is nothing to guarantee that the precommitment will bind to optical policies. Constitutionalism may generate confidence that some policies will not be changed but there are good constitutions and bad constitutions. And, conversely, if Grossman and Noh (1990) are correct, Olson's claim that autocrats cannot credibly precommit themselves is false: if the incumbent autocrats are sure to stay indefinitely in office by pursuing optimal policies and if they are likely to be deposed if they do not pursue such policies, then they will commit themselves to optimal policies and this commitment will be credible, with or without time inconsistency.

Finally, various claims have been made to the effect that democracy generates and uses more information useful for allocating resources. Prima facie this claim is obviously true: a free press, electoral competition, and freedom of association serve groups and individuals to reveal their preferences and information about their productive endowments. A more complex question is whether decision making by an assembly yields a better allocation of resources than decisions by dictators or bureaucracies. Recent literature concerning the Condorcet (1785) Jury Theorem favors majority rule but only when there are no conflicts of interests and information is costless. In turn, Sah and Stiglitz (1988)

166 *Adam Przeworski and Fernando Limongi*

come to the conclusion that while majority rule does have a privileged status in project evaluation, the optimal decision rule depends on a number of factors, including the quality of the portfolio from which projects can be chosen and the costs of information.

Hence, democracy is said to be better at allocating resources because (1) it imposes accountability on governments, which are therefore prevented from stealing or squandering resources, (2) it creates a stable economic climate, including the protection of property rights, and (3) it generates and uses more information in allocating resources.[5]

To close this discussion, note that the arguments that dictatorships mobilize more resources and that democracies allocate them better may both be true. And if they are, then regimes may have no net effect on growth: the rate of investment may be higher under dictatorships, allocative efficiency higher under democracy, and growth rates about the same. Hence, we must examine the effect of regimes on investment before assessing their effect on growth.

Thus far we reviewed arguments concerning the effects of regimes on the average rates of economic growth. But one can argue that regimes affect the variance of these rates, specifically, that democracies are less likely to generate both miracles and disasters than dictatorships.[6]

One argument to this effect is that democracies are less likely to engage in big projects. Suppose that the total resources add up to 100 and that nature offers a choice among three projects, A, B, and C, each of which may bring double or nothing with the same probability. The dictator prefers A over other projects and spends 100 on it. Under democracy, a majority coalition must be formed. Say the majority consists of supporters of A and B, and they are adopted, each at the cost of 50. The expected value is the same under two regimes. But the variance is lower under democracy. A series of successful 100 bets makes a miracle: South Korea pulled it off with steel and with shipbuilding. But losing a 100 is a disaster, like the South Korean petrochemicals, and innumerable Soviet projects, for example, massive irrigation that succeeded in lowering the yield of Ukrainian soils.[7]

Drèze's and Sen's (1989) "early warning function" supports, in turn, the notion that democracies are less likely to pursue risky projects. Since the observation that democracies never experience famines and their analysis of the reasons for it are well known, we will couch this argument in somewhat more general terms. Suppose that big projects, good or bad, take time to bear fruit and are costly in the meantime. The "alarm function" permits democracies to abort or correct projects that impose excessive intertemporal costs, up to threatening survival. Hence, the

Democracy and development

effect of democracy is again to reduce the variance of economic performance.

We introduced these considerations about variance to warn against identification of growth with warfare. An assured minimum may be valued by people more than a high average. Hence, if the variance of growth is indeed lower under democracies, they may be superior on welfare grounds even if they grow slower. Moreover, to open a complicated topic, different indicators may give different pictures of welfare: just one example is that under-five infant mortality declined between 1960 and 1985 in all countries that experienced negative growth rates (Sen 1993).[8]

Selection, comparisons, and counterfactuals

Classifying regimes each year as democracies and dictatorships[9] and calculating average rates of growth of per capita income shows that democracies grew at the average rate of 2.44, while dictatorships had an average rate of 1.88, a statistically and economically significant difference.[10] Running regressions with regimes as a dummy variable brings the same conclusion: democracies grow faster. More than twenty studies examined the impact of regimes in one of these two ways. And since we just gave our answer, you may now wonder what the rest of this chapter could conceivably be about.[11]

Yet such results are biased: they reflect the fact that these regimes existed under different conditions. Regimes are likely to be endogenous with regard to their performance. And if they are, then the observed world of institutions is not a random sample of the underlying population (Pudney 1989: chapter 2). In turn, if observations are selected by a non-random mechanism then inferences based on them are biased and inconsistent, even if we are dealing with the entire observable population, as we are.[12]

The problem we face is the following. We want to examine the effect of political regimes, dichotomized as democracy and dictatorship, on economic growth. We observe Chile in 1980 and discover that it was a dictatorship which grew at 5.7 percent. Would it have grown less or more had the regime been a democracy? The information we have, the observation of Chile in 1980, does not answer this question. But unless we know what would have been the growth of Chile in 1980 had it been democratic, how can we tell if it would have grown faster or slower than under authoritarianism?

Had we observed in 1980 a Chile that was simultaneously authori-

168   *Adam Przeworski and Fernando Limongi*

tarian and democratic, we would have had the answer. But this is not possible. The standard way out is to proceed quasi-experimentally: we look for some country that was exactly like Chile in all respects other than its regime and, perhaps, its rate of growth, and we match this country with Chile. But if regimes are endogenous with regard to economic growth or if regimes and growth are jointly determined by some unobservable factors, then an observation that matches Chile in all respects other than the regime and the rate of growth will be hard to find: there will be observations without a match.[13] And then the selection of cases will bias our conclusions.

Consider the following possibility: suppose that democracies are in general more vulnerable to economic crises than dictatorships, that is, democracies are more likely to "die," becoming dictatorships, when they face adverse economic conditions. Then we will observe dictatorships under a broad range of conditions, good and bad, and democracies only under good conditions. The observed mean of growth for democracies will be higher than the mean for dictatorships even if in fact regimes have no impact on growth, that is, even if they would have had the same mean had they existed under ceteris paribus conditions. The observed variance of growth rates, in turn, will be smaller for democracies. These differences result from selection bias. We can see it by performing a computer experiment: assume that both regimes have the same average rate of growth, $G = 2.11$, plus or minus a random shock. Use the observed probabilities that a regime survives a particular year, conditional on its rate of growth. Run thousands of histories of the 139 countries, with their initial regimes taken as observed. Compute the average rates of growth for the two regimes. The result will be exactly, down to a decimal, what we observe in the real world: democracies will appear to have grown faster!

The evidence for endogenous selection is presented in Table 9.1. Democracies, in particular poor ones, are in fact more vulnerable to bad economic conditions.[14] They are less likely to survive any particular year in which per capita income declines than dictatorships and they are less likely to survive in poor countries. Democracies which experience economic growth $(G > 0)$ at any level have an expected life of sixty-eight years; those that face economic decline $(G < 0)$ have an expected life of eighteen years.[15] The respective numbers for dictatorships are fifty-three years when they grow and forty-one when they decline. Bad economic performance in poor countries makes democracy particularly vulnerable: in a declining economy with per capita income of less than $1,000, democracy can be expected to last on the average less than four years.

Democracy and development 169

Table 9.1. *Regime transitions as a function of the level of development and the rate of growth: annual data*

	All transitions	To democracy	To dictatorship
LEVEL < 1,000	1.65 (17/1,028)	0.53 (5/937)	13.19 (12/91)
G < 0	2.73 (12/439)	0.98 (4/408)	25.81 (8/31)
G > 0	0.85 (5/589)	0.18 (1/529)	6.67 (4/60)
1,000 < LEVEL < 2,000	3.72 (35/940)	3.10 (22/709)	5.63 (13/231)
G < 0	4.73 (14/296)	4.29 (9/210)	5.81 (5/86)
G > 0	3.26 (21/644)	2.61 (13/499)	5.52 (8/145)
2,000 < LEVEL < 3,000	2.44 (12/492)	1.99 (6/302)	3.16 (6/190)
G < 0	3.62 (5/138)	1.20 (1/83)	7.27 (4/55)
G > 0	1.98 (7/354)	2.28 (5/219)	1.48 (2/135)
3,000 < LEVEL < 4,000	3.77 (13/345)	2.67 (5/187)	5.06 (8/158)
G < 0	6.12 (6/98)	4.00 (2/50)	8.33 (4/48)
G > 0	2.83 (7/247)	2.19 (3/137)	3/64 (4/110)
4,000 < LEVEL < 5,000	3.56 (8/225)	5.22 (7/134)	1.10 (1/91)
G < 0	5.88 (3/51)	6.25 (2/32)	5.26 (1/19)
G > 0	2.87 (5/174)	4.90 (5/102)	0.00 (0/36)
5,000 < LEVEL	0.49 (5/1,011)	3.45 (5/145)	0.00 (0/866)
G < 0	1.01 (2/198)	4.65 (2/43)	0.00 (0/155)
G < 0	0.37 (3/813)	2.94 (3/102)	0.00 (0/711)
ALL	2.23 (90/4,041)	2.07 (50/2,414)	2.46 (40/1,627)
G < 0	3.44 (42/1,220)	2.42 (20/826)	5.58 (22/394)
G > 0	1.70 (48/2,821)	1.88 (30/1,588)	1.46 (18/1,233)

Note: transition probabilities are given first, numbers of transitions and of total observations are in parentheses.

These descriptive findings are confirmed by an analysis of rates of transitions between the two regimes. Table 9.2 shows partial derivatives of survival probabilities of both regimes with regard to rates of growth, evaluated at different values of the latter.[16] Both regimes are more likely t.· survive when they grow: all signs are positive. Yet democracies are more vulnerable to bad economic performance: all the coefficients are significant for democracies but not for dictatorships. At the mean, 2.11 per year, an acceleration of growth by 1 percent increases the chance of survival of a democracy by 2.35 percent and of a dictatorship by 0.39 percent.

To correct for non-random selection, we must use the observations we have to generate the counterfactuals we miss. To make such inferences, we model the process by which observations enter the particular states. Then we revert to an artifice: a distribution from which the observed and the unobserved cases were generated. Having identified

170 Adam Przeworski and Fernando Limongi

Table 9.2. *Marginal changes of the probability of survival of each regime due to economic growth (t-ratios in parentheses)*

	Changes of marginal probabilities of survival, with regard to growth rate	
Evaluated at the rate of growth equal to	Dictatorships dP_{AA}/dG	Democracies dP_{DD}/dG
Mean $- 2*SD = -9.93$	0.1286E-06	0.7783E-06
	(0.802)	(1.634)
Mean $- 1*SD = -3.91$	0.1957E-03	0.1185E-02
	(1.070)	(3.707)
Mean $\quad = 2.11$	0.3875E-02	0.2346E-01
	(1.175)	(4.454)
Mean $+ 1*SD = 8.13$	0.9972E-03	0.6037E-02
	(1.084)	(4.326)
Mean $+ 2*SD = 14.15$	0.3337E-05	0.2020E-04
	(0.822)	(1.809)

Note: these estimates derived from a dynamic probit of regimes (Amemiya 1985). P_{AA} is the probability that a dictatorship (A stands for "authoritarian") survives a given year, P_{DD} that a democracy does.

the rule by which the sample was selected, we can do the rest: we can use the actual observations as a basis for inferences about their counterfactual pairs, compare the rates of growth, and arrive at a conclusion about the impact of regimes on growth. The reasoning is the following: given the observations and the selection rule, one can infer the rest of the distribution. This procedure generates the counterfactual values and allows us to compare, that is, to tell what the rates of growth would have been had a particular country faced the same exogenous conditions under dictatorship and under democracy.[17] This is what the comparative method is all about.

Yet we must be careful not to conjure counterfactuals that are not possible: if some conditions under which political institutions are observed are a systematic effect of these institutions themselves, then constructing ceteris paribus conditions is futile. Hence, we must correct for the selection bias but only whenever it is correctable.

This, then, is our procedure. Applying it, we obtain average values of growth which the two regimes would have experienced had they been exposed to the same exogenous, and only exogenous, conditions. Since these ceteris paribus conditions are those actually observed for each country during the period under consideration, the study is historical in

Democracy and development

Table 9.3. *Investment shares (I/Y), by level of per capita GDP*

Level	Proportion of dictatorships	Investment share (I/Y)		
		All	Dictatorships	Democracies
<1,000	0.917391	3.4358	3.3054	4.8834
1,000–2,000	0.740102	14.6730	14.4546	15.2951
2,000–3,000	0.609901	19.4183	19.2641	19.6595
3,000–4,000	0.542373	21.0806	21.5690	20.5018
4,000–5,000	0.560870	24.4002	24.6903	24.0296
5,000–6,000	0.421875	26.8322	28.4128	25.6787
6,000–7,000	0.125000	25.9480	26.0239	25.9371
7,000–8,000	0.106383	26.9886	31.6420	26.4346
8,000–9,000	0.096774	29.9774	33.7667	29.5714
>9,000	0.050218	27.4873	23.8330	27.6805

the sense that perhaps under other, still ceteris paribus, conditions the results would have been different.

Results

We are not sure how to interpret what we found. Since the story is complex, here is a preview: if we treat population growth as exogenous with regard to regimes, and thus take it as a legitimate counterfactual that these rates are the same, then we will conclude that dictatorships grew faster. But population growth is endogenous: higher under dictatorships. And if we treat it as endogenous, then we arrive at the conclusion that regimes do not differ in their impact on the growth of per capita incomes and that democracy fosters the growth of per capita consumption.

To clear the underbrush, let us begin with investment. The observed average of the share of investment in GDP, I/Y, is 14.97 percent for dictatorships and 22.99 percent for democracies. But the effect of selection is obvious: poor countries invest less and they are predominantly dictatorships. Hence, it is the mixture of regimes at different levels of development that accounts for the observed difference in investment behavior, not the regimes themselves.

Once selection is corrected for, the difference disappears. If the two regimes faced the same aggregate demand (LEVLAG), if they were exposed to the same world demand (WORLD), and to the same relative prices of investment goods (RELPINV), and to the same interest rates

172   *Adam Przeworski and Fernando Limongi*

(PRIME), they would have had almost identical investment shares: 18.2 percent.[18]

Hence, we find no support for the hypothesis that dictatorships are more effective in mobilizing resources for investment. Indeed, among the poorer countries, all the way to per capita income of $3,000 (always 1985 PPP USD), democracies have slightly higher investment shares.

For reasons that will become apparent, we must be also concerned with population growth. It turns out that population growth is faster under dictatorships. The observed means are 2.09 for all countries, 1.48 for democracies, and 2.51 for dictatorships. In the entire sample, population growth declines with levels of development, as it does among democracies. But wealthy dictatorships exhibit an extraordinary high population growth.

Correcting for selection does not reduce this difference. If the two regimes had the same per capita incomes (LEVEL), the same concentration of dominant religious (RELIGION) and ethnic groups (ETHNIC), if they were or were not former colonies (NEWC) and specifically British colonies (BRITCOL), dictatorships would still have much higher population growth. The same is true (we checked but do not report it in Table 9.6) if they were oil producers or if they were all located in the Middle East.[19] The same is also true if we put in lagged population growth.[20]

This finding has major consequences for our central question, namely, the effect of regimes on the growth of per capita incomes. To clarify what is involved, we need to go over the standard derivation of econometric growth equations.

The most general model of production is

$$Y = AF(K, L), \tag{1}$$

where Y stands for total output, and the standard way to derive the growth equation is to differentiate both sides with regard to time, and divide by Y, yielding (* are time derivatives)

$$Y^*/Y = A^*/A + F_K(I/Y) + F_L(L^*/Y). \tag{2}$$

Assuming that the rate of technical progress is constant and the same across countries, $A^*/A = \alpha$, and multiplying the last term by (L/L) yields

$$Y^*/Y = \alpha + F_K(I/Y) + \beta(L^*/L), \tag{3}$$

where β is the marginal elasticity of output with regard to labor.[21]

Democracy and development

Table 9.4. *ML estimates of investment, with selection*

Dictatorships $N = 2,344$ adjusted R-squared = 0.90

Variable	Coefficient	Std. error	t-ratio	Prob$|t| \geqslant x$
Constant	1.9829	0.3776	5.251	0.00000
INVLAG	0.90327	0.7091E-02	127.379	0.00000
LEVLAG	0.93977E-04	0.3859E-04	2.435	0.01489
WORLD	0.11860E-01	0.4842E-01	0.245	0.80649
RELPINV	−0.37730	0.6881E-01	−5.483	0.00000
PRIME	0.36358E-02	0.2045E-01	0.178	0.85890
Sigma (1)	2.9825	0.2205E-01	135.264	0.00000
Rho (1, 2)	0.76533E-02	0.6691E-01	0.114	0.90894

Democracies $N = 1,547$ adjusted R-squared = 0.92

Variable	Coefficient	Std. error	t-ratio	Prob$|t| \geqslant x$
Constant	1.9939	0.4031	4.947	0.00000
INVLAG	0.91261	0.8824E-02	103.426	0.00000
LEVLAG	0.40549E-04	0.2636E-04	1.538	0.12404
WORLD	0.28849	0.4347E-01	6.636	0.00000
RELPINV	−0.72052	0.1646	−4.378	0.00001
PRIME	−0.24340E-01	0.1786E-01	−1.363	0.17288
Sigma (0)	2.3607	0.2951E-01	79.995	0.00000
Rho (0, 2)	−0.92045E-01	0.8001E-01	−1.150	0.24999

Selection-corrected values of investment

Under	Mean	Std. dev.	Minimum	Maximum	Cases
Dictatorship	18.185	9.3575	−2.853	50.75	4,041
Democracy	18.229	9.5740	−7.389	51.40	4,041

Note: this table is based on a joint ML estimation of selection and investment equations. Only the investment results are presented here. R-squared is derived from OLS estimations.

Variables:

INVESTMENT	the share of investment in GDP.
INVLAG	lagged value of investment.
LEVLAG	lagged value of per capita GDP/1,000.
WORLD	the average rate of growth of the world during given year.
RELPINV	the ratio of the price of investment goods to general price level.
PRIME	the US prime rate during the given year.

174 *Adam Przeworski and Fernando Limongi*

Table 9.5. *Population growth, by level of per capita GDP*

Level	Proportion of dictatorships	Rate of population growth		
		All	Dictatorships	Democracies
<1,000	0.918970	2.64263	2.65208	2.53553
1,000–2,000	0.743966	2.63778	2.64590	2.61418
2,000–3,000	0.611336	2.27852	2.47314	1.97241
3,000–4,000	0.547550	1.80575	1.97100	1.60577
4,000–5,000	0.568889	1.57659	1.93281	1.10653
5,000–6,000	0.428571	1.09722	1.30309	0.94282
6,000–7,000	0.128571	1.52844	2.58774	1.37215
7,000–8,000	0.107914	1.58095	2.76804	1.43735
8,000–9,000	0.087912	1.25033	2.27496	1.15157
>9,000	0.039735	0.87374	4.71036	0.71499

Note that Y^*/Y is the rate of growth of total output, GDP. Our dependent variable, however, is the rate of growth of per capita income, or Y/P. This rate is

$$\frac{1}{Y/P} \frac{d(Y/P)}{dt} = (Y^*/Y) - (P^*/P). \qquad (4)$$

Substituting (4) and writing the LHS as G yields

$$G = \alpha + F_K(I/Y) + \beta(L^*/L) - (P^*/P), \qquad (5)$$

where P stands for population. Replacing L by P gives in turn[22]

$$g = \alpha + F_K(I/Y) + (\beta - 1)(P^*/P). \qquad (6)$$

Note that since $0 < \beta < 1$, the coefficient on population growth should be negative.

If population growth is taken as exogenous, regardless of the estimation method, dictatorships have a statistically and economically higher selection-corrected average rate of growth. This result should be interpreted as follows: if each country during each year faced under different regimes the same international demand (OECD), if it had the same level of per capita income (LEVEL), if it had the same investment share (INV), *and the same population growth rates* (POPG), then it would have grown faster under dictatorships. Yet if the two regimes experienced the same exogenous conditions specified above, then their population would not have grown at the same rate. Hence, at least within

Democracy and development 175

Table 9.6. *ML estimates of population growth, with selection*

Dictatorships adjusted R-squared = 0.48

Variable	Coefficient	Std. error	t-ratio	Prob$\lvert t \rvert \geqslant x$
Constant	1.7719	0.1438	12.320	0.00000
RELIGION	0.13502E-01	0.1377E-02	9.808	0.00000
ETHNIC	−0.73666E-02	0.1349E-02	−5.462	0.00000
NEWC	0.28867	0.6882E-01	4.194	0.00003
BRITCOL	0.46077	0.7103E-01	6.487	0.00000
LEVEL	0.29172E-04	0.1337E-04	2.181	0.02917

Democracies adjusted R-squared = 0.57

Variable	Coefficient	Std. error	t-ratio	Prob$\lvert t \rvert \geqslant x$
Constant	2.3549	0.1832	12.855	0.00000
RELIGION	0.11278E-03	0.1223E-02	0.092	0.92652
ETHNIC	−0.77464E-02	0.1377E-02	−5.626	0.00000
NEWC	−0.68977	0.6277E-01	−10.988	0.00000
BRITCOL	0.39522	0.5830E-01	6.779	0.00000
LEVEL	−0.91141E-04	0.8754E-05	−10.411	0.00000

Selection-corrected values of population growth

Under	Mean	Std. dev.	Minimum	Maximum	Cases
Dictatorship	2.6032	0.34878	1.559	3.908	4,016
Democracy	1.3523	0.42788	−0.444	2.401	4,016

Note: this table is based on a joint ML estimation of selection and population growth equations. Only the population results are presented here. R-squared is derived from OLS estimations.

Variables:

RELIGION	the share of the largest religious group in the population.
ETHNIC	the share of the largest ethnic group in the population.
NEWC	a dummy variable for countries that became independent after 1950.
BRITCOL	a dummy variable for former British colonies.
LEVEL	per capita GDP.

our historical time span, ceteris paribus population growth is not a valid counterfactual.

The results based on matching all exogenous conditions *other than the rates of population growth* show little difference between regimes.

176   *Adam Przeworski and Fernando Limongi*

Table 9.7. *Growth by regime: summary of results*

Regime	Observed			Selection-corrected G with POPG as			
				exogenous	endogenous		
	Y^*/Y	P^*/P	G	(b)	(a)	(b)	β
All	4.21	2.09	2.12	—	—	—	—
Dictatorships	4.41	2.51	1.89	2.81	2.37	2.52	0.29
Democracies	3.92	1.48	2.44	2.06	2.03	2.33	0.59

Note: selection-corrected values of G are based on two-way random effects panel estimation. (a) Not controlling for data quality. (b) Controlling for data quality. β is the labor share.

These results differ slightly depending on the estimator, but only one estimator yields a difference that is economically consequential (see Appendix II). Moreover, when we control for data quality, these differences are even smaller (see Appendix III).[23]

The reader will now appreciate that our reference to metaphysics was not facetious. The conclusion hinges on a counterfactual: whether we think that a world in which dictatorships have the same population growth as democracies is a possible one. Since we do not know how to resolve this issue, we leave it at that.

But let us interpret the results as they stand. We find that labor productivity is significantly higher under democracy,[24] while population, and presumably labor force, grows faster under dictatorship. This is why the observed average rate of growth of total income is higher under dictatorship (4.41 vs. 3.92 percent) while the observed average rate of growth of per capita income is lower under dictatorship (1.89 vs. 2.44 percent). Dictatorships grow by using more of cheap labor, democracies by using less of better paid labor.[25] Perhaps, therefore, dictatorships are not concerned about population growth because they can repress labor demands.[26] Had all the exogenous conditions, including the rate of population growth, been the same under the two regimes, per capita income would have grown faster under dictatorships. But since dictatorships achieve growth by using more of less productive labor, matching the two regimes for conditions other than the population growth leads to the conclusion that their per capita incomes would have grown at almost the same rate.

Moreover, it appears that dictatorships also use capital stock less efficiently.[27] And this difference has consequences for the rate of growth

Democracy and development 177

Table 9.8. *Two-way random effects estimates of growth, with selection*

Dictatorships $N = 2,404$ adjusted R-squared = 0.11

Variable	Coefficient	Std. error	t-ratio	Prob $|t| \geqslant x$
Constant	1.1305	0.6474	1.746	0.08075
LEVEL	−0.1147	0.1028	−1.117	0.26418
OECD	0.2728	0.1126	2.422	0.01543
INV	0.1274	0.0213	5.976	0.00000
POPG	−0.7113	0.1261	−5.639	0.00000
PPPQUAL	0.1221	0.1125	1.086	0.27756
LAMBDA	−2.5697	0.6888	−3.731	0.00019

Democracies $N = 1,637$ adjusted R-squared = 0.16

Variable	Coefficient	Std. error	t-ratio	Prob $|t| \geqslant x$
Constant	−0.48356	0.7544	−0.641	0.52155
LEVEL	−0.02256	0.0521	−0.433	0.66536
OECD	0.52483	0.0815	6.434	0.00000
INV	0.17326	0.0224	7.735	0.00000
POPG	−0.41228	0.1606	−2.567	0.01027
PPPQUAL	−0.27191	0.1060	−2.566	0.01028
LAMBDA	0.20736	0.2829	0.733	0.46349

Note: this table is based on estimating a dynamic probit model to obtain LAMBDA and on a two-way random effects panel estimation of growth equations.

Variables:
OECD   average growth of the OECD countries during particular year.
LEVEL   per capita GDP/1,000.
INV   share of investment in GDP (I/Y).
POPG   rate of population growth (P^*/P).
PPPQUAL   data quality.

of per capita consumption. Dictatorships still have a higher rate of growth of per capita consumption when population growth is considered to be exogenous, but this difference is smaller than with regard to the growth of per capita income. In turn, when population growth is taken to be endogenous, democracies show to have a higher rate of consumption growth (see Appendix II). Hence, while regimes do not affect the investment share, dictatorships are inferior in terms of allocative efficiency, and, as a result, per capita consumption grows faster under democracy. And, ultimately, it is consumption that matters.

Conclusions

Since the conclusions hinge on something about which we are far from certain, one is tempted to heed Flaubert's warning that "La bêtise, c'est de conclure." But let us go out on a limb.

When we report our findings, we often hear that they are "negative": no difference. But if there is indeed no difference, we would see these results as most positive. What they would imply is that there is no trade-off between development and democracy: democracy need not generate slower growth. In turn, we know that democracy is more likely to survive when the economy grows (Przeworski and Limongi 1994). Together, these findings imply, therefore, that economic growth increases the chances that democracy would survive, while democracy does not impede economic growth.

Viewed in this perspective, the vision of the relationship between development and democracy that dominated the intellectual mood and served to orient US foreign policy during the Cold War years appears strangely convoluted. While Lipset (1960) treated development as exogenous, his contemporaries were persuaded that dictatorship is the inevitable price of development.[28] Galenson (1959: 3) claimed that "The more democratic a government is, . . . the greater the diversion of resources from investment to consumption." La Palombara (1963: 57) thought that "if economic development is the all-embracing goal, the logic of experience dictates that not too much attention can be paid to the trappings of democracy." De Schweinitz (1959) argued that if the less developed countries "are to grow economically, they must limit democratic participation in political affairs." And this was also the belief of Huntington and Dominguez (1975: 60):

The interest of the voters generally lead parties to give the expansion of personal consumption a higher priority vis-à-vis investment than it would receive in a non-democratic system. In the Soviet Union, for instance, the percentage of GDP devoted to consumption was driven down from 65% in 1928 to 52% in 1937. It is most unlikely that a competitive party system would have sustained a revolution from above like this.

Dictatorships are needed to generate development: as Huntington and Nelson (1976: 23) put it, "political participation must be held down, at least temporarily, in order to promote economic development."

Since in this view of the world dictatorships generate development while development leads to democracy, the best way to democracy was said to be a circuitous one. Yet common sense would suggest that in order to strengthen democracy we should strengthen democracy, not

Democracy and development

support dictatorships. Poor countries can develop under democracy and democracy can flourish in poor countries if they develop.

Appendix I Classifying political regimes[29]

Democracy is a regime in which some governmental offices are filled as a consequence of contested elections. This definition has two parts: "offices" and "contestation."

In no regime all governmental offices are filled as a consequence of elections. What is essential to consider a regime as democratic is that two kinds of offices are filled, directly or indirectly, by elections: the chief executive office and the seats in the effective legislative body.

Contestation occurs when there exists an opposition that has some chance of winning office as a consequence of elections. Whenever in doubt, we classify as democracies only those systems in which incumbent parties actually did lose them.

Operationally, a regime was classified as a democracy if it did not fail under any of the four rules listed below. Thus, a regime is classified as a dictatorship if at least one of these conditions holds:

> **Rule 1** "executive selection." The chief executive is not elected.
>
> **Rule 2** "legislative selection." The legislature is not elected.
>
> **Rule 3** "party." There is no more than one party. Specifically, this rule applies if (1) there were no parties or (2) there was only one party, or (3) the current tenure in office ended up in the establishment of a non-party or one-party rule, or (4) the incumbents unconstitutionally closed the legislature and rewrote the rules in their favor.
>
> **Rule 4** "type II error." A regime passes the previous three rules, the incumbents held office in the immediate past by virtue of elections for more than two terms or without being elected, and until today or the time when they were overthrown they have not lost an election.[30]

Alternation in office overrides the party rule: Jamaica, where a single party held at one time 100 percent of the seats in the legislature yet subsequently yielded office having lost an election, was classified as democratic during the entire period.

Our timing rules are the following. We code the regime that prevailed at the end of the year, even if it came to power on December 31, as for example dictatorship arrived in Nigeria in 1983. Transitions to authoritarianism are signalled by a coup d'état. Transitions to democracy are dated by the time of the inauguration of the newly elected government, not of the election. In the few cases, like those of the Dominican Republic in 1963, where a democratic regime lasted six months, or Bolivia in 1979, where the situation changed several times, the information about regimes that began and ended within the same year is lost.

180 *Adam Przeworski and Fernando Limongi*

Altogether, we observed 229 regimes, 101 democratic and 128 authoritarian. The lowest per capita income we observed in the entire sample is \$212 (Burma in 1950), the highest is \$19,627 (United Arab Emirates in 1985).

The resulting classification is closely related to several other scales of democracy: the Coppedge–Reinecke scale for 1978 predicts 92 percent of our regimes, the Bollen 1965 scale predicts 85 percent, while the Gurr scales of Autocracy and Democracy for 1950–1986 jointly predict 91 percent.

Appendix II **Alternative estimators of selection models**

This Appendix concerns some estimators of binomial selection models.

We want to compare the effect of being in states C_j, $j = 0, 1$, which are respectively democracy and dictatorship, on a "performance" variable $G \mid X$, which is the rate of growth of per capita income. Individual observations consist of the state C_{it}, the performance G_{it}, and the independent variables. We observe each individual $i = 1, \ldots, N$ only in one state at each time $t = 0, \ldots, T$. If an individual i is in state $C_{it} = 1$ at time t, then the performance of this individual in state $C_{it} = 0$ is not observed, and vice versa. Hence, the structure of observations does not allow direct comparisons of G_{it} for the same individuals in state $C_{it} = 1$ and $C_{it} = 0$.

It is useful to think of performance as two variables: G_1 is the performance in state $C = 1$, "dictatorial growth," and G_0 the performance in state $C = 0$, "democratic growth." These variables are then defined as follows:

$$G_0 = \begin{array}{ll} G_0, & \text{if } C = 0 \\ G_0^*, & \text{otherwise,} \end{array} \tag{II.1a}$$

and

$$G_1 = \begin{array}{ll} G_1, & \text{if } C = 1 \\ G_1^*, & \text{otherwise,} \end{array} \tag{II.1b}$$

where the starred quantities are not observed and, in general,

$$G_0 = X_0\beta_0 + u_0, \tag{II.2a}$$

$$G_1 = X_1\beta_1 + u_1. \tag{II.2b}$$

If the difference in performance between being in $C = 1$ and $C = 0$ is constant, then

$$G_0 = X\alpha + u_0, \tag{II.3a}$$

$$G_1 = G_0 + C\delta + u_1 = X\beta + C\delta + u_1. \tag{II.3b}$$

Democracy and development

When selection into the states $C = 0, 1$ is not random, then the covariance $(Cu_j) \neq 0$ and $E(G \mid X, C) \neq G$. As a result, estimates of coefficients are consistent and biased, and

$$E(G_1 - G_0) = E(X_1\beta_1 - X_0\beta_0) + E(u_1 - u_0),$$ (II.4)

where $E(u_1 - u_0) \neq 0$.

Assume that selection into the states C is ruled by

$$C^\star = F(V\tau) + u,$$ (II.5)

where $V = \{Z, X\}$ is a vector of observable exogenous variables and u is a vector of variables not observed by the investigator. The index variable $C^\star$ is related to the observed states C by the rule

$$C = \begin{array}{ll} 1, & \text{iff } C^\star > 0 \\ \\ 0, & \text{otherwise.} \end{array}$$ (II.6)

The covariance between C and u_j may be different from zero for two reasons: (1) because some of the observed variables $V = Z, X$ are correlated with u_j or (2) because the unobserved determinants of selection, u, are correlated with u_j. Following Heckman (1988), we will say that in the first case selection occurs on observables, in the second case on unobservables.

The estimators of the selection models differ depending on the assumptions about the covariance (Cu_j), on the specification of the selection equation (5), and the methods for estimating the performance equations (2) or (3).

Once we obtain unbiased estimates of β, to compare the performance of an individual in the two states, we need to calculate $(G_{1it} - G^\star_{1it})$ if the individual is observed in state $C = 0$ or $(G_{1it} - G^\star_{0it})$ if the individual is in state $C = 1$. To assess the average difference in performance between being in state $C = 1$ and state $C = 0$, we calculate

$$(1/N^*T)\left\{ \sum_{C=1} (G_{1it} - G^*_{0it}) + \sum_{C=1} G^*_{1it} - G_{0it}) \right\}$$

$$= (1/N^*T)\left[\sum_{C=1} G_{1it} + \sum_{C=1} G^*_{1it} \right] - (1/N^*T)\left[\sum_{C=1} G_{0it} + \sum_{C=1} G^*_{0it} \right]$$

$$= (1/N^*T)\, (\Sigma \hat{Y}_1 - \Sigma \hat{Y}_0) = \mu_1 - \mu_0.$$ (II.7)

When population growth is treated as endogenous, the average values of G corrected for selection are generated by calculating for each $\mathcal{J} = 0, 1$

$$GHAT(\mathcal{J}) = (1/N) \sum^{i=N} (XG\text{-}POPG)\,\beta + (1/N_j) \sum^{i=N_j} POPG(\mathcal{J})\,\beta_{POPG}.$$ (II.7a)

182   *Adam Przeworski and Fernando Limongi*

The first term of (7a) is the average rate of economic growth that would have occurred under given j had all the values of the independent variables been the same under $j = 0, 1$. The second term corrects for the fact that population growth is endogenous with regard to institutions and, hence, should not be taken to be the same. Here we take the rates of population growth specific to each j.

Selection occurs on variables that are not observed by the researchers when both $E(Cu_j) \leq 0$ and $E(Cu_j \mid Z, X) \neq 0$, that is, when controlling for the observed determinants of selection does not remove the covariance between the states and the errors in performance. Selection on unobservables may occur whenever (1) the selection process is based on some variables not observed by the researcher or (2) the determinants of selection are measured with error. The general method in this case is to get an instrument for the state C and introduce it into the performance equation. The Heckit estimators are based on probit and use hazard rates as instruments; the IV estimators use errors from OLS. Models 1 through 6 use different Heckit estimators; models 7 and 8 use instrumental variables.

Models 1–6 follow the same general steps:

(1) Estimate by probit the reduced form of (5), using C as the dependent variable:

$$C = F(V, \tau) + u = F(C) + u. \tag{II.8}$$

(2) From (8) calculate the hazard rate, LAMBDA.
(3) Estimate the performance equation(s), using LAMBDA as an instrument for C.
(4) Calculate the net effect of C, as given by (7).

The probit equation (8) can be modeled in static or dynamic terms. In turn, performance equations can be estimated by GLS, MLE, or panel methods.

Static probit is based on the assumption that the present state is independent of past states (Amemiya 1985: chapter 11):

$$E(C_t = 1 \mid C_{t-1}, C_{t-2}, \ldots) = E(C_t = 1), \tag{II.9}$$

A dynamic model assumes dependence of the current on past states. Our data obey a first-order stationary Markov process. Such processes are defined by (ignoring individual variations):

$$E(C_t = 1 \mid C_{t-1}, C_{t-2}, \ldots) = P(t)C_{t-1},$$

where $P(t)$ is the matrix of transition probabilities, with elements $p_{jk}(t)$. Assume that

$$p_{01}(t) = F(V_t \kappa),$$

$$p_{11}(t) = F[V_t(\alpha + \kappa)],$$

Democracy and development 183

where F is the CDF of normal distribution. Then to estimate α and κ, from which one can calculate p_{01} and p_{11}, and thus $p_{00} = 1 - p_{01}$ and $p_{10} = 1 - p_{11}$, all we need to do is probit on

$$C_t = F(V_t\kappa + V_t\alpha C_{t-1}) + u. \tag{II.10}$$

We estimate this model with $C(0)$ as given.

To estimate the performance equations, we need to augment the RHS of (2) by the expected value of $u_j | C$, which is $\sigma_{ju}\lambda_j$, where λ_j is the hazard rate and σ_{ju} is the regression coefficient

$$G_1 = X_1\beta_1 + \sigma_{1u}\lambda_1 + u_1^* \tag{II.11a}$$

and, similarly for G_0,

$$G_0 = X_0\beta_0 + \sigma_{0u}\lambda_0 + u_0^*, \tag{II.11b}$$

and to calculate the average difference given by (7) using the estimated values of β.

Heckman (1978) originally estimated (11) by OLS. Yet the OLS estimator is not efficient, since the errors u_j^* are heteroscedastic (Greene 1990: 743). Model 1 is based on static probit and OLS in performance; model 3 on dynamic probit and OLS. The alternative is to estimate these equations by MLE. Since the log-likelihood function is fully separable, it makes no difference whether performance in the two states is estimated separately or together. Model 2 is based on static probit and MLE; model 4 on dynamic probit and MLE.

Neither the OLS nor the MLE versions of Heckit take into account the panel structure of the data. Ideally we would be able to do panel on the entire model. But we have too many periods to do panel on selection. At most, we can do a dynamic probit in selection and a panel in performance. The Breusch–Pagan Lagrange multiplier tests show that neither the dictatorship nor the democracy sample is homogeneous. The Hausman test indicates a preference for two-way fixed effects, but we cannot recuperate the expected values with this method. Hence, we use two-way random effects or one-way fixed effects. Testing for autocorrelation shows the presence of AR1. Since the results are the same whether we use static or dynamic probit, only the results for dynamic probit are presented.

Heckman (1988: 24) presents an alternative method for estimating selection models based on unobservables. Suppose that there exists at least one variable, W in Z, such that $\text{Cov}(W, C) \neq 0$ but $E(Wu_j) = 0$. This variable is correlated with C but contemporaneously uncorrelated with the errors in performance.

Selection can be then estimated by OLS on

$$C = \tau_0 + \tau_1 W + e, \tag{II.12}$$

where $E(e) = 0$ and $E(eW) = 0$.

A constant effect of being in state $C = 1$, as compared to $C = 0$, can be estimated by OLS on (model 7)

$$G = \times\beta + C\delta + e\mu + (u - e\mu). \tag{II.13}$$

184   *Adam Przeworski and Fernando Limongi*

Allowing the slopes to differ between the two states, one can estimate (model 8)

$$G = \times\beta_0 + C(X\beta_1) + e\mu + (u - e\mu), \qquad (\text{II}.14)$$

where the average impact of being in state $C = 1$ is given by

$$\text{DHEK} = (1/N) \, \Sigma \, X\beta_1.$$

Finally, selection on observables occurs when $E(u_j \,|\, C, V) = E(u_j \,|\, V)$, that is, the correlation between u_j and C is due only to the correlation between the observed variables $V = Z, X$ and u_j. To put it differently, $E(u_j \,|\, C) \neq 0$ but $E(u_j C \,|\, V) = 0$.

Assume that the coefficients β_j in (2) are the same for $j = 0,1$ and the only difference between performance in the two states is due to a constant effect δ, so that

$$E(G_1 \,|\, X = x - G_0 \,|\, X = x) = C\delta + E(u_1 \,|\, C, Z, X - u_0 \,|\, C, Z, X). \quad (\text{II}.15)$$

According to Heckman (1988: 18), simply controlling for Z in performance equation will be sufficient to get unbiased estimates. The constant effect of being in state $C = 1$ can be estimated by (model 9)

$$G = V\beta + C\delta + u^\star, \qquad (\text{II}.16)$$

where $u^\star = u - E(u \,|\, Z, X)$.

Slope coefficients can be estimated by (model 10)

$$G = V\beta_0 + C(V\beta_1) + u^\star, \qquad (\text{II}.17)$$

where the average impact of being in state $C = 1$ is given by DHEK.

To summarize, we can estimate the effect of regimes in at least the following ways:

SELECTION ON	SELECTION EQUATION	PERFORMANCE ESTIMATOR	MODEL #
UNOBSERVABLES			
	STATIC PROBIT	OLS	1
		MLE	2
		PANEL	3
	DYNAMIC PROBIT	OLS	4
		MLE ALL	5
		PANEL	6
	OLS	IV CONSTANT EFFECT	7
		IV INDIVIDUAL EFFECT	8
OBSERVABLES			
	NONE	CONSTANT EFFECT	9
		INDIVIDUAL EFFECT	10

Democracy and development   185

Table 9.II.1. *Alternative estimators of the growth of per capita income*

#	Model	G1	G0	G1P	G0P	REG	DHEK
0	BIASED	1.89	2.44			0.44 (1.91)	0.20 (0.50)
1	STATIC, OLS	2.32	1.17	2.06	1.53		
2	STATIC, MLE	2.32	1.59	2.06	1.90		
4	DYNAMIC, OLS	2.50	1.97	2.23	2.24		
5	DYNAMIC, MLE	2.50	1.96	2.23	2.23		
6a	DYNAMIC, 2R0	2.68	1.84	2.37	2.03		
6b	DYNAMIC, 1F1	2.82	1.46	2.41	1.73		
7	IV, CONSTANT					0.33 (1.23)	
8	IV, INDIVIDUAL						−0.03 (−0.04)
9	OBSERVABLE, CONSTANT					0.57 (2.35)	
10	OBSERVABLE, INDIVIDUAL						0.29 (0.66)

Note: G1 and G0 are average rates of growth of per capita income corrected for all exogenous variables. G1P and G0P are average rates corrected for all variables other than POPG. REG is the coefficient on Regime. DHEK is defined in the text: it takes POPG as is. t-statistics are in parentheses. 2R0 stands for two-way random effects model; 1F1 for a one-way fixed effects with AR1.

In the results presented below, the standard list of exogenous variables determining selection is

$$Z = \text{STRA,ODRP,ETHNIC,RELIGION,NEWC,BRITCOL.}$$

The standard list of exogenous variables determining growth (the same in the two states) is

$$X = \text{ONE,LEVEL,OECD,INV,POPG.}$$

The results are presented in Table 9.II.1. Altogether, the substantive conclusion of the chapter stands very firmly: If population growth is considered exogenous, dictatorships do better; if they are considered endogenous, there is little difference in regime performance.

The results with the growth of per capita consumption (DCONSDG) are presented in Table 9.II.2.

Note that the appropriate panel with regard to consumption is GLS-AR1. The qualitative picture is similar but these results are more favorable to democracy.

186   *Adam Przeworski and Fernando Limongi*

Table 9.II.2. *Alternative estimators of the growth of per capita consumption*

#	Model	G1	G0	G1P	G0P	REG	DHEK
0	BIASED	1.72	2.51				
1	STATIC, OLS	2.09	0.64	1.73	1.40		
2	STATIC, MLE	2.09	1.48	1.73	2.14		
4	DYNAMIC, OLS	2.38	2.11	2.00	2.71		
5	DYNAMIC, MLE	2.40	2.04	2.02	2.64		
6a	DYNAMIC, GLS-AR1	2.39	1.89	2.10	2.48		
6b	DYNAMIC, GLS-AR1	2.58	1.94	2.30	2.57		
7	IV, CONSTANT					0.28 (0.66)	
8	IV, INDIVIDUAL						0.19 (0.77)
9	OBSERVABLE, CONSTANT					−0.07 (−0.16)	
10	OBSERVABLE, INDIVIDUAL						−0.34 (−0.37)

Note: G1 and G0 are average rates of growth of per capita consumption corrected for all exogenous variables. G1P and G0P are average rates corrected for all variables other than POPG. REG is the coefficient on Regime. DHEK is defined in the text: it takes POPG as is. t-statistics are in parentheses. Model 6a includes data quality, PPPQUAL, in growth equations.

Appendix III **Data quality**

One source of potential bias may originate from the quality of the economic data. It is well known that the PWT data are of very uneven quality for different countries. To assess data quality, Summers and Heston (1988) used letter grades, from A to D, with pluses and minuses, which we converted into a 10-point scale, in increasing quality (our variable is PPPQUAL). Data quality differs systematically across regimes: the average quality for dictatorships is 2.53, while for democracies it is 6.54. The regime-specific growth equations show that data quality is a source of bias: democracies with higher quality of data tend to report lower growth rates while for dictatorships data quality is unrelated to reported growth rates. The results including data quality, with growth of per capita income as the dependent variable, are presented in Table 9.III.1.[31]

Note that the differences between corrected values in model 6 are smaller when data quality is considered: controlling for data quality provides an even stronger confirmation that there is little difference between regimes when population growth is taken as endogenous.

The two-way random effect model is reported in Table 9.8.

Democracy and development

Table 9.III.1. *Alternative estimators of growth of per capita income, controlling for data quality*

#	Model	G1	G0	G1P	G0P	REG	DHEK
0	BIASED	1.89	2.44			0.47 (1.89)	0.15 (0.34)
1	STATIC, OLS	2.65	1.53	2.40	1.86		
2	STATIC, MLE	2.65	1.82	2.40	2.14		
4	DYNAMIC, OLS	2.75	2.03	2.49	2.34		
5	DYNAMIC, MLE	2.73	2.03	2.48	2.34		
6a	DYNAMIC, 2R0	2.81	2.06	2.52	2.33		
6b	DYNAMIC, 1R1	2.54	1.79	2.29	2.06		
7	IV, CONSTANT					0.61 (2.34)	
8	IV, INDIVIDUAL						−0.08 (−0.94)
9	OBSERVABLE, CONSTANT					0.40 (1.48)	
10	OBSERVABLE, INDIVIDUAL						0.04 (0.04)

Note: G1 and G0 are average rates of growth of per capita income corrected for all exogenous variables. G1P and G0P are average rates corrected for all variables other than POPG. REG is the coefficient on Regime. DHEK is defined in the text: it takes POPG as is. *t*-statistics are in parentheses. 2R0 stands for two-way random effects model; 1R1 for a one-way random effects with AR1.

NOTES

We appreciate the collaboration of Mike Alvarez, José Antonio Cheibub, and Alejandro Lopez. We have attempted to answer several comments by participants in the Symposium, in particular those of Kenneth Arrow, Surjit Bhalla, Partha Dasgupta, Amartya Sen, Georg Sorensen, and Lawrence Whitehead. Surjit Bhalla generously shared with us his data. This work was supported in part by a grant from the National Science Foundation, No. SES-9022605.

1 As Baghwati (1994) points out, the implicit assumption in the 1960s was that all regimes in the less developed countries are developmentalist; the only question was whether dictatorship or democracy is better at generating development.

2 For a review of these models, see Przeworski and Cheibub (1994).

3 North and Weingast (1989) came closest in their analysis of the English eighteenth-century parliament but they failed to notice that only the propertied enjoyed political rights. In a seminal study, Cheibub (1994) compared the absolute values of annual changes of tax rates under dictatorships and democracies and discovered that they are slightly larger under democracies.

188 *Adam Przeworski and Fernando Limongi*

4 See the argument in Przeworski and Limongi (1993) and Elster's (1994) critique of it.

5 A different argument is offered by Dasgupta (1993) who argues that liberty is a productive input.

6 The following two paragraphs are based on discussions with Raj Sah.

7 On the *gigantomania* under the Soviet regime, see a beautiful piece by Zalyguine (1987).

8 But see Kakwani (1993), who shows that per capita GDP correlates highly with indices of standard of living based on infant mortality and life expectancy in a cross-section of eighty developing countries between 1971 and 1990. Moreover, while infant mortality declined in all countries, even those that experienced a negative growth during the 1980s, there was still a strong positive relation between income and infant mortality during this period. Dasgupta (1993) also found that these indicators correlate among the poorest countries.

9 See Appendix I for our definition of democracy and the operational rules we used to classify regimes.

10 All the references to levels of development and growth rates are expressed in constant US dollars computed at purchasing power parities and expressed in 1985 prices, based on Penn World Tables (PWT5.5). Thus all $ numbers refer to 1985 PPP USD. The caveats about intertemporal and international comparisons of GDP would take a separate paper: even if we ignore the problems inherent in the measurement of GDP in one country at one time, different approaches to conversion into a common currency and to aggregation yield highly disparate results. The impact of data quality on our results is discussed in Appendix III.

11 For a review of these studies, see Przeworski and Limongi (1993). The results are about equally balanced in favor of democracy and dictatorship. Strikingly, studies published before 1988 never show democracy to be superior; those published after 1987 never show dictatorship to be better.

The only analyses which used simultaneous equations are Helliwell (1993), who found a slightly negative effect of democracy, and Bhalla (in this volume), who found a positive effect. Yet both use 2SLS, an estimator which is based on the assumption that errors in selection and in performance are not contemporaneously correlated across equations. In the presence of non-random selection these errors will be correlated and the performance equation will suffer from an omitted variable bias. Our reanalysis of the Bhalla results shows that this is indeed the case (his specification fails the RESET test) and the instrumental variables estimation of his model (see Heckman 1988 and Appendix II) shows that the overall effect of regime is not significant.

12 The literature on selection bias is already enormous. For a technical exposition and references, see Przeworski and Limongi (1992) and Appendix II.

13 As Heckman (1988: 23) warns, "selection bias conditioning on observed characteristics may be worse than selection bias when there is no conditioning."

14 Prima facie, one could expect democracies to be less vulnerable to bad economic conditions because they derive legitimacy from more than economic

Democracy and development 189

performance and one could expect dictatorships to weather economic crises better since they can repress discontent. Both mechanisms probably operate, and what we see is their balance.

15 Expected life is the inverse of the transition probability from a given state.

16 These results are based on a dynamic probit model (Amemiya 1985: chapter 11). In any non-linear model $Y = F(C\beta)$, the partial derivative is $dY/dX = f(X\beta)\beta$, so that it depends on the value of the independent variable at which it is evaluated.

17 Since we make inferences about tails of distributions, methods for correcting selection are not robust: different methods can generate different results. (Gary King made us sensitive to this point.) Stolzenberg and Relles (1990) have shown that the Heckit OLS estimator often fails when selection is weak. Yet paradoxically, the very fact that different estimators generate different results constitutes evidence that selection operates (Heckman 1988).

18 This result is not sensitive to estimation method. The OLS estimates for the two regimes separately, pass the RESET test at 0.05 level. Hence, there is no reason to suspect these equations are misspecified. The proxy for aggregate demand we used in this estimation is lagged GDP. But since the theoretically relevant variable is the GDP expected for the next year, one could use current growth as the proxy, which would result in simultaneity between investment and growth. A FIML estimate of simultaneous equations shows, however, (1) that the model is misspecified (as judged by a negative R-squared in the 2SLS estimate) and (2) that selection-corrected investment shares still do not differ between regimes. They are also almost the same when we use panel estimation (LSDV with AR1): 19.02 for dictatorships and 18.62 for democracies.

19 The averages of population growth by region are:

Latin America	2.31843
Middle East	3.00332
Eastern Europe	0.57696
Africa	2.76596
South Asia	2.40581
East Asia	2.25798
OECD	0.86184

Population growth rates seem to decline in income among Catholic but not among Muslim countries. One possible explanation might be migration: even though the birth rate is lower in the wealthier Muslim countries, there is massive migration to them from the poor Muslim countries. A cursory examination of fertility and crude birth rates indicates that, except for Saudi Arabia, these are somewhat lower among the Muslim oil producers but still much higher than among Catholic countries with equivalent incomes. Another explanation may be that demographic transition is exceptionally rapid among oil countries, which became rich fast, so that mortality rates declined significantly while fertility rates did not. A cursory glance at the numbers provides some support for this explanation, again with the exception of Saudi Arabia.

Obviously, we need to pursue these puzzles further.

20 Panel methods generate results that are even more dramatic: a one-way random effects model with AR1 (which is high for both regimes) yields a selection-corrected mean of 2.40 for dictatorships and −0.66 for democracies. Moreover, religious and ethnic composition as well as the former colonial status matter for dictatorships, while level does not; for democracies the effect of level is enormous, while among other factors only ethnic homogeneity is significant.

21 Note that F_K is the marginal product of capital but β is the marginal elasticity of labor: they do not have the same interpretation. Obviously, one could have written (3) in terms of elasticities alone but then we would get a term (K^*/K) which is avoided because there are no good data about capital stock and there are data about investment. With a capital share equal to about 1/3 and the average marginal output/capital ratio also equal 1/3, we should get estimates of F_K of about 1/9: 0.11, somewhat lower than we get. The estimates for β, the labor share, are also reasonable.

22 One problem encountered in empirical work is that data on L, the labor force, are not available; only data on population, P, are, and this is what almost everyone uses. But using P in place of L can bias β. In fact, $L^*(t) = P^*(t - k)$, where k is the average age when people enter the labor force. But, again, we do not have good data on $P^*(t - k)$ for the entire period. Hence, we use $P^*(t)$ in place of $L^*(t)$. Now, suppose that population growth declines during the period from $t - k$ to t according to $P^*(t + 1)/P(t + 1) = \pi[P^*(t)/P(t)]$, $0 < \pi < 1$. Then $P^*(t)/P(t) = \pi_k[P^*(t - k)/P(t - k)]$. The estimated value of labor force contribution is $\beta\pi_k[P^*(t - k)/P(t - k)]$ instead of $\beta[P^*(t - k)/P(t - k)]$. Hence, the true value of β, $\beta^\wedge = \beta/\pi^k > \beta$: when population growth slows down between $t - k$ and t, we underestimate the contribution of labor. Conversely, if it increases we overestimate it. Similarly, it can be shown that we underestimate the contribution of labor if the proportion of active population declines and overestimate it if this proportion increases.

23 The selection-corrected values based on one-way fixed effects with AR1, not controlled for data quality, imply that per capita income doubles under dictatorships in about twenty-nine years and under democracies in about forty years. But when we control for data quality, a one-way random effects model with AR1 reduces this difference to thirty years for dictatorships and thirty-four for democracies.

24 All methods of estimation show much higher coefficients on population growth for democracy than for dictatorship. But a rough comparison of average population growth rates by decades shows that they have been declining faster under dictatorship: hence, in the light of n. 21, we may be somewhat overestimating this difference.

25 Under competitive conditions, labor share equals β.

26 This explanation contrasts with Sen's (1994) argument that voluntary methods of family planning are more effective than what he calls the "override" approach. The question open for further analysis is whether dictatorships try less to control fertility growth or are less effective at doing it.

27 The difference between the coefficients on investment in Table 9.8 is quite

Democracy and development

large and the estimates are very tight. The coefficients on investment are somewhat sensitive to the method of estimation. They are always higher under democracy, but estimates that do not entail panel methods show a smaller difference.

28 Lipset (1960: 84) too, however, refers to "the 'premature' triumph of the democratic left" as a threat to democracy in Africa and Asia.

29 For a full explanation and historical details, see Alvarez, Cheibub, Limongi, and Przeworski (1994). We refer to our data set as the ACLP Data Base.

30 This rule is controversial and it allocates 9.1 of the sample. To check its effect, we reclassified Type II dictatorships as democracies. The dynamic probit–MLE estimator gives results almost identical to Model 5 in Table 9.II.1: the average rate of growth (with population growth as endogenous) is 2.37 percent for dictatorships and 2.27 percent for democracies.

31 Since data quality is a time-invariant variable, only the random effects model can be estimated.

REFERENCES

Alvarez, Mike, José Antonio Cheibub, Fernando Limongi, and Adam Przeworski. 1994. "Classifying political regimes for the ACLP data set." Working Paper #3. Chicago Center on Democracy. University of Chicago.

Amemiya, Takeshi. 1985. *Advanced Econometrics*. Cambridge, Mass.: Harvard University Press.

Bhagwati, Jagdish. 1994. "Democracy and development: new thinking on an old question." The Rajiv Gandhi Lecture, New Delhi, October 22.

Bollen, K. A. 1980. "Issues in the comparative measurement of political democracy," *American Sociological Review* 45: 370–390.

Cheibub, José Antonio. 1994. "Democracy and property rights: is there a link?" Paper presented at the Annual Meeting of the American Political Science Association, New York City.

Condorcet. 1986 (1785). "Essai sur l'application de l'analyse à la probabilité des décisions rendues à la pluralité des voix." In *Sur les élections*. Textes choisis et revues par Olivier de Bernon. Paris: Bayard.

Coppedge, Michael, and Wolfgang H. Reinicke. 1990. "Measuring polyarchy," *Studies in Comparative International Development* 25: 51–72.

Dahl, Robert A. 1971. *Polyarchy*. New Haven: Yale University Press.

Dasgupta, Partha. 1993. *An Inquiry into Well-Being and Destitution*. Oxford: Clarendon Press.

Drèze, Jean, and Amartya Sen. 1989. *Hunger and Public Action*. Oxford: Clarendon Press.

Elster, Jon. 1994. "The impact of constitutions on economic performance." Paper presented at the Annual Bank Conference on Development Economics. Washington, DC: World Bank.

Evans, Peter B. 1989. "Predatory, developmental, and other apparatuses: a comparative political economy perspective on the Third World state," *Sociological Forum* 4: 561–587.

192 Adam Przeworski and Fernando Limongi

Ferejohn, John A. 1986. "Incumbent performance and electoral control," *Public Choice* 50: 5–25.

Findlay, Ronald. 1990. "The political economy: its explanatory power for the LDCs," *Economics and Politics* 2: 193–221.

Galenson, Walter. 1959. "Introduction" to Walter Galenson, ed., *Labor and Economic Development*. New York: Wiley.

Greene, William H. 1990. *Econometric Analysis*. New York: Macmillan.

Grossman, Herschel I., and Suk Jae Noh. 1990. "A theory of kleptocracy with probabilistic survival and reputation," *Economics and Politics* 2: 157–171.

Gurr, Ted Robert, Keith Jaggers, and Will H. Moore. 1990. "The transformation of the Western state: the growth of democracy, autocracy, and state power since 1800," *Studies in Comparative International Development* 25: 73–108.

Haggard, Stephan. 1990. *Pathways from Periphery. The Politics of Growth in the Newly Industrializing Countries*. Ithaca, N.Y.: Cornell University Press.

Heckman, James J. 1978. "Dummy endogenous variables in a simultaneous equations system," *Econometrica* 46: 931–961.

1979. "Sample selection bias as a specification error," *Econometrica* 47: 153–161.

1988. "The microeconomic evaluation of social programs and economic institutions," in *Chung-Hua Series of Lectures by Invited Eminent Economists, No. 14*. Tapei: The Institute of Economics, Academia Sinica.

1990. "Selection bias and self-selection," in John Eatwell, Murray Milgate, and Peter Newman, eds., *The New Palgrave. Econometrics*. New York: W. W. Norton.

Helliwell, John F. 1993. "Empirical linkages between democracy and economic growth," *British Journal of Political Science* 24: 225–248.

Huntington, Samuel P. 1968. *Political Order in Changing Societies*. New Haven: Yale University Press.

Huntington, Samuel P., and Jorge I. Dominguez. 1975. "Political development," in F. I. Greenstein and N. W. Polsby, eds., *Handbook of Political Science*, vol. III. Reading: Addison-Wesley.

Huntington, Samuel P., and Joan M. Nelson. 1976. *No Easy Choice: Political Participation in Developing Countries*. Cambridge, Mass.: Harvard University Press.

Kakwani, N. 1993. "Performance in living standards. An international comparison," *Journal of Development Economics* 41: 307–336.

La Palombara, Joseph, ed. 1963. *Bureaucracy and Political Development*. Princeton: Princeton University Press.

Lipset, Seymour M. 1960. *Political Man*. Garden City, N.Y.: Doubleday.

Macaulay, Thomas B. 1990. *Complete Writings*, vol. XVII. Boston and New York: Houghton-Mifflin.

Marx, Karl. 1952. *The Class Struggle in France, 1848 to 1850*. Moscow: Progress Publishers.

Democracy and development

North, Douglass C., and Barry R. Weingast. 1989. "Constitutions and commitment: the evolution of institutions governing public choice in seventeenth-century England," *Journal of Economic History* 49: 803–832.

O'Flaherty, Brendan. 1990. "Why are there democracies? A principal agent answer," *Economics and Politics* 2: 133–155.

Olson, Mancur, Jr. 1991. "Autocracy, democracy and prosperity," in Richard J. Zeckhauser, ed., *Strategy and Choice*. Cambridge, Mass.: MIT Press.

Powell, G. B., Jr. 1990. "Holding governments accountable: how constitutional arrangements and party systems affect clarity of responsibility for policy in contemporary democracies." MS.

Przeworski, Adam, and José Antonio Cheibub. 1994. "Political regimes, government, and economic growth." MS. Chicago Center on Democracy. University of Chicago.

Przeworski, Adam, and Fernando Limongi. 1992. "Selection, counterfactuals and comparisons." Working Paper 11. Chicago Center on Democracy. University of Chicago.

1993. "Political regimes and economic growth," *Journal of Economic Perspectives* 7: 51–69.

1994. "Modernization: theories and facts." Working Paper 14. Chicago Center on Democracy. University of Chicago.

Przeworski, Adam, and Michael Wallerstein. 1988. "Structural dependence of the state on capital," *American Political Science Review* 82: 11–29.

Pudney, Stephen. 1989. *Modelling Individual Choice. The Econometrics of Corners, Kinks and Holes*. Oxford: Blackwell.

Sah, Raj, and E. Joseph Stiglitz. 1988. "Committees, hierarchies and polyarchies," *The Economic Journal* 98: 451–470.

de Schweinitz, Karl, Jr. 1959. "Industrialization, labor controls and democracy," *Economic Development and Cultural Change* 7: 385–404.

1964. *Industrialization and Democracy*. New York: Free Press.

Scully, Gerlad W. 1992. *Constitutional Environments and Economic Growth*. Princeton: Princeton University Press.

Sen, Amartya. 1993. "Economic regress: concepts and features," *Proceedings of the World Bank Annual Conference on Development Eonomics*: 315–334.

1994. "Population: delusion and reality," *New York Review of Books* 61 no. 15.

Stokes, Susan C. 1994. "Democratic accountability and policy change: economic policy in Fujimori's Peru." Working Paper 18. Chicago Center on Democracy. University of Chicago.

Stolzenberg, Ross M., and Daniel A. Relles. 1990. 'Theory testing in a world of constrained research design," *Sociological Methods and Research* 18: 395–415.

Stolzenberg, Ross M., and Daniel L. Relles. 1990. "Theory testing in a world of constrained research design," *Sociological Methods and Research* 18: 395–415.

Summers, Robert, and Alan Heston. 1988. "A new set of international comparisons of real product and price levels estimates for 130 countries, 1950–1985," *The Review of Income and Wealth* 34: 1–26.

Westphal, Larry E. 1990. "Industrial policy in an export-propelled economy: lessons from South Korea's experience," *Journal of Economic Perspectives* 4: 41–60.

Zalyguine, Sergeuei. 1987. "Le 'projet du siècle': détournement des fleuves, détournement de la science par la bureaucracie," *Les Temps Modernes* 42: 171–192.

10 Freedom and economic growth: a virtuous cycle?

Surjit S. Bhalla

Abstract

This chapter investigates the relationship between freedom and economic growth. Two components of freedom are considered – political and economic. While political freedom measures have frequently been used, this chapter offers three separate variables to measure a major, and much neglected, determinant of economic growth – namely, economic freedom. The relationship of freedom with respect to welfare is examined through the use of *five* separate indicators of welfare: – per capita income growth, measured in constant dollars and purchasing power parity (PPP) dollars; total factor productivity growth (TFPG); growth in secondary school enrollment and decline in infant mortality. Data for over ninety countries are used for the time period 1973–1990.

The results are robust and *invariant* to alternative specifications. In particular, both political and economic freedom are positively associated with economic growth. For example, a 1 point increase in political freedom (on a 7 point scale) leads to an increase in per capita growth of approximately 1 percent; and an opening up of international capital markets (as proxied by the black market premium on the currency) leads to an increase of 1.6 percent in the per capita growth rate. These results hold regardless of whether the estimation is ordinary least squares (OLS) or in the context of a simultaneous equation model. Further, the results hold for all three educational attainment variables (World Bank 1991; Barro and Lee 1992, 1993b; and Nehru, Swanson, and Dubey 1993).

One reason why these results differ markedly from the "no (or negative) freedom–growth" relationship observed in the literature is because of the improved specification of the growth model developed in this paper, i.e., a model which incorporates

195

196   *Surjit S. Bhalla*

both economic and political freedom. The incorporation of the two freedoms in the modeling also helps to explain the "anomalies," e.g., India with high political freedom grows slowly (low economic freedom) and the East Asian economies with low political freedom grow considerably faster (high economic freedom). One additional result is that *no* initial education externalities are found once political and economic freedom variables are introduced in the growth model. Instead, education is found to yield increasing returns *only* when economic freedom is present. This result suggests that an important explanator of growth in developing countries is the presence of an interaction effect between economic freedom (economic openness) and education.

SECTION 1: INTRODUCTION

The last decade has been witness to a virtual explosion in the number of countries that have moved towards a democratic form of government. Two continents – Latin America and Europe – have been transformed into (almost) exclusive democracies, while most of Asia, and parts of Africa, are converging towards a democratic norm. Not as emphasized, but equally important, is the *economic* revolution that has accompanied this political revolution.

While the effects of this revolution on freedom are unambiguous, the effects on economic growth are not. Both the political science, and the economics literature, have offered "mixed" conclusions, i.e., some studies find the effects of democracy on growth to be negative, some find it positive, and some find no effect.[1] The emphasis towards a negative effect increases as one moves towards policy makers and the popular media. For example, a successful leader of a very successful country, Singapore, recently stated: "I do not believe that democracy necessarily leads to development. I believe that what a country needs to develop is discipline more than democracy. The exuberance of democracy leads to indiscipline and disorderly conduct which are inimical to development" (Lee Kwan Yew 1992).

Policy makers, especially in democratic developing countries, are envious of the authoritarian success of countries like Singapore. It is not uncommon, therefore, to find Indian policy makers (politicians and bureaucrats) explain their own failure by stating that Indian policies would be more growth-friendly if the shackles of freedom and democracy were absent. Obviously, there is a profound self-interest which

Freedom and economic growth: a virtuous cycle?

guides political leaders towards a distrust of freedom, especially economic freedom.

The view in the popular media is perhaps best exemplified by the following quotes from a magazine which is *critical* of authoritarianism. In a cautious article entitled "Freedom and prosperity" (June 29, 1991) the *Economist* magazine stated "For the past 25 years Asia has had the world's fastest-growing economies. It has not had the best democracies. Just a coincidence? . . . In Asia, authoritarian governments may find it easier than democratic ones to haul countries out of poverty." However, the *Economist* in 1994 (August 27, p.17) reached a different conclusion: "Dictatorships with wise economic policies can achieve rapid economic growth: but they are rare, and, being dictatorships, will lack the economic strengths of stable democracy. Far from inhibiting growth, democracy promotes it."

A large part of the popular impression about the ill-effects of democracy or the growth-inducing effects of authoritarianism stems from observing the East Asian experience *and* contrasting it with that of democratic countries like India. The record is clear and harsh – India, a democratic country for all but three years since 1947 grew at a 1.9 percent per capita rate from 1960 to 1987; the three East Asian dictatorships – Singapore, South Korea and China (Taiwan) – grew at a 6.4 percent rate during the same time period. The important exclusion here is that of Hong Kong – it had considerably greater political freedom than the other three East Asian countries and grew at the same rate as Singapore – 5.9 percent. While the Hong Kong experience points to the mixed nature of the evidence, the impression remains that authoritarianism is the preferred policy option. This conclusion is reinforced by authoritarian China's spectacular growth record since the late seventies.

Given the extraordinary improvement of freedom in the last decade, it is a moot question whether the world will have to forego some growth, and development, in order to enjoy the fruits of this newly found freedom. If so, what can policy makers do to help reduce the costs of freedom? Alternatively, is it likely that a faster pace of growth comes with *more* freedom?[2] If so, are freedom and growth locked in a virtuous cycle? These questions are the main motivation for the analysis.

Estimation of the partial impact of freedom on growth involves a hypothesis/model of the determinants of economic growth. Traditional, or "new" growth theory models,[3] are deficient in two aspects: first, these models completely ignore the role of political and (especially) economic freedom. In contrast, the model of growth offered in this chapter assigns

198   *Surjit S. Bhalla*

a critical role to both types of freedom. Second, and following from the first omission, the growth theory models miss the important interactive (synergistic) role played by the simultaneous presence of *both* education and economic freedom. The results show that this interaction (rather than education *per se* or any other factor) possibly accounts for a large part of the observed "excess" in East Asian growth rates. Further, omission of this interaction term may have yielded the pervasive, and possibly spurious, result that there are externalities associated with education. Thus, this chapter is both about a revised explanation of the process of economic growth and about the role of freedom. And this revised view suggests that the Solow model *is* an adequate explanator of growth, with the caveat that the flow of technology *not* be assumed exogenous (as in the Solow model).

The concept of freedom is obviously complex and not easily reducible to quantitative measurement. Yet extensive use of quantitative measures of freedom is made in this chapter. Further complexity is generated by the fact that changes in freedom impact upon welfare change with "long and variable lags." This chapter does not attempt to model the complex lag structure. Thus, the drawbacks of this study are apparent. However, these caveats should not detract from the strong finding that emerges from the extensive analysis presented in this chapter and in Bhalla (1992): no matter how freedom is measured, and no matter how welfare change is defined, there is a strong and positive relationship between the two.

This is in striking contrast to some of the recent studies on the subject, e.g., Alesina *et al.*: "Democracies do not appear to show a different growth path than non-democracies" (1992: 22); or Helliwell: "Aggregate evidence does not support any significant linkage between the level of democracy and subsequent economic growth" (1992: 19); or Przeworski and Limongi: "we do not know whether democracy fosters or hinders economic growth" (1993: 64).

Why does this study offer different results? Four reasons are possible: (i) different time period of analysis, 1973–1990 (this study) vs. 1960–1988; (ii) use of a more appropriate educational *attainment* variable (this study) rather than educational *enrollment* variables; (iii) use of *three* economic freedom variables vs. *none* in the other studies; (iv) differences in instrument variables;[4] and (v) use of PPP growth rates (most studies) rather than constant dollar growth rates (this study). The inclusion of economic freedom variables appears as the single most important difference between this and other studies. Tables 10.3 and 10.4 contain "sensitivity" results of models which include different specifications and variables. These alternative specifications reinforce the strong conclusion that political and economic freedom are jointly important in affecting economic growth.

This chapter is concerned with freedom and growth. Democracy is a form of government strongly *associated* with greater freedom. As the analysis will make clear, the hypothesis to be tested is one between greater individual freedom (political, civil, *and* economic) and growth. Democracies vary in the type of individual freedom (especially economic freedom) they provide to their population. In particular, as emphasized by Hayek (1944), economic freedom is at least equally important as political freedom. Past studies, by not controlling for economic freedom, may have estimated an inappropriate relationship between (political) freedom and growth. This, therefore, is the first important departure of this study from previous research. It analyzes the *independent* individual impacts of political and economic freedom on economic growth.

Four other differences of this study need to be highlighted. First, it is likely that there is a simultaneous relationship between freedom and growth, i.e., freedom is hypothesized to lead to higher growth, and higher growth can often lead to greater demands for more freedom. These joint effects need to be modeled in a statistically appropriate fashion. This chapter does so. Helliwell (1992) also estimates a simultaneous equation model, but reaches different results, perhaps because of exclusion of variables representing economic freedom. Second, there are other correlates of growth which if not appropriately controlled for can lead to the estimation of a spurious relationship between freedom and growth. The most important of these variables is the average educational level of the population. *Three* different measures of educational attainment are used to help estimate an unbiased relationship between freedom and growth. (Other studies have loosely proxied educational attainment with an inappropriate flow variable, namely the percentage of students *enrolled* in primary or secondary school in an "initial" year.) Third, this chapter makes an explicit attempt to estimate the relationship between freedom and growth including, and excluding, the unusual East Asian experience. Recognition of the unusual nature of East Asian growth can help to isolate the effects of individual determinants on economic growth. Finally, this chapter uses *five* different welfare variables to proxy for economic development. These consist of two variables which measure per capita growth (in constant dollars and in PPP dollars à la Summers and Heston [1988]), total factor productivity growth, improvement in education (secondary school enrollment) and health (decline in infant mortality).

The plan of the chapter is as follows. Section 2 discusses why a dichotomous variable representing democracy is flawed and why it is

200   Surjit S. Bhalla

preferable to use variables relating to individual freedom. It also discusses the need for a variable to correct for the likely two-way causation between freedom and growth. Section 3 discusses data and measurement issues related to the complexity of freedom variables, and variables related to welfare improvement. In particular, it is suggested that economic freedom (a heretofore neglected variable) is an important determinant of economic growth. Section 4 discusses why it is important for growth models to adjust for the reality of the exceptional growth experience of six East Asian (Confucian) economies. It is suggested that if such adjustment is not made, then most estimates may yield biased results. Section 5 discusses the results obtained on the basis of the various specifications estimated here (eighteen) and in Bhalla (1992). Section 6 concludes and offers some forecasts based on the extraordinarily robust relationship that is obtained between freedom and growth.

SECTION 2: DEMOCRACY, FREEDOM, AND GROWTH – A MODEL

Democracy vs. freedom

There are both positive and negative effects of democracy on growth. The positive effects have to do with the presence of a liberal regime at the center – a form of government which respects various rights of individuals. *The most important of these rights is probably the right to property.* Other rights *associated* with democracy, but not necessarily required by this form of government, are the economic rights characterized by a market-friendly system. The political right which democracy confers on its citizens is the right to change governments. This right, theoretically, can have a positive effect on growth because the rulers know that their retention of power is (partially) based on economic performance.

In theory, democracy need not confer any of the above-mentioned *economic* rights on its citizens. In practice, democratic governments have allowed their citizens extremely varied amounts of economic freedom, and often erred on the low side. Nationalization of industries, foreign exchange controls, investment regulations and restrictions, wage and price controls, etc., are all policies that democracies have arrogantly introduced and rigidly implemented. Parties in power have also attempted to stall, through non-democratic means, the evolution of opposition parties. Even the right to change governments has been delayed by a declaration of a "state of emergency", e.g., India and Sri Lanka in the seventies.

Just as democracies can have a wide range of freedom, so can non-

Freedom and economic growth: a virtuous cycle? 201

democracies. Some non-democratic governments are associated with few economic or political freedoms (e.g. Eastern Europe prior to 1990); some with considerable amounts of economic freedoms (e.g. East Asian economies like Singapore, China (Taiwan), and Korea); and some with considerable amounts of freedom (both political and economic) but no voting rights (Hong Kong). The high variance of freedoms associated with both democracies and authoritarian regimes means that a measured relationship between democracy and economic growth is likely to be heavily contaminated with error. It is preferable, therefore, to analyze economic growth with respect to important attributes of a "proper" democracy, i.e., presence of political and economic freedom. And especially so if data on freedom are available on a somewhat continuous scale (in contrast to the dichotomous nature of a variable representing democracy).[5]

The above arguments pertaining to the role of freedom implicitly involve an acceptance of a particular process of economic growth. Rejected explicitly are growth processes associated with less freedom, e.g., economic growth associated with authoritarianism, forced savings, planned industrialization, high tariffs, etc. Such policies restrict economic freedom and prevent competition from playing its allocative role; these restrictive policies ensure that relative factor prices and technology prevailing in the domestic market are different (and inferior in the case of technology) than those prevailing internationally.

A "new" model of growth

This chapter is both about a "new" model of growth as well as the role of freedom in generating growth. A heuristic model of the growth process can be stated as follows. A developing country has a manna advantage in that it is a late-comer. This implies that improved production possibilities are available on the "shelf" ready to be adopted, rather than to be achieved through research and development, as in the developed countries. This advantage leads to *relatively* faster growth, i.e., convergence. However, the developing country needs the means to exploit its backwardness. Education can help attain development. But education may only be a necessary condition – otherwise, countries like Sri Lanka and India would have been success stories by now. What allows education to achieve its maximum return is economic openness, a subset of economic freedom, i.e., the freedom to import technology, a freedom constrained in most developing countries by the policy makers, or planners, or bureaucrats. With economic openness, capital is allowed to seek the highest return domestically and internationally, and countries can

202   *Surjit S. Bhalla*

move along the path of their dynamic comparative advantage. If two countries are equally open, *then* education differences are likely to matter – both because of the ability to select the appropriate technology and the ability to adapt the technology, if needed.[6] Thus, there is synergy between education and economic freedom. An interactive effect between the two leads to faster economic growth, and faster convergence.

In production function terms, the differences between the model outlined above and others can be illustrated as follows. Let the production function be written as

$$Y(t) = A(t)f(K(t), L(t)) \tag{1}$$

where Y represents income, K represents capital, L represents labor, and t is time. The neoclassical Solow model assumes $A(t)$ to be exogenous and available to all producers. In their modification of this model, Mankiw, Romer, and Weil (1990), suggest that in the *initial* time period, $A(t)$ varies amongst countries by a random term, i.e., $A(0) = b + x$, where b is a constant and x represents random "fixed-effect" differences. Like Solow, the growth rate of A is assumed to be exogenous, and constant, across countries. The "new" growth theory literature (Romer 1986; Lucas 1988; Barro 1991) rejects the assumption that $A(t)$ is exogenous, and suggests that its evolution is determined by the level of human capital in the economy. Human capital can lead to increasing returns because the productivity of all workers is enhanced when managers and co-workers have higher education. Considerable empirical support has been achieved for the proposition that higher amounts of initial human capital leads to higher economic growth, i.e., confirming the hypothesis of increasing returns (externalities) to education.

The literature on the "new" growth theory is voluminous, and several determinants of $A(t)$, in addition to education, have been offered.[7] The model offered above is in the same tradition. The *difference* is in the role accorded to education, and freedom. It is hypothesized that a considerable portion of the returns (increasing or otherwise) to education result from increased openness to international markets and technology; that for closed (non-economic freedom) economies – as most developing countries were till the late eighties – the contribution of education is limited. That the magnitude of education may have relatively little to do with the transfer of technology in the presence of government restrictions is abundantly confirmed by the example of Eastern Europe prior to 1990.

Once a country becomes developed, i.e., catch-up is achieved, and technology is similar in all countries, the "traditional" determinants of

Freedom and economic growth: a virtuous cycle? 203

growth (innovation, entrepreneurship, research and development expenditures) become more relevant. Hence, this model of growth is more about developing, than developed, societies.

The role of freedom in the above model is as a determinant of A(t), along with education. If policy makers restrict foreign technology or foreign competition, they are refusing to let (foreign) prices determine (domestic) resource allocation. In a non-free environment, domestic producers and/or consumers cannot allocate resources in the most profitable or welfare enhancing manner. Economic freedom results in increased economic opportunities; political and civil liberties help ensure that the "exploiters" of these increased opportunities are dictated by merit rather than fiat.

Summarizing, the argument in favor of a causative relationship from freedom to growth is one which emphasizes the prevalence of political and economic checks and balances in the system. The assumption is that a free society can help allocate resources more efficiently than a non-free society. Further, in a free society, errors by the government or leadership or bureaucrats can be corrected through the ballot, the press or the judicial system. In particular, political freedom means that a country need not be stuck with a bad policy – or a bad ruler. The removal of bad rulers (political freedom), or a movement towards efficient resource allocation (economic freedom) has the same result – better economic performance.[8]

Freedom and growth – a two-way causation

This "new" growth model – one incorporating economic and political freedom in addition to other determinants – is the one estimated in this chapter. If there is only one-way causation from freedom to growth, then unbiased estimates of the coefficients can be obtained by OLS (Table 10.2). However, a strong theoretical possibility exists of reverse causation from economic growth to political freedom, i.e., countries first obtain growth, and then move towards "luxury" items like freedom and democracy. This argument was first offered by Lipset (1959) via his observation that democracy and level of per capita income are positively related. At present, the example of East Asia is most often alluded to in this regard, i.e., after attaining economic development, these countries have moved towards democratic systems.[9]

An exogenous variable which directly affects freedom but not growth is required in order that possible simultaneous effects be purged. Such a variable is difficult to identify since most determinants of freedom affect growth as well. For example, higher education can be expected

204   *Surjit S. Bhalla*

to lead to greater demands for democracy, and also to higher growth. The same argument holds for high initial levels of income.

Freedom and growth – identification

This chapter constructs an "institutional (colonial) heritage" variable to identify the freedom equation. Until recently, several of the developing countries were under a colonial regime. It is reasonable to assume that the institutions now present in these countries are in part a function of the colonial regime – and in part a function of the indigenous culture, and "initial conditions." Towards this end, countries were classified into five "colonial heritage" categories: (i) British colonialism in sub-Saharan African countries, e.g., Tanzania; (ii) British colonialism in non-sub-Saharan African countries, e.g., Egypt, India;[10] (iii) American influence countries, e.g., Panama, Liberia, Philippines, South Korea; (iv) non-British (e.g., French, Dutch) colonial countries; and (v) non-colonial independent countries, e.g., Brazil, Thailand.[11]

In most senses of the term, the colonial heritage classification offered above is truly exogenous. Further, it is quite *likely* that the nature of colonial influence prior to the 1970s (and starting as early as the nineteenth century) had an impact on the kind of political institutions the colonized countries eventually adopted; and it is quite *unlikely* that this institutional heritage systematically affected future growth performance in any way.[12]

There is, however, one linkage between colonialism and subsequent growth. It can be argued that apart from their influence on political institutions, colonialism probably affected infrastructural development, e.g., railroads, schools, etc. Such differences in infrastructure are likely to affect future growth. However, the growth model used has two infrastructure control variables – initial per capita income in 1972, and initial educational attainment levels in 1972. Hence, the effect of colonial heritage estimated below is *after* controlling for the effects of colonial infrastructure development. The contention is that while the direct effect of colonialism on growth ended around the late fifties, and certainly by the late sixties, the indirect effect of colonialism on institutions like democracy lingers on.

It is important to note that the investments resulting from different patterns of colonialism in the past *do* affect the *level* of income in the future. In this regard, colonialism variables are correlated with per capita income in the initial period of estimation, namely 1972. However, use of colonial heritage as an instrument is invalid if colonialism (till approximately the late 1940s) were to affect the *growth* rate from 1973

Freedom and economic growth: a virtuous cycle? 205

to 1990. It is highly unlikely that colonial heritage does that – if it did, one would have to observe either explosive, or implosive, growth rates in perpetuity.

SECTION 3: DATA AND MEASUREMENT

Rights – political, civil, and economic[13]

Broadly, freedom can be thought of as consisting of three separate rights: political rights, defined as "rights to participate meaningfully in the political process," i.e., rights which allow the leaders to be changed; civil rights, defined as the "rights to free expression, to organize or demonstrate, as well as rights to a degree of autonomy such as is provided by freedom of religion, education, travel, and other personal rights" (Gastil 1987); and economic rights.

While political and civil rights have been extensively discussed, the same cannot be said of economic freedom. Indeed, there is a larger dichotomy – political freedom has been deemed politically correct, and economic freedom (first suggested by Hayek 1944 and then followed up by Scully and Slottje 1991 and Bhalla 1992) deemed politically *incorrect*. Only recently has the tide begun to shift with both Freedom House (publisher of the political freedom rankings used in this chapter) and the Heritage Foundation announcing plans to measure economic freedom on a systematic basis.

Economic freedoms generally reflect rights provided by a free (competitive) environment, e.g., property rights, external and internal openness (right to buy and sell goods to whomever one wishes and at prices the competitive market determines); rights to set up investments without a license, rights to foreign travel, rights to hire and fire (with due process); rights of domestic and international movement of labor and capital, etc.

Omitting the freedom to immigrate, labor freedom means the right to work anywhere in national boundaries and at wages the impersonal market determines, rather than the "face-less" bureaucrat. Capital freedom means the freedom to obtain the highest return on one's capital either domestically or abroad – hence, negative real rates of interest domestically would suggest a need for freedom to transfer one's capital abroad. Produce freedom implies a right to sell abroad at favorable prices, or to import from abroad if import products are cheaper.

The above broad definitions (but no less precise than political freedom) suggest several variables which can be used to capture components of economic freedom, e.g., nature of property rights (land

206   *Surjit S. Bhalla*

ownership, urban land ceilings, patent rights, etc.), high trade taxes,[14] unionization, licensing procedures, capital market controls, minimum wages, etc. Each constraint on market behavior (excepting that of monopolists and actions that ignore externalities) constitutes an infringement of economic freedom.

Empirical measures of freedom

Given the diversity of rights, it is difficult to envision an all encompassing *single* measure. Consequently, *four* separate measures of liberty are used in the empirical analysis.

Political and civil rights – Gastil data

Gastil (and now Freedom House) has conducted an annual survey of rights in most countries of the world since 1973. The survey ranks all countries (and territories) according to over thirty specific criteria. Some of the criteria for political rights are: whether the chief authority was elected by a meaningful process; whether there were fair election laws, whether there was a significant opposition vote, etc. A partial listing of the criteria for civil rights includes: freedom of the press, freedom of assembly and demonstration, freedom to organize unions, personal social rights – including those to property, internal and external travel, choice of residence, etc. Two indices, one each for political rights and civil rights, each ranging from 1 (worst) to 7 (best) are constructed.[15] There exists a high degree of correlation between the two – over 0.9. Further, there is hardly any intra-country variability in the indices for a particular country–year. For example, in 1982 (mid-point year for the survey data which exists from 1973 to 1992) out of a total sample of 112 countries, there were 49 countries with the same estimate, 58 countries whose values were within a point and only 5 countries whose values differed by two points. Given this large association between the two, a simple average is used as a measure of political and civil liberties.[16]

How accurate are the Gastil indices? One test is whether the indices conform to most "priors" in pair-wise comparisons, and in ranks. Table 10.1 lists the average value of political and civil liberties (1 lowest and 7 highest) for 1973–1992 for selected countries. The most free country in Africa is Mauritius (5.8) with Botswana (5.6) only slightly behind. The least free is Burundi (1.4) with Kenya (2.8) at a higher level and Nigeria (3.4) even higher. The results for Latin America also seem

Freedom and economic growth: a virtuous cycle? 207

Table 10.1. *Political and civil liberties, 1973–1992 – selected countries*

Country	Average PCL
Africa	
Botswana	5.57
Burundi	1.43
Kenya	2.80
Mauritius	5.78
Nigeria	3.35
East Asia	
China	1.66
Indonesia	2.82
Malaysia	4.30
Middle East	
Egypt	3.22
Malta	6.13
Syria	1.65
Latin America	
Costa Rica	7.00
Haiti	2.07
Jamaica	4.20
South Asia	
India	5.43
Pakistan	3.28
Sri Lanka	4.85

Notes: Figures refer to the average of political and civil liberties for the time period 1973–1992. Both the political liberty and civil liberty indices are ranked from 1 (worst) to 7 (best). These indices are reversed from the original (Gastil) where 1 is best and 7 is worst. See Appendix 10.III for data for other countries.
Source: Gastil 1987.

plausible – Haiti (2.1) with low freedom and Costa Rica (7.0) a free country with "maximum" freedom.

Economic freedom

Three measures of economic freedom are used in this chapter. One measure pertains to openness to the international *goods* market; the second pertains to openness to the international *capital* market; and the third pertains to the openness of the domestic capital market. Unfortunately, comparative data on other important aspects of internal economic freedom (e.g., freedom of labor movement, unionization, effectiveness of minimum wages, licensing procedures, etc.) are not available.

208   *Surjit S. Bhalla*

However, it is likely that the three measures used are correlated with excluded aspects of internal economic freedom.

Economic openness

Openness to world markets is a *subset* of economic freedom. The more economically open a society, the more economic freedom is likely to be present. As an agent, one should be free to import, export, manufacture, and consume tradable goods at *international* prices. Thus, in a completely open society, the domestic price level for tradables should be equivalent to the world price level, exclusive of taxes and transportation costs. The hypothesized relationship of economic freedom (openness) with growth is straightforward. When policies allow domestic prices to move towards international prices, the increase in the efficiency of resource allocation, and in the appropriateness of technology adoption, allows economic growth to accelerate. In other words, movement towards openness allows "catch-up" to proceed at a faster pace. This phenomenon can be reflected through use of a variable which measures the *change* in the relative prices of tradable goods – the relative price being the domestic price of tradables, in constant dollars, relative to the international price of tradables, in constant dollars. As a crude proxy, the US price of tradables is taken as a reference international price.[17] (See Appendix I for further details.)

Black market premium on domestic currency

An additional measure of economic freedom (and first used as such by Scully and Slottje 1991, and World Bank 1991, is the black market premium on a country's *official* exchange rates. This variable can be thought of as a proxy for freedom to move financial capital across borders. Such data are available on an annual basis from the *Pick's Currency Yearbook*. Black market premia can reflect distortions in the exchange rate. It can also reflect the presence of exchange controls and controls on imports – all variables connected with economic rights. In addition, however, black market premia can reflect short-term political uncertainty. Given this caveat, black market premia is used (as a second measure) to reflect degrees of economic liberty.

Confucian dummy

The East Asian economies have enjoyed spectacular growth over the last three decades and Section 4 discusses some of the oft-cited reasons

Freedom and economic growth: a virtuous cycle? 209

for this "miraculous" performance. There are six countries – China, China (Taiwan), Hong Kong, Japan, Singapore, and South Korea – that form part of East Asia and share a common cultural "Confucian" heritage.[18] There is considerable evidence (see the literature cited in World Bank 1993) to suggest that these six countries also enjoyed, in parallel to their common Confucian heritage, common economic realities over the last three decades. For various economic criteria – *saving rates, investment rates, positive (and competitive) real interest rates, low inflation rates, financial market development* – all the six countries rank in the top tenth or top fifth of the developing countries. For example, *each* of the six countries had an average savings rate above 28 percent for the time period 1973–1987. High saving rates (and other factors) can (and do) influence growth. Exceptional performance on several economic factors like savings, inflation, etc., are likely to be the result of well-developed *domestic financial markets*.

Unfortunately, for each domestic financial markets variable, there are several countries for which such data are missing. Hence, use of individual variables to capture this effect is not feasible. Instead, a short-cut and rough proxy for relative development of domestic financial markets is through the use of the Confucian dummy variable.

The parallel between the black market premium and Confucian dummy is straightforward. The former reflects restrictions on capital seeking the highest return internationally; the latter is indicative of whether capital is allowed to seek the highest return in the domestic market. Thus, use of a Confucian dummy (one if the country is one of the six East Asian economies mentioned above, zero otherwise) is a convenient proxy for greater internal economic freedom and/or an economic environment that facilitates financial development.

As with all *proxies*, other interpretations of the above three economic freedom variables are possible. For example, the black market premium could be narrowly construed as reflecting price distortions; the economic openness variable as reflecting the maintenance of an overvalued exchange rate; and the Confucian dummy as reflecting cultural differences. What makes the first two measures reasonable economic freedom proxies is the contention that such distortions/overvaluations could not be maintained for long time periods *without* an extensive system of controls, i.e., without restraining economic freedom. What makes the Confucian dummy an *economic freedom variable* is its extremely high correlation with variables which reflect development of the domestic financial market.

While some measurement error is possible, the maintained hypothesis is that the three measures of economic freedom do capture the

210 Surjit S. Bhalla

underlying reality. The measure of economic openness is a summary of the *change* in price distortions of tradables, i.e., the change in the relative price of a large number of commodities. Partial adjustments to this measure – off-setting tariffs and subsidies on some goods – are unlikely to be significant. Analogously, the black market premium variable is not a measure prevailing in a given year, nor is it an average of values over several years. Rather, it is a constructed dichotomous variable, with a broad classification, i.e., countries are in a zero black market premium category if their premia is in the bottom 25 percent of the developing countries considered (in reality this corresponds to a fifteen-year average premia of less than 6 percent), and one otherwise.

Perhaps the most convincing reason to use the black market premia as a measure of economic freedom (along with, and analogously, the relative price-based measure of openness, and the Confucian dummy) is because it accurately reflects aspects of economic control prevailing in the economy. This was first elaborated upon by Hayek (1944: 92, italics mine):

The extent of control over all life that economic control confers is nowhere better illustrated than in the field of foreign exchanges. Nothing would at first seem to affect private life *less* than a state control of the dealings in foreign exchange, and most people will regard its introduction with complete indifference. Yet the experience of most Continental countries has taught thoughtful people to regard this step as the decisive advance on the path to totalitarianism and the suppression of individual liberty . . . Once the individual is no longer free to travel, no longer free to buy foreign books or journals, once all the means of foreign contact can be restricted to those of whom official opinion approves or for whom it is regarded as necessary, the effective control of opinion is much greater than that ever exercised by any of the absolutist governments of the seventeenth and eighteenth centuries.

Economic performance – selected dependent variables

Five variables are used to measure various aspects of economic performance – three reflect income improvement while two reflect improvement in social sectors. The income variables are: per capita income growth (in constant 1987 dollars at official exchange rates), per capita income growth in PPP dollars à la Summers and Heston (1991), and (TFPG).[19] The two social indicators are declines in infant mortality and increases in secondary school enrollment.[20]

SECTION 4: THE EXCEPTIONAL CONFUCIAN (EAST ASIAN) EXPERIENCE

It is extremely important for growth models (especially those pertaining to capture the reality of developing countries) to specifically account

Freedom and economic growth: a virtuous cycle? 211

for the divergent, and seemingly extreme, behavior of the Confucian countries. This can be conveniently done so via the use of a dichotomous variable. Use of this variable achieves two purposes – first, it helps to achieve an unbiased estimate of the impact of the *other* included variables, and, second, its coefficient can indicate the magnitude of "excess" growth still left unexplained by the estimated model. As the rest of this section will demonstrate, *non-use* of the Confucian dummy can lead to possibly *erroneous* evaluations of the determinants of growth.

The Confucian classification is useful because it alerts one to the dangers of basing *general* observations on growth on the *specific* experience of six countries which share one, or several, common economic phenomena. Explanations based exclusively on these countries are liable to blow up in the face of the analysts. The reason is simple – almost *any* factor can be "successfully" shown to be an important explanator as long as it was somewhat common to the Confucian growth experience. Econometrically speaking, this mishap occurs because of inadequate attention to a seemingly gargantuan identification problem.

Inadequate attention to identification has meant that analysts have "found" *several* important explanators for the East-Asian "miracle". A brief description of each explanation follows.

(i) Authoritarianism Excepting Hong Kong and Japan, the EAC countries have had non-free political regimes through most of the development period, 1960–1990. It is an observed reality that all these countries have grown at growth rates above 5.5 percent, 1960–1990. Thus, some casual observers have conjectured that perhaps the discipline of authoritarianism is a prerequisite for growth now and freedom later.

The above reasoning is fraught with problems. The most important problem may be definitional – the observed negative relationship is not between freedom and growth, but rather between a type of government (dictatorship) and growth. Further, in these countries relatively *small amounts of political freedom* have coexisted with relatively *large amounts of economic freedom*. This makes any judgments about the relationship between freedom *per se* and growth problematical, to say the least. The causal relationship to be tested is not between authoritarianism and growth but between a complex freedom structure and successful economic performance. It is important, therefore, to adequately identify the contribution of the separate channels of influence of freedom on growth – a task attempted in the next section.

(ii) Land reform A more equal initial distribution of land (wealth) made agricultural productivity grow which fueled growth in

212   *Surjit S. Bhalla*

the urban centers. Four countries – Japan, Korea, China and Taiwan (China) – had land reform in their early development period.

(iii) Managed growth   This is one of the most popular explanations, and has gained currency lately with the US Administration seemingly wanting to emulate the EAC growth experience by following the managed growth prescription. The premise is that government involvement in the private sector helps facilitate rapid growth. The assumption is that many more winners than losers are picked by the bureaucrats. Support for this argument is obtained from the robust empirical observation that all EAC countries (except Hong Kong) had managed government. See Wade (1990).

(iv) High savings rates   A "taste" for higher savings, and investment, has made rapid growth possible. All EAC countries (except Korea in the sixties) have had significantly higher savings, investment, and growth.

(v) Education   The new growth theory's emphasis on externalities to education has revived interest in the explanation that EAC countries grew well because in the early sixties they had significantly higher levels of education. The sample of sixty-eight developing countries for which education data were constructed by Bhalla, Lau, and Louat (see Appendix II) shows an average education level of the labor force of 2.5 years in 1960, compared with 4.7 years for the EAC countries and 2.3 years for the non-EAC countries.

(vi) Female education   As argued in the *World Development Report* (World Bank 1991: chapters 2 and 3), Bhalla and Gill (1991), and Gill and Bhalla (1992)) the more important externality is one due to higher *female* levels of education. In 1960, the average level of female education was 1.9 years, with EAC countries registering 3.9 years and non-EAC countries 1.8 years. Bhalla, Kharas, and Nabi (1993) advance the argument that female education and increased female participation in the urban labor force was an important explanator of the Malaysian growth experience. Indeed, they suggest that export-led growth was often a case of female-led growth.

(vii) Confucianism   The reasoning is based on culture – the Confucian countries grew faster because of their cultural philosophy. This view has many followers, and many still evaluate Japanese success (both past and expected future growth) in these non-economic terms.

Freedom and economic growth: a virtuous cycle? 213

All the arguments, except perhaps the one pertaining to Confucianism, have been seriously offered in the literature – and all have merit. It is unclear on a heuristic basis as to which of the above seven explanations should be accepted. Especially since each explanation involves at least one of the three fallacies noted below in interpreting the EAC growth experience.

Fallacies about Confucianism, authoritarianism, and growth

There are three major fallacies in proffering the East Asian Confucian experience in support of a "model of growth." The fallacies are – (i) interpreting a common factor amongst the Confucian countries as an important distinguishing variable; (ii) ignoring the differing experiences within the same common factor experience; and (iii) generalizing from the Confucian experience, i.e., ignoring probability.

The *first fallacy* is an act of near tautology. Find a factor common to East Asian countries, and offer that as an explanator. The popularity of this method was outlined above with the discussion of *seven* explanations for the "unique" East Asian experience. Since nothing succeeds like success, any common factor among the EAC can be construed as *the* factor responsible for "excess" growth.

The *second fallacy* pertaining to East Asia is that the conclusion – less freedom equals more growth – is more in the nature of an act of commission by omission. Both North and South Korea faced an equal, and uncertain future, after the Korean war. Yet few observers argue that North Korea has been helped by authoritarianism.[21] Ditto the case with East and West Germany. Some have argued (see Wade 1990) that it is the *specific* kind of authoritarianism (and market intervention) practiced by the East Asian economies that has led them to success. Since this kind of authoritarianism is presumed to be *sui generis*, the reasoning is too close to a tautology to be of comfort.

Analogous to the South Korea – North Korea example is the case of pre-reform/post-reform authoritarian China. Over the 1960–1991 time period the Chinese economy registered an average growth rate of 6.0 percent, and a per capita growth of 4.2 percent.[22] These statistics are indicative of spectacular performance – hence, the argument that authoritarianism in China has not been costly. One can argue that the Chinese path to development via "positive" authoritarianism is worthy of emulation. However, if one looks at the pre-reform period, 1960–1977, the average growth rate was 4 percent; post-reform, 1978–1991, the economy grew at more than twice the rate at 8.4 percent. This

214   *Surjit S. Bhalla*

confounds the dilemma, and makes one wish for precision in the measure of authoritarianism, i.e., which authoritarianism should one applaud – pre-reform or post-reform? It may be the case that the reforms contributed to success. If so, what evidence is there that political reforms are *harmful* to growth? It is manifestly the case that China did not become free with market-oriented reforms. However, it *is* the case that reforms brought *greater* freedom. In terms of gains in economic freedom, the increase was large. Thus, the Chinese economy data are strongly supportive of the argument that greater freedom leads to greater, not lesser, growth.

The *third fallacy* involving the miracle growth of the EACs is more serious – the problem lies with probability. Since authoritarianism was present in the EACs, and *all* of them grew well, a simple probabilistic leap would indicate that authoritarianism is good for growth. However, for every single Confucian authoritarian success, there are at least ten non-Confucian authoritarian failures.[23] For example, a little discussed fact is that the African continent has had both a considerably lower level of freedom *and* a lower level of growth. For the period 1973–1990, sub-Saharan Africa averaged a political and civil liberties (PCL) average of 2.5 and an average per capita growth rate of –0.1 percent per annum; in contrast, the Confucian countries averaged a higher PCL level of 3.9 and an average per capita growth of 4.9 percent per annum. Within sub-Saharan Africa, the example of Botswana is noteworthy – it had a high PCL average of 5.6, and a high per capita growth of 7.4 per cent per annum.

As Raaj Sah (1991) argues, the conclusion that authoritarianism is *bad* for growth is to be expected on *a priori* grounds. "A less centralized society has the advantage of a greater diversification of its performance across a larger number of preceptors. This is because diversification here dilutes the impact of the ability, *or the lack thereof*, of each preceptor on the aggregate societal performance" (71, italics added).

SECTION 5: RESULTS

The growth model outlined in Section 2 is tested with data from a large sample (over ninety) of countries for the time period 1973 to 1990. The beginning year 1973 is dictated by the availability of Gastil data on political and civil liberties. (However, the results are not sensitive to the choice of a larger time period, 1960–1990; see below.) Table 10.2 reports the results for three specifications of the model estimated both as OLS and two-stage least squares (TSLS).

The three specifications pertain to (i) a (misspecified) preliminary model without any regional dummies; (ii) model in (i) plus five regional

Freedom and economic growth: a virtuous cycle? 215

Table 10.2. *Growth and political and economic freedom – basic model (OLS and TSLS)*

Variables	Ordinary least squares			Two-stage least squares		
	Basic model			Basic model		
Constant	4.74	5.74	4.89	5.04	4.64	5.07
	(2.52)	(3.31)	(1.79)	(2.33)	(2.10)	(2.88)
Log of initial 1972	−0.76	−0.64	−0.86	−1.03	−0.84	−1.03
per capita income	(2.22)	(1.97)	(2.89)	(2.45)	(2.05)	(3.02)
Mean years of	0.56	0.13	0.37	0.20	−0.06	0.12
education in 1972	(3.21)	(0.91)	(2.40)	(0.71)	(0.24)	(0.54)
Freedom						
Black market	−1.82	−1.51	−1.43	−2.11	−1.54	−1.57
premium (0, 1)	(3.57)	(3.30)	(3.25)	(3.49)	(2.98)	(3.23)
Economic openness	0.28	0.16	0.25	0.43	0.30	0.34
	(1.93)	(1.24)	(2.03)	(2.33)	(1.54)	(2.34)
Political and civil	0.38	0.40	0.53	1.34	1.15	1.14
liberties	(1.74)	(2.08)	(2.79)	(2.29)	(1.58)	(2.52)
Confucian countries			3.64			3.98
(0,1)			(4.68)			(4.57)
Regional dummies	No	Yes	No	No	Yes	No
Adj. R-squared	0.41	0.64	0.57	0.22	0.55	0.49
RMSE	1.90	1.47	1.62	2.18	1.66	1.76
# of obs.	68	68	68	68	68	68

Notes: dependent variable – per capita income growth, 1987 constant dollars. The five regional dummies are (i) sub-Saharan Africa; (ii) Latin America; (iii) East Asia; (iv) Europe, Middle East and North Africa; and (v) South Asia. The Confucian dummy consists of the following six countries: China, China (Taiwan), Hong Kong, Japan, South Korea, and Singapore. For definition of the various variables, see Appendix 10.I.

dummies and (iii) the basic model which is the preliminary model in (i) and an economic freedom (quasi-regional) dummy for the "Confucian" countries.

The rationale for presenting the preliminary OLS model is that it most closely corresponds to the specifications reported in the literature, i.e., OLS without regional dummies. Inclusion of the regional dummies is to see if any of the coefficients are affected, i.e., presence of omitted variable bias.

As Table 10.2 shows, the results are extremely robust across the three specifications, and whether or not instrument variables were used. In the "worst" equation (TSLS with regional dummies), the political and civil liberties variable is significant at the 11 percent level. The magni-

216   *Surjit S. Bhalla*

tude of this variable stays relatively constant at around 0.4 for the OLS regressions, and 1.15 for the TSLS regressions. The three economic freedom variables are also generally significant across equations.

Another robust result pertains to the coefficient for initial education. Once simultaneity considerations are introduced into the equation, the coefficient of this variable drops by more than half (from 0.56 to 0.1 and under) *and* it becomes insignificant. The only occasion in which initial education is significant is in the misspecified OLS regression. The insignificance of initial education in the fully specified model suggests that the oft-cited result of externalities to initial education (Romer 1986; Lucas 1988; and Barro 1991) might have been caused by the correlation of initial education with economic and/or political freedom. The lack of significance of initial education in the growth equation in no manner implies that human capital does not play an important role in economic development; but it does imply that externalities to *initial* education are not present or as pronounced as claimed by the "new" growth theory.

There are two alternate ways in which the role of *initial* education in affecting future growth can be viewed. First, that education acts via the political (and economic) freedom variables. Second, and as strongly supported by the results reported in Table 10.5, initial education has an important role when accompanied by large doses of economic freedom, e.g., relatively high education can be taken advantage of via the successful introduction of foreign technology.

Apart from the six specifications reported in Table 10.2, twelve others are reported as part of a sensitivity analysis in Tables 10.3 and 10.4. The regressions are reported for the sake of completeness; the point estimates reported below generally refer to the basic model (final TSLS regression in Table 10.2). The sensitivity results strongly support the following conclusion: the joint specification of *both economic and political freedom* variables is what yields the markedly different, and robust, results obtained in this chapter.

(i)   Political and civil liberties

A strong, and consistent, result is that political and civil liberties matter. The effect varies in magnitude (from 0.7 to 1.4 in the growth rate equations) but is (almost) invariably significant at the 5 percent level. The coefficient magnitude implies that countries can increase their growth rates by about 1 per cent per annum, ceteris paribus, for each one point move in political freedom.[24] Or that a one standard deviation change (1.5 points in PCL) improves the average annual growth rate by 1.5 percent. Further, the positive and significant effect of political freedom occurs *after* the effect of three different economic freedom vari-

Freedom and economic growth: a virtuous cycle? 217

Table 10.3. *Growth and political and economic freedom – sensitivity analysis (a)*

Variables	Regressions					
	1	2	3	4	5	6
Constant	7.93	5.15	4.21	4.47	5.91	7.36
	(3.14)	(3.32)	(2.80)	(2.94)	(2.68)	(3.38)
Log of initial 1972	−1.33	−1.03	−0.80	−1.49	−1.23	−1.38
per capita income	(2.01)	(3.35)	(2.76)	(4.71)	(2.32)	(2.99)
Mean years of education	0.12	0.02	0.16	0.07	0.05	0.02
in 1972	(0.54)	(0.10)	(1.03)	(0.36)	(0.18)	(0.12)
Freedom						
Black market premium	−1.89	−1.43	−1.36	−1.20	−1.74	−1.86
(0,1)	(2.17)	(3.44)	(3.31)	(2.75)	(2.31)	(3.11)
Economic openness	0.30	0.36	0.29	0.24	0.41	0.24
	(1.99)	(2.97)	(2.21)	(1.79)	(2.16)	(1.79)
Political and civil liberties	0.95	1.23	0.93	1.20	1.34	1.00
	(1.40)	(3.35)	(2.96)	(2.99)	(2.36)	(2.26)
Confucian countries	4.01	4.40	3.38	3.10	3.77	3.87
(0,1)	(2.46)	(5.78)	(4.98)	(3.94)	(3.32)	(3.37)
Additional variable (1)				0.16	0.02	0.16
				(3.46)	(0.14)	(1.18)
Additional variable (2)						0.02
						(0.45)
Adj. r-squared	0.24	0.47	0.52	0.61	0.46	0.53
RMSE	1.95	1.63	1.40	1.55	1.88	1.64
# of obs.	31	86	68	68	53	54

Notes: see notes to Table 10.2. The basic model used is the two-stage least squares model reported as the final regression in Table 10.2. This model is estimated for the time period 1973–1990 and uses data for sixty-eight countries defined as developing in 1960 (including Japan). The educational attainment data is from Bhalla, Lau, and Louat (1990). The per capita initial income in 1972, and the per capita growth rate, are calculated on the basis of World Bank/IMF data on constant dollar values. Any modification to this structure is reported as part of sensitivity analysis below.

Regressions in Table 10.3

1 Uses only thirty-one observations which have original (rather than imputed) data on the relative price of tradables, or economic openness.
2 Uses data on eighteen developed countries which increases the sample to eighty-six observations.
3 Uses data from 1960 onwards, rather than 1973 onwards as with the basic model. This estimation has the drawback that the political and civil liberties data for 1960–1990 is assumed to be the same as that from 1973–1990.
4 Uses the share of investment in GDP (IGDP) as an additional explanatory variable.
5 Assumes that IGDP is not exogenous and uses IGDP from 1960–1972 as an instrument for IGDP 1973–1990.
6 Uses the investment (equipment and non-equipment) data from De Long and Summers (1991) as additional explanatory variables. These investment data are assumed to be exogenous (as do De Long and Summers) to the growth process.

218   *Surjit S. Bhalla*

Table 10.4 *Growth and political and economic freedom – sensitivity analysis (b)*

Variables	Regressions					
	1	2	3	4	5	6
Constant	9.30	4.84	2.71	4.59	1.82	5.01
	(2.88)	(1.40)	(1.86)	(2.58)	(0.72)	(2.96)
Log of initial 1972 per	−1.95	−0.80	−0.78	−0.86	−0.63	−0.98
capita income	(1.45)	(1.33)	(2.78)	(2.80)	(1.55)	(2.83)
Mean years of education	0.09	−0.08	0.07	0.06	−0.61	0.20
in 1972	(0.37)	(0.29)	(0.38)	(0.32)	(1.15)	(0.74)
Freedom						
Black market premium	−1.95	−1.44	−1.32	−1.30	−1.26	−1.53
(0,1)	(1.45)	(2.66)	(3.29)	(2.52)	(1.88)	(3.21)
Economic openness	0.09	0.50	0.12	0.32	0.46	0.31
	(0.44)	(2.75)	(0.96)	(1.91)	(2.29)	(2.06)
Political and civil liberties	1.01	1.25	0.73	0.93	1.96	0.95
	(1.44)	(2.07)	(1.97)	(2.18)	(2.05)	(1.64)
Confucian countries (0,1)	3.98	4.84	1.71	4.59	5.40	3.88
	(2.45)	(3.81)	(2.37)	(4.46)	(3.52)	(4.48)
Additional variable (1)	−3.70					
	(0.76)					
Adj. R-squared	0.48	0.29	0.18	0.47	0.18	0.53
RMSE	1.76	2.03	1.45	1.83	2.13	1.69
# of obs.	29	68	68	77	62	68

Notes: see notes to Table 10.3.
Regressions in Table 10.4.

1 Uses inequality in income distribution around 1972 (Gini coefficient, Fields 1989) as an additional explanatory variable.
2 Uses the latest data from Summers and Heston on purchasing power parity basis (growth rates and initial income in 1972).
3 Uses TFPG (calculated from production function estimation, see World Bank (1991) and Bhalla (1992)) as the dependent *variable*.
4 Uses the educational attainment data as reported by Barro and Lee (1992). As reported in the text, use of the new Barro and Lee (1993b) data does not affect the results.
5 Uses the educational attainment data as reported by Nehru, Swanson, and Dubey (1995).
6 The instrument used in the basic model to identify political and civil liberties was based on colonial heritage. This variable classified British colonialism into two: sub-Saharan Africa and non-sub-Saharan Africa. In this regression, British colonialism appears as a single variable.

Freedom and economic growth: a virtuous cycle? 219

Table 10.5 *Inter-active effect of education and freedom on growth*

	Low economic freedom (BMP > 15.41)	High economic freedom (BMP <= 5.41)
Low education (Educ <= 3.16)	−0.33 (18)	0.59 (16)
High education (Educ > 3.16)	0.47 (14)	3.60 (20)
	Low economic freedom (Eqinv <= 2% of GDP)	High economic freedom (Eqinv > 2% of GDP)
Low education (Educ <= 3.16)	0.16 (19)	0.26 (7)
High education (Educ > 3.16)	0.18 (10)	2.72 (18)
	Low political freedom (PCL <= 3.24)	High political freedom (PCL > 3.24)
Low education (Educ >= 3.16)	−0.35 (25)	1.35 (9)
High education (Educ > 3.16)	1.87 (9)	2.22 (25)

Notes: all the freedom variables are separated into low and high categories on the basis of the median observation for the countries selected. The education level is the years of education in the initial year, 1972. Equipment investment data are from De Long and Summers (1993). The figures represent the average per capita growth rate of the countries in the sample for the period 1973–1990. The number of countries is indicated in the parentheses.

ables have been incorporated – this suggests that the relationship between political freedom and growth is neither accidental nor illusory.

(ii) *Economic freedom*

(ii.a) Change in the relative price of tradables This economic freedom variable is also a measure of openness. That openness contributes to growth is *now* part of the conventional wisdom. The most popular measure of openness has been export growth, which critics have claimed is inappropriate because of circularity or simultaneity considerations. Given the *unique* price-based construction of this openness measure – movement of tradables prices towards international prices – and

220 Surjit S. Bhalla

lack of any simultaneity of this variable with growth, the results strongly reinforce the notion that a significant determinant of success is economic openness. The results suggest that each sustained 10 percent increase in openness (over approx. ten to fifteen years) leads to an annual increase of 0.3 per cent increase in per capita income growth.

(ii.b) Presence of black market premium This economic freedom variable is consistently significant. Its magnitude is relatively unaffected by the choice of economic growth proxy or education proxy (Tables 10.3 and 10.4). The robust result is that economies with few external capital controls (average black market premium below 6 percent) grow at about a 1.5 per cent faster rate.[25]

(ii.c) Confucianism The results on internal economic freedom pertaining to domestic capital markets (Confucian dummy) are *invariant* with respect to the different variables, or specifications. The robust result is that per capita economic growth during 1973–1990 was higher by 3 to 4 percentage points in these countries. TFPG, however, was only higher by about 1.7 percent (regression 3, Table 10.4), suggesting that higher use of factors (capital) accounted for almost 60 percent of the extra "miracle" growth in the Confucian countries.

(iii)   Convergence

The results confirm a strong tendency towards convergence – initial per capita income is consistently, and significantly, negative in the regressions. A coefficient of 1.03 (regression 6, Table 10.2) suggests that convergence takes place at the rate of 1.2 percent per year – a result somewhat less than the Barro and Lee (1993a) result of convergence at 3.1 percent per year.[26] One possible explanation for this difference could be due to the time period of analysis – Barro and Lee evaluate growth from 1960 onwards while the analysis here is for data post-1972. Though not reported, it is the case that the coefficient on (log) income per capita increases once freedom (political and economic) variables are introduced into the equation. For example, the coefficient of log per capita income increases from 0.71 (without freedom variables) to 1.03 (with freedom variables). This change translates into an increase in the speed of convergence from 0.8 percent per annum to 1.2 percent per annum. Thus, another explanation is that Barro and Lee overestimate the role of convergence because of misspecification, i.e., exclusion of political and economic freedom variables.

Freedom and economic growth: a virtuous cycle?

(iv)   Education externalities

Very little support for education externalities, as typically estimated, are obtained. Regardless of which one of three educational attainment variables are used, initial education is *not* significant. But as noted earlier, initial education likely affects subsequent growth in an *indirect* manner, e.g., via political and economic freedom (economic openness – see below).

In the discussion about the theoretical basis for the growth model estimated in this chapter, an interaction effect between education and openness was alluded to. Estimation of an interaction term with conventional methods (e.g., a multiplicative term involving openness and education) was inconclusive – the coefficients had the right sign, but were insignificant (possibly due to multicolinearity). However, if the sample is stratified into open/not open economies according to the black market premium,[27] and the De Long and Summers equipment investment variable (which is likely to be a good proxy for openness since capital goods were mostly imported by the developing countries), then two results are obtained: (i) education is *not* significant in explaining relative growth rates among non-open countries; and (ii) education is somewhat significant in explaining relative growth rates among open economies. The movement of a country from a low education–low openness to a high education–high openness results in 3.93 percent and 2.56 percent gain in per capita growth depending on whether black market premium or equipment investment is used as an openness variable (Table 10.5). Relatively less of this gain results in a movement from low education to high education, while a larger percentage of the gain results from greater openness by itself. The logic behind these results is straightforward – only if a country is open, can it expect to fully take advantage (via education) of foreign technology. In a closed economy, education has only limited use.[28] These results also help explain the consistently high magnitude (around 4 percent) and significance (t-statistic greater than 3) of the Confucian dummy in the regressions reported in Tables 10.2, 10.3, and 10.4. Recall that these countries score high on education and economic freedom during the early stages of their development. It is (likely) not a coincidence that their *estimated excess growth is not much different than the excess observed due to the joint presence of high education and high economic freedom.*

Sensitivity analysis

As well documented by Levine and Renelt (1992), growth regressions are extremely suspect to alternate specifications. Biases in estimation

222 *Surjit S. Bhalla*

can occur due to simultaneity, measurement error, or specification error. The use of the institutional heritage variable should correct for simultaneous equation bias; errors due to measurement or omitted variables can be assessed via alternative specifications.

The "basic" model used is the TSLS model reported as the final regression in Table 10.2. Tables 10.3 and 10.4 report on *twelve* separate specifications. *These specifications involve different dependent and independent variables.* Regardless of the specifications, the results are very similar, i.e., freedom variables (political and economic) retain their significance, and the education externality variable, educational attainment in the initial year, is never significant. Details follow.

(i) No imputation of missing observations

Data on economic openness are available for only thirty-one countries, while data for all other variables are available for a minimum of sixty-eight developing countries. The best subset regression technique (see Kmenta 1990: 379–388) was used to impute values for openness for countries with missing data (regressions in Table 10.2). This technique involves some assumptions and it is of interest therefore to estimate the model on the reduced, "no missing data" sample. Regression 1, Table 10.3, contains the results. Little change is observed in the magnitude of the coefficients. Standard errors on all the coefficients are larger, and the PCL variable is significant at the 17 percent level.

(ii) Estimation inclusive of developed countries

As emphasized in Section 3, the growth model estimated is applicable mostly to developing countries. The growth literature, however, is agnostic about the inclusion of developed country data. Regression 2, Table 10.3, includes data on eighteen developed countries in addition to the sixty-eight developing countries. Almost no change is observed in either the magnitude or significance of *any* of the coefficients.

(iii) Larger time period, 1960–1990

The model can be estimated for the time period 1960–1990. However, no data for the period 1960–1972 are available for political and civil liberties. If the average level of political and civil liberties for 1973–1990 are assumed to be broadly similar to that prevailing for the period 1960–1990 (a questionable assumption) then the larger time-period regression can be estimated. This regression is reported as regression 3, Table

Freedom and economic growth: a virtuous cycle? 223

10.3. Some change is observed in the magnitude of the coefficients; however, the significance levels stay similar to the reference regression (time period 1973–1990). The education variable retains its insignificance, and the political freedom and economic freedom variables remain highly significant.

(iv)   Investment as a determinant of growth

Most researchers (e.g. Romer 1990; Mankiw Romer, and Weil 1990; Helliwell 1990; De Long and Summers 1991 include some type of an *investment* variable in the growth equation. While investment undoubtedly affects growth, there is a strong possibility of reverse causation, i.e., higher growth leads to greater investment. Regressions 4 and 5, Table 10.3, report the results with investment share in the time period 1973–1990 as an exogenous variable, and as an endogenous variable, respectively. (Regression 5 uses the investment share in the earlier time period, 1960–1972, as an identifying variable.) Whether investment is assumed exogenous (as done by the other studies) or endogenous, little difference is observed in either the magnitude, or significance, of the variables in the basic model. However, what is revealing is that the investment variable becomes highly *insignificant* once the exogeneity assumption is relaxed (regression 5, Table 10.3).

(v)   Equipment investment

De Long and Summers (1991) argue convincingly that what is appropriate in a growth equation is not a variable representing total investment, but rather the magnitude of a particular type of investment – namely, equipment investment. Regression 6, Table 10.3, uses their data on equipment, and non-equipment investment. Like other alternative specifications, little difference is observed in either the magnitude or significance of the freedom variables (e.g., magnitude of PCL changes marginally from 1.14 to 1.0, its t-statistic from 2.53 to 2.26). However, unlike the De Long and Summers specification, the equipment investment variable now becomes insignificant (t-statistic of 1.18). This is suggestive of the fact that equipment investment is a reasonable proxy for economic openness.

(vi)   Effect of inequality on growth

There is a revived interest in the relationship between growth and inequality. However, unlike the earlier interest in the Kuznet's curve or

224   *Surjit S. Bhalla*

the effect of growth on inequality, interest now is with the reverse effect (see Persson and Tabellini 1994; and Alesina and Rodrik 1993). Regression 1, Table 10.4, reports the results for a regression with inequality in the early seventies, as represented by a Gini coefficient (data are from Fields 1989, and are the same as used by Alesina and Rodrik). Again, the results pertaining to the basic variables are relatively unaffected (but note that this regression has only twenty-nine observations). However, initial inequality appears to be insignificant in affecting subsequent growth – coefficient of −3.70 (correct sign) but a t-value of only 0.76. (Additional results [not reported here] suggest that the inequality variable is highly sensitive to the inclusion/exclusion of the East Asian economies. See discussion on Confucian fallacies above.)

(vii)   *Alternative dependent variable – TFPG*

The results for the effect of freedom on TFPG are similar with their effect on per capita growth – regression 2, Table 10.4 (see World Bank 1991 and Bhalla 1992 for details on the estimation of TFPG). The only variable whose significance changes from the basic specification is economic openness – its t-statistic falls to 0.96 and its magnitude to 0.12. However, both the other two economic freedom variables – black market premium and Confucian economies – as well as political freedom remain significant. The magnitude on the Confucian dummy declines significantly to 1.71 from 3.98 suggesting that larger use of inputs, particularly capital, caused the contribution of this variable to be significantly higher in the growth equation. This result suggests that freedom leads to greater capital accumulation as well as greater productivity. The coefficient of initial education, like the result on economic growth, is insignificant.

(viii)   *Alternative dependent variable – output growth as measured by PPP*

Most of the empirical literature on the "new" growth theory has eschewed the use of conventional constant dollar data on growth and instead used the Summers and Heston (1988, 1991) estimates on per capita growth. The pioneering estimates on PPP are invaluable when the goal is to compare *levels* of income across countries. It is not clear how much *extra* information the PPP *growth* rates provide, since an important input into the computation of PPP growth rates are the constant dollar growth rates themselves. Further, the PPP growth rate calculations are hampered by the omission of extra "new" data on several

Freedom and economic growth: a virtuous cycle? 225

economies. For example, in 1970 only twenty-two countries were sampled for new information, with only one country in Africa; in 1975, the coverage increased to sixty countries, but only three of these were in Africa. In 1980, the coverage was increased to sixty-two countries, with fifteen countries in Africa. In 1985, the coverage remained large (sixty-two countries) but unfortunately, no countries in Latin America were sampled.

Given this spotty and varied *intertemporal* coverage (the cross-sectional coverage remains exhaustive), the belief is that for *growth* rates one might be better off with the conventional data. However, since PPP growth data have very often been used, regression 3, Table 10.4 reports the results using the latest version of the Summers and Heston data. Again, the results are only marginally different from the alternative constant dollar data regressions. And the coefficient on initial education is still insignificant.

(ix)   *Alternative educational attainment variables*

Models based on two alternative measures of educational attainment, Nehru, Swanson, and Dubey (1993) and Barro and Lee (1992),[29] are reported as regressions 4 and 5 in Table 10.4. Little difference is observed in the results and initial education level still remains insignificant.

Social welfare

Analogous to the growth model, a reduced form model for social welfare changes is as follows:[30]

social welfare change = (initial education, economic growth,
political and civil liberties)   (2)

Two variables of welfare change are considered – infant mortality decline and secondary school enrollment.[31] The time period of analysis is 1973–1990 and the results are reported in Table 10.6. Three results are noteworthy: (a) political and civil liberties are significant in explaining improvements in welfare – the magnitude of the coefficient (approx. 0.2 and 0.1 for mortality and secondary education, respectively) suggests that for each 1 point (17 percent) improvement in political freedom, there is approximately a 17 percent increase in the rate of infant mortality decline, and approximately a 10 percent increase in the rate of secondary educational enrollment; (b) income growth is significant in the infant mortality decline equation but not in explaining

226   *Surjit S. Bhalla*

Table 10.6. *Social welfare change and freedom*

Variables	Infant mortality decline	% secondary school enrollment changes
Constant	−0.93	−2.86
	(2.69)	(12.72)
Per capita income growth	−0.19	0.03
	(2.94)	(0.80)
Mean years of education in 1972	−0.38	0.45
	(4.36)	(8.13)
Average level of PCL	−0.21	0.12
	(1.83)	(1.61)
Adj. r-squared	0.59	0.73
# of obs.	67	66

Notes: dependent variables are the average of the change in the *logistic* of infant mortality, and secondary school enrollment, 1973–1990. The data on mean years of education of the labor force in 1972 are from Bhalla, Lau, and Louat (1990). Data on political and civil liberties are from Gastil (1987), and are the average for the time period 1973–1992.

secondary school enrollment changes; (c) initial education levels are strongly significant in both the equations. The elasticities are also similar at roughly unity.[32] These results suggest that there is an externality to initial education – but it comes about in social welfare changes, rather than in economic growth.

SECTION 6: CONCLUSIONS

The purpose of this study was to empirically address the question "Does freedom lead to improved economic performance?" Analysis of this question involved the suggestion of a "new" growth model; a model which explicitly incorporated the role of political and *economic* freedom in generating growth. The estimation of a model involving political freedom required use of an identification variable to remove the simultaneity bias between freedom and growth. Such a variable, colonial heritage, was offered and successfully used. Three variables for economic freedom: black market premium on domestic currency, movement in the relative price of tradables, and a Confucian dummy representing in large part greater *domestic* capital market freedom (developed financial markets) were also tested.

The results pertaining to the impact of political and economic freedom on economic growth are robust. After controlling for the impact

Freedom and economic growth: a virtuous cycle? 227

of variables like (log) initial per capita income, initial education (*three* different educational attainment series), the variables pertaining to political and economic freedom are positively, and significantly, associated with improvements in economic welfare (measured by *five* different variables).

Data from over ninety countries for the time period 1973–1990 were used; the results, surprisingly, are strongly in favor of the proposition that political and civil liberties, and economic freedom, help improve economic performance. Specifically, if countries are ranked à la Gastil in terms of political and civil liberties into seven categories (with USA as 7 and Burundi as 1) then, empirically, each single point increase in freedom (approximately 17 percent) leads to an increase in per capita growth of 1 percent, and TFPG of 0.7 percent. Note that these effects are partial effects, i.e., after the effects of other variables are removed. Regarding economic freedom, all three variables tested were found to be significant. Lack of black market premium (proxy for open international capital markets) results in a 1.6 percent faster growth rate; each 10 percent (permanent) increase in domestic tradables prices towards international prices results in a 0.2 percent increase in the growth rate.

Inclusion of both economic and political freedom in the growth model helps explain some of the "anomalies" observed by researchers; e.g., if political freedom is important, then why have countries like India, Sri Lanka, and Costa Rica grown at a considerably slower pace than the authoritarian regimes of East Asia. If a growth model has both economic and political freedom, then the mystery resolves itself; i.e., the above democracies all had low economic freedom, and the East Asian dictatorships had high economic freedom. The partial ceteris paribus effect of political freedom (and economic freedom) remains strongly positive.

Estimation of this "new" model also helps in explaining the externality to education result obtained in recent research. In particular, it is found that once freedom variables are incorporated, the positive externality effect of initial education becomes *insignificant*. One possible explanation of this "different" and unexpected result is that in contrast to studies that find initial education to be a significant determinant of future growth, this study incorporates economic freedom variables in the model. And the presence of these variables likely renders the coefficient on initial education to be insignificant.

At a theoretical level, it was suggested that education is likely to play an important role in the appropriate selection, and transfer, of foreign technology. This view of education is supported by the data – while

228   *Surjit S. Bhalla*

education by itself does not yield increasing returns (as claimed by recent results on the "new" growth theory), there is a strong interactive effect between education and economic freedom (economic openness, both domestic and foreign), i.e., the joint presence of education and openness does yield increasing returns.

A simple model relating social welfare (infant mortality decline and increase in secondary school enrollment) to political and civil liberties was also tested. The results suggest that each 1 point increase in freedom leads to a 17 percent faster decline in infant mortality and an 11 percent faster increase in secondary school enrollment.

This chapter has conducted extensive tests, using a large body of data, on the relationship between freedom and welfare. The conclusion is straightforward and against the conventional wisdom – more freedom is unambiguously good for both growth and social development. Since most developing countries (and Eastern Europe) were near the bottom end of the freedom range in 1987, improvement in freedom augurs well for future post-Berlin Wall economic performance. This is in direct contrast to the conventional view that freedom either is unrelated to, or hampers, growth.

The results suggest that economic development is likely to be successful if countries follow the right economic and political policies. In other words, countries should get their prices right, and their politics right. The right policies can be defined *ex ante* – economic policies which allow the maximum freedom to individuals. As a short cut such policies should ensure that domestic tradable prices are close to international tradable prices, investors should be allowed freedom, and exchange rates should be allowed to move freely. The right political policies are ones that provide the maximum freedom to individuals. The short cut to this goal is the provision of a free press and a "free-wheeling" democracy. In conclusion, free markets, and free societies, are the important ingredients to rapid economic development.

Finally, there is a forecast that follows from the above results. In recent years, countries across the developing world – Africa, Latin America, Asia and Eastern Europe – have proceeded to open up their markets and their politics. The education level in most of these countries is relatively high, at least compared to the early sixties and seventies. Thus, the nineties for the less developed countries should be the beginning of sustained and successful economic development. This high growth is likely to result in even more freedom. Growth and freedom can indeed be locked into a virtuous cycle.

Appendix I **Construction of variables**

(i) *Economic growth* Given data on output, population, and labor, per capita and per worker growth rates can easily be derived (time period 1973–1990). The PPP dollar growth rates are based on the Summers and Heston (1991) data (latest set available) and pertain to the time period 1973–1992.

(ii) *PCL* Simple average of the variable reflecting (a) political and (b) civil liberties. The data are from 1973 to 1992.

(iii) *Black market premium* This is a dummy variable which takes on the value of zero if the average premium (defined as the percentage difference between the official and unofficial exchange rates) was less than 6 percent during 1973–1990, and 1 if greater. 6 percent represents approximately the 25th percentile of the distribution of the average premium.

(iv) *Economic openness* It is hypothesized that economic openness is correlated, if not synonymous, with economic liberty. Bhalla and Lau (1992) use this variable in assessing the impact of openness on productivity growth. This measure reflects the movement towards international prices of the tradable goods in an economy. National income series on construction, services and GDP were used to derive an index of tradables (defined as GDP minus Construction minus Services). Actual tradable price data from Kravis *et al.* (1975 and 1980) were used to convert a relative to US *index* series (US is defined as the most open economy) to a relative to US *price* series.

This primary relative price series (call it zo) is used to construct the changes in economic openness series. Three steps are involved. (a) First, percentage changes are calculated and assigned to zo1 if the change was progressive (increase in prices if zo below 1 and decrease in prices if zo above 1); and assigned to zo2 if the change was regressive (decrease in prices if zo below 1 and increase in prices if zo above 1). Note that this assignment means that when zo1 is non-zero zo2 is zero and vice versa. (b) Empirically, the coefficients of zo1 and zo2 are found to be of (statistically) equal magnitude and opposite in sign. (See World Bank 1991: 159; zo1 has a plus sign and zo2 a negative sign.) (c) Consequently, the two effects can be added and the term (zo1 – zo2) yields the change in openness in any given year. (This result is equivalent to the statement that improvement in openness is the same irrespective of whether the relative prices in a country moved from 2 to 1 or from 0.5 to 1). The average of this series yields the economic openness term in Appendix III, and is the value used in the regressions.

(v) *Education of labor force in 1972* Three variables are used (separately) to measure the average education of the labor force in 1972. See Appendix II.

(vi) *TFPG* The definition of productivity growth is straightforward – it is that portion of growth that is "unexplained" by growth in inputs. The inputs considered are physical capital, labor, and land. Construction of physical capital is based on the perpetual inventory method using gross investment data, a depreciation rate of 5 percent, and the assumption that the initial capital stock was zero in 1945. These estimates of capital are then adjusted by a capacity

230   *Surjit S. Bhalla*

utilization rate (derived by the convex hull method) to obtain estimates of utilized capital. Several instruments are then used to obtain an "instrumented" estimate of capital growth. See Bhalla and Lau (1992) for details.

(vii) *Social indicator variables*   Data on infant mortality and secondary school enrollment (percentage) are used and transformed into a logistic. This is done since both infant mortality and secondary school enrollment are subject to a floor (approximately zero) or a ceiling (100 percent). The average annual change in this logistic is used in the regressions.

Appendix II   **Educational attainment**

Presently, three different data sets exist on the educational attainment of the population. These data sets are potentially of great use for research on human capital, growth theory, production functions, etc.

(i) *Bhalla, Lau, and Louat*   This series was constructed in two stages. The first stage involved estimation for the World Bank's 1990 *World Development Report*, Lau, Jamison, and Louat (1991). The methodology employed in this pioneering study was as follows: school enrollment data from the sixties and seventies were used to project enrollment backwards to 1902. Total number of person-school-years in the working age population were then computed using the perpetual inventory method.

The above methodology was revised by Bhalla, Lau, and Louat (1990); especially see Louat (1991). Enrollment data from 1950 were used, when available; an improved backcasting method was employed; and most importantly, mortality data were used to adjust the education cohorts. Male and female enrollments were used separately; the reported figure is a simple average of the two. This is the only education series which reports data for both female and male education. Unfortunately, lack of migration data meant that the education series could not be adjusted for this important phenomenon. This non-adjustment leads to biased estimates for Hong Kong and Israel. For these two countries, census data as reported in Pscharapoulos and Arriagada (1986) were used to "benchmark" the figures. The education figures are for the working-age population 15–65 years.

(ii) *Nehru, Swanson, and Dubey* (1993)   This series replicates the Bhalla, Lau, and Louat methodology with one addition – the enrollment data are adjusted for drop-out rates. Separate data for male and female education are not available, though the figures reported are for the entire working-age population, 15–64 years. The figures are not adjusted for migration and are therefore likely to be in error for Israel (no figures are reported for Hong Kong).

(iii) *Barro and Lee* (1992)   Census data are used for population above 25 years of age. Separate data for male and female education are not available though the reported figure is for the entire population.

The results in this paper are invariant with respect to the education series chosen. A revised version of Bhalla and Gill (1991) contains an analysis of the similarities and differences in the three series. A peculiar feature of the Barro and Lee series is that for several countries (especially in Latin America) it shows

Freedom and economic growth: a virtuous cycle?

a *declining* level of average education. For some African countries, the education level in the Barro and Lee data is either too low (0 and 0.4 years for Egypt in 1960 and 1965) or too high (6.74 for Tanzania in 1960).

Appendix III

Country	lydu	bmp	zopen	zydu	zysh	tfpg
Algeria	7.72	147.70	—	0.78	1.78	−1.88
Argentina	7.93	49.39	−0.34	−0.78	−0.63	−0.86
Bangladesh	4.87	117.61	—	1.92	3.28	0.93
Barbados	8.41	9.31	—	1.66	0.50	—
Benin	5.88	2.16	—	−0.16	−0.91	−1.80
Bolivia	6.65	37.36	−5.50	−0.75	−1.29	−1.34
Botswana	6.02	18.19	—	7.42	5.95	—
Brazil	7.22	32.28	0.02	1.78	2.51	−0.36
Burkina Faso	5.43	2.16	—	1.44	2.14	−0.05
Burma	5.33	341.69	—	1.01	2.75	—
Burundi	5.16	20.40	—	1.54	1.72	−2.06
Cameroon	6.47	2.16	−3.55	1.71	2.67	1.12
Central Africa	6.10	2.16	—	−1.25	−1.05	0.00
Chile	7.30	44.79	−6.14	1.08	−0.13	−0.71
China	4.75	79.66	—	5.64	5.72	1.02
Colombia	6.77	7.91	0.45	1.97	1.95	−0.23
Congo	6.55	1.62	—	2.15	2.20	1.58
Costa Rica	7.30	55.98	−1.69	1.06	1.07	−2.05
Côte d'Ivoire	6.95	2.16	—	−1.53	−1.23	−1.18
Dominican Republic	6.35	36.92	—	1.03	1.01	—
Ecuador	6.65	22.05	—	2.19	2.20	—
Egypt	5.85	40.77	—	4.05	4.41	1.23
El Salvador	6.90	58.22	−1.63	−0.39	−0.03	−3.09
Ethiopia	4.86	82.70	—	−1.36	0.13	−0.13
Gabon	8.31	1.86	—	−0.67	3.67	−3.40
Gambia	5.61	8.21	—	0.78	0.72	—
Ghana	6.21	324.50	—	−1.21	−1.42	−1.30
Greece	8.18	6.93	—	1.79	1.82	0.16
Guatemala	6.75	21.05	—	0.05	0.20	−1.62
Guyana	6.29	265.10	—	−1.71	−1.64	—
Haiti	5.85	12.82	—	−0.76	0.01	−3.05
Honduras	6.70	85.83	—	0.17	1.18	—
Hong Kong	8.13	−0.52	—	5.48	6.04	2.05
Hungary	7.33	186.84	−0.75	1.96	3.22	0.98
India	5.46	30.85	−1.49	2.40	1.26	0.61
Indonesia	5.50	737.27	1.57	4.17	4.45	−1.27
Iran	8.24	335.82	—	−1.58	0.81	—
Iraq	8.36	92.19	—	−5.63	0.41	—
Israel	8.84	16.62	—	1.39	1.30	0.54
Jamaica	7.47	27.53	−4.46	−1.24	−2.11	−2.88
Japan	9.45	2.34	−3.06	3.25	3.15	0.45

Appendix III (*cont.*)

Country	lydu	bmp	zopen	zydu	zysh	tfpg
Kenya	5.81	18.69	−3.24	0.79	−0.49	−0.20
Korea, South	6.97	18.15	−0.29	7.30	6.26	1.66
Lesotho	4.93	6.82	—	3.49	5.70	—
Liberia	6.64	0.00	—	−2.99	−2.62	−2.13
Madagascar	5.88	26.96	−3.75	−2.51	−3.20	−2.14
Malawi	5.00	43.00	—	0.49	−0.64	−0.06
Malaysia	7.00	1.18	1.36	4.21	3.55	−0.61
Mali	5.41	3.94	—	0.63	0.57	0.29
Malta	7.43	3.21	—	6.63	5.89	3.55
Mauritania	6.38	85.17	—	−1.04	−1.46	−4.37
Mauritius	6.85	5.20	—	4.53	4.26	0.42
Mexico	23.00	5.05	−1.39	1.44	1.00	−1.74
Morocco	6.38	9.14	−3.85	2.07	2.21	−0.57
Nepal	4.93	35.55	—	1.05	1.30	—
Nicaragua	7.69	2,124.60	—	−4.16	−2.38	−4.08
Nigeria	5.76	96.65	—	−0.30	−2.11	−4.07
Pakistan	5.36	45.85	−3.08	2.87	2.61	1.36
Panama	7.50	0.00	—	0.40	1.58	0.36
Papua New Guinea	6.84	14.85	—	−0.60	−1.35	—
Paraguay	6.47	26.25	—	2.34	2.84	—
Peru	7.10	45.04	−2.11	−1.22	−0.23	−0.65
Philippines	6.25	10.85	0.39	0.83	1.40	−1.34
Portugal	7.89	4.84	−5.84	2.31	2.78	−0.57
Rwanda	5.65	37.81	—	−0.42	0.71	−1.88
Senegal	6.60	2.16	−7.73	−0.56	−0.29	−0.29
Sierra Leone	5.09	164.60	—	−0.56	−2.65	—
Singapore	8.12	0.85	—	5.36	5.41	0.56
South Africa	7.79	4.05	—	−0.15	0.35	—
Spain	8.67	2.58	−5.02	2.12	1.56	−0.22
Sri Lanka	5.52	61.15	−3.74	3.25	2.26	−0.69
Sudan	6.55	103.05	—	−0.39	−0.92	−0.91
Swaziland	6.63	12.37	—	0.29	−0.43	—
Syria	6.69	108.44	0.22	1.88	2.19	−1.48
Taiwan	7.57	0.00	—	6.46	5.93	1.72
Tanzania	5.13	127.16	—	−0.20	1.48	−1.37
Thailand	6.18	0.25	0.46	5.21	4.23	1.14
Togo	6.02	2.16	—	−0.71	−0.23	−2.12
Trinidad	8.33	38.20	—	−0.64	−1.60	—
Tunisia	6.80	33.10	—	2.17	1.95	—
Turkey	6.77	23.41	—	2.42	2.07	0.43
Uganda	5.99	295.82	—	−1.38	0.20	−0.83
Uruguay	7.58	12.47	—	1.14	0.97	—
Venezuela	8.06	33.52	−9.07	−0.93	0.80	−3.00
Yugoslavia	7.57	18.88	—	1.53	2.54	0.31
Zaire	5.76	104.03	—	−2.60	−2.45	−3.50
Zambia	6.05	111.12	−4.75	−2.76	−4.18	−1.21
Zimbabwe	6.55	65.30	0.25	−0.23	0.29	−1.07

Appendix III *(cont.)*

Country	pcl	educ1	educ2	educ3	insth	zimrh	zenrh
Algeria	2.13	2.36	1.28	2.16	4	−4.21	−0.55
Argentina	4.78	5.71	7.60	6.22	5	−3.06	0.25
Bangladesh	3.68	2.52	1.08	2.46	2	−1.86	−1.45
Barbados	6.95	—	11.17	—	2	−6.40	1.72
Benin	1.53	1.09	0.27	—	4	−1.77	−1.85
Bolivia	4.30	3.34	4.56	3.84	5	−3.07	−0.69
Botswana	5.57	—	2.31	—	1	−5.30	−1.21
Brazil	4.72	2.93	3.96	2.89	5	−2.83	−0.76
Burkina Faso	2.76	0.26	—	—	4	−1.59	−3.40
Burma	1.40	—	1.41	1.49	2	−2.82	−1.29
Burundi	1.43	0.97	—	—	1	−1.43	−3.47
Cameroon	2.20	2.18	1.48	1.40	4	−1.90	−1.43
Central Africa	1.57	1.03	0.57	—	4	−1.61	−2.05
Chile	3.07	5.76	7.07	5.81	5	−7.82	0.36
China	1.66	3.20	—	3.14	5	−4.29	−0.19
Colombia	5.45	3.11	4.77	3.21	5	−3.79	−0.23
Congo	1.72	2.89	—	—	4	−0.52	—
Costa Rica	7.00	4.96	6.51	5.78	5	−6.48	−0.28
Côte d'Ivoire	2.53	0.89	—	0.72	4	−1.8	−1.61
Dominican Republic	5.63	—	4.70	—	5	−2.25	−0.43
Ecuador	4.70	—	4.80	3.88	5	−3.18	−0.10
Egypt	3.22	3.37	1.53	3.37	2	−4.83	0.25
El Salvador	4.53	3.23	3.40	3.31	5	−3.68	−1.14
Ethiopia	1.47	0.28	—	0.18	4	−1.11	−2.27
Gabon	2.13	2.76	—	—	4	−2.00	−1.72
Gambia	5.45	—	0.51	—	1	−1.81	−1.89
Ghana	2.45	2.76	2.73	2.74	1	−1.52	−0.53
Greece	5.75	6.08	6.27	7.78	5	−4.86	1.74
Guatemala	4.20	2.25	2.48	2.54	5	−2.66	−1.80
Guyana	3.85	—	6.06	—	2	−2.68	0.37
Haiti	2.07	1.97	1.44	1.76	4	−2.10	−1.93
Honduras	4.57	—	2.89	3.03	5	−3.21	−1.18
Hong Kong	4.93	6.73	6.19	—	2	−5.18	0.47
Hungary	3.00	7.05	8.77	—	5	−4.27	0.81
India	5.43	2.78	2.85	2.17	2	−2.42	−0.73
Indonesia	2.82	3.13	3.83	2.71	4	−4.00	−0.84
Iran	2.35	—	1.52	1.67	5	−2.01	−0.26
Iraq	1.14	—	1.44	2.08	5	−2.28	−0.11
Israel	5.85	8.86	9.24	4.40	3	−4.80	1.05
Jamaica	5.85	6.66	4.50	6.97	2	−5.32	0.39
Japan	6.78	8.88	8.68	10.69	3	−5.04	2.68
Kenya	2.80	2.45	2.02	2.25	1	−2.31	−1.54
Korea, South	3.50	6.06	6.26	4.80	3	−5.81	1.30
Lesotho	3.03	—	4.61	—	1	−2.11	−1.49
Liberia	2.57	1.55	1.24	1.10	1	−1.89	−1.53
Madagascar	2.97	2.53	—	2.15	4	−2.45	−1.34
Malawi	1.53	3.23	3.11	3.41	1	−1.49	−3.26

234 *Surjit S. Bhalla*

Appendix III *(cont.)*

Country	pcl	educ1	educ2	educ3	insth	zimrh	zenrh
Malaysia	4.30	6.78	4.93	4.10	2	−5.46	−0.00
Mali	1.57	0.49	0.37	0.32	4	−1.30	−2.55
Malta	6.13	6.41	7.64	—	2	−3.60	1.03
Mauritania	1.78	0.25	—	—	4	−1.84	−2.33
Mauritius	5.78	5.99	4.78	5.23	1	−5.56	−0.14
Mexico	4.28	3.93	4.76	4.02	5	−3.49	−0.18
Morocco	3.57	1.81	—	1.21	4	−3.60	−1.08
Nepal	3.72	—	0.14	—	2	−1.53	−1.44
Nicaragua	3.28	3.53	3.14	—	5	−3.68	−0.66
Nigeria	3.35	1.24	—	1.28	1	−2.03	−1.56
Pakistan	3.28	1.63	1.62	1.38	2	−1.90	−1.67
Panama	2.93	5.69	6.17	5.39	3	−4.10	0.37
Papua New Guinea	5.84	—	1.05	—	2	−3.62	−2.04
Peru	4.25	5.31	5.13	4.49	5	−2.89	0.17
Philippines	3.93	6.80	6.34	5.79	3	−2.74	0.57
Portugal	5.72	4.98	1.87	4.48	5	−6.78	0.05
Rwanda	1.97	2.19	0.81	2.08	1	−0.92	−3.36
Senegal	3.90	0.91	3.02	0.77	4	−2.60	−2.01
Sierra Leone	2.85	—	1.24	1.02	1	−1.83	−1.86
Singapore	3.35	5.62	4.96	4.38	2	−5.75	0.46
South Africa	2.82	—	5.83	—	1	−3.18	—
Spain	5.50	5.61	5.33	5.81	5	−5.27	1.78
Sri Lanka	4.85	7.80	6.45	5.10	2	−5.17	0.29
Sudan	2.40	0.83	0.62	0.69	1	−2.19	−1.69
Swaziland	2.85	—	3.15	—	1	−1.63	−0.46
Syria	1.65	4.11	2.56	3.18	5	−4.34	0.02
Taiwan	3.25	5.72	5.49	—	3	—	—
Tanzania	2.05	1.17	4.39	1.06	1	−0.68	−3.36
Thailand	4.15	5.36	5.15	4.49	5	−5.03	−1.03
Togo	1.80	1.78	0.88	—	4	−2.38	−1.18
Trinidad	6.35	—	6.46	—	2	−3.09	0.80
Tunisia	2.78	—	1.39	2.65	4	−5.84	−0.84
Turkey	4.68	3.35	2.66	2.87	5	−5.06	−0.53
Uganda	2.35	1.64	1.92	2.04	1	0.69	−2.77
Uruguay	4.20	—	6.74	5.75	5	−4.72	0.46
Venezuela	6.32	3.95	4.30	4.00	5	−2.14	−0.26
Yugoslavia	2.47	5.95	7.24	—	5	−3.86	1.37
Zaire	1.60	3.11	1.94	2.38	4	−1.87	−1.09
Zambia	3.00	2.21	3.23	2.17	1	−0.99	−1.61
Zimbabwe	3.13	3.48	3.81	3.48	1	−3.70	−1.45

Definitions of variables

    (i)   lydu: log of income per capita, constant 1987 dollars, in 1972.

    (ii) bmp: average black market premium, 1973–1990. A dummy variable based on this variable is used in the regressions; this dummy has a value 1 if the bmp is less than 6 percent, and zero otherwise.

Freedom and economic growth: a virtuous cycle? 235

(iii) zopen: economic openness; average percentage change in the relative price of tradables, 1973 onwards. End date varies with availability of data. See Appendix I for details.
(iv) zydu: average rate of per capita growth, constant 1987 $, 1973–1990.
(v) zysh: average rate of per capita PPP growth, 1973–1990.
(vi) tfpg: average rate of total factor productivity growth, 1973–1987.
(vii) pcl: average of political and civil liberties, Gastil data, 1973–1992.
(viii) educ1: mean years of education of the labor force in 1972, Bhalla, Lau, and Louat data, population 15–65 years.
(ix) educ2: mean years of education of the labor force in 1972, Barro and Lee data, population > 25 years.
(x) educ3: mean years of education of the labor force in 1972, Nehru *et al.* data, population 15–65 years.
(xi) insth: institutional or colonial heritage classification
insth = 1, British rule, Africa
insth = 2, British rule, non-Africa
insth = 3, American influence
insth = 4, non-British rule
insth = 5, independent
(xii) zimrh: average percentage change in the logistic of infant mortality 1973–1990.
(xiii) zenrh: average percentage change in the logistic of secondary school enrollment, 1973–1990.

NOTES

This chapter formed part of a background study for the 1991 *World Development Report* of the World Bank. I am grateful to Angus Deaton, Farrukh Iqbal, Lawrence Lau, T. N. Srinivasan, Lawrence Summers, and Vinod Thomas for helpful discussions, and to Sudhir Anand, Pranab Bardhan, Jere Behrman, Clive Crook, Partha Dasgupta, William Easterly, Stanley Fischer, Homi Kharas, Robert Lawrence, and Lant Pritchett for comments on earlier drafts. Comments of participants at seminars at the World Bank (Aug. 1992 and Aug. 1993), Princeton University, MIT, International Monetary Fund, the Nobel Symposium – 1994 on Democracy, and Harvard University were helpful. The views expressed in this chapter are those of the author and not of the institutions to which he belongs, or has belonged.

1 See Dasgupta (1990), Sirowy and Inkeles (1990), World Bank (1991), and Przeworski and Limongi (1993) for a sampling of this rapidly burgeoning literature.
2 This conclusion was explicit in Hayek (1944) and implicit in Friedman (1962). However, as Sirowy and Inkeles (1990) document in their review, and Przeworski and Limongi (1993) concur, little empirical support has been found (to date) for this "radical" proposition.
3 The traditional Solow model emphasizes the role of factor inputs; the "new" growth theory models à la Romer (1986), Lucas (1988), and Barro (1991) emphasize the increasing returns externality associated with higher *initial* levels of education.
4 The only other study to use an instrument variable to identify the political freedom and growth relationship is Helliwell (1992); his identifying variable

236   *Surjit S. Bhalla*

is Bollen's (1990) estimate of political freedom in 1965. Thus, Helliwell's instrument suffers from the drawback that it is more in the nature of a lagged variable.

5 Gastil (1987) recognized the problems associated with evaluating countries on the basis of the form of government and instead offered measures of freedom – in particular, measures of political and civil rights. His measures are the ones most used in the literature and also are used in this chapter.

6 A prime example of this is the introduction of high-yielding varieties of wheat and rice which were developed in the late sixties. These varieties needed adaptation to succeed in local conditions, and the education level of domestic researchers, as well as the education level of the farmers, were important in affecting the improvement in agricultural productivity.

7 See the special issue of the *Journal of Monetary Economics*, Dec. 1993, for a sampling of the various determinants.

8 The political freedom role has been emphasized by Sen (1983) and Dreze and Sen (1991). Sen argues that the presence of a free press (greater freedom) has contributed significantly to the absence of famines (better economic performance) in India.

9 As Section 4 documents, the East Asian experience has been used to support almost *any* thesis of development.

10 The rationale for separating the British colonial experience into two categories is because of the assumption that the effectiveness of colonialism in affecting institutional development was dependent on initial conditions: e.g., the initial level of education of the indigenous population. In any case, the results are unaffected if British colonialism is combined as one variable – see regression 6, Table 10.4.

11 A separate colonialism category for Japan was created, i.e., Korea and China (Taiwan). None of the results are affected by this alternative specification.

12 One possible counter-argument is that the colonizers conquered (chose ?) their colonies on the basis of future growth potential. If so, one would need to argue, based on growth performance in the 1970s and 1980s, as to which colonialists (British, French, Dutch, etc.) had more accurate vision in the nineteenth century.

13 The terms rights, liberties, and freedom are used interchangeably in this chapter.

14 Non-trade taxes diminish freedom, but public good expenditures can enhance economic freedom. The net influence of domestic taxation and domestic expenditure on economic freedom is a subject for future research.

15 The original Gastil rankings are the exact opposite, i.e., 1 is best and 7 is worst but have been transformed for this chapter in order that a positive sign in the regressions indicates a positive relationship.

16 An alternative measure of freedom is available, i.e., Humana (1986). Unfortunately, this index is only available for 1985. For that year, its correlation with the Gastil average for political and civil liberties is quite high – 0.86. Thus, it is unlikely that the results are affected by the choice of a particular freedom variable.

17 This measure was first developed by Bhalla and Lau for use in the World Bank's *World Development Report* (1991). See Appendices I and II for details.

Freedom and economic growth: a virtuous cycle? 237

18 The possible role of Confucianism in affecting growth is not unlike that of the Protestant ethic. Since this chapter is about developing countries, the role of the latter is ignored.

19 TFPG is based on the following estimate of the production function:

$$Y = .415 * K + .043 * T + d*ui + ei$$
$$(15.9) \ (1.25)$$

where Y, K, T reflect percentage changes in output per worker, capital per worker, and land per worker. Dummy d is a dummy which takes on the value 0 and 1 for 1960–1973, and 1974–1987 respectively; ui reflects individual country dummies and ei is the error term. The coefficient of ui for the time period 1974–1987 is the estimate of TFPG used in this chapter. Further, this estimate is *inclusive* of human capital. See Appendix I for construction of data on capital.

20 Infant mortality decline and increases in secondary school enrollment are both represented by the change in the logistic of the variable. For example, the logistic of infant mortality at a point in time is given by

imrl = ln[(infant mortality/1,000)/{1 − (infant mortality/1,000)}]

The preference for the logistic is based on the assumption that improvements in the indicators are more difficult the closer one gets to the floor (around 0 for infant mortality) or the ceiling (100 percent for secondary school enrollment).

21 Indeed, as suggested by Farrukh Iqbal, one could ask that if South Korea proves that authoritarianism works, what does North Korea prove?

22 Incidentally, these growth rates, along with the World Bank assessment of Chinese per capita income as $370 in 1990, suggest that China had a per capita income of approximately $92 in 1960, 1987 prices. This figure is put in perspective by noting that with this income, China ranks as the *poorest* developing country in 1960 followed by Lesotho ($93), Burundi ($99), and Ethiopia ($103). The Summers and Heston data are not so ridiculous – out of 118 countries China ranks 66 from the bottom.

23 As Dasgupta plaintively asks "How is one to choose a benign dictator"?

24 Note that a one-point move in political freedom is about 16 percent.

25 Note that these regressions report long-term effects. A country not only has to have a low black market premium, but should have done so, on average, for the entire 1973–1990 time period.

26 The formula for converting the coefficient on initial log per capita income into a speed of convergence is given in Barro and Sala-i-Martin (1992). It is given by $(1 - \exp(-bT))/T = - c$, where c is the estimated coefficient, b is the convergence rate and T (equal to eighteen years, 1973–1990) is the observation interval.

27 Lack of enough observations prevented the use of this method with the economic openness (relative prices) variable.

28 The result on interaction is consistent with the Solow growth model. This model assumes that technology is costlessly available to all countries. The emphasis here is that governments do not allow this manna to flow so easily, *and* that education is needed to take full advantage of new technology.

238   Surjit S. Bhalla

29 The Barro and Lee data used and reported in Appendix III is based on their 1992 paper. Revisions to these data are reported in Barro and Lee (1993b). Use of the revised Barro and Lee data does not affect any of the conclusions – initial education remains insignificant (0.25, t-statistic of 1.18) and PCL remains significant (0.76, t-statistic of 1.93).

30 Unlike the growth equation, this model does not have an "initial per capita income" variable. This is because there is no theory of "convergence" relating to infant mortality or secondary education. Any convergence due to natural limits is already included in the specification of the logistic form for the dependent variable. Further, lack of relevance of simultaneity means that political and civil liberties can enter the regression in their normal (non-instrumented) form.

31 See Bhalla and Gill (1991) for the specification and estimation of a detailed model of social welfare changes.

32 In Bhalla and Gill (1991) it is shown that *female* education has a greater bearing on welfare changes (both infant mortality and secondary school enrollment) than male education.

REFERENCES

Alesina, Alberto, and Dani Rodrik. 1993. "Distributive politics and economic growth." Mimeo, Harvard University, October.

Alesina, Alberto *et al.* 1992. "Political instability and economic growth." NBER Working Paper # 4173. Cambridge, Mass.

Bardhan, Pranab. 1993. "Symposium on democracy and development," *Journal of Economic Perspectives* 7: 45–49.

Barro, Robert J. 1991. "Economic growth in a cross section of countries," *Quarterly Journal of Economics* 106: 407–443.

Barro, Robert J., and Jong-Wha Lee. 1992. "International comparisons of educational attainment, 1960–1985." Mimeo, Harvard University, June.

   1993a. "Losers and winners in economic growth." NBER Working Paper # 4341, Boston, April.

   1993b. "International comparisons of educational attainment," *Journal of Monetary Economics* 31: 313–394.

Barro, Robert J., and Xavier Sala-i-Martin. 1990. "Economic growth and convergence across the United States." NBER Working Paper, July.

   1992. "Public Finance in Models of Economic Growth." London: Centre for Economic Policy Research.

Bhagwati, Jagdish N., and T. N. Srinivasan. 1975. *India*. Special Conference Series on Foreign Trade Regimes and Economic Development 6. Cambridge, Mass.: National Bureau of Economic Research.

Bhalla, Surjit S. 1992. "Free societies, free markets and social welfare." Mimeo, World Bank, Aug. 1992. Final Revision, Feb. 1994.

Bhalla, Surjit S., and Indermit S. Gill. 1991. "Social expenditure policies and welfare achievement in developing countries." Background paper for the *World Development Report* 1991, Washington, DC: World Bank.

Bhalla, Surjit S., and Lawrence Lau. 1992. "Openness, technological progress, and economic growth in developing countries," in progress.

Bhalla, Surjit S., Homi Kharas, and Ijaz Nabi. 1993. "Female-Led growth." Mimeo, World Bank, July.

Bhalla, Surjit S., Lawrence Lau, and Frederic Louat. 1990. Background papers for the *World Development Report* 1991, Washington, DC: World Bank.

Bollen, Kenneth A. 1990. "Political democracy: conceptual and measurement traps," *Studies in Comparative Development* 25: 7–24.

Dasgupta, Partha. 1990. "Well-being and the extent of its realisation in poor countries," *Economic Journal* 101: 22–26.

Dasgupta, Partha, and Martin Weale. 1992. "On measuring the quality of life," *World Development* 20 (1): 119–131.

De Long, Bradford J., and Lawrence H. Summers, 1991. "Equipment investment and economic growth," *Quarterly Journal of Economics* 106: 446–502.

De Long, Bradford J., and Lawrence H. Summers, 1993. "How strongly do developing economies benefit from equipment investment?" *Journal of Monetary Economics* 31: 395–415.

Dreze, Jean, and Amartya Sen. 1990. *Hunger and Public Action*. Oxford: Oxford University Press.

Dreze, Jean, and Amartya Sen, eds. 1991. *The Political Economy of Hunger*. Oxford: Clarendon Press.

Economist. 1991. "Freedom and prosperity" June 29.

1994. "Why voting is good for you" August 27.

Fields, Gary S. 1989. "A compendium of data on inequality and poverty for the developing world." Mimeo, Cornell University, March.

Friedman, Milton. 1962. *Capitalism and Freedom*. Chicago: University of Chicago Press.

Gastil, Raymond D. 1987. *Freedom in the World*. New York: Freedom House Inc.

Gill, Indermit S., and Surjit S. Bhalla. 1992. "Externalities in new growth theory: the importance of female human capital." Paper presented at the Western Economic Association Meetings, San Francisco, July 9–13.

Hayek, Friedrich August von. 1944. *The Road to Serfdom*. Chicago: University of Chicago Press.

1988. *The Fatal Conceit: The Errors of Socialism*, ed. by W. W. Bartley III. Chicago: University of Chicago Press.

Helliwel, John F. 1990. "Empirical linkages between democracy and economic growth," *British Journal of Political Science*.

1992. "Empirical linkages between democracy and economic growth." NBER Working Paper # 4066. Boston.

Humana, Charles. 1986. *World Human Rights G*. London: Economist Publications.

Huntington, Samuel. 1968. *Political Order in Changing Societies*. New Haven: Yale University Press.

Journal of Monetary Economics. 1993. "Special issue on national policies and economic growth: a World Bank conference." Dec.

Kim, Jong-Il, and Lawrence J. Lau. 1993. "The role of human capital in the economic growth of the East Asian newly industrialized countries." Mimeo, Stanford University, Dec.

Kmenta, Jan. 1990. *Elements of Econometrics*. New York: Macmillan.

240   *Surjit S. Bhalla*

Kravis, Irving, Alan Heston, and Robert Summers. 1982. *International Comparisons of Real Gross Product*. Baltimore: Johns Hopkins University Press.

Kravis, Irving B. *et al.* 1975. *System of International Comparisons of Gross Product and Purchasing Power*. Baltimore: Johns Hopkins University Press.

Lau, Lawrence, Dean T. Jamison, and Frederic F. Louat. 1991. "Education and productivity in developing countries: an aggregate function approach." PRE Working Paper 612. Background paper for World Development Report. 1990, Washington, DC: World Bank.

Lee Kwan Yew. 1992. Statement to an audience in the Philippines; also quoted in *Economist* August 27–1 September 2 (1994).

Levine, Ross, and David Renelt. 1992. "A sensitivity analysis of cross-country growth regressions," *American Economic Review* 82: 942–963.

Lipset, Seymour M. 1959. "Some social requisites of democracy: economic development and political legitimacy," *American Political Science Review* 53: 69–105.

Louat, Frederic. 1991. "Time-series of educational attainment of the labor force: a cross-country data base, 1960–1987." Mimeo, World Bank, June.

Lucas, Robert. 1988. "On the mechanics of economic development," *Journal of Monetary Economics* 22: 3–42.

Mankiw, G., D. Romer, and D. Weil. 1990. "A contribution to the empirics of economic growth." NBER Working Paper # 3541.

Nehru, Vikram, Eric Swanson, and Ashutosh Dubey. 1993. "A new database on human capital stock." Working Paper Series # 1124. World Bank, April. 1995. "A new database on human capital stock in developing countries: sources, methodology, and results," *Journal of Development Economics* 46: 379–401.

Persson, Torsten, and Guido Tabellini. 1994. "Is inequality harmful for growth?," *American Economic Review* 84: 600–621.

Pourgermani, Abbas. 1988. "The political economy of development: a cross-national causality test of development-democracy-growth hypothesis," *Public Choice* 58: 123–141.

Przeworski, Adam, and Fernando Limongi. 1993. "Political regimes and economic growth," *Journal of Economic Perspectives* 7: 51–69.

Psacharopoulos, George, and Ann-Maria Arriagada, 1986. "The educational attainment of the labor force: an international comparison." World Bank, October.

Romer, Christiana D. 1990. "New evidence on the monetary transmission," *Brookings Papers on Micro-Economic Activity*.

Romer, Paul. 1986. "Increasing returns and long-run growth," *Journal of Political Economy* 94: 1002–1037.

Sah, Raaj K. 1991. "Fallibility in human organizations and political systems," *Journal of Economic Perspectives* 5: 67–88.

Scully, Gerald W. 1988. "The institutional framework and economic development," *Journal of Political Economy* 96 no. 3: 652–662.

Scully, Gerald W., and Daniel J. Slottje. 1991. "Ranking economic liberty across countries," *Public Choice* 69: 121–152.

Sen, Amartya. 1983. "Development: which way now?," *Economic Journal* December.

Sirowy, Larry, and Alex Inkeles. 1990. "The effects of democracy on economic growth and inequality: a review," *Studies in Comparative International Development* 25: 126.

Robert Summers, and Alan Heston. 1988. "A new set of international comparisons of real product and price levels for 130 countries, 1950–85," *Review of Income and Wealth*, Income and Wealth Series 30: 1–25.

1991. "The Penn world table (mark 5): an expanded set of international comparisons, 1950–88," *Quarterly Journal of Economics* 106 (2): 327–368.

Wade, Robert. 1990. *Governing the Market*. Princeton: Princeton University Press.

Westphal, Larry E. 1990. "Industrial policy in an export-propelled economy: lessons from South Korea's experience," *Journal of Economic Perspectives* 4: 41–60.

World Bank. 1991. *World Development Report 1991*. New York: Oxford University Press.

1993. *The East Asian Miracle: Economic Growth and Public Policy*. Policy Research Report, July. New York: Oxford University Press.

11 Democratization and administration

Göran Hydén

Introduction

Development discourse in the 1990s has focused primarily on how to liberalize markets and democratize societies. A number of authors have devoted their attention to the relationship between market and democracy (eg, Przeworski 1991; Rueschemeyer, Stephens, and Stephens 1992; and Lipset, Seong, and Torres 1993). Very little scholarly work, however, has been carried out on the impact of economic and political reforms on public administration. Do these have a positive or negative effect on the quality of public administration? The purpose of this chapter is to explore this topic using largely African data to illustrate it. The rest of this presentation will initially cover a brief review of the classical literature on the rise of capitalism, democracy, and modern administration and then a look at the efforts in the 1960s to study administration through the lens of political development. The next section will address the challenges of improving public administration in the contemporary African setting. Specific attention will be paid to questions that are pertinent to the issue of democratization: (1) how to make the administration more public and transparent, and (2) how to make it more accessible to the public.

Capitalism, democracy, and bureaucracy

Much of our understanding of the rise of modern public administration is derived from the experience of Western European countries. Although not exclusively focused on that part of the world, Max Weber's analysis of the interrelations between capitalism, democracy, and bureaucracy forms the starting point for much of the thinking on this subject. He saw economy, politics, and administration as being closely linked and constantly interacting with each other within a given society. Without arguing, as Marx did, that politics and administration are mere derivatives of economic relations, Weber maintained that economy, politics,

Democratization and administration

and administration tended to reflect each other. He conceptually captured these similarities with his notion of "ideal types" that in a historical perspective could be identified in an evolutionary fashion. For example, in medieval times politics and administration were characterized by the ruler typically seeking to extend his domain and increasing the dependence of the notables of the realm on him and his immediate entourage, and with the local notables in turn trying to exact guarantees of rights and extension of privileges for the services demanded of them. Among the devices used by the ruler in gaining firmer control over the nobility was expansion in the number and capacity of the royal servants upon whom he could rely. Although the extent of monarchical dominance varied from country to country in Europe, it was generally aided by two important factors in the sixteenth to the eighteenth centuries. The first was the development of a money economy and the emergence of a new middle class ready to enter into alliance with the monarch against the old aristocratic class. As Eisenstadt (1963) has noted, this led to the growing importance of non-ascriptive rural and urban groups. The other factor was the increasing claims to power by jurists who reinterpreted concepts of Roman law by transferring the Roman imperium to the monarch and identifying the imperium of the monarch with the individual's private property. The "right" of sovereignty was vested in the monarch. The state then was "owned" by the monarch, and sovereignty belonged to him personally. He alone could legally exercise it, transmit it to his heirs, or otherwise dispose of it (Chapman 1959). Sovereignty was the right to command, and those commanded had a duty to obey. Laws were the tangible expression of the will of the monarch, and there was no higher authority to which further appeal could be made.

This system of established privileges was destroyed by the French Revolution and the Napoleonic era, producing a fundamental reformation of the nature of the state by replacing the king with the nation (Heady 1966: 35–36). The fiction of royal sovereignty was swept away, and the link between governmental authority and inherited privilege was broken. Sovereignty was now seen to rest with the people making up the nation. The concept of citizenship is universalized; formally, all citizens participate equally in public affairs (Bendix 1964).

The political transition from feudalism to absolutism to the nation-state was accompanied by extensive administrative changes as well. Put in simple terms, the royal household was converted into the royal service, which in turn was transformed into the public service. In Weberian terminology this marked the transition from patrimonial to bureaucratic administration. Weber used the concept of patrimonialism to charac-

244   *Göran Hydén*

terize a system of authority in which the royal household and the royal domains are being managed by the king's personal servants. Their power is arbitrarily granted them by the ruler.

The emergence of the absolutist monarchy was accompanied by a dramatic expansion of the scope of services undertaken by government. During the Middle Ages defense and justice had been the primary responsibilities of the king, but increasingly intervention took place in social and economic fields. Furthermore, matters that previously had been under local jurisdiction became matters of national concern. This meant an elaboration and centralization of field services. The most thoroughgoing attempts to reform the administrative structure of the state were made in late seventeenth – and early eighteenth-century Prussia where a corps of professional civil servants directly responsible to the crown was created through special training programs and appointments based on merit. Here, and subsequently in other European nations, the whole basis of public administration was transformed. The state was depersonalized; the nation replaced the king and organized public services for its own purposes rather than as the patrimony of the king. The public official was no longer the servant of the crown but of the state and thus, indirectly, of the nation.

The foundation of modern administration had been laid before capitalism, and democracy further transformed European society. It is important to remember that it was precisely in the countries where bureaucratic administration had been most firmly rooted – notably Germany and France – that democracy proved particularly difficult to introduce. In Great Britain and other parts of northern Europe, the state could more easily be transformed and tamed for democratic purposes. The rapid rise of a market economy also created alternative means of resource control that allowed other groups in society to exercise influence. Nonetheless, in all these societies undergoing a transition to capitalism, there was a contradictory impetus for bureaucracy in government and democracy in society. Industrialization and the growth of an urban working class accelerated this conflict between democracy and bureaucracy which can be summarized in the following way:

Democracy	*Bureaucracy*
— plurality and diversity	— unity
— dispersion of power; equal access	— hierarchy and authority
— liberty and freedom	— command and control
— elected officials	— appointed officials
— short-term mandate	— long-term tenure
— opportunity to participate	— limited participation
— openness	— secrecy; control of information

Democratization and administration 245

The subordination of bureaucracy to the principles of democracy could not have been achieved without the strength of the market. Not only did the latter serve as a competitor and alternative to state rule and regulation. It also served to promote the generation of new classes in society which had an interest in subjugating the state to serve their own interests. Administration eventually emerged as an instrument not just of the nation but of the *democratic* nation.

To a considerable extent, in all industrialized democracies today, bureaucrats share the norm that they are not supposed to "usurp" the rule-making function. Many go to some pains to convince themselves and others that their essential role is primarily instrumental. These men eschew politics even when it is strikingly apparent that they are deeply involved in the rule-making process. Even so, the tension between the principles of democracy and those of bureaucracy continue to afflict modern society. Citizens complain of the difficulty of access to government offices and the information they possess. Others lament the social distance that often exists between officialdom and the public. Such tensions, however, are generally handled within the existing political machinery for resolving conflicts. There are institutionalized means of resolving them in ways that do not shake society.

Bureaucracy and political development

Some thirty years ago when African nations gained their independence, the issue of the relationship between democracy and bureaucracy was very much in the forefront of the academic debate. Cast as this debate was in the light of the ambition to achieve rapid economic and social development, one issue of concern was how far the Western experience served as a guide to the developing nations of Africa and other Third World regions. Development, or "modernization" as it was often called, implied an imitation of the major achievements of the already developed countries: a market economy, industrialization, physical infrastructure, secular education, lower mortality, and fertility rates, and so on. This is how one prominent analyst of the day, Edward Shils, put it: "The elites of the new states have lying before them, not the image of a future in which no one has as yet lived or of a still living and accepted past, but rather an image of their own future profoundly different from their own past, to be lived along the lines of the already existent modern states, which are their contemporaries" (Shils 1962: 47–48). Yet there was also recognition made of the different circumstances facing the developing nations. Africa, like other developing regions, was expected to catch up with the West; that called for a strong leadership and

246   *Göran Hydén*

government to accelerate economic and social transformation. Africa had only a relatively small cadre of educated officials; that tended to make development policy-making elitist. Africa had weak political parties; that became a call to reliance on the administrative services to take a greater role in development.

"Developmentalism" tended to overshadow the considerations of what should be done with bureaucracy and democracy in the new nation-states of Africa. Two debates were particularly instructive of the ideas dominating the early 1960s. The first centered on the relative power of the political realm over the administrative one. The second focused on the need for a peculiar type of "development administration."

The first of these debates started from the assumption that political organs in the developing countries were relatively weak because the colonial powers had not let them develop any degree of strength of their own. To the extent that political development meant democratization, some analysts argued that in the absence of strong associations and political parties to represent the public, the bureaucracy may usurp power or merely fill the vacuum left by these other organizations. Eisenstadt (1963) argued that bureaucrats may become omnivorous consumers of resources and even dominate the articulation of political demands by virtue of the weakness of other institutions in society. The notion that bureaucrats appropriate the political function in the absence of strong political organs was also advocated by Fred Riggs (1964). The latter drew attention to the great expansion of governmental agencies and a proliferation of functions that accompanied the transition to independence in African and Asian countries. By contrast, parliamentary bodies were, in the main, proving ineffectual and their role in public policy making was being questioned. Both authors maintained the desirability of political control over the administration in ways that could already be found in industrialized Western societies. Riggs concluded that political development (read: democratization) is itself a fundamental requisite for a better life, for the world and the people of the new nations, and that progress in public administration and economic growth will not automatically promote political development. The latter should be treated as an independent variable in these countries.

Others in this debate accepted that administrative institutions must, and should, play a greater role in development in the new nations. The imitative character of African public administration was a given in ex-colonial countries. There was not much that could be done to change this historical legacy. Kingsley (1963), for example, illustrated how the traits of the colonial administration carried over in both francophone

Democratization and administration 247

and anglophone West African countries: "The *fonctionnaire* slouched at his desk in Lomé or Cotonou, cigarette pasted to his underlip, has his counterpart in every provincial town in France; and the demeanor of an administrative officer in Accra or Lagos untying the red tape from his files would be recognizable to any one familiar with Whitehall or, more specifically, the Colonial Office" (Kingsley 1963: 303). Others were even more explicit in terms of arguing for a strong and centralized administration. The development imperative had Merghani (1964) advocate the need for a strong administrative machinery as an end in itself. A few years later, Huntington (1968) warned against strengthening political organizations responsible for articulating public demands, because other institutions in society were too weak to cope with the "revolution of expectations" that independence had brought to new nations.

The second debate focused more specifically on the nature of administration itself. Participants in this debate generally accepted that administrators in developing countries had to play a new and different role. This role was defined in relation to both "classical" administration in the West and colonial administration. These two types of administration were largely oriented towards maintaining law and order and had never been asked to play a developmental role. Administrators in developing countries had to play a more activist role. They had to have a different perception of their job than that found among administrators in the West. This is how a specific "development administration" evolved. Victor Thompson (1964) suggested that organization theory provided insights that would be useful for such an administration, notably the idea that it should be adaptive and innovative. Dresang (1973), who had conducted field work in Zambia, argued that civil servants could, and should, play an entrepreneurial role, i.e., seizing the initiatives to get things done without always waiting for political direction from cabinet ministers. After all, in the spirit of national independence, every one shared the same aspiration of social and economic development. If ministers were slow or ineffectual in giving direction, civil servants should not just wait.

The other side in this debate was taken by Bernard Schaffer (1969) who maintained that advocates of development administration failed to recognize the peculiarities of bureaucratic administration. He suggested that these people were also naive in trying to blend participatory modes of program implementation, e.g., community development, with what is essentially a hierarchical model of organization that has little or no room for such approaches. Development administration, according to Schaffer, therefore, found itself in a deadlock.

248   *Göran Hydén*

The debate about the relationship between democracy and bureaucracy in the 1960s died a natural death as political trends of events in many Third World countries began going in an autocratic direction. The notion of a strong government, and by implication a directive bureaucracy, was sustained for much of the 1970s on the assumption that it was a requisite for development. The achievements of Communist countries were often held up as examples that the relation between autonomous political associations and government bureaucracy could be defined in ways different from that found in the West.

Liberalization, democratization, and public service reform

The issues discussed in this chapter experienced a revival in the late 1980s and early 1990s as the Cold War came to an end and the Communist model of development literally collapsed before the eyes of the world. As indicated at the beginning of this chapter, however, the focus of this new debate has been largely on economic liberalization and political democratization. Administrative reform, or public service reform, as it is now typically called, has been relegated to a secondary or tertiary position in this debate. Above all, such reforms have been treated as separate from the issues of democratization. Much of this can be explained by the different perception of the role of the state in development that prevails in the 1990s. A comparison with the period immediately after World War II may be instructive.

The role of the state during that period was perceived to be expansive and interventionist. Keynesian economics reigned in the minds of politicians and experts alike. The state had responsibility for pump-priming the economy at times of recession by providing social security benefits that enabled people to generate a greater demand for consumer goods. The economic wheels were to be accelerated by a demand-side approach.

The political consequences of such an approach to macro-economic management was to legitimize a redistributive type of politics. In Western Europe Keynesian economics facilitated the integration of the working class into the existing framework of democratic politics. In Latin America, where much the same thinking prevailed, the principal effect of these policies was to strengthen domestic economic actors vis-à-vis foreign competitors. The beneficiaries were not really members of the low-income groups but the middle class. Thus, it is not a coincidence that the former were for a long time denied political rights and that democracy kept being associated with the interests mainly of the

Democratization and administration

better-off groups in society. Such an association notwithstanding, the notion of an activist state helped Latin American governments to at least attempt reaching out to the poorer segments of the population.

The Keynesian economic outlook dominated also the African scene in the days of decolonization and after independence. Foreign aid, for example, was viewed as complementing local investments and thus serving the same pump-priming function as deficit financing was doing at times of recession in Western Europe and Latin America. There is one important difference, however, between these two regions and Africa. In the latter this approach was never employed to promote political goals, such as democratization, only administrative ones.

In spite of attempts by some scholars to link political development to administrative development, the prevailing outlook in policy circles was largely technical. The notion of an expansive and interventionist state translated foremost into how its executive capacity could be enhanced in African countries. The answer to the question which in Western Europe and Latin America had very significant political dimensions was in Africa to provide technical assistance in the field of public administration and provide training for nationals of these countries. At least in part because of the dominance of external donors, the political challenge was ignored in favor of the more narrow and more manageable administrative one.

When the issues of economic liberalization, democratization, and public service reform are reemerging in the 1990s, the circumstances are very different. Keynesian economics is out and neo-classical economics in. This means that there is very little sympathy for demand-side solutions to economic issues. These are instead sought in the market, in the form of incentives and other supply-side measures. One of the most important consequences of this outlook has been to reduce the size of the public services. The World Bank and other donors have been instrumental in getting African governments to cut back on the number of employees in the public services as a means of reducing the national budget deficit and offering a more realistic salary to those employees remaining in service.

African countries, like those in Eastern Europe and the former Soviet Union, therefore, are being asked to engage in political democratization at a time when the state is expected to contract rather than expand. While governments in the first thirty years after World War II could gain legitimacy from redistributing resources and benefits to groups in society, the governments today are expected to earn that same legitimacy by abstaining from such redistributive interventions. As the experience from several African countries and the Soviet Union indi-

250   *Göran Hydén*

cates, most governments find this new "political asceticism" hard to comply with. It is often only the pressures from the international finance institutions that keep these policies alive. It is not clear, however, how effective these institutions are in keeping these governments in line.

The point is that whichever way governments in Africa, Eastern Europe, or the former Soviet Union turn, they find themselves in a dire predicament when it comes to realizing democracy. If they stay with neo-classical economic reforms, they may get the economy in better shape but their chance of being reelected in the next elections is most probably severely reduced because macro reforms do not immediately translate into micro-economic benefits for the majority of the population. If, on the other hand, they abandon the reforms, they worsen the economic situation and thereby lower the chances of getting democratic forms of governance realized.

No one can really say which of these two scenarios may be better but it is understandable if political leaders in these regions are bewildered. For instance, we do not know how big a macro-economic failure democracy or democratic forces in society can take. Huntington (1991: 259) reminds us that democracy survived the Great Depression (although it must be added that it was only in some countries in Western Europe and North America). Does democracy in the 1990s have more or less capacity to resist rapid economic deterioration than it had in the late 1920s? Such a comparison cannot really be done with any degree of certainty, but if there is some malleability or robustness today, it may be due to factors that were not necessarily present in the 1920s. Jeffrey Herbst (1993: 171), for instance, argues with reference to Ghana that state weakness may in fact help economic and political reform efforts, because the demands on a weak and discredited state are not likely to be that strong. People in Ghana – and, I believe, in other parts of Africa and much of Eastern Europe and the former Soviet Union – deliberately avoid the state and seek solutions to their problems through private and voluntary means. Civil society grows simply because the state is incapable of carrying out the things it used to do.

It is this interface between state and society that needs to be further examined with the role of public administration in mind. The literature on democratization in the past five years has focused almost exclusively on the input side of the political equation: how societal interests can be more effectively articulated through private and voluntary associations. There has been much less interest in the output side, i.e., how state and civil society interact through public administration (Pierre 1994). In other words, in order to fully understand the constraints and oppor-

Democratization and administration

tunities for democratization in Africa we need to obtain a better grasp of how public administration relates to the policy-making process and its key institutions and actors as well as to civil society. Two issues are of special interest in the contemporary African context: (1) how can government administration be made more public? and (2) how can the public gain easier access to this administration?

Making administration more public

One of the dominant features of post-independence politics in Africa has been the emergence of patrimonial forms of government (Callaghy 1984; Joseph 1987). With the departure of the colonial power and the Africanization of power relations (Chabal 1992), politics in Africa has taken on new dimensions. Particularly striking has been the tendency to treat public policy making as a closed and private affair. This is a legacy that virtually all African countries have to cope with as they consider political, economic, and administrative reforms in the 1990s.

As political analysts we tend to take for granted that the most important thing a government does is to produce public policy. We evaluate its performance accordingly. What might be called "policy government," however, is but one conception of government. Government can and has operated in accordance with other principles or indeed with *no* principles, only a blind faith in charismatic leaders. Government actions have been authorized solely by documents (or other tokens) bearing the "seal" of the ruler. Such a government is run through patronage and personal loyalty rather than policies and procedures. It operates not by formulating and implementing public policies by means of a public bureaucracy, but rather by allowing the representatives of communities to occupy offices and to use considerable personal discretion in exercising authority. We saw in the first section of this chapter how patrimonial administration is an example of this type of "non-policy" government.

Policy government, by contrast, is both analytical and impersonal. It does not usually attend to the unique circumstances of persons but to the common needs and problems of categories of individuals and to specified cases within each category. Neutral words like "cases," "applicant," "subscriber," and "resident," which identify persons narrowly as members of analytical categories, are characteristic of the vocabulary of policy government. Their effect is to depersonalize and routinize the relations between bureaucrats and citizens, making those relations conform as much as possible to the impersonal norm of government–public relations (Jackson 1977). In short, policies never particularize persons:

252   *Göran Hydén*

they stipulate qualifications by which individuals can claim to belong to the policy domain. It is uncharacteristic for policies to particularize precisely because particularism entails discrimination and favoritism.

Policy government, then, is public government. Public policies are formulated, deliberated, debated, adopted, announced, and enforced. To be enforced, they must be known, just as the law is known. Policies suggest choice and thus inspire debates and consideration of "reasoned argument." In this sense, policy government encourages an institutional openness that is congenial to democratic forms of governance.

Non-policy government is different. It operates by means of spoils and preferments that take into account the particular situations of persons and communities. Such government tends to be "private government," both in the sense that government offices are treated as private property and in the sense that spoils, unlike policies, must be managed in a discreet and even clandestine fashion. They cannot be advertised, nor can they be publicly debated. Spoils provoke disputes rather than debates. Such disputes arise over access to spoils and the privileges surrounding such access. The allocation of spoils, if carried out in public view, would provoke quarrels; hence, it cannot be announced and declared. As Jackson (1977: 45) notes, the politics of spoils is a type of distributive politics. It does not inevitably imply privilege and injustice, as one might be inclined to believe. There is a redistributive logic to the system based on the notion that spoils have to be divided and allocated in accordance with prior contributions. From the viewpoint of policy government, spoils systems are unjust for failing to take account of other merits such as qualifications for holding office or citizenship.

In the case of most African countries, government is not policy government in the sense we have described it above. There is little debate and decisions are made in secret, often in terms of spoils and preferments. In short, the ruler tends to reward his followers in accordance with contributions they have made in the past. Such contributions may include loyal support in various public settings, donations to causes advocated by the ruler, or ability to neutralize potential enemies of his. Many of the economic problems of African countries stem from the consequences of adopting a patronage approach to governance. Because policies are very often not based on "reasoned arguments" in the same sense as we assume in the context of policy government, they typically contradict the logic of economic rationality. Government is not concerned with efficiency but with redistributing spoils so as to sustain itself in power. For example, this became painfully apparent in Kenya in connection with the 1992 general elections, in anticipation of which the ruler and his incumbent government had new money printed for spoils purposes with the effect that in 1993 the country's economy went into a serious inflationary spin.

The patrimonial tendencies in African politics have not disappeared with recent democratic reforms. While the form of governance may have changed in most African countries, its content remains much the same. The public service remains subject to the interference by political spoils considerations with the consequence that it is secretive and private rather than open and public in its orientation towards the citizenry. Efforts in recent years to reform the public services have focused more on form than content. For example, the recommendation often made by consultant experts to improve the pay for public servants as a way of enhancing the efficiency of administrative organizations completely overlooks the political dimensions that sustain a patrimonial rather than a bureaucratic orientation. It is clear that a very big question mark will continue to hang over African democratization efforts as long as patrimonialism dominates political behavior. It will prove extremely difficult to enhance government legitimacy in the eyes of the public as long as the ruler and his supporters in public office continue to treat these as their private domains. Democratization to date has not changed this behavior and it is unlikely to happen as long as the consequences of patrimonialism for government administration are overlooked.

Enhancing public access to administrative services

Much political rhetoric has been spilled on decentralization over the past thirty years in Africa. Little has been accomplished in practice, the main reason being that advocates of decentralization have made the wrong assumption that African governments are policy governments; that they actually operate on the basis of reasoned argumentation. As long as patrimonialism prevails, all such advocacy is bound to be in vain because patrimonial forms of governance are centralized. As was suggested in the first section of this chapter, patrimonialism implies not only that the public realm is confused with that of the ruler but also that the latter controls his subordinates through the application of spoils and preferments.

Any effort to delegate political authority to local governments as part of a plan to democratize society is likely to run into serious difficulties because the ruler can only proceed along such lines at the risk of losing control of the political situation. There may be rulers who are ready to cede such authority and accept political defeat, but a much more likely scenario is one in which the ruler will use his control of the public realm to perpetuate patrimonialism. The biggest challenge to democratization

254   *Göran Hydén*

in Africa – and in other countries displaying the same social characteristics – therefore, is how to rid the political system of patrimonialism
without creating political chaos or anarchy.

Africans opposed to such form of governance and donors demanding
greater transparency are trying to deal with this issue but in no African
country has patrimonialism really been displaced by one that combines
the features of political accountability and rational-legal administration.
Spoils and preferments continue to prevail both in the political and the
administrative spheres. It is becoming increasingly clear that in order
to really make governance in African countries more oriented towards
rule of law and transparency, the social forces in Africa so inclined and
the donors must act in unison to overhaul the system. This can be done
neither by the African opposition nor the donors alone.

One possible avenue is to encourage the development of intermediate
funding structures that are jointly controlled by the donors and those
who believe in the establishment of a rational-legal structure of authority
as a precondition for democratization. Groups of Africans are already
working in the direction of setting up development funding mechanisms
which are independent of the ruler. The legal framework for such funds
exists in many countries but would have to be introduced in others in
order to pave the way for such institutions. What these groups of
Africans are having in mind are a set of sectoral development funds, e.g.,
for public health, agricultural improvement, education, or women in
development, which operate on a national basis with a mandate to finance projects requested on a competitive basis by governmental or non-
governmental organizations, cooperatives or private sector institutions.
Instead of giving funds directly to governments or NGOs, donors would
channel their support for development activities in the social and economic development sectors via these funds, where an independent board
of trustees would make the allocation. The composition of these boards
is crucial to the success of the funds. They must not be allowed to fall
into the hands of a head of state or cabinet minister, because that means
almost inevitably the perpetuation of patrimonialism. Instead, ways
must be found to make these funds answerable to other actors. One
possible way that is being considered assumes that one third of these
boards are appointed by the national legislature, one third by the financial investors – most likely donor agencies – and the remaining third by
the board itself. This way no single actor can control the institution for
its own purposes and there are sufficient checks and balances built into
the system that tendencies toward patrimonialism and other forms of
personalized appropriation of funds can be minimized.

Democratization and administration 255

Trustees would be asked to sign legally binding contracts before taking their position on the board so as to make it possible to hold them legally responsible for their actions while serving as such. Preliminary investigations in African countries demonstrate that many persons are ready to serve in these positions even with these legally binding obligations hanging over them. Such persons include members of the clergy, representatives of the legal and other professions, and former public servants who have retired honorably.

For the donors, this system marks a distinct departure from previous practices in that it assumes a readiness on their part to give up direct control of the money that they give to Africa. Because the funds would be legally incorporated in the recipient country and decisions made by the boards, this is a form of decentralization that is absolutely necessary if African countries are going to have a chance to democratize in ways that the donors themselves advocate. The latter must be ready to give the African countries a chance to prove their own ability to govern themselves in more transparent and accountable ways. Because the resources controlled by the sectoral development funds are available to any institution, including any level of government, this system paves the way for a genuine delegation of authority to local government structures that has been impossible to achieve as long as funds, including those provided by the donors, are centrally controlled. The funds, therefore, have a role to play in making people hitherto left out of politics more involved in their own development.

Some donors may at first glance find giving up control over their funds to be a step in the wrong direction, particularly in view of the frequent allegations now being made that African governments are corrupt. Corruption in Africa, however, is by no means inherent in society. It is structurally determined, largely by the way African governance has been centralized in the hands of one person. It is precisely because such centralization is so closely wedded to patrimonialism, private and secretive forms of governance, that this system must be brought to an end. The donors can help put constructive pressure on African political systems by making sure that the money they make available for these funds is subject to withdrawal in case the boards fail to live up to their mandate. In signing agreements with African governments about how their assistance can be used, donors may wish to insert a clause that makes it possible to move contributions to these development funds if the donors lose confidence in their ability to finance sustainable development or fund management displays serious faults. By being able to fall back on the threat of moving their money from one fund to another,

256   *Göran Hydén*

the donors are able to create a competitive climate in which fund trustees know that they have to prove their professional and managerial competence in order to continue being in business.

Because so many actors involved in development in African countries are poor and hence unable to benefit from regular commercial credit, these funds may wish to operate through three separate windows. One would support training and education and would operate through grants. A second window, relying on soft loans, would make finances available to groups and organizations who are unable to go to a bank for credit. These actors, however, would be required to demonstrate some form of matching contribution. Furthermore, they would be expected to pay back their loan on terms that are realistic. A third window may be created for persons and organizations capable of receiving finances on regular credit terms. This would be like an ordinary bank although its funding mandate would be confined to a particular sector activity.

Although the fund model is still in need of empirical testing, it holds promise where other efforts in the past forty years have failed. This approach has the advantage of dealing with both the political and the administrative aspects of governance in ways that enhance indigenous capacity and allows donors to interact with recipient countries in ways that are more constructive than the practices of control now in place. The model allows citizens access to public authority in ways that have the potential of restoring legitimacy to Africa's hard-pressed and compromised public institutions. It holds the promise of facilitating both political and administrative development; of making both democracy and bureaucracy (in the rational-legal sense) reality.

Conclusions

This chapter has tried to make four points. The first is that research on democratization and governance tends to overlook public administration, although it is an important component of ongoing reform processes. By failing to take into consideration the output side and how government performance affects its legitimacy, much of the debate about democracy is incomplete. Simply focusing on civil society is not enough, because it centers more on the input side than the output side of the political system. There are good reasons, therefore, to incorporate issues of administrative development in the analysis of political reform.

The second point relates to where we may seek inspiration for further work on these issues. As I have tried to demonstrate in this chapter, we

Democratization and administration 257

need not reinvent the wheel again. Many of the contemporary issues of administrative and political reform have been covered by classical writers like Max Weber and in the 1960s by a number of scholars interested in the interface between administrative and political development. In revisiting these issues, however, it is important to bear in mind that the structural conditions are different today. For example, I referred to the different role of the state in the 1990s compared to what it was in the 1960s. This and other structural differences need to guide the research of tomorrow.

The third point concerns the substance of political behavior in Africa. There has been an unquestioned assumption for far too long that governments in that part of the world are policy governments. The literature should by now have laid that to rest. Yet the implications of the persistence of patrimonialism on efforts to promote democracy and a rational-legal form of administration have not been examined. It is not unreasonable to hypothesize that the single biggest hurdle to realizing existing reform objectives is the prevalence of patrimonial behavior in government circles. Scholars need to study this issue closer and not merely assume that African political systems are in transition from some form of neo-patrimonial rule. The latter is still very much present.

The fourth point is about what can be done to overcome this patrimonialist legacy. It is unlikely that such a transformation can be achieved by African political actors alone. They certainly will find it hard to sustain any such transformation. It is important, therefore, that donors acknowledge their own role in this process and facilitate change to more transparent and accountable forms of governance by changing their own modes of operation along lines suggested in the last section of this chapter. Patrimonialism is not inevitable in Africa today. The notion that African societies find themselves at levels of development corresponding to medieval Europe is mistaken. Current structures set the stage for patrimonialism and donors must accept that their mode of dispensing aid to African governments has reinforced these structures. At a time when African governments are extensively dependent on donor funding, the latter can be used constructively to make a difference in the direction of democratic governance and more rational administration. The approach discussed above has the added advantage of being promoted by Africans themselves. In that respect, the next move rests with the donors. Will they be ready to transcend the limited horizons of their own organizational dynamics to allow Africans to realize the objectives of political and administrative reform that we all share today?

258   *Göran Hydén*

REFERENCES

Bendix, Reinhard. 1964. *Nation-Building and Citizenship.* New York: John Wiley & Sons.

Callaghy, Thomas M. 1984. *The State–Society Struggle: Zaire in Comparative Perspective.* New York: Columbia University Press.

Chabal, Patrick. 1992. *Power in Africa: An Essay in Political Interpretation.* New York: St. Martin's Press.

Chapman, Brian. 1959. *The Profession of Government.* London: George Allen & Unwin.

Dresang, Dennis. 1973. "Entrepreneurialism and development administration," *Administrative Science Quarterly* 18: 76–85.

Eisenstadt, S. N. 1963. "Bureaucracy and political development," in Joseph LaPalombara, ed., *Bureaucracy and Political Development.* Princeton, N. J.: Princeton University Press.

Heady, Ferrel. 1966. *Public Administration: A Comparative Perspective.* Englewood Cliffs N. J.: Prentice-Hall.

Herbst, Jeffrey. 1993. *The Politics of Reform in Ghana, 1981–1991.* Berkeley, Calif.: University of California Press.

Huntington, Samuel P. 1968. *Political Order in Changing Societies.* New Haven and London: Yale University Press.

1991. *The Third Wave: Democratization in the Late Twentieth Century.* Norman, Okla.: Oklahoma University Press.

Jackson, Robert H. 1977. *Plural Societies and New States: A Conceptual Framework.* Berkeley, Calif.: Institute of International Studies, University of California.

Joseph, Richard. 1987. *Democracy and Prebendal Politics in Nigeria.* New York: Cambridge University Press.

Kingsley, Donald J. 1963. "Bureaucracy and political development, with particular reference to Nigeria," in Joseph LaPalombara, ed., *Bureaucracy and Political Development.* Princeton, N. J.: Princeton University Press.

Lipset, S. Martin, Hyoung-Ryung Seong, and John Charles Torres. 1993. "A comparative analysis of the social requisites of democracy," *International Social Science Journal* 45: 155–75.

Merghani, Hamzah. 1964. "Public administration in developing countries – the multilateral approach," in Burton A. Baker, ed., *Public Administration a Key to Development.* Washington, DC: Graduate School, US Department of Agriculture.

Pierre, Jon, ed. 1994. *Bureaucracy in the Modern State.* Aldershot: Edward Elgar Publishing House.

Przeworski, Adam. 1991. *Democracy and the Market.* New York: Cambridge University Press.

Riggs, Fred. 1964. *Administration in Developing Countries – The Theory of Prismatic Society.* Boston: Houghton Mifflin Company.

Rueschemeyer, Dietrich, Evelyne Huber Stephens, and John D. Stephens. 1992. *Capitalist Development and Democracy.* Chicago: University of Chicago Press.

Schaffer, Bernard. 1969. "The deadlock in development administration," in Colin Leys, ed., *Politics and Change in Developing Countries*. Cambridge: Cambridge University Press.

Shils, Edward. 1962. *Political Development in New States*. The Hague: Mouton & Co.

Thompson, Victor. 1964. "Administrative objectives for development administration," *Administrative Science Quarterly* 9: 91–108.

Part 5

Democracy and globalization

12 Globalization, sovereignty, and democracy

Jagdish Bhagwati

Introduction

Like everyone else, economists like to break out of the narrowness of their discipline and speculate on a larger theme, painting on a bigger canvas. Like John Kenneth Galbraith, they may even make money while having fun. In the process, they may even illuminate and inform, doing good while doing well.

The task I have been assigned is an intellectually challenging one: does the growing globalization of the world economy and the presumed growth then in interdependence promise to constrain national sovereignty; and, does it equally threaten to compromise democratic accountability within nation-states? I feel daunted by the task: it is both extremely broad in scope and at the same time inadequately amenable to conventional analysis within any discipline. My analysis, while grounded in my understanding of the globalization process that is ongoing, must therefore remain essentially speculative in character. Few such speculations, especially those that contain within them a prognosis of the future, have turned out, if the past is any guide, to stand the test of time (though, I derive comfort from the fact that the worth of an idea lies in what it stimulates, even if by provocation, even while it is itself wildly wrong).

Since a major element of the globalization process today is international trade and since we economists tend to think of international trade as essentially a technology (in the sense that it adds to one's productive potential yet another way of transforming goods into one another, via external exchange), the great failure of such speculation that comes to mind, of course, is that of the celebrated pessimists George Orwell and Aldous Huxley. The authors of *Nineteen Eighty-Four* and *Brave New World* imagined modern technology as the enemy of freedom and the unwitting tool of authoritarianism; things, however, turned out for the better, not worse. Modern technology was supposed to make Big Brother omnipotent, watching you into submission;

263

264   *Jagdish Bhagwati*

instead, it enabled us to watch Big Brother into impotence. Faxes, video cassettes, CNN have plagued and paralyzed dictators and tyrants, accelerating the disintegration of their rule. As a wit has remarked, the PC (personal computer) has been the deathknell of the CP (Communist Party).[1]

But closer to home, both to me and to the broader theme of this volume, has been the failure of the early intellectual thinking on the relationship of democracy to development.[2] Thus, when reflection on strategies for the newly liberated countries began in the 1950s, there was considerable skepticism about the ability of democracies to compete in the race against totalitarian regimes. In fact, it seemed evident that democratic ideas and countries were fated to suffer a disadvantage in this contest. To understand why, it is necessary to recollect the mind-set at the root of the conception of development that then prevailed.

The Harrod–Domar model, much used then, analyzed development in terms of two parameters: the rate of investment and the productivity of capital. For policy-making purposes, the latter was largely treated as "given," so debate centered on the question of how to promote investment. This approach favored by mainstream economists coincided with the Marxist focus on "primitive accumulation" as the mainspring of industrialization and also with the cumbersome quasi-Marxist models elaborated in the investment-allocation literature that grew up around Maurice Dobb.

But if the focus was on accumulation, with productivity considered a datum, it was evident that democracies would be handicapped vis-à-vis totalitarian regimes. Writing in the mid-1960s, I noted "the cruel choice between rapid (self-sustained) expansion and democratic processes" (1966: 204). This view, which the political scientist Atul Kohli has christened the "cruel choice" thesis, was widely shared by economists at the time (1986: 155). Later emphasis would shift away from raising the rate of savings and investment (dimensions on which most developing countries did well) to getting the most for one's blood, sweat, and tears (dimensions on which developing countries performed in diverse ways). Indeed, by the 1980s it was manifest that the policy framework determining the productivity of investment was absolutely critical, and that winners and losers would be sorted out by the choices they made in this regard. Democracy then no longer looked so bad: it could provide better incentives, relate development to people, and offset any accumulationist disadvantage that it might produce. Indeed, as Kohli has emphasized, the growth rates of democracies have not been noticeably worse than those of undemocratic regimes (1986).[3]

I also think that the common view, that the undemocratic nature of

Globalization, sovereignty, and democracy 265

the regimes in South Korea, Taiwan, Singapore, and Hong Kong was the key to their phenomenal growth, is false. This is a *non sequitur*, a choice example of the *post hoc ergo propter hoc* fallacy. These regimes owe their phenomenal success to their rapid transition to an export-oriented trade strategy (which first enabled them to profit from the unprecedented growth in the world economy through the 1960s, and then positioned them to continue as major competitors in world markets),[4] as well as to their high rates of literacy (which economists now generally acknowledge to be an important "producer good"). Both of these growth promoters were present in part because of the geographic proximity of Japan and the power of its example. Similarly, I would argue that the dismal performance of India owed to her poor choice of developmental strategy, with excessive reliance on import substitution and degeneration into mindless bureaucratic controls, as also low rates of literacy (whose roots lie in social and political factors discussed insightfully by the political scientist, Myron Weiner, in his recent book [1991]), the former failing to be blamed in large part on the intellectual affinity that its governing classes harbored for both Fabian politics and Cambridge economics.[5]

East Asian authoritarianism and Indian democracy are thus not the key to explaining their relative performance: the proponents of the contention that democracy aids, or at minimum does not hamper, development have little to fear from the comparative performance of these two regions.

Clearly, then, the "cruel choice" thesis was wrong; and, for us who value democracy, the error hurts our ego while warming our hearts. Here we have therefore an excellent illustration of how speculation grounded in the best thinking of the time failed the test of time, simply because we were using the wrong road map. I am therefore conscious, as I address the tasks before me, that some years down the road, the reality that I seek to grasp will have proven to be elusive again.

The questions

The central questions that I will address now are:

- Is sovereignty being lost by nation-states because of the interdependence implied by the increased globalization of the world economy?
- Is there also a decline, for this and other reasons, in the democratic accountability that national governments owe to their citizens?

266   *Jagdish Bhagwati*

Environment vs. trade: an illustration

These questions have acquired considerable political salience today. They are readily illustrated, though neither in all their complexity nor with the analytical rigour that I hope to use below, by the often-acrimonious debate between the proponents of free trade, the General Agreement on Tariffs and Trade (GATT) and the World Trade Organization (WTO), on the one hand, and many environmentalists, on the other.

To a large extent, of course, this conflict is inevitable. It reflects partly differences of philosophical approaches to nature that are irreconcilable. Several environmentalists assert nature's autonomy whereas many economists see nature as a handmaiden to mankind. The environmentalists' anguish at the effect of human activity on the environment is beautifully captured by Gerald Manley Hopkins when, in *Binsey Poplars*, he writes:

> O if we but knew what we do
>   When we delve or hew –
> Hack and rack the growing green!
>   Since country is so tender
> To touch, her being so slender,
> That, like this sleek and seeing ball
> But a prick will make no eye at all,
> Where we, even where we mean
>   To mend her we end her,
>   When we hew or delve:
> After-comers cannot guess the beauty been.
>   Ten or twelve, only ten or twelve
>   Strokes of havoc unselve
>   The sweet especial scene,
>   Rural scene, a rural scene,
>   Sweet especial rural scene.

It is indeed hard to find an echo of Hopkins in the utilitarian, cost-benefit calculus that many economists bring to bear on the question of the environment.

Then again, the conflict reflects other contrasts. Thus, trade has been central to economic thinking since Adam Smith discovered the economic virtues of specialization and of the markets that naturally sustain it, whereas markets do not normally exist to protect the environment and must often be specially created. Trade therefore suggests abstention from regulation, whereas environmentalism suggests its necessity. In turn, trade is exploited and its virtues extolled by corporate and multinational interests, whereas environmental objectives are embraced typi-

Globalization, sovereignty, and democracy 267

cally by non-profit organizations which are generally wary of, if not hostile to, these interests.

In the end, however, the hostility of the environmentalists to trade and the institutions such as the GATT that oversee it arises from precisely the two issues posed earlier: the threat that trade, increasingly resulting from the globalization of the world economy, poses to sovereignty and to democratic accountability.[6] Let me elaborate.

Thus, concerning sovereignty, the environmentalists feel that their ability to maintain the High Standards that they have achieved in their countries will be constrained and eroded by free trade and free capital flows with the Low Standards countries. Their concern is reminiscent of the classic problem of "socialism in one state." Just as capital and labour outflows will undermine the socialist objectives in a country going it alone, so will environmental (and labor) standards erode if they are lower elsewhere. In economists' language, the "political equilibrium" will shift in favor of those who oppose High Standards as industries decline through competition with foreign rivals operating under Low Standards. Moreover, there may ensue an interjurisdictional competition to attract capital and jobs through lowering environmental (and labor) standards, so that the trading countries may wind up with an inferior Nash equilibrium, characterized also by lower standards in one or all jurisdictions, than would emerge in a cooperative equilibrium.[7]

The environmentalists also fear the undermining of their High Standards via the alternative route of the Low Standards countries challenging the High Standards as "unscientific" or as "closet protectionism." In this instance, when the High Standards are subject to such challenge at the GATT (and now, the WTO which is replacing the GATT) by other trading nations, the environmentalists see the problem as the second one posed above: the undermining of democratically enacted legislation by "faceless bureaucrats" at the GATT. Again, they argue that "the process of negotiating international agreements [such as the GATT's Uruguay Round of multilateral trade negotiations, concluded in April 1995 at Marrakesh] is less subject to public scrutiny, and therefore a threat to democratic accountability."[8]

In fact, some environmentalists have gone even further and alleged that trade liberalization is in part a strategy for circumventing the health and welfare regulations legislated democratically within the nation: the title of a celebrated article by Walter Russell Mead in *Harper's Magazine* (September 1992), embracing this thesis, is: "Bushism, Found: A Second-Term Agenda Hidden in Trade Agreements."

Thus, the questions concerning the impact of globalization, and

268   *Jagdish Bhagwati*

the integration of one's economy into the world economy, on sovereignty, and on democratic accountability are central concerns in the political arena. A systematic examination of these questions is manifestly necessary. I will therefore turn to each of these questions. But, prior to doing so, I will consider briefly the nature and extent of globalization to date.

Globalization

The process of globalization of the world economy has occurred on several dimensions: trade, capital flows, human migrations (voluntary and involuntary). I will sketch these with great brevity.

Trade flows have dramatically increased in the last two decades, with most countries doubling the share of their trade in GNP and more. The increased trade reflects the continuing reduction of trade barriers with successive multilateral trade negotiations and also, in the case of developing countries, a substantial amount of unilateral, non-reciprocal trade liberalization which can be attributed to a mix of aid-conditionality and self-enlightenment in light of the postwar example of successful outward-oriented countries.[9]

A contribution to this phenomenon has also been made by the expansion of transnational production by multinational firms to a point where many have now made the claim that it is impossible now to say whether a product is American or Japanese or European: a claim that is perhaps premature but certainly destined to be validated in the near future. The trade flows have expanded, not just in manufactures, but explosively in services. In turn, that has meant, because services must be supplied often by taking the provider to the user, that the trend towards foreign establishments and (temporary) migration of skilled labor such as lawyers and accountants has greatly accelerated.

Investment flows have increased. True, we forget that the East India Company and the Dutch East Indies Company dominated commerce and the economic life of their countries, so in the long historical sweep, it is probably untrue to talk of the increased dominance of direct foreign investment (DFI). But, in recent decades, it has certainly grown; and its composition is now more evenly balanced between rich-to-poor and rich-to-rich countries. Much DFI occurs now in services, partly piggybacking on manufacturing DFI from their home country. Again, while DFI leads to trade, trade leads to DFI; the entry of Spain into the EC triggered a substantial influx of DFI to access the EC market and President Salinas realistically hoped for a similar bounty for Mexico from the North American Free Trade Arrangement (NAFTA).

Globalization, sovereignty, and democracy 269

The growth of the international flow of *short-term funds* is perhaps the most dramatic change in the world economy. Their staggering size and their volatility that recently devastated Mexico is a continuing and painful reminder, of the vulnerability that they equally bring, to the finance ministers and Central Bank chairmen and governors of even powerful countries like France, England, Japan, and the United States.

By contrast foreign *aid* flows have continued to shrink in real terms. But they remain important, bilaterally from the triad (the EU, USA, and Japan) and multilaterally. (They bring explicit conditionality with them, unlike the private funds which exact only the implicit conditionality that the task of wooing them or else losing them implies.)

An important dimension on which countries interface has been humanity itself. *Illegal* flows have become dramatic as, now that information and networks exist, the rich countries have become targets for entry. Immigration controls have been evaded, as controls invariably are; it is not too farfetched to say that borders are getting to be beyond control.

The problem is compounded for the *refugees*, both as narrowly defined in UN Covenants, and in terms of the wider definition of flight from civil wars and mortal danger. The UN High Commissioner for Refugees finds her hands full and her purse empty as the refugees have multiplied with civil wars brought about by ethnic strife, famine, and deprivation.

Conventional concerns: benign versus malign impacts

Economists generally see the increasingly interdependent world, with its growing exchange of goods and services and flows of funds to where the returns are expected to be higher, as one that is gaining in prosperity as it is exploiting the opportunities to trade and to invest that have been provided by the postwar dismantling of trade barriers and obstacles to investment flows. This is the conventional "mutual-gain" or "non-zero-sum game" view of the situation. I would argue that it is also the appropriate one.

But it is not a view that has had a clear run at the best of times. That integration into the world economy is a peril rather than an opportunity, that it will produce predation at one's expense instead of gain, has never been wholly absent from the policy scene. The substance of the disagreement among policy makers and among mainstream economists has, however, been defined by disagreements concerning the impact of such integration or globalization on conventionally defined economic welfare whereas only recently have broader concerns about sovereignty

270   *Jagdish Bhagwati*

and democratic accountability risen from the fringe to command attention in policy circles.

An ironic reversal

But I must point to an irony: where the developing countries (the South) were earlier skeptical of the benign-impact view and the developed countries (the North) were confident of it, today the situation is the other way around.

(i) The earlier situation   Thus, if you look back at the 1950s and 1960s, the contrast between the developing countries (the South) and the developed countries (the North) was striking and made the South strongly pessimistic about the effects of integration into the world economy while the North was firmly optimistic instead.

The South generally subscribed, not to the liberal, mutual-gain, benign-impact view, but to *malign-neglect* and even *malign-intent* views of trade and investment interactions with the world economy.[10] It was feared that "integration into the world economy would lead to disintegration of the domestic economy." While the malign-neglect view is manifest most clearly in the famous *dependencia* theory that President Cardoso of Brazil formulated in his radical youth as Latin America's foremost sociologist, the malign-impact view was most vividly embodied in the concept and theory of *neocolonialism*.

Trade thus had to be protected; investment inflows had to be drastically regulated and curtailed.[11] The inward-oriented, import-substituting (IS) strategy was the order of the day almost everywhere. Only the Far Eastern economies, starting mainly in the early 1960s, shifted dramatically to an outward-oriented policy posture: the results, attributable principally to this contrast in orientation to the world economy but partly also to initial advantages such as inherited land reforms and high literacy rates, were to produce the most remarkable growth experiences of this century (and, as I shall presently argue, to facilitate by example the reversal of the inward-looking policies in recent years). But, at the time, the developing countries were certainly in an inward, cautious mode about embracing the world economy.

By contrast, the developed countries, the North,[12] moved steadily forward with dismantling trade barriers through the GATT Rounds, with firm commitment to multilateralism as well, subscribing essentially to the principles of multilateral free trade and of freer investment flows as the central guiding principles for a liberal international economic order that would assure economic prosperity for all participating nations.[13]

Globalization, sovereignty, and democracy

(ii) Role reversal: the turnaround Today, however, the situation is almost reversed. The fears of integration into the world economy are being heard, not from the developing countries which see great good from it as they have extensively undertaken what the GATT calls "autonomous" reductions in their trade barriers, i.e., unilateral reductions outside the GATT context of reciprocal reductions. Of course, not all these reductions, and increased openness to inward DFI, have resulted from changed convictions in favor of the liberal international economic order and its benefits to oneself, though the failure of policies based on the old pro-inward-orientation views and the contrasting success of the Far Eastern countries following the pro-outward-orientation views have certainly played an important role, especially in Latin America and Asia. But some measure of the shift must also be ascribed to necessity resulting from the conditionality imposed by the World Bank and, at times, by the International Monetary Fund (IMF), as several debt-crisis-afflicted countries flocked to these institutions for support in the 1980s, and equally from their own perceived need to restore their external viability by liberal domestic and international policies designed to reassure and attract DFI.

But if the South has moved to regard integration into the world economy as an opportunity rather than a peril, it is the North that is now fearful. In particular, the fear has grown, after the experience with the decline in the real wages of the unskilled in the United States and with their employment in Europe in the 1970s and 1980s, that by trading with the South with its abundance of unskilled labour, the North will find its own unskilled at risk.[14] The demand for protection that follows is then not the old and defunct "pauper-labor" argument which asserted falsely that trade between the South and the North could not be beneficial. Rather, it is the theoretically more defensible, income-distributional argument that trade with countries with paupers will produce paupers in our midst, that trade with the poor countries will produce more poor at home.

Now, it is indeed true that the real wages of the unskilled have fallen significantly in the United States during the previous two decades. In 1973, the "real hourly earnings of non-supervisory workers measured in 1982 dollars . . . were \$8.55. By 1992 they had actually *declined* to \$7.43 – a level that had been achieved in the late 1960s. Had earnings increased at their earlier pace, they would have risen by 40 percent to over \$12" (cf. Lawrence 1994). The experience in Europe has generally been similar in spirit, with the more "inflexible" labor markets implying that the adverse impact has been on jobs rather than on real wages (*Employment Outlook* 1993).

272   *Jagdish Bhagwati*

But the key question is whether the cause of this phenomenon is trade with the South, as unions and many politicians feel, or rapid modern information-based technical change that is increasingly substituting unskilled labor with computers that need skilled rather than unskilled labor. As always, there is debate among economists about the evidence: but the preponderant view today among the trade experts is that the evidence for linking trade with the South to the observed distress among the unskilled to date is extremely thin, at best. In fact, the main study by labor experts that first suggested otherwise has been shown to be methodologically unsound in not appreciating that if real wages were to fall for unskilled labor due to trade with the South, the goods prices of the unskilled labor-intensive goods would have to have fallen (see Bhagwati 1991a); and subsequent examination of the US data on prices of goods shows that the opposite happened to be true.[15]

While therefore the consensus currently is that technical change, not trade with the South, has immiserized our proletariat, the fear still persists that such trade is a threat to the unskilled. In Europe, there has thus been talk of the difficulty of competing with "Asiatic ants"; such talk leads to talk of protectionism, in turn.

Alongside this is the fear that multinationals will move out to take advantage of the cheaper labor in the poor countries, as trade becomes freer, thus adding to the pressure that trade alone, with each nation's capital at home, brings on the real wages of the unskilled. Of course, this too is unsubstantiated fear: but it has even greater political salience since the loss of jobs to trade is less easily focused on specific competing countries and their characteristics than when a factory shuts down and opens in a foreign country instead. As it happens, I suspect that, at least in the United States, the flow of capital also is in the wrong direction from the viewpoint of those who are gripped by such fear. For, during the 1980s, the United States surely received more DFI than it sent out elsewhere, both absolutely and relative to the 1950s and 1960s. Besides, if foreign savings are considered instead, the 1980s saw an influx, corresponding to the current account deficit that has bedeviled US–Japan trade relations for sure.

The fears in the developed countries are fairly potent, nonetheless, and drive a number of other demands, such as those for harmonizing and imposing higher environmental and labor standards on the poor countries: not primarily because of moral concerns reflecting a sense of transborder moral obligation but often with a view to somehow and anyhow raising the costs of production in the poor countries to reduce the pressure of competition that is feared to depress one's wages and take away one's jobs. I will return to these aspects of the question below.

Globalization and sovereignty

Evidently then, I regard the foregoing critiques and fears of the globalization process in the developed countries to be unsound, and the reverse enthusiasm for globalization among the developing countries today to be sensible. In fact, I embrace (with necessary nuances) the current "Washington consensus," which I embraced in fact long before it reached Washington, that successful and robust development requires two pillars: democracy (whose merits I began my analysis with) and markets (which, in turn, imply integration into the world economy).

But there are new concerns which have arisen, which cut across the rich and poor countries and in fact afflict the latter even more pointedly, concerning the loss of sovereignty as also of democratic accountability following the globalization phenomenon. These are important concerns, especially since, if integration into the world markets for trade, investment, and people is undercutting democracy, then the two legs on which the Washington consensus seeks to walk will be pulling in different directions. These concerns therefore need to be carefully assessed.

Let me begin with the question of sovereignty. Two different ways can be distinguished in which this question may be approached. Both concern the poor nations more than the rich nations, since the latter are politically and economically the stronger.

Increased cost of certain policy options

One way is to consider sovereignty as adversely affected if the globalization, while welfare-improving, increases the cost of certain policy options so dramatically as to impair, in effect, our *ability* to adopt them.

Thus, the increasing trade opportunities and flows of funds and of DFI in today's world economy are increasing the ability of different countries to achieve greater income or even significantly accelerated growth rates. At the same time, however, the increased reliance on trade, external funds, and DFI may constrain the ability of individual nation-states to pursue social agendas.

This may happen, for instance, because the politically weaker nations may find themselves unable to pursue more egalitarian agendas, for example, without serious consequences such as outflows of capital. This used to be, in fact, the problem of "socialism in one state": if you went socialist, while the world around you was not, your capital and people would exit, forcing such immense economic costs that the option of socialism was effectively ruled out.

Then again, to recount a more pertinent problem today, consider the

274   *Jagdish Bhagwati*

Mexican debacle in early 1995. Integration into the capital markets of the world through capital account convertibility aided Mexico's prosperity for sure by enabling her to gain from short-term capital inflows and by avoiding the efficiency losses that exchange control restrictions entail. But then such integration and openness to volatile short-term capital inflows demands extremely difficult fiscal and monetary discipline in whose absence the economy becomes seriously vulnerable. When things go wrong, as they did in Mexico, putting the economy on the rack to restore credibility with Wall Street becomes Hobson's choice: the alternatives are even worse. Policy options shrink dramatically before and during crises.

One may well ask: if governments choose to integrate and take these risks and corresponding constraints on their policy options, is this not a calculated and rational surrender of sovereignty? By and large, I think that this is a valid way to look at the question. But some observations are in order.

Governments may not adequately grasp the full implications of globalization when they choose to integrate in specific ways into the world economy. Evidently the many macro-economists, who have dominated Mexico's recent politics, did not. Then again, even if they did, they may overdiscount the downside scenarios, leading to a regret phenomenon.

Unfortunately, the reversal of mistaken policies may not be easy. It is hard to imagine that Mexico will be able to get out from under Wall Street's yoke now that it is financially crippled thanks to embracing Wall Street with abandon.

Besides, governments are not unitary actors. A decision to integrate, for example, that constrains (by increasing greatly the cost of such a shift) the ability to shift to more egalitarian policies down the road may weigh greatly on some groups. These groups will then continue to regard and to oppose the decisions to integrate the economy into the world economy as a surrender of sovereignty even when the decision is taken democratically and is best seen as a welfare-improving one.

These groups also see several recent institutional arrangements underlying and embodying the globalization as being explicitly designed to *preempt* future options to reverse the integration process. Thus, during the NAFTA debate in the United States and Mexico, the most popular argument for NAFTA's passage by the US Congress was precisely that, once Mexico had entered NAFTA, it would politically "lock in" Mexico's markets-oriented and outward-looking proglobalization reforms. Presumably, the cost of withdrawal from NAFTA would be so great that no political party could succeed in reversing the reforms which were integral to the NAFTA arrangements. The political ability to

Globalization, sovereignty, and democracy 275

reverse the "reforms" later would be constrained, signifying to those who wish to work for such reversal that there has been a loss of "sovereignty" in this sense.[16]

Strategic action by governments and non-governmental organizations (NGOs)

What I have said so far suggests reasons why globalization is seen as reducing sovereignty, even though it increases efficiency, income, and wealth, simply because it is felt to be reducing the ability to exercise certain policy options. This reduced ability is, however, simply a reflection of the market forces as reflected in the globalization process. No "conspiracy" or "strategic" behavior by any foreign governments or agents is involved; the country is simply a victim of autonomous, "structural" developments in the world economy.

But strategic behavior impacting on one's sovereignty also may be an increasingly important factor in a globalized economy. Thus, the strong nations, exploiting their increased leverage through globalization, may successfully impose on the weak ones demands that improve the distribution of gains from trade and investment in their favour, either bilaterally through aggressive actions that reflect the increased vulnerability of internationally integrated weak nations to such threats (as in the case of the use by the United States of market-access-closing threats under the Special 301 provisions of its trade legislation against selected developing countries that do not accept the maximalist US version of desirable intellectual property protection) or multilaterally (as when socially suboptimal, excessive intellectual property protection was demanded and successfully translated into concessions by the weaker nations in multilateral trade negotiations at the Uruguay Round which culminated in the transformation of the GATT into the WTO).[17] In these instances, the weaker nations are forced into renouncing policy options that are clearly useful in the pursuit of their interest: the integration in to the world economy and the dependence brought by it increases the cost to the weaker countries of not yielding to such demands for the abandonment of their welfare-improving policy options.

But such strategic behavior also comes today through the proliferating NGOs, many of which have active international agendas (aimed at exploiting the leverage implied by the increased globalization of the world economy through trade, private capital and DFI flows, foreign aid programs, etc.), not with a view to shifting *economic* advantage in their constituents' favour, but motivated instead by *moral* consider-

276   *Jagdish Bhagwati*

ations. Today, there is a veritable explosion of NGOs around the world, even among the developing and the former socialist countries.[18] But there is little doubt that, on the international stage, as it impacts on national sovereignty, the well-financed and organized NGOs of the rich countries, whose impassioned one-page advertisements in leading newspapers such as *The Financial Times* and *The New York Times* cannot have missed catching your attention, call the shots. And the efforts of these NGOs are often aimed at the developing countries: e.g., at Mexico's environmental standards, at India's Narmada Dam, at Thailand's safety standards, indeed at an increasing number of issues.

A noteworthy aspect of these NGO efforts at intruding on the sovereignty of nations in regard to matters which the NGOs are targeting is that it reflects an enhanced sense of the obligation that we as human beings owe one another, transcending national borders. In turn, this phenomenon has contributed to an important shift in the current approach to questions of sovereignty: namely, that the nation-state is no longer accepted by many as necessarily the legitimate and exclusive arbiter of its citizens' welfare.

The sense of transborder moral obligation is of course ancient, long predating the modern nation-state. As John Dunn, the Cambridge political theorist, has reminded us eloquently in tracing the origins of the notion of a "human community," and the consequent answer to the question of what human beings owe one another:

an old answer [to the question of what we owe to others] with deep Greek and Christian roots, is that there is just one human community, "that great and natural community" . . ., as John Locke called it, of all human beings as natural creatures, whose habitat is the whole globe and whose obligations to one another do not stop at any humanly created – any artificial – boundary. Locke had a very powerful explanation of why this was so, an explanation which tied human obligations immediately to the purposes of God himself . . . A pale shadow of Locke's conception, with God tactfully edited out, still lives on in modern secular understandings of human right . . . and, even more diffusely, in anthropocentric interpretations of the collective ecological imperative to save a habitat for the human species as a whole. (Dunn 1993)

Obligation implies rights. If then transborder obligations to others elsewhere are accepted, so must the notion that these others have rights which *we* are expected to sustain.

It follows then that the assumption in international relations since the Treaty of Westphalia, that nation-states have exclusive domain over their subjects such that treatment of these subjects is a matter of domestic sovereignty and international relations therefore must respect moral pluralism, is no longer acceptable. As Raymond Plant has put it

Globalization, sovereignty, and democracy

succinctly: "The principle of cuius regio euius religio may have been central to the Treaty of Westphalia but the principle of cuius regio, eius jus is not compatible with the idea that there are basic human rights the moral authority of which crosses frontiers" (1993).

The problem, of course, is that the mere assertion of morality does not automatically put these NGOs on higher ground. Often, the demands they make are culture-bound and have no overriding moral force as when environmentalists in the United States seek to attack Mexico with trade sanctions for using purse seine nets to catch tuna and killing dolphins in the process; surely these demands appear to Mexicans to be morally defective in putting dolphins ahead of the Mexican poor (since purse seine nets are more productive). Also, Mexicans may well wonder why there is no equivalent condemnation of equally cruel hog farming or chicken batteries within the United States itself, suggesting compellingly that there is no morally coherent approach here to the issue of cruelty to animals and of animal rights.

Often the NGOs, based in the North, also focus on the failings in the South rather than admitting the commonality of these failings everywhere and turning the spotlight equally on the moral turpitude in their own backyards. Thus, for instance, the labor-standards lobbies have typically used the example of a deadly fire in a toy factory in Bangkok, Thailand, where several women workers died, unable to use the exit doors which had been closed to prevent theft. But a similar fire had occurred in North Carolina in a chicken parts plant, with exit doors closed again to prevent theft, and was a far more serious matter since it was in the world's richest country. Why not use that example instead or alongside? Then again, the demand to include a Social Clause in the WTO has also been couched overwhelmingly in terms of the developing countries indulging in practices leading to unfair competition rather than focusing on the universality in practice of the failures in regard to the practices (such as, for instance, virtual slavery through bonded labor, say in India, and through cruel abuse of migrant labor, say in the US) chosen to be put in the Clause. Equally, one fails to see good faith efforts to include within the Clause practices where some of the developed countries would be more serious culprits (e.g., in regard to the effective as against the notional right to unionize, the right to worker representation in management, the treatment of immigrant labour, etc.).

The feeling has steadily grown, therefore, among the developing countries that the morality that many of the NGOs advance to override national sovereignty via the use of trade and aid sanctions is selective, aimed at the developing countries rather than universal, is often a mask for protectionist intentions, and is hypocritical in throwing stones at

278   *Jagdish Bhagwati*

other countries' glass houses while building fortresses around one's own.[19] The NGOs' efforts are therefore unlikely to succeed until these fundamental flaws are fixed, as I optimistically expect that they will eventually as the NGOs mature and their activities and influence expand.

Globalization and democracy

The arguments above about the effect of the globalization process on national sovereignty have an obvious relationship, of course, to the ability of citizens to participate effectively in the democratic choice of policies within the nation-state. On the other hand, there is much that is positive for the spread of democracy in the developing countries when globalization is seen on the dimension of freer mobility of people and of ideas that goes with greater integration. The idea of democracy itself has spread through the postwar period, a role being played in the dramatic turn of the Third World to democracy by the increased awareness among the peoples there of the institutions of democracy in the developed world. Trade and investments have drawn the elites, the bourgeoisie, into deeper contacts with the democracies and have surely prompted their successful demands for democracy in their own countries.

Also, the *quality* of democracy has certainly improved with the increased trade and investments that, alongside the growth of foreign education and the availability of information through the medium of television (which brings telling images of individualism, political freedom, liberated women, etc., to vast audiences via CNN, BBC and other worldwide services), are serving as catalysts for bringing ever more of the traditionally peripheral groups such as women increasingly into an assertive, and often a political, role in their own societies. To give just one telling example: the enormous expansion of Japanese multinationals in the European Union and in the United States in the last fifteen years, and the accompanying explosion in the number of corporate wives and children living in the West, has been a source of cultural change in the direction of modernizing the elite women (and men) of Japan and encouraging their inclusion in Japan's strengthening democracy and polity.[20] I can only applaud such outcomes.

NOTES

1 In Huxley's instance, the irony is greater still when one contemplates that mescalin was seen by him as opening the doors of perception when today its progeny, LSD, etc., are seen as closing these doors.

Globalization, sovereignty, and democracy 279

2 For a short commentary on this question, see Bhagwati (1992), and, in particular, see the extended analysis in Bhagwati (1995a).
3 This conclusion is certainly not refuted by the more intensively statistical chapters in this volume on this subject. While Surjit Bhalla appears to deduce that "political freedom," or democracy, has a benign influence on growth, Przeworski and Limongi are more skeptical of this benign relationship. Neither concludes, however, as the cruel-dilemma thesis did, that democracy harms growth.
4 The question of the reasons for the East Asian "miracle" have been the subject of much controversy among economists recently. My own view, developed in many writings, is that their external orientation since the late 1950s enabled these countries to raise their investment and hence savings rates to phenomenally high levels, while the high export earnings and high investment rates meant that imports of new-technology-embodying capital goods also increased dramatically, enabling these countries to profit additionally from the technological inflow.
5 I have discussed the role of these intellectual antecedents, and of misplaced economic theorizing by some of India's leading economists, on India's dismal economic performance (Bhagwati 1994a).
6 The threat to sovereignty was also a principal objection to signing the Uruguay Round accords by many legislators in the two democracies, India and the United States. Ironically, the former feared that the weak countries would lose sovereignty to the strong ones, the latter feared that the strong countries would lose it to the weak ones.
7 The theoretical aspects of this argument, which has attracted a huge economic literature, have been nicely reviewed and synthesized by Wilson (in Bhagwati and Hudec 1996).
8 This claim is quoted in Robert Hudec's excellent article (1993), containing the proceedings of a conference on "The Morality of Protectionism" at the New York University Law School in November 1992.
9 This value of example has certainly worked in South America and in India, where such unilateral trade liberalization has occurred. It would have greatly pleased Cobden and Bright, leading lights in Britain's repeal of the Corn Laws, who were unilateral free traders and felt that the example of British success from her free trade, rather than reciprocity, would effectively spread free trade elsewhere. Cf. Bhagwati (1988).
10 These different economic-philosophical positions are discussed in depth in Bhagwati (1977: chapter 1).
11 This attitude extended to other areas too: the outward flow of skilled manpower was thus considered a "brain drain" rather than an opportunity for one's citizens to train and work abroad that would lead to a beneficial impact as this diaspora expanded.
12 They were called the West, of course, then. The changing nomenclature of the poor and rich countries reflects a shift from a historical, cultural, and imperial divide into East and West to a contemporary, post-colonial and development-related divide into South and North.
13 See, for example, Bhagwati (1988), on the question of free trade, and Bhagwati (1991b) on the issue of multilateralism.

280   *Jagdish Bhagwati*

14 The evidence in support of this phenomenon in the 1980s, both for the United States and for several other countries, is reviewed and synthesized nicely by Marvin Kosters (in Bhagwati and Kosters 1994: chapter 1).
15 This empirical work by Robert Lawrence and Matthew Slaughter is reviewed in Bhagwati and Dehejia (1994). A subsequent empirical study by Sachs and Schatz (1994) claims to overturn the Lawrence and Slaughter findings by taking out computers (a procedure that is debatable at best). Even then the coefficient with the changed sign is both small and statistically insignificant. So, while Noam Chomsky has educated us that two negatives add up to a positive in every language, it is wrong to claim that the two negatives of a statistically insignificant and small parameter of the required sign add up to a positive support for the thesis that trade has been depressing the real wages of the unskilled! The work of Adrian Wood (1994) argues in support of the trade-hurting-real-wages-of-the-unskilled thesis but his arguments have been effectively criticized by Lawrence (1994). See also the most recent review of the theory and evidence in Bhagwati (1995c).
16 Mind you, this is not the same thing as Ulysses chaining himself voluntarily to resist the sirens; here, he is chaining also others who have no such fear of the sirens.
17 On these questions, see Bhagwati (1991b).
18 Salomon (1994) calls this the global "associational revolution" and studies the diverse cultural and political roots of this phenomenon.
19 I have dealt with these problems in greater depth, in the context of environmental and labour standards demands at the WTO, in several writings. See, for example, Bhagwati (1995b).
20 I have dealt with this question of Japan's political, economic, and cultural evolution and convergence in the context of a critique of the Clinton administration's Japan policy (Bhagwati 1994b).

REFERENCES

Bhagwati, Jagdish. 1966. *The Economics of Underdeveloped Countries*. London and New York: Weidenfeld and Nicolson and McGraw-Hill.
    ed. 1977. *The New International Economic Order: The North–South Debate.* Cambridge, Mass.: MIT Press.
    1988. *Protectionism.* Bertil Ohlin Lectures, 1987. Cambridge, Mass.: MIT Press.
    1991a. "Free traders and free immigrationists: strangers or friends?." Working Paper No. 20. New York: Russell Sage Foundation.
    1991b. *The World Trading System at Risk.* Harry Johnson Lecture. Princeton: Princeton University Press.
    1992. "Democracy and development," *Journal of Democracy* 3: 37–44.
    1994a. *India in Transition.* Radhakrishnan Lectures, Oxford University, 1992. Oxford: Clarendon Press.
    1994b. "Samurais no more," *Foreign Affairs* 73: 7–12.
    1995a. "Democracy and development." First Rajiv Gandhi Memorial Lecture, delivered on October 22, published in *Journal of Democracy* 6: 50–64.

Globalization, sovereignty, and democracy

1995b. *Free Trade, "Fair Trade" and the New Protectionism.* Harold Wincott Lecture, 1994. London: Institute for Economic Affairs.

1995c. "Trade and wages: choosing among alternative explanations," *Federal Reserve Bank of New York Economic Policy Review* 1: 42–47.

Bhagwati, Jagdish, and Vivek Dehejia. 1994. "Freer trade and wages of the unskilled – is Marx striking again?," in Bhagwati and Kosters 1994.

Bhagwati, Jagdish, and Robert Hudec, eds. 1996. *Fair Trade and Harmonization: Prerequisites for Free Trade?.* Cambridge, Mass.: MIT Press.

Bhagwati, Jagdish, and Marvin Kosters, eds. 1994. *Trade and Wages: Leveling Wages Down?* Washington, DC: American Enterprise Institute.

Dunn, John. 1993. "The nation-state and human community: life chances, obligation and the boundaries of society." Mimeograph, King's College, Cambridge.

Employment Outlook. 1993. Paris: OECD.

Hudec, Robert. 1993. " 'Circumventing' democracy: the political morality of trade negotiations," *Journal of International Law and Politics* 25: 311–322.

Kohli, Atul. 1986. "Democracy and development," in John P. Lewis and Valeriana Kallab, eds., *Development Strategies Reconsidered.* Washington, DC: Overseas Development Council.

Lawrence, Robert. 1994. "Trade, multinationals, & labor." NBER Working Paper No. 4836. Cambridge, Mass.: National Bureau of Economic Research.

Plant, Raymond. 1993. "Rights, rules and world order." Mimeograph, University of Southampton.

Sachs, Jeffrey, and Howard Schatz. 1994. "Trade and jobs in US manufacturing," in *Brooking Papers on Economic Activity* 1: 1–84.

Salomon, Lester. 1994. "The rise of the nonprofit sector," *Foreign Affairs* 73: 109–122.

Weiner, M. 1991. *The Child and the State in India: Child Labor and Education Policy in Comparative Perspective.* Princeton: Princeton University Press.

Wood, Adrian. 1994. *North–South Trade, Employment and Inequality.* Oxford: Clarendon Press.

13 Dangerous liaisons: the interface of globalization and democracy

Claude Ake

Preliminaries

At the end of the Cold War, democracy seems triumphant and unassailable, its universalization only a matter of time. But if democracy is being universalized, it is only because it has been trivialized to the point that it is no longer threatening to power elites around the world, who may now enjoy democratic legitimacy without the notorious inconveniences of practicing democracy.

The trivialization of democracy occurred under the pretext of sorting out a complex and confusing political concept. That was an ideological blind, however. For a political concept, democracy is uncharacteristically precise. Democracy means popular power or in a famous American restatement, government of the people, by the people for the people. The Greeks who invented it understood it in that sense. Indeed, every faction in the ideological camps of ancient Greek society including conservatives such as Aristotle agreed on this definition despite their strong political disagreements. They also operationalized it meticulously in practical political arrangements. They left us not only a precise and non-controversial definition but also a historical practice of democratic governance complete with institutions. The Athenians took democracy seriously enough to devise, at great pains, political arrangements which actually realized the ideal of popular power. All citizens formed the Sovereign Assembly whose quorum was put at 6,000. Meeting over forty times a year, it debated and took decisions on all important issues of public policy including issues of war and peace, foreign relations, public order, finance and taxation. The rigors of direct control of the people was carried to the executive function. The business of the Assembly was prepared by a Council of 500 which also had a Steering Committee of fifty headed by a President who held office for only one day. The executive function of the polis was carried out by Magistrates, invariably a committee of ten, usually elected for a non-renewable term of one year. Even if there was a chance that anyone had difficulties with the very precise Athenian conception of democracy, these political arrangements leave no doubt what it is as a form of government. The supposed confusion over the meaning of democracy is a mystification. It is not lexical but political, a manifestation of an endless political struggle raging over the appropriation of democratic legitimacy.

The French Revolution was the watershed of this struggle. That revolution had reached back to the Athenian idea of democracy as popular power, as was clear from its theory of inalienable human rights, universal citizenship, and popular sovereignty. However, in doing this, it created formidable impeccable enemies not only against itself but also against democracy. The rising European bourgeoisie had welcomed the French Revolution for supplying the impetus for the liquidation of the economic and political institutions of feudalism. However, they were appalled by its radical egalitarianism, especially its theory of popular sovereignty. They understood only too well what it meant for private property and the prerogatives which they enjoyed by virtue of their status.

Not surprisingly they rejected democracy and replaced it with liberal democracy. Liberal democracy has significant affinities to democracy but it is markedly different. Instead of the collectivity, liberal democracy focuses on the individual; it substitutes government by the people with government by the consent of the people. Instead of sovereignty of the people it offers sovereignty of the law. Rather than emphasize universality it celebrates specificity. Most importantly, liberal democracy completely repudiates the notion of popular power.

What is at issue here is not a conflict of meaning or interpretation but deliberate political choices arising from a careful appraisal of substantive interests. Indeed, all the major opponents of democracy understood it as popular power and that was precisely why they opposed it. This is true of James Madison who argued that universal suffrage would mean "permanent animosity between opinion and property." It was true of Thomas Macaulay who argued that democracy in the form of universal suffrage would be "the end of property and thus the end of civilization" and also of David Ricardo who wanted suffrage only for those with no interest in abolishing private property. Alexander Hamilton and James Madison knew that democracy meant popular power. This was why they rejected it and offered an alternative called "representative democracy" which renounced the core value of popular power. It is instructive that they did not adopt representation as a concession to the practical problems of scale and complexity but rather as an alternative to what they deemed to be a dangerous doctrine. Rather than arguing as might have been expected that representative democracy was expedient in a

284 *Claude Ake*

large republic, they argued that a large republic was desirable because it makes representation necessary. Indeed Madison argued that "the larger the republic the better, since the ratio of representatives to represented would thereby be reduced" (Hamilton, Madison, and Jay 1961).

Contemporary social science has contributed significantly to the demise of democracy. With minor exceptions, scholarly projects of clarifying the meaning of democracy have paraded a manifest function of clarification to conceal the latent function of suppressing the meaning of democracy and replacing it with a conception of democracy which rationalizes particular political practices or interests.

To illustrate briefly, the group theory of politics, for instance, totally evades the meaning of democracy and pushes the idea that the essence of democracy is that the dynamics of group competition in a democratic polity prevents the monopoly of state power by one or a few groups and also allows the emergence and accommodation of the broad concerns of many groups. The interest group theory of politics is just as evasive. The citizen of the democratic polity is no longer a real or potential law maker, a participant in sovereignty, but only a supplicant for favorable policy outputs in consonance with articulated interests. The protective theory of democracy is worse still. For this theory, the democratic polity is one in which the citizen is protected against the state (Held 1987). It is a polity which has a vibrant civil society to check the state. Sovereignty disappears as does participation as we settle for protection against excesses. In the *civic culture* theory the failures of contemporary democratic practice become virtues as we are instructed that political apathy is good for "democratic political stability" (Almond and Verba 1963, 1980).

More recently, in the zeal to spread democracy at the end of the Cold War, democracy has been reduced to the crude simplicity of multiparty elections to the benefit of some of the world's most notorious autocrats such as Arap Moi of Kenya and Paul Biya of Cameroon and Campaore of Burkina Faso who are now able to parade democratic credentials without reforming their repressive regimes (Ake 1991). In the light of these reflections, the celebration of the universalization of democracy in the contemporary world is somewhat premature. Democracy is clearly not thriving and it is by no means clear whether we should be celebrating the triumph of democracy or lamenting its demise.

However, there is one redeeming feature in this embattled history of democracy. For all the attacks, subversion, displacement, and trivialization of democracy, there was an unstated consensus on the legitimacy of democracy. Indeed all the problems of democracy arose precisely from an attempt to appropriate democratic legitimacy for concepts or

Dangerous liaisons: the interface of globalization and democracy 285

practices of democracy that are less than ideally democratic to the benefit of particular economic, cultural, or political interest. So in a paradoxical sense, even the attempts to trivialize, undermine, and redefine democracy in self-serving ways were also affirmations of the ideal of democracy.

Against this background we can see in clearer relief the implications of globalization for democracy. My thesis is that the process of globalization attacks democracy in a manner that is uniquely different and extremely threatening. It does not redefine democracy in theory or practice or bend it to the service of specific interests. It does not seek appropriation of democratic legitimacy for something else. It does not trivialize democracy or even reject it. It is simply rendering democracy irrelevant and in this it poses the most serious threat yet in the history of democracy.

Globalization and democracy

Globalization is conceived here as the stretch of processes, practices, and structures across space, especially the national space to globality. It is the transnationalization of things. This is a highly simplified definition of an extraordinarily complex process which is replete with ambiguities, variations, uncertainty, and incompatibilities (Robertson 1992). For instance, globalization concentrates and decenters, uniformizes and differentiates; it universalizes particulars and particularizes universals. It is a leveling process which also hierarchizes. The manifestations and effects of globalization are not uniform and predicable because they are always mediated in historical actualities.

And yet it is all too easy to be mesmerized by the complexities of globalization and to forget that it is economically driven. Its core phenomenon is the irresistible expansion of capitalism, its conquest and subsumption of other modes of production and circulation, and the hegemonization of its values across the globe. By all indications, the dynamics of capitalism has virtually turned the world into a single system of production and distribution, a single market whose exploitation is producing a global mass culture which is the sedimentation of global marketing and its ever-developing communications technology. To be sure, globalization entails more than the globality of industrial capitalism but that is its core and its defining element.

The demise of the nation-state

We have assumed for a long time that the nation-state is the inevitable basic political organization of humankind. In the wake of globalization,

286   *Claude Ake*

this assumption is beginning to look too easy. For global processes are putting the nation-state under pressure from two ends. One side is the pressure for transcendence and amalgamation of nation-states, a trend represented by the European Economic Community (EEC) and the North American Free Trade Area (NAFTA). In these instances, the impetus for aggregation is predominantly economic and the emergence of these entities simultaneously reflects the transnationalization of economic activities and gives impetus to further transnationalization.

The other side are pressures towards decomposition into constituent linguistic, national, religious, or ethnic components as we have witnessed in the decomposition of the Soviet Union, Yugoslavia, Czechoslovakia, Ethiopia, and Somalia. Like the aggregative pressures, the pressures for decomposition occur because of the diminishing relevance and viability of the nation-state especially as the basis of collective identity. The ruptures, tensions, uncertainties, and anxieties of globalization nurture an orientational upheaval which the abstract universalism of civil identity in the nation-state cannot contain. As we shall see later, these conditions elicit particularistic but holistic cultural identities such as national, religious, communal, or ethnic identity. As we have seen in Yugoslavia and Somalia, these identity switches tend to be associated with violent implosions.

As the relevance of the nation-state diminishes, so does that of democracy, especially liberal democracy. For democracy is ideally articulated in the context of a national organization of politics and power. The nation-state, the traditional repository of sovereignty has consummate power which monopolizes the means of coercion to an extent which no substate or superstate political formation can legitimately claim or exercise. The consummate power including the power of life and death within the national territory of the nation-state is the other side of democratic freedom and self-realization. For it is what gives concreteness to them since there is no freedom in powerlessness and no point in democratic arrangements when power resources do not exist and the exercise of power cannot arise. Not surprisingly, insofar as we apply the concept of democracy to any social or political formation apart from the nation-state, its use is largely metaphorical. We can apply and do apply the concept of democracy to the governance of a family, but that is clearly not a strict usage of the term. The democratic intensity of the family is low because a natural sense of mutual obligations makes democratic arrangements less compelling as does the family's lack of anything remotely close to consummate power. Similarly, political formations such as the EEC, North Atlantic Treaty Organization (NATO), trade unions or the United Nations are democratic in a largely analogical sense; they too have low democratic intensity, lacking consummate power.

One of the ways in which global processes have been significant for democracy is precisely that they have been whittling away the power of the nation-state, a major repository of its democratic intensity. With the transnationalization of more and more things, especially economic activities, decisions which affect people's lives and shape public policies decisively are made in distant places, often anonymously, by agents and forces we can hardly understand much less control. Therefore it is not always very clear what people are choosing or controlling, if anything, at national elections. The dilemma is that the political entity which ideally "materializes" popular sovereignty and the fullness of freedom has less and less power, while the amorphous space of transnational phenomena which is not amenable to democratic control has more power. A polarization appears to be occurring: on one side, democracy without empowerment and, on the other, power inaccessible to democratization.

The demise of the social

Global processes are affecting the prospects of democracy even more radically still by threatening the annulment of the social. This is connected to the constitution of capitalist hegemony at the end of the Cold War which has given the market an entirely new status. Already, liberal theory privileged the market over the state, studiedly prohibiting the state from being an entrepreneur to avoid giving it any financial independence and positing that the less the state is present and active the better. But now the status of the market is higher still, something close to a global theology. The market looms so large it effectively subsumes society as well. Market society is no longer simply a metaphor, or an analytic concept. It is a living reality.

As society becomes a market the values and operative norms of the market become salient to society as well. That is why consumption, the driving force of the market has assumed a special significance in the contemporary world. Consumption is no longer a convenience or a means or even a necessity. It has become existential, the veritable badge of identity. As we consume so we are. Our economic identity as consumers is increasingly overriding our civic and even our human identity, a fact reflected in the profound alienation of our large underconsuming population, in the correlation between consumption power and social standing and in the tendency to treat those with marginal or no consumption power as a problem, or worse. For example, it is said increasingly that if Africa and all its 500 million inhabitants should suddenly

288   *Claude Ake*

perish, it would not be missed or even noticed. Perhaps a cruel reprimand to Africa but that is not the point of this remark. The point is about consumption; the significance of the point is that those who do not command the effective demand to register as consumers might as well be dead for they are of no use to themselves or to anybody else.

As the market subsumes society and consumer identity becomes the overriding identity democratic politics, any politics for that matter, becomes virtually impossible. Not surprisingly, because the market is the moment of particularity, self-seeking, and purely private concerns, while democratic politics is the moment of universality. Democratic politics is about a collective enterprise, about how common concerns are to be addressed. Indeed without the presupposition of common cause and the relative "homogeneity" of the population which makes common cause possible in the first place, the basis for democratic participation disappears. This politics presupposes the constitution of political society as "a public," a solidarity of some shared characteristics, common concerns and common cause.

The concept of "a public" is perhaps best understood by referring to Hegel's treatment of civil society in *The Philosophy of Right*. Here civil society is the second movement in the dialectical triad of family, civil society, and the state. The family is the moment of unity, its members typically bound biologically and emotionally. As families reproduce, society expands, becomes more impersonal, a division of labor of growing complexity emerges especially with pervasive commoditization, the moment of particularity is framed. The collectivity of the family gives way to individuality, intimacy yields to impersonality, biological and emotionalities to contractual relations, cooperation to competition. However this moment of particularity is also one of homogeneity. The members of civil society are homogeneous by virtue of being self-interested commodity bearers with a common interest in formal equality and freedom to pursue self-interest. The dissolution of the family and the atomization of society calls into being a higher unity arising from what Hegel calls "the system of wants." Civil society, a network of complementarities and reciprocities, constitutes an organic solidarity. This "public" is the domain of the discourse of civil morality, citizenship, political obligation, public interest, and public opinion. The state itself is a public asset for managing the affairs of this public. So it is entirely appropriate and accurate that the state was referred in the past as *res publicae* or commonwealth.

Globalization is moving the desocialization of market society in the direction of removing the conditions which make political consciousness and the political public possible. Phenomenal advances in communi-

Dangerous liaisons: the interface of globalization and democracy 289

cations technology driven by global marketing and the information revolution which it has spawned is reconstituting consciousness as information, information delivered in ever-increasing profusion and speed. And yet having established itself as consciousness, this information bears hardly any social experience. To begin with, it is not only a product of technology, it is technology. Form and content, message and medium are intertwined in what is really a subsumption, the subsumption of information into technology. In its technological materiality information is not communication, but non-communication. It does not allow for reciprocity especially antagonistic reciprocities which is more dynamic; it is what Jean Baudrillard calls "speech without response."

Since information is only a record encrusted in technology and carries no social experience, it does not integrate socially – this is just the other side of its non-communication. Rather it isolates, partly because of the way in which it is delivered and consumed. The technology connects us as discrete units in an electronic coherency while isolating us socially for information is delivered through the privacy of modems, storage devices, and computer screens, and once it is delivered and received it becomes just a record or an environment disconnected from social praxis.

Global processes have framed a syndrome of isolation and desocialization at the confluence of the singularities of the new communications technology, information, and the public sphere. For a start the technology delivers the information to us in relative isolation largely devoid of social experience. The information itself is isolating. Then, both technology and information define a new public sphere which is mediated in complex ways that desocialize it. This is not the bourgeois public sphere of Habermas so conducive to democratic politics (Habermas 1989, 1992) for it is decidedly non-dialogical. Our visibility to each other in this new public sphere is abstract as is the space itself. It has hardly any boundaries. It is too fluid and too amorphous to elicit a sense of sharing in a social entity or to nurture political projects and democratic activism.

In this context there can only be a politics of disempowerment for here is a context in which the critical role of political mobilization is abstractized and concentrated in the mass media, a context in which political will and political choice achieve concreteness only as opinion polls. Some like Hans Enzensberger (1970) find the dominance of the mass media liberating especially for the masses who are enabled to participate in the productive process. But they participate not as energizing subjects but as objects. The mass media constitute and instrumentalize contemporary politics in a manner that amounts to self-constitution.

290   *Claude Ake*

They promise politics and participation only to deny them by crystalizing into a formidable power, and a formidable obstacle to politics. They deny them by creating a realm of necessity which demands submission rather than creating a realm of freedom which facilitates and enjoins creativity.

As for opinion polls, they only mock political will and political choice. Opinion polls present political will and political choice as facts and statistics to the total destruction of their democratic significations. The essence and saliency of political will and political choice in democratic politics is that they are dynamic processes, the living experience of preferring and willing, expressing the will and actively negotiating consensus on matters of common concern. The opinion poll precisely subverts this political process by virtue of the fact that it is still-born, passive, intransitive, a statistic which has nothing to do with social participation, aggregation, or social exchange.

Difficulties for democratic struggles

The process of globalization is framing a global environment in which emancipatory struggles including democratization are unable to find focus or meaning. The Cold War was a harrowing experience which cannot be missed. But at least in that era, everything was charged with political significance which was invariably about the possibilities of democracy. The great ideological divide was conspicuous and intrusive, pressing everything into the political arena and compelling everyone to make political judgments and to assume political postures constantly. We were always soldiering for a political cause with an ubiquitous presence full of historical importance.

In the Cold War era, allies and opponents were easily identified and generally understood. There were specific power centers to focus on, there were grand ideologies which readily suggested how to interpret events and how to proceed and there were ready-made allies to mobilize and tested modalities of struggle to utilize. Most significantly, even though both sides in the Cold War spoke different languages, bristled with hostility, and believed that their differences were deep and irreconcilable, both camps were in fact a dialectical unity. For each camp had a vision of a world of progress, rationality, and democracy, a vision to which it was passionately committed.

All that has changed. There is now no epic ideological struggle to politicize every difference and every social space. Since the substance of this politicization was progress, rationality, and democracy, these

Dangerous liaisons: the interface of globalization and democracy 291

concerns have largely lost their importance. Now, there is only one vision of a rational world society which has been supposedly realized at "the end of history." What remains are minor adjustments and final touches which call for no serious politics, only some administration and private initiatives. For those who see in the triumph of this world view the meeting of the real and ideal, there would be no point in lamenting the atrophy of politics. For them, the non-feasibility of democratic politics and democratic struggles poses no problem. On the contrary, it merely attests to what has been achieved.

But the real is not yet the ideal and history is far from over. There are many who see a world of increasingly asymmetrical power relations in which their weaknesses are reproduced endlessly. These people are conscious of their marginality, their tenuous control over their lives, their lack of access to democratic participation, and their exposure to abuse and oppression. There are large numbers of entire countries in the world which feel this way. There is a greater number yet of people within all nations including the most developed who share these feelings and for whom there exists a need for politics and for emancipatory and democratic struggles.

How to wage these struggles is the problem. As we have seen, because of globalization, there are hardly any power centers to attack, the oppressors are not easily identified. Political mobilization is very difficult because of the subsumption of the social into the market, the isolation of individuals due to the primacy of information over communication, the general desocialization of life, and the ever-increasing number of social activities (such as shopping, education, meetings, sports, and cultural events) which technology now delivers to us in isolation.

The difficulties of democratic struggles are compounded by the porosity of the nation-space caused by transnational phenomena. How can people organize against oppressive power which is impersonal, invisible, and fluid, power which is always flowing into spaces beyond our grasp and immune to the institutional checks on power in our locality. It is not just power that is fluid. We too are "fluid", and also despatialized for our interests are increasingly tangled with people and events far from us. Consequently, our local or national space is increasingly unlikely to encompass the interest groups which are critical to us. The international or global space gets ever more relevant. Unfortunately, the expansion and porosity of our space does not enhance our power by facilitating a larger, more powerful coalition but gives us only a disorienting sense of spacelessness and little room for political action. Political mobilization, especially interest aggregation and interest articulation, is

292 *Claude Ake*

all but impossible in the fluidity and anonymity of this new political space. Even if mobilization was possible, how would the struggle be focused? At what power centers, and with what power resources?

Misdirected hostilities and irrelevant struggles

Globalization has been credited with being a source of anxiety and tension. The difficulties of finding political expression or mounting emancipatory struggles is clearly a source of this anxiety. For the purpose of understanding the interface of global processes and democracy it is useful to stress how global processes are suffused with tension and anxiety. Perhaps the best way to begin is to remember that globalization is driven by a vigorous, triumphant capitalism which is aggressively consolidating its global hegemony. As always its impetus is profit-seeking, efficiency, and competition. What is unique in this instance is that these values of the capitalist mode of production are inscribed with a new intensity.

For instance the very notion of globalization suggests the finitude of capitalist expansion in space and the exhaustion of new geographical frontiers. That means a shift from spatial extension to intensity which will be associated with a qualitative leap in the rigor of efficiency and competition. In addition to this, the necessities of a global production system as well as a global market have produced large powerful multinationals with enormous resources and unprecedented reach. They are playing for very high stakes in a competition of immense rigor. But this syndrome is not confined to the top; it is decidedly pervasive. Every player, even the most marginal, is in its vortex because the process of globalization is bringing every one into close proximity, shrinking everything into one small intimate space which has to be fought over incessantly. Globalization has created a highly charged competitive economic environment which causes a great deal of anxiety even for the "winners."

The anxieties of globalization are compounded by the openness of boundaries which exposes everyone, everywhere, to the unblinking view and judgment of a global society. There is no place to hide, no respite from scrutiny and assessment or from maneuvering eternally in a changing order of precedence. Shrinking physical space, increasing proximity, and enforced intimacy cause tensions and anxiety by crowding us into ever smaller space with all our differences and mutual suspicions intact. Even when globalization tries to induce common values for instance through the global market, it does not reduce the tensions; if anything it increases them by inducing convergence on the same values and by

Dangerous liaisons: the interface of globalization and democracy 293

focusing demand on the same scarce resources. The process of globalization engenders anxiety by the sheer magnitude of the changes associated with it and by its uncertainties and its contradictions, its rupture of traditional solidarities, its homogenizing effects. It causes anxiety by transforming cultures including those which it is supposed to be universalizing, and by making a global environment where there is a pervasive sense of losing control of one's affairs even in the case of the most powerful actors.

Finally there is the question of the dominant materialist technocratic culture of capitalism which thrusts itself aggressively everywhere. Following the subsumption of society into the market this technocratic culture is reconstituting us radically in terms of a consumer identity. This is an important source of anxiety, tension, and disorientation because the majority of people are marginal or insignificant consumers. At any rate, so they see themselves. Consumer identity is problematic because even for those who command effective demand, consumption cannot satisfy. Indeed consumption is programmed to satisfy only superficially and temporarily and to elicit desire for more consumption so that the productive system can be sustained. In conception and reality, consumer identity carries a formidable tension, for identity is about collectivization, about sharing and solidarity but consumption is about appropriation, privatization, and self-gratification. In a world of ubiquitous change and an uncertain future, in which considerable anomie and disorientation is already problem enough, the aggressive incursion of the materialistic technocratic culture appears to have driven many to desperation and hostility.

But how to fight this debilitating and oppressive presence is a problem. By all indications, people are doing so by embracing new identities. Overwhelmingly, they appear to be embracing "primary" identities especially national, ethnic, religious, racial, and communal identities. This preference for primary identities apparently arises from the fact that the threat which is being met is generalized and cultural and demands nothing less than the crystalization of the self holistically, which is precisely what primary identities do.

For instance ethnic identity, like all other primary identities is cultural and more importantly holistic. As self-reflexivity, it takes itself and all its claims for granted. By the same token it does not take rival identity claims seriously except in the oppositionality by which it determines and invigorates itself by negation. For those who respond to ethnic interpellations, the claims of ethnicity are totalistic, ethnicity presumes to articulate all signifying practices and to encapsulate the members' whole way of life.

294 *Claude Ake*

The problem is that while resort to primary identity may be the logical response to the threat in question, it is by no means a relevant one. For when solidarity is thus formed and the struggle against the threat is waged, it is unfortunately against the wrong enemies – Bosnians, Hutus, Afghans, Moslems, foreigners, blacks, immigrants, Catholics. These false enemies are aggressed with violent intensity, for once people are mobilized to fight in these social formations, the conflict is necessarily intense because they are inclined to believe that they are defending their whole way of life. We have seen the tragic enormity of this in Burundi, Rwanda, Bosnia, Sudan, and Algeria.

No wonder some are beginning to envision the era of the clash of civilizations. However, appearances notwithstanding, there is no clash of civilizations. There is only one overweening materialistic technocratic culture which is so entrenched and dominant, it has no serious competitor. What we call the clash of civilizations are contradictions in the local space of a necessary but misdirected struggle against this dominant culture as people in their desperation to attack an unbearably oppressive but totally invisible enemy, lash out in confusion against superficially plausible but wrong targets.

Since the threat is an oppressive power, it cannot be met without power, without engineering through political power, fundamental changes in economy and society, and in cultural experience. However, the identities which the threat elicits are static identities that are not really conducive to framing a serious political project or mounting a political movement of the enormous spread and depth which is required by the threat and our new amorphous political space.

Despite their rhetoric, the rash of primary identity struggles which we are witnessing in Bosnia, Somalia, Sudan, Rwanda, etc., are not really about power or even about politics except in a metaphorical sense. They are about human dignity, they express a stirring of life, the affirmation of humanity. In lashing out, however aimlessly against the oppressive materialistic technocratic culture, people are signaling that they are alive and asserting their human dignity. Unfortunately, what this means is that the struggle for human dignity is now tendentially dissociated from politics and from democracy which is odd and rather tragic.

These reflections do not mean that democracy is to be written off. Globalization may be rendering democracy irrelevant, yet democracy remains the only answer to the problems of fractured modernity and its oppressive fetishised technology and materialism. For the answer lies in a renewed commitment to democracy and to human dignity and autonomy; it lies in asserting the will to freedom, in refusing to be confined to a path of movement prescribed by technology and market opportunities.

Dangerous liaisons: the interface of globalization and democracy 295

REFERENCES

Ake, C. 1991. "Rethinking Democracy in Africa," *Journal of Democracy* 2 no. 1: 32–44.

1992. "Devaluing Democracy," *Journal of Democracy* 3 no. 3: 33–37.

Almond, A., and S. Verba, 1963. *The Civic Culture: Political Attitudes and Democracy in Five Nations.* Princeton, N. J.: Princeton University Press.

eds. 1980. *The Civic Culture Revisited.* Boston: Little, Brown & Co.

Archer, M. S. 1990. "Foreword," in M. Albrow and E. King, eds., *Globalization, Knowledge and Society.* London: Sage Publications.

Aristotle. 1981. *The Politics.* Harmondsworth: Penguin.

Arnason, J. P. 1990. "Nationalism, globalization and modernity," *Theory, Culture and Society* 7 (2–3): 207–236.

Baudrillard, J. 1980. "The implosion of meaning in the media and the implosion of the social in the masses," in K. Wordward, ed., *The Myths of Information Technology and Post Industrial Culture.* Madison: Coda.

Beetham, D. 1981. "Beyond liberal democracy," in Ralph Miliband and John Saville, eds., *Socialist Register.* London: Merlin Press.

Berelson, B. 1952. "Democratic theory and public opinion," *Public Opinion Quarterly*, 16: 313–330.

Berelson, B., P. F. Lazarfeld, and W. McPhee. 1954. *Voting.* Chicago: University of Chicago Press.

Boyne, R. 1990. "Culture and the world-system," in M. Featherstone, ed., *Global Culture.* London: Sage.

Burnheim, J. 1985. *Is Democracy Possible?* Cambridge: Polity Press.

Cohen, J., and J. Rogers. 1983. *On Democracy.* New York: Penguin.

Dahl, R. A. 1956. *A Preface to Democratic Theory.* Chicago: University of Chicago Press.

1961. *Who Governs? Democracy and Power in an American City.* New Haven, Conn.: Yale University Press.

1971. *Polyarchy: Participation and Opposition.* New Haven: Yale University Press.

1979. "Procedural democracy," in P. Laslett and J. Fishkin, eds., *Philosophy, Politics and Society*, Fifth Series. New Haven: Yale University Press.

Der Derian, J., and J. Shapiro, eds. 1989. *International/Intertextual Relations: Postmodern Readings of World Politics.* Lexington, Mass.: Lexington Books.

Economist. 1991. "Global village, traveling peasants," *Economist* 321: 20.

Enzensberger, H. 1970. "Constituents of a theory of the media," *New Left Review* 64: 13–36.

Featherstone, M. 1991a. "Global culture: an introduction," *Theory, Culture and Society* 7 (1): 1–16.

1991b. "Consumer culture, postmodernism, and global disorder," in R. Robertson and W. R. Garrett, eds., *Religion and Global Order.* New York: Paragon.

Friedman, J. 1990. "Being in the world: globalization and localization," *Theory, Culture and Society* 7 (2–3): 311–328.

Fukayama, F. 1992. *The End of History and the Last Man.* New York: Free Press.

296   *Claude Ake*

Ghai, D. 1992. *Structural Adjustment, Global and Social Democracy*. Geneva: UNSRID.

Giddens, A. 1991. *Modernity and Self-Identity: Self and Society in the Late Modern Age*. Stanford, Calif.: Stanford University Press.

Habermas, J. 1976. *Legitimating Crisis*. London: Heinemann.

1989. *The Structural Transformation of the Public Sphere: An Inquiry into a Category of Bourgeois Society*. Cambridge: Polity Press.

1992. "Further Reflections on the Public sphere," in C. Calhoun, ed., *Habermas and the Public Sphere*. Cambridge, Mass.: MIT Press.

Hamilton, Alexander, James Madison, and John Jay. 1961. *The Federalist Papers*. New York: New American Library.

Hegel, F. 1967. *Philosophy of Right*, transl. T. M. Knox. Oxford: Oxford University Press.

Held, D. 1987. *Models of Democracy*. Cambridge: Polity Press.

Hobsbawm, E., and T. Ranger, eds. 1983. *The Invention of Tradition*. Cambridge: Cambridge University Press.

Locke, J. 1963. *Two Treatises of Government*. Cambridge and New York: Cambridge University Press.

Mazrui, A. A. 1980. *Cultural Forces in World Politics*. London: James Currey.

Meyer, J. W. 1980. "The world polity and the authority of the nation-state," in A. Bergesen, ed., *Studies of the Modern World System*. New York: Academic Press.

Offe, C. 1984. *Contradictions of the Welfare State*. London: Hutchinson.

Robertson, R. 1992. *Globalization: Social Theory and Global Culture*. New York: Sage Publications.

Schumpeter, J. 1976. *Capitalism, Socialism and Democracy*. London: Allen and Unwin.

Smith, A. D. 1990. "Toward a global culture?," *Theory, Culture & Society* 7 (2–3): 171–192.

Truman, D. B. 1951. *The Governmental Process*. New York: Knopf.

Wolff, J. 1991. "The global and the specific: reconciling conflicting theories of culture," in A. D. King, ed., *Culture, Globalization and the World-System*. London: Macmillan.

14 Exploring the problematic triumph of liberal democracy and concluding with a modest proposal for improving its international impact

Philippe C. Schmitter

The celebrations that have accompanied the wave of transitions from autocracy to democracy since 1974 have tended to obscure two serious dangers. Together, they presage a political future that, instead of embodying "the end of history," promises to be tumultuous and uncertain. Far from being secure in its foundations and practices, modern democracy will have to face unprecedented challenges in the 1990s and beyond.

First, with regard to **established liberal democracies** (ELDs), the very absence in the present context of a credible "systemic" alternative is bound to generate new strains. The apologists for ELDs have long argued and their citizens have generally agreed that, whatever the defaults, this mode of political domination was clearly preferable to any of several forms of autocracy. Now, these external criteria for comparison have (largely) disappeared and, in any case, are no longer supported by the propaganda and military might of a great power. All that remains are the internal standards for evaluation, embedded in the pages of a vast *corpus* of normative democratic theory and in the expectations of a vast majority of normal democratic citizens. What will happen when the rulers of ELDs are held accountable in their well-entrenched practices to these long subordinated ideals of justice and equality – not to mention those of participation, accountability, responsiveness, and self-realization?

Second, with regard to **fragile neo-democracies** (FNDs), the widespread desire to imitate the basic norms and institutions of ELDs does not guarantee that these efforts will be successful. Nothing demonstrates that democracy is inevitable or irrevocable. It is not a necessity. It neither fills some indispensable functional requisite of capitalism, nor does it correspond to some ineluctable ethical imperative in social evolution. There is every reason to believe that its consolidation demands an extraordinary and continuous effort, which many countries are not likely to be able to make. What will happen when the inevitable

297

298   Philippe C. Schmitter

desencanto begins to undermine citizen confidence in the precarious institutions of FNDs, and their rulers are forced to admit that democratization alone cannot bring the long-awaited benefits of well being, justice, and equality?

The system of sovereign national states

What links the ELDs and the FNDs is the international (or, better, interstate) system. Even when the countries on both sides of the North–South and the East–West divide have adopted domestic regimes that have (more or less) the same domestic institutions and respect (more or less) the same human rights, their foreign relations will remain problematic. Whatever their convergence in the way they govern themselves internally, two things cannot be overlooked in the way they relate to each other externally:

(1) the absence of any arrangement for ensuring justice that transcends the jurisdictions of the countries involved in these regime changes; and
(2) the persistence of multiple forms of inequality in size, economic development, military capacity, and political influence across their national borders.

It is certainly comforting that, so far, no well-established democracy has gone to war with another democracy and it is widely expected that accountable government will open up more favorable perspectives for investment and growth, but nothing guarantees that the countries involved or, even less, their individual citizens will have comparatively greater access to the good life. No matter how much their newly democratized regimes strive to improve the domestic administration of justice and the domestic production of goods and services, international differences in the access to justice and equality will persist. Moreover, the goals these FNDs are seeking to attain are moving ahead of them, as the rate of economic development and the distribution of political rights in ELDs continues to grow faster than in most FNDs. There is even growing evidence that, in the short to medium run, the uncertainty of regime change is likely to depress rates of economic growth and disturb export performance, thereby magnifying these differences, at least, until the FNDs become somehow consolidated and can benefit fully from the freedoms they have attained.

The major reason for these persistent injustices and inequalities – and, hence, the major weakness of liberal democracy as the basic principle for founding a "new world order" – is the system of sovereign national

The problematic triumph of liberal democracy 299

states (SNSs). Neither liberalism nor democracy produced this system. It was a European invention of the fifteenth to sixteenth centuries which antedated the full development of capitalist economic relations and the widespread demand for popular sovereignty. Needless to say, it strongly influenced the subsequent emergence of both. The unfortunate fact is that complex historical forces – balances and imbalances of power, foreign and domestic warfare, dynastic rivalries and marriages, religious conformity and dissent, ethnicity and language use, state strengths and weaknesses, and *virtù* and *fortuna* – produced a set of autonomous political units in Europe of very uneven size, population, natural resources, geo-strategic location, and military capacity. Colonialism, imperialism, and diffusion spread this pattern around the world. The success of subsequent movements for national liberation merely consolidated it.

The ideologically consistent economic or political **liberal** should be indifferent to these "accidental" boundaries. He or she should have no national affiliation or bias. His or her principles are supposed to be universal in nature and application. The fact that a given exchange increases employment in another country more than in one's own, or that a given policy improves citizen rights in a neighboring polity that may be used to make claims against one's own, should be cause for approval not regret. In the abstract, the goal of liberals should be to enhance the freedom and welfare of the global system as a whole, not of any particular part of it.

Nor can ideologically consistent **democrats** afford to ignore the impact of national boundaries. One of their most sacred principles is deeply antithetic to the system of sovereign national states as it developed historically – namely, the universal right for citizens to have an equal voice in all issues that collectively affect their freedom and well being. Admittedly, in modern democracies, this right has rarely been exercised directly by individuals, but indirectly through processes of representation. Nevertheless, the fact that some territorial demarcation cuts across the functional boundaries surrounding the constituency of a given issue should be irrelevant for its resolution. In principle, separation into distinctive national jurisdictions should not be exploited – especially when it involves the borders of two or more SNSs with very unequal capacities and high levels of interdependence – to deny citizens or their representatives their rights, their mutual *droits de regard*, in matters that jointly affect their freedom and well being.

Liberal democracy cannot guarantee that all affected citizens will be equally benefited or harmed by a specific policy – within or across national boundaries – but it can and should ensure that they have an equal opportunity to express their preferences with regard to that policy

300   *Philippe C. Schmitter*

and that the distribution of its effects not be systematically biased only because of the existence of an artificial political jurisdiction.

The (out-moded) presumption of autonomy

Since its origins in classical Greece through its transformation by liberalism in the eighteenth and nineteenth centuries, democratic theory has always presumed the existence of political units that were autonomous, both in their ability to satisfy the interests of their citizens and in their immunity from the actions of other polities. Neither is any longer the case, if it ever was. Under contemporary conditions of increasing trade interdependence and financial liberalization, none of the ELDs, no matter how large and resourceful, and certainly none of the FNDs, can be described as sufficiently autonomous to be self-governing. Their decisions, no matter how democratically taken, are bound to be limited by prior decisions made outside their borders and, in turn, will inevitably affect the welfare of citizens elsewhere. The territorial jurisdictions of national authority are no longer congruent with the functional domains of public policy.

Previously, the central problems with the international system were **aggression** and **exploitation**, i.e., the likelihood that stronger states would be able to conquer weaker ones by force or coerce them into accepting unequal exchanges by military threats. The subsequent emergence in a few democratized regions of the world of what have been called "security communities" in which states voluntarily and permanently abjure recourse to force to settle their disputes has shifted the nature of the problem. Nowadays, what threatens to destroy the accountability of rulers to citizens within national boundaries are **extra-territorialities** and **externalities**. Actors have emerged – transnational industries, financial intermediaries, professional service agencies, and international crime syndicates – that cannot be controlled by any SNS. Actions are frequently taken by one SNS which produce negative and uncontrolled effects in other, usually lesser developed, SNSs. Both of these conditions violate the central principle upon which liberal democracy is founded: that rulers be held accountable by citizens for all their public actions, regardless of the jurisdictions within which they occur.

The (unfortunate) reality of national liberalisms

In the real world, of course, these jurisdictional boundaries are frequently and routinely used to deny such a right, all in the name of "non-interference in the domestic affairs of another state." The seem-

The problematic triumph of liberal democracy

ingly inexorable trend toward greater international interdependence, even toward globalization, may have drastically reduced the number of issues that are purely domestic in nature, but it has yet to make much of a dent in the institutional armature of national sovereignty. Only in Western Europe – and, there, only with great difficulty – have new institutions of supranational authority emerged to shift the boundaries of jurisdictions and representations. And, even in the EC, the "democracy deficit" remains substantial.

Another way of putting this is that most self-proclaimed economic or political liberals are also nationalists. As politicians, they may not consciously practice "realism" by incessantly seeking to maximize the power and wealth of their own country without regard for others, but they are held exclusively accountable by their fellow nationals for the benefits they produce at home, not for those they provide abroad. Moreover, if they deliberately or inadvertently provide foreigners with "disbenefits," they are almost never punished for it by their *concitoyens*.

Other than pious, unconvincing, and ineffectual protestations of cosmopolitanism, liberal democrats have largely dealt with injustice and inequality in the international system by ignoring both. Some have been comforted by the widely disseminated notion that only rich societies can afford democracy, and the disparities among these Northern and Western countries are of lesser concern. Naturally, liberals in these fortunate countries applaud when their less-fortunate brethren adopt and practice their economic and political principles. Governments in ELDs may even officially promote such outcomes and their citizens can devote considerable resources through a myriad of non-governmental organizations to bringing about the demise of political autocracies and statist economic policies. However laudable these efforts are – and both have tended to increase – they do not directly address the issue of persistent international injustices and inequalities.

Doctrinaire liberal democrats could respond to these charges by arguing that "good governance" will eventually bring about higher growth rates and that this, along with "crowding-out" and "trickle-down" effects, will produce a long-term convergence of FNDs with the more just, egalitarian, and developed ELDs. They could also point out that liberalization should bring about greater respect for the law and other norms which, in turn, should enhance the effectiveness of international law. Neither of these arguments seem very convincing to me – least of all, when some of the best installed liberal democracies do not themselves always practice "good governance" and when they have repeatedly ignored international law if it seemed convenient for their national interests.

302   *Philippe C. Schmitter*

What can be done?

Faced with this embarrassing inconsistency between principle and practice, the usual answer of liberal democrats is: "Nothing right now, but wait until the global effects of liberal democratization are felt; then, we will be able to do something." And that something is thought to be **world government**, obviously according to liberal, representative, democratic, constitutional, and probably federalist principles. Only such an overarching arrangement of supranational authority can be expected to develop the normative preconditions for solidarity and to administer the necessary policies of redistribution that will produce lasting justice and equality across the nation-states of the world. In the meantime, it may be possible to make some marginal improvements in **intergovernmental organizations** (IGOs) and to continue to expand the role of **non-governmental organizations** (NGOs), but they can hardly be expected to have much impact upon the substance of the matter.

Which is not to say that a lot of less formal and more pragmatic arrangements have not grown up around attempts to cope with these issues of international injustice and inequality. The **channels of diplomacy** – noisy or quiet – have long been used to send messages and register protests. Adjacent countries often have a myriad of joint agencies and commissions to resolve disputes crossing their borders. **Summit meetings** between chief executives have been known to deal with such matters. Lesser ministerial officials can meet more often and less obtrusively. **Arbitration boards** handle a growing volume of commercial complaints, and more and more interest associations seem to be opening up their memberships and even their offices to persons from other countries. But by far the most important political adjustment mechanism and the one most beyond the control of national governments seems to be **lobbying by foreign interests**. Washington has been literally invaded by representatives of foreign firms, consortia, governments, associations, foundations, and movements. Nor have they confined their activity just to influencing US national legislation and administrative regulations. They have not hesitated to address manifestos to the general public, to attempt to manipulate the content of mass media, to fund ostensibly American think-tanks, and even to attempt to influence the direction of supposedly scholarly research. Analogous efforts – even on a smaller scale – in the capitals of more peripheral and less powerful countries would most certainly constitute an unwelcome intrusion into domestic affairs.

One could, of course, argue that all this is desirable and exemplifies the exercise at the international level of rights of speech, association,

The problematic triumph of liberal democracy 303

assembly, and petition that are well entrenched at the national level in all ELDs. Nevertheless, this is a form of organized influence which is only open to a fortunate few and which frequently operates in a nether land between illegality and unconfessability. It would surely be preferable if the cross-national representation of interests were available to a broader range of affected groups and could express itself in a more open and publicly accountable way.

A modest proposal for reform

In the remaining portion of this chapter, I will propose a concrete (and, I hope) feasible reform of existing institutions of representation that is intended to address more directly and consequentially the limitations that national boundaries have placed on the practice of "real-existing" liberal democracies. It does not depend upon the advent of world government or even a substantial improvement in existing IGOs. For many countries, it may not even require a constitutional amendment and might even be perceived as non-threatening by existing office holders, although that remains to be seen. It is the sort of reform that is designed in terms of process not goal or end-state. Initially, it would produce modest, even symbolic, effects but my assumption is that these will accumulate and expand with the passage of time and the additional experience of the actors involved.

My purpose, the reader will recall, is to mitigate the effect of the unequal distribution of political units in the international system and to compensate for the absence of reliable, fair, supra-state mechanisms for ensuring justice across national borders. My solution rests on the assumption that information flows are an increasingly important component of modern governance and, therefore, that it is worth the effort to make citizens and politicians in different countries more sensitive to each other's interests and passions. If one could establish publicly an arrangement that would inform each other about intended actions and anticipated reactions, then it might be possible to identify and even to preempt conflicts before they emerge, rather than waste resources in coping with their emergent effects or by compensating their eventual victims. The best way I could think of doing this was to incorporate an international component within the domestic legislative process.

I call my proposal **reciprocal representation** (RR). Under its auspices, formally SNSs would accord each other seats in their respective national legislatures. The number of seats – perhaps two or three – could vary, depending on mutual perceptions of the degree of interdependence, as well as the total number of deputies in each legislature.

304　*Philippe C. Schmitter*

Normally, these would be seats in the upper house, where it exists and especially where it has special responsibilities for foreign affairs as in the United States.

Under all circumstances, the reciprocal representatives would have the right to speak on the floor and insert material in the official record. They would have the same salaries, services, and perquisites, serve on committees (except for those dealing with sensitive security matters), and receive information on drafts and hearings just like any "native" member of the legislature. Their terms in office should coincide with the host country's electoral cycle. It seems very unlikely that they would initially be permitted to vote, particularly in situations where theirs would be the deciding ballot. However, if the experience were to prove successful, eventual voting rights should not be excluded, again, on a reciprocal basis.

Who would these representatives be? My preference would be for their indirect election by each of the respective legislatures, rather than for direct popular election. As was the case until 1979 with the European Parliament, I would hope that (where there was more than one) their distribution would be roughly proportional, with both the governing party or coalition and the opposition being represented. My further assumption is that it would be in the interest of the respective legislatures to select individuals with considerable national prestige – perhaps, former presidents or prominent former ministers – and a strong command of the language and culture of the country to which he/she was being sent. If this opportunity were exploited to appoint political cronies, defeated politicians, or personal friends, then we could be sure that its importance would rapidly be discounted.

Which countries might be expected to participate in and profit from such an arrangement? Neighboring states are the most likely candidates, although nothing would preclude polities as far away as the United States and Japan or the United States and the European Community from exchanging representatives, if the reciprocal will were there. To a certain extent, the feasibility of RR depends on the relative size of the legislatures involved and the number of neighboring or consenting states. For example, the US Senate has 100 members and borders with only three countries – six if you count the sea lanes between Florida and Cuba, and Alaska and Russia. The Canadian Senate has 112 members and only one international border, if one discounts the straits and seas separating it from Greenland, Saint Pierre et Miguelon, and Russia. Mexico's Senado has sixty-four elected members and three bordering countries. It is only when we turn to Europe that the formula begins to look unmanageable. Germany has nine immediate neighbors. If each

The problematic triumph of liberal democracy 305

were accorded two seats in the Bundestag, that would amount to over 25 percent of the present total (eighteen of sixty-eight). In the case of Russia, the "reciprocals" from adjacent states and former republics would almost overwhelm the "natives"!

Where RR seems especially important to me is in the context of free trade areas. A genuine common market, like the European Community, comes with a central policy process and an attendant representative assembly, the European Parliament, however limited its present powers may be. Free trade areas are designed to increase economic, social, and environmental interdependencies without subjecting their members politically to anything more than an episodic arbitration procedure for resolving the conflicts that will inevitably arise. In such a context, some more permanent arrangement for registering mutual sensitivities than diplomatic exchanges, summit meetings, or expert consultations would seem very desirable. Whether RR would be sufficient to preclude the demand for forming specialized councils on labor and the environment, as presently called for by the Clinton Administration, is doubtful, although it would provide a more visible and publicly accountable forum for airing these same issues. The North American Free Trade Area (NAFTA) and MERCOSUL could both benefit considerably from RR and, in the process, they would be credited by the international community for taking a pioneering step beyond the present national-territorial limitations of liberal democracy.[1]

If the arrangement works as envisaged, the "reciprocals" would serve as important adjuncts to the normal channels of diplomatic representation and to the abnormal channels of foreign interest representation. They would constitute an "early warning system" for drafts of legislation or regulatory measures that might adversely affect groups or persons in their home country. Their interventions in committee or on the floor, plus any amendments they might introduce, could conceivably change the actual content of the policies adopted. If not, the publicity surrounding their efforts should have some impact on the public as a whole, and certainly could be used to bolster their country's case before global and regional IGOs. It is not even beyond the possibility that when the "reciprocals" return home, they might be better able to explain the reasoning and intention behind legislative initiatives in the other country than if national politicians relied solely on diplomatic messages and press reports. That has certainly been one of the functions that Euro-deputies have performed vis-à-vis their national constituencies.

Nor must RR stop at the national level. It could be profitably extended to relations between adjacent subnational states and municipalities. Moreover, by establishing a precedent of mutual trust and

306   *Philippe C. Schmitter*

respect, its principles could be applied to other contentious issues and confidence-building gestures. For example, mutual monitoring of elections, of court proceedings, of prison conditions, and even of police stations where both countries have persons or interests at stake might be a possibility. Within the European Community the breakthrough to the Single Market rested ultimately on a very similar notion, that of **mutual recognition**, not just of the technical specification of products, but of the quality of services and professional diplomas.

Finally, it is important to stress what RR does **not** accomplish. It is not a surreptitious mechanism for international or regional integration or for the creation of a new overarching political identity. It does not impose uniform standards and leaves the countries that participate free to govern themselves according to national laws and customs. Sovereignty may be limited by a process of mutual disclosure and deliberation, but it is not transferred to a supranational institution.

Moreover, RR is a voluntary arrangement that does not last any longer than the countries involved wish it. Should one persistently ignore the other's preferences or should one diminish the power of its representative institutions, then the other could withdraw and, thereby, destroy the arrangement at relatively low cost and with rather dramatic effect.

In short, RR would not by any means eliminate all injustice and inequality between democratically governed polities in the international system. It does little to resolve the issues of extraterritoriality – that would require either general supranational authority or specialized international regimes – but it does address the problems associated with externalities. It should contribute to making the existing international system function better without, however, transforming that system into a world or regional polity that might eventually eliminate the sources of injustice and inequality between states.

NOTES

Originally prepared for the International Seminar on Liberty and Justice in Modern Societies, Secretaria de Desarrollo Social, Mexico, D.F., June 3–5, 1993.
1. If NAFTA and MERCOSUL were to institute reciprocal representation and to accord each other two seats in their respective upper houses, the distribution would be as follows:

The problematic triumph of liberal democracy

I. NAFTA

Country	Number of seats in upper house	Number of reciprocal representatives
Canada	112	4
Mexico	64	4
United States	100	4

II. MERCOSUL

Country	Number of seats in upper house	Number of reciprocal representatives
Argentina	46	6
Brazil	81	6
Paraguay	36	6
Uruguay	30	6

Part 6

Promoting democracy

15 Promoting democracy in the 1990s: actors, instruments, and issues

Larry Diamond

Since 1974, a "third wave" of global democratization has dramatically increased the number of democracies.[1] If we choose as our operational standard of democracy the presence of a civilian, constitutional, multi-party regime, with competitive elections, one could count as many as 114 "democracies" in the world at the end of 1994 (Karatnycky 1995: 5). This is almost twice the number of formal democracies in 1984.[2] If, however, we insist on looking beyond constitutional form and even electoral conduct, and consider as well real levels of political freedom and civil liberties, a different picture emerges. In its annual survey of freedom in the world for 1994, Freedom House counted seventy-six countries as "free." This is a substantial increase from forty-two in 1972, and fifty-three in 1985. Yet, by this calculus, a third of the formal democracies in the world (thirty-eight) do not rate as "free" because the power of democratically elected leaders is seriously constrained by unaccountable groups, particularly the military (as in Pakistan, Turkey, and Guatemala); or because political and ethnic violence mar individual freedom and the integrity of political competition (as in India, Colombia, and El Salvador); or because the actual performance and accountability of formal democratic institutions pushes the quality of political competition, representation, organization, and/or expression below a critical threshold (as in Venezuela, the Philippines, and Zambia, in the judgment of Freedom House). Clearly, there is a large gap between democratic form and reality in the world, and this bears serious implications for the challenge of democratic consolidation, which, I argue, must be the ultimate goal of international efforts to promote democracy.

I use the term "democracy" as roughly equivalent to Dahl's "polyarchy," or "liberal democracy." This encompasses not only a civilian, constitutional, multiparty regime, with regular, free, and fair elections and universal suffrage, but organizational and informational pluralism; extensive civil liberties (freedom of expression, freedom of the press, freedom to form and join organizations); effective power for elected officials; and functional autonomy for legislative, executive, and judicial

312   *Larry Diamond*

organs of government (Dahl 1971: 1–9; Diamond, Linz, and Lipset 1995).

Important normative and political issues are at stake in the way we define democracy. If we rest content to promote the mere constitutional form of democracy, pressure for democratization will cease once the structural form is put in place, and assistance may go mainly to strengthen formal institutions and assist economic reform and development. Those are necessary objectives for democratization, but they are not sufficient. In a great many "near-democracies" and partial, "poor," "low-quality," or struggling democracies, democratic capacities must also be strengthened outside the formal system, in civil society, and the international community must continue to pay attention to problems of military domination and impunity, and ongoing political violence and human rights violations. Such an analytical and strategic approach implies a different and more comprehensive mix of democracy promotion programs. It also directs attention to countries whose political systems might, from a more superficial conception of democracy, be considered too "advanced" or established to warrant international attention and assistance.

This chapter proceeds in three principal sections. First, it describes some of the many national and multinational actors now engaged in democracy assistance, and assesses their distinctive advantages and limitations. Second, it considers the principal policy instruments for democracy promotion, including diplomacy and aid conditionality, and analyzes some of the problems and opportunities that arise with their usage. In conclusion, I consider several issues – communication, coordination, consistency, and coherence among actors – that will help to determine the effectiveness of democracy promotion efforts.

Actors

Governments of the leading industrialized democracies remain the most important and resourceful promoters of democracy, but they increasingly share the arena with a wide variety of non-governmental organizations (NGOs). Official democracy assistance comes from countries with long histories and lingering ties of colonialism (especially Britain and France) and of foreign intervention and occupation in the name of democracy (especially the United States), as well as countries wishing to develop or deepen trading partnerships by promoting democracy among their neighbors (Japan). However, a number of smaller democratic countries have given the promotion of democracy and human rights a more and more prominent place in their foreign policy and foreign aid – Canada, Sweden, Norway, Denmark, the Netherlands. The Swedish International Development Authority (SIDA), for example, has a carefully conceptualized program of support for democracy and human rights. Moreover, the first country to establish explicit institutions for democratic assistance, and still one of the largest donors for this purpose relative to its GNP, is a post-World War II democracy with a traumatic authoritarian history, Germany.

States and state agencies[3]

Established democratic states are engaged in democracy promotion through diplomatic pressure and initiatives, the mobilization and conditioning of multilateral policies and resources, and through their official overseas development or aid agencies. I will leave for later consideration the former two dimensions and consider here state actors in the aid relationship.

Almost certainly the largest official democratic assistance program today in terms of sheer volume and funding is that of the US Agency for International Development (AID). By one estimate, AID spent some $400 million in fiscal year (FY) 1994 on democracy assistance programs around the world, but any such estimates involve a good deal of judgment because a multipurpose organization like AID has many programs which serve several multiple goals (Carothers 1991: 124).[4] Since its creation in 1961, AID has been engaged in activities that serve democratization indirectly (such as strengthening independent educational and research institutions, and enhancing participation at the local level), but until 1990 its focus was mainly on social and economic development (including health, population, and environment). From modest beginnings with human rights projects in the late 1970s, AID programs expanded during the 1980s to assist the administration of justice, the conduct of democratic elections, dialogue between civilians and the military (mainly in Latin America).[5] With the announcement of its "Democracy Initiative" in December 1990, AID established the promotion of democracy as one of its central aims, involving it extensively in assistance programs for free and fair elections, constitutional drafting, legislatures, judicial systems, local government, anti-corruption efforts, regulatory reform, civic education, and independent organizations and media in civil society (including human rights, legal aid, women's, professional, and church groups). AID's involvement in democracy promotion was deepened further with the inauguration of President Clinton, who had featured the promotion of democracy worldwide as one of the few foreign policy themes of his 1992 campaign (see Joel Barkan's

314   *Larry Diamond*

chapter in this volume and US Agency for International Development 1994).

The US government has also been involved for some time in democracy promotion through its US Information Agency (USIA). Partly an exchange and propaganda organ during the Cold War, USIA (and the associated anti-communist Radio Liberty and Radio Free Europe) nevertheless did much in that period to puncture the totalitarian lid of secrecy and advance pluralist, democratic ideas. Today USIA administers a wide range of activities to explain and advocate the concept of democracy; to provide information and counsel on institutional and policy options for those trying to consolidate democracy; and to facilitate links with American institutions toward those goals. In addition to its Fulbright scholarly exchanges, USIA brings hundreds of foreign professionals to the US each year for month-long visits; places "professionals in residence" for limited periods (up to six months) to help establish democratic legislatures, media, and judicial systems; sponsors lecture tours and consultations by various American experts (which often highlight relevant comparative dimensions of American experience); helps train East European journalists; and provides books on the theory and practice of democracy. Thematic foci include elections administration, rule of law, constitutional reform, civil society, transparency and government ethics, conflict resolution, and economic reform. By 1992 USIA missions in eighty-five countries had undertaken 132 major projects under the agency's initiative for "Building Democratic Institutions," as well as another 215 projects addressed to related themes such as market-oriented economic reform and the free flow of information (Diamond 1992b: 35). By 1995, almost all of USIA's Africa posts listed democracy programming as the number one theme in their country plans (US Information Agency n.d.).

NGOs

NGOs (some of which are called "quasi-governmental" because they are primarily publicly funded but independently operated and directed) have long been engaged in the transmission of financial and technical assistance for democratic development. Over the past two decades these efforts have burgeoned to the point of breathtaking diversity that is almost certainly beyond the knowledge of any single entity.

The earliest explicit effort at non-governmental (or quasi-governmental) assistance for democracy came in the 1950s with the creation of the German party foundations or *Stiftungen*: the Friedrich Naumann Foundation, the Friedrich Ebert Foundation, the Konrad

Adenauer Foundation and the Hans Seidel Foundation (each affiliated with a major German political party). Like USIA and AID, these organizations have a number of purposes (including fostering educational exchanges, scholarships, and international understanding). But democracy promotion abroad has long figured prominently (if not always explicitly) in their work. In fact, until recently the combined spending of the four foundations on assisting democratic associations, trade unions, media, and political institutions equaled or exceeded that of all US publicly funded institutions.[6] In 1991, the Friedrich Ebert Foundation alone dispersed DM88.5 million (about $55 million) in 67 countries in the developing world, with the assistance of 97 German experts abroad and over 500 local personnel.[7] A large proportion of these projects was devoted to supporting autonomous civil society organizations, decentralized and democratic local government structures, enhanced citizen participation, more effective trade unions, market-oriented economic development, and other activities that were more or less related to democracy promotion. The Friedrich Naumann Foundation works with over 500 partner organizations in over 80 countries on similar programs to train journalists and political leaders, promote civic education, strengthen civil society organizations, and foster the regular exchange of information and ideas about democracy. The Konrad Adenauer Foundation has similar training, education, and institutional assistance programs, with political assistance targeted on Christian Democratic and like-minded (centrist or center-right) parties and organizations.

Influenced to some extent by the model of the German *Stiftungen*, the Reagan Administration established in 1983 the National Endowment for Democracy (NED) with congressional funding but an independent, bipartisan board of directors.[8] NED's mandate is explicitly to promote and assist democracy abroad. It was appropriated $35 million for this purpose in FY 1994, when it made over 300 grants in some 80 countries. NED makes grants directly (through its "discretionary" program) and through four "core" grantees that receive about two-thirds its annual program funding and have their own independent boards and staffs: the two party institutes – the National Democratic Institute for International Affairs (NDI) and the International Republican Institute (IRI) – the Free Trade Union Institute (FTUI), and the Center for International Private Enterprise (CIPE).[9] FTUI is affiliated with the predominant US labor federation, the AFL-CIO, and CIPE with the US Chamber of Commerce. While labor already had several regional institutes active before the creation of NED, the other three core grantees were established in 1984 following the creation of NED.[10]

316   *Larry Diamond*

Despite its relatively small size and congressional budgetary appropriation,[11] NED has been on the cutting edge of democratic change in numerous countries over the past decade. Its extensive efforts in Poland, Chile, and Nicaragua provided critical support to the democratic movements that brought down those dictatorships. Throughout Eastern Europe it helped to build the independent civic infrastructure that undermined Communism in the late 1980s (most notably, through sizable assistance to Poland's anti-Communist trade union, Solidarity). NED efforts were also credited with an important role in facilitating the transitions to democracy in Namibia, Haiti, Zambia, and South Africa, in part through international election observing efforts (see below). While most governmental and publicly funded democracy promotion organizations now focus mainly or exclusively on assisting the consolidation of new or partial democracies, NED continues to devote substantial funds (mainly through its discretionary grants) to supporting beleaguered democratic movements in (and in exile from) authoritarian and closed societies. It has become a major (sometimes the primary) source of funding for human rights and pro-democracy groups, and the independent flow of information, in numerous countries, including China, Tibet, Burma, Vietnam, Serbia, Bosnia, Cuba, Iraq, Egypt, Zaire, Sudan, Nigeria, Liberia, and Kenya.

The NED family also funds a wide variety of grants that aim to consolidate democratic political institutions and civil societies in the post-Communist and developing worlds. In several dozen new or partial democracies in Central and Eastern Europe, the former Soviet Union, Latin America, Asia, Africa, and the Middle East, it provides training, capacity-building, infrastructure and (for some societal groups) operational resources for democratic political parties, legislatures, election monitoring and administration, and local governments; and for independent social movements, civic education and human rights organizations, policy publications and research institutes, conflict resolution efforts, anti-corruption and accountability initiatives, mass media, and democratic trade unions. Among the NED's civil society grantees in 1994 were the Moscow Human Rights Research Center, a network of fifteen human rights groups that offers citizens legal counseling, advises on legislation and policy, and monitors implementation of the law; GERDDES, a Benin-based citizens' organization, with contacts in more than thirty African countries, that promotes civic education, election monitoring, and democratic development across the continent (Guie 1993); and Mexico's Civic Alliance, whose unprecedented election monitoring efforts resulted in the least fraudulent presidential election Mexico has had in decades.[12]

Promoting democracy in the 1990s

Through CIPE, NED supports innovative efforts in many countries to demonstrate the need for economic reform, advise legislatures on economic issues, train economic and business journalists, enhance the skills of business associations, improve corporate governance and accountability, strengthen the codes and enforcement of business and commercial law, and promote the teaching of private entrepreneurship and modern business management. In its first decade, CIPE has sponsored over 100 projects in some 48 countries. By broadening the base of understanding for and participation in the economic reform process (and the market economy more generally), such training and capacity-building programs mitigate the presumed tensions between democracy and market reform, thereby exploding the myth that it takes a Pinochet or Chinese-style dictatorship to accomplish it (Sullivan 1994).[13]

In its work throughout the post-Communist societies of Central and Eastern Europe and the former Soviet Union, FTUI seeks to level the structural advantages of the old Communist trade unions and the managerial *nomenklatura* (which are often closely allied with one another). Early on after the fall of Communism it rushed in "liberation technology" (computers, local-language software programs, printers, fax machines) and then printing equipment. It has also supported democratic newspapers and radio and TV shows; taught courses on the role and responsibilities of free trade unions, the techniques of labor organizing and collective bargaining, and the mechanics of financing and democratically governing a trade union; encouraged (on a non-partisan basis) voter participation; provided advanced training for union organizers; and facilitated cross-country interaction among free trade union leaders from throughout the region. In Russia, FTUI's rule of law project is helping to build the legal infrastructure of democratic trade unionism by supporting the work of Russian lawyers on labor legislation and assisting unions with registration, local disputes, and illegal dismissals or privatization schemes (Somogyi 1995). Similar programs by FTUI's regional affiliates seek to strengthen the democratic capacities (for advocacy, organization, and coalition-building) of independent trade unions in Africa, Asia, and Latin America.

The two NED party institutes are heavily involved in institutional development in new and emerging democracies. By 1994, NDI had sponsored political party training in twenty-seven countries, legislative strengthening in thirteen countries, local government programs in five countries, civil-military dialogues in four Latin American countries, and civic and voter education efforts in twenty-nine countries (NDI 1994a: 4–5).[14] Its efforts draw on twenty field offices throughout the developing and post-Communist worlds, a staff of regional and functional experts

318   Larry Diamond

in Washington, and democratic politicians, civic organizers, election monitors, and other practitioners from more than seventy countries who are recruited to volunteer their time to share their experiences. (In this important respect, NGOs like NDI, IRI, NED, and the Asia Foundation have the flexibility, which USIA does not, of using non-American teachers and trainers to promote diffusion of democratic knowledge and enable developing democracies to learn from one another. The international democratic networks they thereby generate constitute one of the most important legacies of their work.) Supporting free and fair elections, through monitoring and voter education, and strengthening political parties and institutions have also figured prominently in the mission of IRI, which has eleven field offices (mainly in the former Communist countries, including Cambodia) and projects in some fifty countries around the world. During 1990 to 1993, IRI organized eighteen international election observing missions during the first rounds of post-Communist elections, and it has also observed in Africa and other regions. With NDI and others, it sponsored the highly successful South African Election Support Project that assisted parties and civic organizations with voter education, registration, communication, and pollwatching for the historic April 1994 elections (IRI 1994).

A number of other private, non-profit, US organizations also have independent identities and structures of governance, while relying heavily or almost entirely on public funds in performing a variety of democracy promotion functions. For example, the International Foundation for Electoral Systems (IFES), established in 1987, monitors, supports, and strengthens the mechanics of the election process in emerging democracies. It offers technical assessments of the electoral process in particular countries, on-site technical assistance, training of poll workers, voter and civic education, and assistance with monitoring and administration on election day. During its first five years, IFES sent over twenty pre-election surveys to five continents and aided the election councils of nine (mainly newly emerging) democracies.

The Asia Foundation, founded in 1954 and based in San Francisco, now devotes more than half of all its grant spending (about $8 to 10 million per year during fiscal years 1993 to 1995) to democracy promotion. These activities cluster in five areas: building the institutional capacities of legislatures, and promoting more effective citizen participation in and monitoring of legislative processes; developing an effective justice system, through training and technical support for governmental institutions and through aid to human rights organizations, bar associations, and legal assistance programs; supporting journalism training programs, journalists' associations, and liberalizing reforms of media

Promoting democracy in the 1990s

laws; aiding the development of thousands of NGOs in civil society through start-up support, staff training, research and publication projects, and encouragement of indigenous philanthropy; and strengthening democratic governance in several dimensions, such as electoral administration, local government, civil military relations, and public accountability and probity at all levels. With a total cash budget of $41.7 million in FY 1994, it is considerably larger than the NED discretionary grant program and has the advantage of more than a dozen field offices in Asia, which give it intimate knowledge of each country, sensitivity to its culture, and a long-term presence that allows for an emphasis on incremental change.[15]

Similarly straddling the boundary between public and private is the Eurasia Foundation, established in 1993 with funding from USAID to support economic reform and democratic institution-building in the New Independent States (NIS) of the former Soviet Union. Based in Washington, with five field offices in the NIS, it makes grants in four areas: economic reform, governmental reform, the non-profit (civil society) sector, and mass media and communications. In its first year of operation, it awarded about $7.5 million in grants to support (*inter alia*) the conversion of military plants to peacetime production, business and management training, public opinion polling, strengthening NGOs, book distribution, and electronic publishing (Eurasia Foundation 1994). A current priority is to expand access to computer communications and support new e-mail networks throughout the former Soviet Union (IDEE 1995: 34).

Outside the US, the NED example has inspired the creation of at least two counterpart organizations, both of which also are funded almost entirely by annual parliamentary appropriations. The International Centre for Human Rights and Democratic Development was established by the Canadian Parliament in 1988 and operates on an annual federal grant of $5 million. The Centre's mission is both narrower than NED's, in that it focuses on promoting human rights and democratic societies, and broader, in that it gives "equal emphasis" to social, economic, and cultural, as well as civil and political rights. It provides financial, political, and technical support primarily to NGOs, such as human rights and women's organizations and independent trade unions, struggling for such goals as due process, press freedom, and elimination of child slavery and violence against women. In contrast to NED, it is also an advocacy organization, lobbying governments, multilateral institutions, and regional organizations on human rights and democracy issues (such as the promotion of women's rights). It works with over 300 partners and projects primarily in a more limited set of

320   *Larry Diamond*

thirteen countries in the Americas, Africa, and Asia (International Centre for Human Rights and Democratic Development 1993–1994, 1994).[16]

Established in 1992 by the British Parliament, the Westminster Foundation follows more closely the American NED model of sponsorship by the principal political parties (in this case three), which (as with NED) are represented on the Foundation's governing board along with non-party figures from business, the trade unions, academia, and civil society.[17] About half of the Foundation's annual budget (£2 million in 1993–1994, twice the initial grant) is directed through British political parties and the other half is allocated to all-party or non-partisan projects. Even more than NED, Westminster seeks to leverage its limited resources with many small grants (some only a few thousand pounds). Thus it was able to fund 236 projects in 1993–1994 (April 1–March 31). Westminster also focuses its grants regionally: fully three-quarters are in Central and Eastern Europe (58 percent) and the former Soviet Union (17 percent), and another 16 percent are in Africa. Most of its projects channeled through the British parties support development, campaign training, and media assistance for like-minded political parties; other grants support civic education, civil society organizations (including free trade unions), mass media development, rule of law, and other programs similar to NED's (Westminster Foundation for Democracy 1994).

A large amount of US financial and technical assistance that originates with governmental organizations like AID is channeled through NGOs (including NED affiliates). Some of these, like Freedom House, the African-American Institute, and the Asia Foundation, have been involved in political assistance and institution-building for decades, and are now engaged in numerous democratic assistance projects (some funded by NED; see Table 15.1).

A number of organizations of varying size are working, typically in close partnership with host institutions, to defend human rights, develop legal systems, and build the institutional and cultural foundations of a rule of law. The American Bar Association provides *pro bono* legal assistance to emerging democracies throughout the world. Its Central and East European Law Initiative linked each law school in the region with at least three American schools, conducted numerous legal assistance workshops, assessed over 172 draft laws, and provided over $20 million worth of legal expertise by volunteer lawyers, judges, academicians, and interns (Stayden 1994).

The New York-based Committee to Protect Journalists (CPJ) and the Vienna-based International Press Institute (IPI) both monitor the state

Promoting democracy in the 1990s

Table 15.1. *Selected US organizations administering NED grants for foreign democratic assistance, fiscal years 1992 and 1993*

ORGANIZATIONS	GRANT ACTIVITIES
African-American Institute	Seven grants to support human rights work, civic education, and democratic mass media in Nigeria and Liberia.
American Federation of Teachers Education Foundation	Two grants to support training for democratic civic education in Nicaragua; and to prepare classroom teachers and education officials in newly democratizing countries to implement education for democracy programs.
America's Development Foundation	Twelve grants to support human rights training, advocacy, and education in Burkina Faso, Ethiopia, and especially Zaire; women's rights in Mali and women's democratic action in the Ivory Coast; the West African democratic civic education group, GERDDES; and civic education and efforts to increase citizen participation in Nicaragua and Panama.
America's Fund for Independent Universities	One grant to promote private sector support for higher education in Latin America.
Center for Foreign Journalists	Two grants to advise publications and help establish a training center for journalists and publishers in Ethiopia; and to provide training and technical assistance to Russian local newspapers.
Central Asian Foundation	One grant to support a conference on strategies for democratization and market reform in the Turkic republics of the former Soviet Union.
Congressional Human Rights Foundation	Eight grants to support human rights advocacy and monitoring programs in Nigeria, democratic civic education in Sierra Leone, and civic groups in Serbia seeking peaceful resolution of the conflict in the former Yugoslavia.
Delphi International Group	Four grants to support education for democracy and human rights in Guinea; a democratic radio station in Nicaragua; and the multifaceted civic education, citizen mobilization, and leadership training efforts of women's democratic groups in Argentina and Paraguay.
East–West Educational Development Fund	Two grants to provide democratic NGOs in developing and former Communist countries with overstock computer equipment and supplies.
Foreign Policy Research Institute	One grant to support a Romanian journal of culture and politics that is a major forum for democratic thought.
Foundation on Democratization and Political Change in the Middle East	Five grants to support two conferences on democracy in the Arab world; Arabic translation and publishing of major works on democracy; and democratic civic education and debate among Palestinians in the Occupied Territories.

322   *Larry Diamond*

Table 15.1. (*cont.*)

ORGANIZATIONS	GRANT ACTIVITIES
Freedom House	Seven grants to assist establishment of a Sakharov Archive in Russia and a democratic public policy institute in Northern Iraq; to distribute democratic books and aid human rights groups in Cuba; and to support independent publications, news gathering, research efforts, and voter education in Russia.
Fund for Peace	Six grants to hold workshops in Ethiopia on establishing human rights and democratic institutions; to assist Sudanese human rights groups and a democratic publication from exile; to support civic education and election monitoring in Ethiopia; civic education and civil society development in Eritrea; and to conduct human rights training for the Horn of Africa.
Institute for Democracy in Eastern Europe	Four grants to support a seminar on democracy in Romania and an independent newspaper in Belarus; to establish centers for pluralism and democratic debate in seven countries; and to assist anti-war civic groups in Serbia.
Inter-American Dialogue	One grant to support a comprehensive study and forum on the status of democracy and requirements for its consolidation in the Americas.
International Human Rights Law Group	One grant to recruit and train three fellows from Africa, Asia, and Latin America in administration of human rights and rule of law programs.
International Rescue Committee	One grant to assist publication of a quarterly Afghani journal promoting freedom, democracy, and human rights.
Joint Center for Political and Economic Studies	Six grants to support voter education and mobilization in Ghana; democratic research, publishing, and discussion in Senegal; a democratic exile publication for Sudan; and democratic training and civil society development in South Africa.
Jamestown Foundation	Four grants to create a press service, improve information gathering about reform, support educational efforts about democracy and market reform, and create a democratic library and resource center in Russia.
League of Women Voters Education Fund	Two grants to assist civic education and grassroots participation efforts by women leaders in Poland.
National Forum Foundation	Two grants to support internship training programs for promising young leaders in the former Soviet Union and support the placement in Russia and Ukraine of American professionals in journalism, business, and other fields.

Promoting democracy in the 1990s

Table 15.1. *(cont.)*

ORGANIZATIONS	GRANT ACTIVITIES
National Peace Foundation	Three grants to support an independent media group in Sarajevo; democratic research, publishing, and education efforts in Georgia; and a conference to encourage women's participation in Armenian, Azerbaijani, and Georgian politics.
Points of Light Foundation	One grant to support efforts at grassroots citizen involvement in the Czech Republic.
Puebla Institute	Three grants to support human rights information gathering in Cuba and international dissemination of its findings.
Resources for Action	Eight grants to support the democratic civic education and leadership training programs of the women's group, Conciencia, in Colombia, Ecuador, and Nicaragua; and to fund independent efforts in Mexican civil society to encourage political reform, prepare for election monitoring, conduct leadership and human rights training, stimulate participation, and mobilize for free and fair elections.
Southwest Voter Research Institute	One grant to support dissemination of basic legal and constitutional information through radio.

Universities	Grants
Central Connecticut State University	One grant to conduct a training seminar in Poland on democratic transformation of the bureaucracy.
Columbia University, Center for the Study of Human Rights	Four grants to support establishment of a human rights resource center, legal aid clinic and related efforts in Liberia; to support efforts to secure strong constitutional human rights protection in Uganda; and to publish and disseminate in China works by Chinese scholars on constitutionalism and the rule of law.
Consortium of Universities of the Washington Metropolitan Area	Three grants to support legal education at the high school and advanced levels and to develop democratic curriculum materials on the law in Chile and Hungary.
Georgetown University	Two projects to support the revision of history textbooks in Poland and three former Soviet Republics, and to support discussion of constitutional reform in Bolivia.
Hofstra University	One grant to support legal reform and judicial training in Eastern Europe.
Ohio State University, Mershon Center	One grant to establish "Centers for Civic and Economic Education" to conduct teacher training and aid course innovation in Poland.
State University of New York (Research Foundation)	To enable the University of the Andes in Bogota, Colombia, to conduct a comparative study of democratic governance in Colombia.

Note: does not include the four core grantees or country-specific aid organizations.

324 *Larry Diamond*

of press freedom in the world, exposing and protesting abuses of press freedom and pressuring for openness and change.[18] Established in 1984 and funded mainly from the private sector, the Center for Foreign Journalists (CFJ) offers foreign journalists and news executives advanced training and consultation in the US and abroad, donates textbooks, and operates related support services. Press training programs are also conducted by IPI; by numerous press fellowship programs, such as the US-based Alfred Friendly Press Fellowships and the Paris-based Journalists in Europe (which offers eight-month programs for young Russian journalists); and by the Independent Journalism Foundation (IJF), which operates Centers for Independent Journalism in Prague, Bratislava, and Bucharest and publishes a journalism quarterly for the region, *KMIT* (IDEE 1995: 30, 37; *TransAtlantic Perspectives* 1994: 36–37).

A similar panoply of private assistance efforts focus on democratic civic education and strengthening civil society. The Institute for Democracy in Eastern Europe (IDEE) makes grants and facilitates communication to support NGO activity in the former Soviet bloc. In cooperation with its sister organization (IDEE Warsaw) it coordinates the flow of information and ideas among 11 "Centers for Pluralism" in ten countries. The American Federation of Teachers (a US trade union) conducts "education for democracy" workshops and numerous other civic education programs; it is now preparing a database of some 300 groups worldwide engaged in civic education for democracy (IDEE 1995: 2–3, 5, 22, 33–36).

One of the most energetic private-sector endeavors in democracy promotion has been the Carter Center of Emory University. Former US President Jimmy Carter has been instrumental in organizing a council of former elected heads of state in the Americas. In collaboration with them, and with a wide variety of other prominent individuals and organizations, he has observed elections in more than a dozen countries around the world, and in several countries – including Nicaragua, Ethiopia, and Liberia – the Center has played a pivotal role in mediating between conflicting or warring parties.

Private foundations have also been devoting an increasing share of their resources to building democratic institutions and civil societies. The Carnegie Corporation of New York lists several sizable grants it has made under the rubric of "strengthening democratic institutions." Among its recent recipients are: the Lawyers Committee for Human Rights to monitor, analyze, and assist legal reform in Russia; Helsinki Watch, for human rights monitoring and training in the former Soviet

Union; the Kennedy School of Government, for programs on democratizing civil-military relations and advising on economic reform and political decision making at all levels of government in the former Soviet Union; and scholarly exchanges between the US and the former Communist countries of Eastern Europe and the former Soviet Union (Carnegie Corporation 1992). In addition to its support for individual scholars, the MacArthur Foundation made grants in 1992 to support democratic legal and institutional reform, including increased accountability of police and military, in Central America, and to advance human rights and democracy in Latin America (MacArthur Foundation 1992). The Ford Foundation has long had an extensive program of grants in this area. In 1992 it made fifteen grants for human rights work to US and European organizations (totalling almost $3 million) and another nineteen grants in developing countries (totalling about $2.25 million). In all, Ford Foundation grants to support human rights and democratic development probably equal in sum the discretionary grant program of NED.

The German Marshall Fund of the United States initiated in 1989 a Political Development Program to support democratization in seven Central and Eastern European countries. Its grants (many with AID funding) seek to alter entrenched cultural patterns of distrust, cynicism, passivity, and deference to authority; to encourage active citizen and NGO engagement with local government; to help NGOs to become effective public advocates for human rights (including minority rights), governmental transparency, and public access to information; and to foster accurate, readable, fact-based reporting (*TransAtlantic Perspectives* 1994).

The boldest and most farreaching private effort has been the network of Soros Foundations established by Hungarian emigre financier George Soros, who contributed more than $15 million in 1990 alone to democratic dissidents and organizations throughout Eastern Europe (*New York Times* 1990). Begun in Hungary in 1984 and now operating in some twenty-two countries, from Poland and Russia to South Africa and Burma, the Soros Foundations seek to promote an "open society" based not only on democracy and the market economy but on tolerance, the rule of law, historical truth, and respect for minorities. Democracy-building projects support human rights (especially the rights of ethnic and national minorities), legal reform, expanded access to electronic mail and the internet, revision of Communist-era school curricula, and mass media training and development. Soros' Open Society Institute, based in New York, also administers numerous projects to research

326   *Larry Diamond*

public policy issues, encourage pluralism and debate, and assist other institutions of higher learning in Central and Eastern Europe (Soros 1994).

Beyond these grant-making institutions, an increasingly wide range of civic organizations is becoming involved in democracy promotion efforts, as suggested by the list in Table 15.1 of selected US organizations that received NED grants to administer for democratic groups abroad in 1992 and 1993. The presence of NGOs historically concerned with economic development, peace, and international exchange issues is noteworthy. So is the involvement of civic and lobbying organizations, like the League of Women Voters and the Joint Center for Political and Economic Studies, whose traditional focus has been on American politics. This not only broadens the base of political support for democracy promotion in the established democracies,[19] it also multiplies the points of autonomous social contact between developed and developing democracies.

Pluralism or fragmentation, public or private?

It is sadly ironic that at a moment of unprecedented democratic ferment and uncertainty in the world, and after a decade in which international democracy assistance organizations have demonstrated often remarkable cost-effectiveness, US organizations that blazed important trails of democracy promotion in the 1980s and early 1990s have become endangered. As pressure intensifies to cut spending to eliminate chronic budget deficits, and as support for liberal internationalist engagement declines, AID and USIA are being targeted by some Congressional budget-cutters. There is also growing sentiment for cutting or eliminating funding for NED, the Asia Foundation, and similar publicly funded NGOs.

There are several reasons why US NGO like NED and the Asia Foundation need to remain vigorously engaged in democracy promotion, with public funding directly appropriated by the US Congress and not tied to specific projects. Each type of effort has its own strengths and weaknesses. AID can be effective at long-term institution-building, particularly with respect to the governmental structures of democracy and large-scale assistance projects.[20] With its years of experience in economic and social development, AID also is well positioned to offer assistance at the nexus between those sectors and the political, for example to universities, and to NGOs and research institutes concerned with development, the environment, economic reform, and the status of women. However, as with any large government bureaucracy, its elabor-

Promoting democracy in the 1990s

ate decision mechanisms and reviewing, reporting, and auditing procedures make it unable to respond quickly to crises and new opportunities, less prone to take risks, and less effective in dealing with smaller and less formal organizations.[21] Because it lacks extensive political development expertise, much of AID's work in this area must be contracted out, and when large amounts of funds must be contracted quickly, some contract recipients are bound to be less experienced, cost-effective, and committed to the substance of democracy promotion than others. NGO donors can be more cost-effective in providing small grants for a wide range of projects, not only because their administration is more compact but because they are able to elicit volunteer and *pro bono* expert participation.[22] In addition, AID faces increasing restrictions on where it can work.

These problems of increased administrative burdens and reduced flexibility and cost-effectiveness apply as well when NGOs receive AID grants to promote democracy abroad, as do most of the major US non-governmental democracy promotion organizations.[23] Heavy dependence on project-specific AID funding also makes it more difficult for NGOs to maintain their own methods and institutional identity, and to engage in long-term financial and program planning and staff development, since they cannot know what their budgets will be from year to year.[24] In terms of both cost efficiency and effectiveness in democracy promotion, it would make more sense to increase – rather than eliminate – direct Congressional funding for these NGOs, by converting into general public grants most of the project-specific funds they are now receiving from AID. Political opposition to this change derives precisely from the fact that it would reduce centralized control over US democracy promotion projects by the executive branch agencies and the Congress.

Other considerations also underscore the need to limit the direct role of US governmental agencies in democracy promotion. "In countries where one of the issues being addressed is the paucity of autonomous civic and political institutions, the fundamental idea that government ought not control all aspects of society is undermined by a too-visible US government hand in the development and implementation of these programs" (NDI 1994b: 11). Furthermore, as agents of the US foreign policy establishment that must serve overall US government interests, both AID and USIA have less scope to assist political opposition forces and groups in civil society that might expose corruption or press for reform of a government with which the US seeks warm bilateral relations. For a big power in the world, this is a big problem: it must have non-governmental instruments that can react quickly and engage

328   *Larry Diamond*

civil society actors who might be suspicious of official, big-power aid agencies, or who might become the object of diplomatic friction between the big power and a hostile host government. Particularly in authoritarian situations, pro-democracy groups are exposed and vulnerable, at greater risk of being discredited (or punished) as tools of foreign interests when they accept money from governmental sources of a superpower like the US, or a regional power like Japan, or a former colonial ruler like Britain or France. There is less risk and suspicion when funding comes from a non-governmental agency, which is not bound by the political direction or constraints that may be imposed by the local American embassy, or from the official aid agencies of a smaller country, like Canada or Sweden, which are less likely to have (or be seen to have) geo-strategic interests at stake (and which have more of the flexible, cutting-edge, challenging character of the publicly funded democracy promotion NGOs in the US). In authoritarian countries, NED has particular freedom of action because (unlike the Asia Foundation and the Ford Foundation in some countries) it does not have to worry about preserving its own in-country presence, with a local office and expatriate staff.

In an endeavor such as democracy promotion, where the challenges are diverse in character, scale, countries, and cultures, there is value in having pluralism of approaches and donor organizations. For countries whose overcentralization of government and public life retards democratic development, centralizing the provision of US (not to mention international) democratic assistance through a single agency would hardly provide a useful model or message. Vigorous pluralism of US democracy promotion actors exposes democratic forces abroad to the diversity (and tolerance of diversity) intrinsic to democracy, and creates a richer repertoire of donors and methods, able to relate effectively to a wider range of potential recipients (NDI 1994b: 11–12).

Globally as well, having donors from a wide range of countries and approaches increases the legitimacy of democracy promotion as a political task, provides a wider range of funding sources from which to choose, and gives civil society organizations at risk the opportunity to shield themselves from political retaliation and reduce future funding uncertainty by broadening their bases of support. As we have seen, some organizations, like NED, still work to foster democratic transitions, while some focus only on consolidation. Some work on a larger scale, some on a small scale. Some focus mainly on democratic governance, some on human rights more broadly, some on multiple dimensions of development (including conventional economic ones that make them

Promoting democracy in the 1990s

appear less threatening to authoritarian regimes). Some have the deep country expertise that comes with an exclusive regional focus, others have the comparative breadth that comes with a global network and reach. Some have an in-country presence that enhances understanding of local conditions, actors, possibilities and risks, and facilitates closer monitoring and evaluation of grants. Official aid bureaucracies move slowly and may need to respond to multiple and conflicting policy goals, but they can commit large funds to institution-building and sustain them over long periods of time. NGOs can respond rapidly to urgent needs and surprise opportunities; emergency help from NED, for example, kept the Sarajevo daily *Oslobodjenje* publishing, as a source of truth and hope, through the brutal winter of 1994. Certainly, it makes sense to have donors like NED and Westminster that are able to offer relatively small grants for limited or short-term projects, or for seed purposes, or for informal organizations; often these smaller grants are the most cost-effective, though unfortunately they are also precisely the most difficult to audit cost-effectively.[25]

The enormous variety of organizations involved in democracy promotion has permitted the development (deliberately and coincidentally) of widely different strengths and areas of expertise, functionally, thematically, and regionally. At first glance, this may appear a welter of confusion and duplication. Instead, it increasingly represents the overlapping, reinforcing, integrating pluralism that marks a healthy, democratic civil society within a country. In the spirit of democracy, such pluralism should remain – full of eclecticism and experimentation, and free of central direction. What would be useful, however, to keep assistance working to maximum benefit, is regular communication and closer coordination among the various donors. Today, that works much better (but still not always well) within countries than across them.

Regional and international organizations

In addition to states and NGOs, regional and international organizations have also become involved in democracy promotion in recent years. Periodically over the years, and quite rapidly since the end of the Cold War, the United Nations has been evolving a concern and capacity to assist the administration of free and fair elections – which Article 21 of the Universal Declaration of Human Rights stipulates as the means for determining "the will of the people" that "shall be the basis of the authority of government." The UN's supervision of the 1989 Namibian elections marked a turning point: its last major observing role as a territorial trustee, and its first engagement in a new, broader type of demo-

330   *Larry Diamond*

cratic intervention that included not only extensive election monitoring but peacekeeping forces, civilian police, civic education, and post-election assistance in institutional development. In February 1990, the UN mounted its first electoral observation mission in a member state, Nicaragua, in a comprehensive effort that began six months in advance of the voting and continued after it. A comparable mission to Haiti followed later in the year. In Haiti, the UN's willingness for the first time to justify its intervention on the basis of a country's internal needs (rather than maintenance of international peace and security) marked a sharp departure from the past. UN engagement was soon institutionalized with the creation of an Electoral Assistance Unit, and then tested with major new missions in El Salvador, Cambodia, Angola, and the Western Sahara (Gershman 1993: 9–11).

The first UN mission failed in Angola (with the resumption of civil war after the September 1992 elections), due in large measure to the lack of adequate human and financial resources (Tvedten 1993: 118). However, its mission in El Salvador (Onusal) – which included monitoring of human rights and a ceasefire, and peacekeeping and civil policing assistance – did provide a crucial mediating framework for the termination of the civil war and incorporation of the rebels into the constitutional process. The United Nations Transitional Authority in Cambodia (UNTAC) was successful in bringing about a peaceful transition to a multiparty, formally democratic system (although it failed to demobilize the Khmer Rouge, control corruption, and prevent campaign violence and malpractices). After a year and a half of what can only be described as UN "occupation", almost 90 percent of voters turned out to the polls, in a surprisingly peaceful and free election that defied enormous logistical obstacles and a daunting legacy of fear and horror. A new coalition government resulted. The most ambitious such undertaking in UN history – investing $2 billion, 16,000 troops, over 3,000 police officers, and 3,000 civilian officials who assumed control of key ministries – UNTAC became the epitome of the UN in the "New World Order," showing inseparable connections between traditional UN functions – such as peacekeeping, disarmament, and repatriation of refugees – and the new democracy-building functions of electoral administration and monitoring, political mediation, and institutional reconstruction (Jeldres 1993).

Of the regional organizations, the European Community (now European Union) was the first to take democracy seriously by imposing as a condition for membership that states manifest "truly democratic practices and respect for fundamental rights and freedoms." This conditionality provided "an important incentive for the consolidation of

Promoting democracy in the 1990s 331

democratic processes in the Iberian peninsula," Greece, and (more recently and less successfully) Turkey (Whitehead 1986: 21–23; see also Huntington 1991: 87–89). It is today a powerful incentive against backsliding into authoritarianism in Eastern Europe, particularly in those more economically advanced countries (Poland, Hungary, the Czech Republic, Slovakia) where admission in the near future is most plausible, and was specifically envisioned – with very explicit democratic conditionality – in the Europe Agreements of 1990 (Pinder 1994: 124–125). Reinforcing this is similar conditionality – democratic pluralism, the rule of law, and protection of human rights – for membership in the Council of Europe, which several East European democracies have recently obtained, and which the former Communist countries view not only "as desirable in its own right" but "as an important step toward the grand prize of membership in the European Community" (Kritz 1993: 25).[26]

The general EC/EU approach to encouraging democratization has been via support for market reform, on the principle that if Eastern Europe's markets become developed like those in the West, its government's will also become more democratic like those in the West. The EU and the Group of 24 (G-24) together with the International Monetary Fund (IMF), have thus given the Central European countries, plus Bulgaria and Romania, $1 billion each in aid, while Poland also received a $16 billion debt write-off.[27] The EU and G-24 have also provided humanitarian aid of food and medicines to ease the shock of economic adjustment, and through the PHARE program, technical and administrative advice, training, and support on building market institutions amounting to some $3 billion per year for the region (Pinder 1994: 128–129, 133).[28] PHARE and its complement for the former Soviet Union, TACIS, also have democracy programs, managed by the European Human Rights Foundation, that support the work of NGOs in building democratic, pluralistic societies and the transfer of expertise and technical skills concerning democracy and the rule of law (IDEE 1995: 39–40).

The twenty-year-old CSCE (now OSCE – Organization for Security and Cooperation in Europe) is more directly engaged in democracy promotion activities in the former Communist countries of Eastern Europe and the former Soviet Union. Stepping beyond its historic (but limited) concern for human rights in that broad region, the CSCE (in its June 1990 Copenhagen meeting) declared "democracy and the rule of law" to be "essential for ensuring respect for all human rights and fundamental freedoms"; defined those various concepts in unprecedentedly explicit and comprehensive detail (incorporated later that year into the

332 Larry Diamond

Charter of Paris for a New Europe); and imposed sanctions against states responsible for flagrant human rights abuses (quoted in Kritz 1993: 19). The EU has also imposed sanctions: A trade agreement with Bulgaria was suspended after the regime's abuse of its Turkish minority in 1989; PHARE assistance to Romania was suspended following the violent repression in 1990; and the aid program for the Soviet Union was suspended following its action against the Baltics (Pinder 1994: 132). Since the downfall of Communism and the transformation of its role in 1990, the CSCE has also established a number of new permanent institutions, including an Office of Democratic Institutions and Human Rights in Warsaw (ODIHR) with a mandate to aid the development of democracy in more than twenty post-Communist CSCE countries. Though lean in staff and funding (with a 1993 budget of $2.4 million) the ODIHR has been active, organizing electoral advice and assistance for new democracies; missions to assess minority rights and interethnic relations in Moldova and Estonia; and seminars on such issues as developing tolerance and drafting constitutions.

In 1990 the Council of Europe (CE) established its own set of democracy promotion activities in Central and Eastern Europe, with a view toward facilitating the eventual integration of these countries into the Council. With a budget of 54 million francs (about $10 million) in 1994, plus voluntary contributions from member states, the CE's Demosthenes project provides practical assistance in many areas, such as drafting legislation on human rights, the mass media, and local government; prosecuting human rights violations and protecting ethnic minorities; the technical aspects of broadcasting; local finance procedures; and seminars on the role of NGOs in a democratic civil society.

Since its founding in 1948, democracy has also been an explicit concern of the Organization of American States (OAS). This rhetorical commitment has been periodically strengthened over time, yet always with equivocation about national sovereignty. Not until the historic June 1991 Santiago meeting was this reticence pierced to some extent with the adoption of Resolution 1080, which mandated an immediate meeting of the Organization's Permanent Council following the rupture of democratic rule anywhere in the region, and the adoption of "efficacious, timely, and expeditious procedures to ensure the promotion and defense of representative democracy" (Muñoz 1993; Hakim 1993: 40).[29]

Until the 1990s, OAS action to enforce the democratic commitment implicit in its charter had been modest and episodic at best, showing the impossibility of any regional organization effectively promoting

Promoting democracy in the 1990s 333

democracy when most of its member states are not democratic. Only when the region had become overwhelmingly democratic, and had passed the Santiago resolution, did it begin to take more concerted action, effectively monitoring elections in Haiti, El Salvador, Paraguay, and Surinam, and sanctioning the coups against democracy in Haiti (in September 1991) and Peru (in April 1992). In the case of Haiti, the member states of the OAS cut off all non-humanitarian aid and imposed a general trade embargo, but this had little impact on the ruthless ruling elite. In the end, only the prospect of an imminent US invasion induced the generals to accept a negotiated exit at the final hour. The milder OAS diplomatic pressure on Peru may have helped persuade President Fujimori to abandon plans for a plebiscite to legitimate his *autogolpe* and to hold OAS-monitored elections for a constituent assembly to draft a new constitution. But human rights abuses continued (Hakim 1993: 40–2).

As Peter Hakim has argued, a principal reason (beyond deep-seated distrust of the US) why the OAS is so notoriously weak and immobile – even more than the UN – is because of its structure, which provides for no independent institutional authority, other than the thirty-four member governments sitting collectively, to manage its affairs. There is no equivalent to the UN Security Council (which Hakim believes is badly needed), and the OAS Secretary General has far less authority and autonomy than his UN counterpart. A few years ago the OAS established a Democracy Unit "to provide program support for democratic development," but it needs more staff resources and broader analytical capabilities. As with the UN, funding constraints are severe (the Organization today spends less than half of what it did twenty years ago) (Hakim 1993: 43–5).

Much less effective still at democracy promotion has been the Organization of African Unity (OAU). Its history shows even more graphically the constraints imposed when most member states of a regional organization are authoritarian. Anti-colonialism, defense of sovereignty, and regional cooperation were its founding purposes – not democracy or human rights. In 1981, a meeting of OAU heads of state unanimously adopted an African Charter on Human and People's Rights, which came into force in October 1986 with forty-eight countries signed on. The Charter was riddled with contradictions and qualifications, however, and lacked any serious enforcement mechanisms. Most member states ignored even its most mild procedural provisions, and the Commission it established to research, investigate, and receive charges of violations has proved timid and ineffectual, with no real power (Nwankwo 1993). By contrast, with a self-activating enforcement mech-

334   *Larry Diamond*

anism, an independent governing board and mandate, and a more forceful, pro-democratic Charter of its parent organization, the Inter-American Commission on Human Rights of the OAS has achieved "a distinguished record of investigating and disclosing abuses and recommending remedial action in many countries of the hemisphere" (Hakim 1993: 44; see also Farer 1989).

Recently, beginning with the historic 1991 Zambian election, the OAU has begun to undertake small electoral observation missions (including ambassadors from member countries and OAU staff). However, these have only been initiated by invitation from the country, and have been hampered by the small size of the team, their narrow mandate, excessive reliance on host governments, the briefness of their stay in the country, and the privacy of their reported findings to the Secretary General (Garber 1993).

Clearly, there is a growing international architecture of collective institutions and formal agreements enshrining both the principles of democracy and human rights and the legitimacy of international action to promote them. Increasingly, the world community is embracing a shared normative expectation that all states seeking international legitimacy should manifestly "govern with the consent of the governed" – in essence, a "right to democratic governance," a legal entitlement (Franck 1992: 50). Already effectively implied by the Universal Declaration of Human Rights and the International Covenant on Civil and Political Rights, this right to democratic governance has been articulated more and more explicitly in the documents of regional organizations like the CSCE and OAS, and affirmed by the growing interventions of those organizations and the UN. For some, this suggests the world is moving (and *should* move) toward establishing a global guarantee of constitutional democracy to every nation (similar to the clause in the US constitution compelling the federal government to ensure "A Republican Form of Government" in every state) (Halperin and Lomasney 1993; Halperin 1993). Such a *universal* guarantee (in anything more than principle) is no doubt years away, at least. But significant erosion of the principle of "non-intervention in the internal affairs of a country" is already discernible (even in Africa). At a minimum, this evolution has done two things. First, it has lowered the political threshold against intervention, not only for the multilateral actors but for states and NGOs as well; and, second, it has emboldened domestic advocates of democracy and human rights. If the world has not yet recognized a universal *legal* entitlement to democracy, it has at least advanced cultural norms and expectations of its *moral* worth.

Instruments

A variety of instruments are available for international actors seeking to promote, foster, or support democracy. Most of the above review has focused on the various donors offering *political assistance* of various kinds. This may be of a financial or technical nature, but its goal is political: to develop democratic institutions, practices, and capacities. *Economic assistance* can also make a difference, if one presumes that (market-oriented) economic development ultimately encourages democratization, and that economic improvement is at some point necessary to legitimate and sustain a new democracy. A major aid instrument that states have at their disposal and are increasingly inclined to use is *conditionality* – tying desired forms of aid to democracy or political liberalization. States may also threaten or cajole other regimes through *diplomatic pressure* (usually behind the scenes), and may employ *sanctions* if diplomatic threats and appeals fail. If those measures fail as well, as a last resort a few powerful nations, or the international system collectively, may resort to *military force*. And where armed conflict has become an obstacle to democracy, *peacekeeping and mediation* may also help to establish more favorable conditions for democratization. Space does not permit review here of the latter two instruments, although I do believe that peacekeeping and military intervention may have legitimate roles to play where, respectively, warring parties are ready to cease violent hostilities and transfer their conflict into the political arena (e.g., El Salvador), and where an overwhelming popular preference for democracy exists and is blocked by a narrow repressive elite (Haiti).

Political assistance

Political institution-building is the premier task of democratic consolidation, although it may begin to have some importance in completing a lengthy, phased democratic transition (as in Brazil or Nigeria). Most new democracies are very weak institutionally. Elections typically begin with a highly fragmented landscape of political parties, few if any of which have significant and stable bases of support, especially outside the major cities. Most parties are heavily dependent on a few elite personalities, or on an ethnic identity, or both. By Huntington's classic criteria of institutionalization, they lack coherence, complexity, autonomy from other social groups, and of course adaptability (since they are new, or newly restored) (Huntington 1968).

Traditional development assistance programs sought to strengthen

336   *Larry Diamond*

the bureaucracy and executive branch. While state strengthening and civil service reform are important targets of World Bank and other economic assistance, and are crucial to the institutionalization of market-oriented reforms, democratic assistance targets the legal and judicial system, and the input and response mechanisms of the state: legislatures, local governments, and elections.

Legislative assistance programs not only improve the legal and technical ability of legislators and staffs to write legislation (which function in many countries has historically been the virtual monopoly of the executive branch), but aim to strengthen a number of other key functions: committee systems; library, information, and research support services; oversight of executive branch agencies (including ultimately the military and intelligence apparatus); communicating with and serving constituencies; drafting and analyzing budgets; computerizing legislative operations; and opening the legislative process to greater citizen access, participation, and scrutiny. The latter goal involves an entire second dimension of engagement with civil society (which the Asia Foundation, among others, has heavily supported), assisting public hearings, public dissemination of legislative proceedings, training for parliamentary reporters, public opinion polling on issues before the legislature, and independent watchdog groups. Like so much in the way of institution-building, this process relies heavily on training (particularly of permanent staff), but is also advanced through the transfer of financial resources, resident advice, organizational forms, and books and equipment, particularly computers. With decades of experience and several specialized organizations, this is one of the best-developed forms of institutional assistance.

Local government assistance nurtures the ability of municipalities and rural districts to govern their own affairs, enhancing the skills both of elected officials and of staffs. Improving communication between officials and local constituents is again an important theme. So are crafting and managing budgets, working with higher levels of government authority, dividing responsibility between mayors and elected councils, and other features of democratic law making and governance at the local level.

Building a legal and judicial system is a much more extensive undertaking than merely training judges, magistrates, clerks, prosecutors, public defenders, police, and investigators – though all of that is centrally involved. Often, a very substantial presence of expert legal advisors from abroad may be useful to help redraft and codify criminal laws and procedures. Computers and other equipment may help to modernize and speed up judicial proceedings. Frequently the courts (and even the national legislatures) need the most basic type of infrastructural assistance to operate effectively – such as money for adequate working facilities. However, a democratic rule of law involves more than the official administration of justice. It requires a supporting culture and institutional framework in society. Even in an institution-building sense, development of a democratic judicial system must involve parallel assistance to train judicial reporters, fund legal aid programs, improve law schools, strengthen bar associations, and disseminate basic human rights and legal education at all levels of society.

Strong advocacy groups in civil society and aggressive, resourceful investigative reporting are especially crucial to the challenge of controlling corruption – an indispensable dimension of a democratic rule of law. This is the aspect of democratic legality that entrenched political, bureaucratic, and clientelistic interests most resist. Foreign donors can invest huge sums of money, expertise, and time in helping to develop effective auditing staffs and procedures, but to no avail if their investigations are sidelined and their reports are buried, and if an auditor-general lacks the autonomy and legal standing to expose and bring to punishment venal officials. The same is true for the judicial system more broadly, which often requires broad structural (and even constitutional) reform to establish more autonomy for the judiciary in budgeting, administration, and review of executive and legislative actions, as well as higher professional standards for appointments.

AID experience with Rule of Law programs suggests the importance of the political context for any effective democratic institution-building. Professional training and modern technology may produce little improvement in judicial (and, for that matter, other democratic) performance "in the absence of a political commitment" at high levels.[30] Similarly, much knowledge has accumulated about how to improve auditing and management information systems, alter incentive structures, circumscribe the discretion of government officials, and narrow the scope for rent-seeking in order to control corruption. But only committed political leadership can make these work (Klitgaard 1991; Diamond 1991). Foreign donors must look for or find ways of using leverage to generate this political commitment, or assistance may be consumed eagerly, but with little impact. This is precisely why a balanced approach is needed, which simultaneously develops societal as well as governmental institutions. Independent NGOs and media are vital in mobilizing the public support for reform and accountability that make possible effective institution-building in the state sector.

Political party-building is a crucial and too often neglected element of democratic development. Despite the advent of television, computer

338   *Larry Diamond*

networks, and public opinion polling, as well as the proliferation of NGOs of all types, political parties remain the indispensable instruments for fashioning diverse identities, interests, and preferences into laws, appropriations, and governments. Without effective parties, democracies cannot have effective governance. Party-building entails more than training party practitioners in campaign organization, use of the mass media, candidate recruitment, etc. It requires training in techniques of membership recruitment, volunteer organization, local branch development, fundraising, public opinion polling, interest group liaison, policy research, message development, constituency contact, and coordination between parliamentary and extra-parliamentary wings. It may involve education about alternative electoral laws and the different incentives and party systems they generate. Often it requires assistance to reform and democratize established parties that have become brittle, corrupt, and unresponsive. Techniques here include competitive primaries to select candidates, transparent procedures, greater scope for participation of grassroots volunteers, and more effective two-way communication between national party headquarters and local branches.

Election assistance involves preparing, conducting, monitoring, and observing a free and fair election.[31] The great fund of technical knowledge accumulated has enabled organizations like NDI and IFES to provide expert, independent recommendations for reforming electoral codes and reorganizing electoral procedures that break deadlock and win the confidence of both government and opposition. With sufficient numbers of trained domestic monitors and international observers, it is not difficult to detect organized efforts at fraud. The premier instrument for doing so is the parallel vote tabulation, by which independent monitors report the results from individual polling stations (either all of them or, if a "quick count" is sought, a statistical random sample) directly to a non-partisan watch group (usually aided by international observers), which then collates and announces its own count (Garber and Cowan 1993). However, observers can only render adequate judgments about the overall freedom and fairness of the election if they begin work sufficiently well in advance of the voting (as much as six months) not only to assess administrative preparations, train monitors, and prepare for election day, but also to observe the election campaign for signs of official intimidation, lack of access to the media, and misuse of government resources by the incumbent party.

Few instruments of democracy promotion have had as immediately and clearly visible an impact as international election observing. Free and fair elections are only one dimension of democracy, and are too often equated with democracy. Still, they are a prerequisite for democ-

Promoting democracy in the 1990s

racy, and often a forbidding obstacle at the dawn of a new regime or in a period of political crisis. At a minimum, a well-organized team of international observers can help to verify the election results so as to enhance the credibility and legitimacy of the declared victor in a polarized contest, as in South Korea in 1987 and Bulgaria in 1990. In some countries, their presence has deterred an authoritarian or incumbent government from rigging the election or forging or canceling the result, as with the 1988 plebiscite that ended Pinochet's rule in Chile; the December 1991 elections in Zambia that defeated President Kenneth Kaunda after twenty-seven years of rule; and the recent founding elections in South Africa and Malawi, where long-ruling parties went down to peaceful defeat.[32] Where fraud does occur, as in Panama under Noriega (1989) and the Philippines under Marcos (1986), observers can demonstrate it and deny it domestic and international acceptance. At times, observers can also go much further, helping bitterly opposed sides to negotiate mutually acceptable terms of the electoral game, and even mediating the implementation of "a collectively guaranteed process of national reconciliation and democratization," as in Nicaragua, El Salvador, and Cambodia. Many times, the international role is truly indispensable, since mediation and observing of elections requires impartial arbiters whom all sides can trust (McCoy, Garber, and Pastor 1991; see also Muravchik 1991: 208–210; Garber and Bjornlund 1993; Bjornlund, Bratton, and Gibson 1992).

As with other forms of political assistance, election observing requires political will to succeed – in this case, will on the part of the international community to hold a particular regime to the same democratic standards as others, and to impose sanctions if it fails to meet them. Election observing failed to advance democratization in some recent instances – notably the 1992 presidential elections in Cameroon and Kenya – because of divisions among international actors. While NDI's observer mission found widespread irregularities in Cameroon's elections and the US-imposed sanctions, France ignored the ample evidence of fraud and embraced the regime. In Kenya, NDI was excluded from the international observing process altogether, and its efforts to aid Kenyan civic organizations to develop a non-partisan election monitoring program were hindered.[33] This left the international responsibility to 160 observers from IRI and the British Commonwealth who were perhaps less aggressive, and proved more inclined to declare the voting itself largely "free and fair," in contrast to independent domestic observers who pointed to numerous irregularities in ten key "swing" constituencies. The lack of unity in assessments, the underemphasis given to malpractices in advance of the election, and the severe divisions in

340   *Larry Diamond*

opposition political ranks undermined the formation of any clear judgment that Moi had stolen the election, and thus enabled the regime to squeak through to reelection with some remnant of political legitimacy and international tolerance (Barkan 1993).

Aiding civil society is a third dimension of political assistance that goes hand in hand with the other two. Election monitoring often stimulates the mobilization of independent civic efforts, because of the large numbers of domestic monitors who must be trained and deployed (3,500 for a small country such as Zambia). Founding elections are often the genesis for civic education organizations, like the Latin American network *Conciencia*, that go on over a period of years to heighten civic awareness, encourage tolerance and compromise, and mobilize women and other excluded groups. Rule of Law assistance programs increasingly seek to strengthen independent media, research, training and advocacy organizations in civil society both to deepen democratic legal capacities and culture and to generate informed political pressure on the state to undertake democratic reforms. These and other examples point to the significant complementarity between state and civil society in the construction of democracy (Diamond 1994b).

Civil society development, however, takes work, and especially in the former Communist countries, must struggle against debilitating legacies of distrust, both in public institutions and in fellow citizens. It is precisely this pervasive distrust that makes the construction of a vibrant civil society (interacting, in particular, with autonomous local government) essential, for "the construction of trustworthy institutions is more likely to happen from the bottom up than from the top down" (Rose 1994: 29). As Robert Putnam has shown in his work on Italy, social trust and cooperation, norms of reciprocity, and networks of civic engagement reinforce one another and undergird the vitality of democracy (Putnam, with Leonardi and Nanetti 1993).

As with political party development, assistance to civil society groups heavily involves education and training (including the training of trainers and associational leaders) in forming, building, and running an organization democratically: drafting a constitution or by-laws, facilitating meetings, recruiting volunteers, eliciting active participation, expanding membership, holding elections, tolerating differences, resolving conflict, raising funds, managing projects, advocating policies, building associational networks, and relating to the press, public, and government. Training in more specialized skills – grant proposal writing, financial accounting, curriculum development, civic education, program evaluation, computer networking, public opinion polling, and statistical analysis – are often also needed, along with equipment, infrastructure,

Promoting democracy in the 1990s 341

project funding, and general operational subsistence. In very poor countries, and in those with massive inequalities and scant civic traditions, it is often unrealistic to expect that groups seeking to reform the political process, empower marginalized groups, and challenge established interests can maintain ambitious agendas while being (or becoming) self-supporting. International donors should provide their grantees in civil society with incentives and skills to develop indigenous funding sources (even in very small amounts from mass memberships), while recognizing the limits of the possible in countries without broad middle classes or enlightened elites.

Aiding civil society also complements and overlaps with more traditional development assistance goals and programs. When a women's group gets assistance to develop a network of cooperatives, or an environmental group to lobby for pollution controls, or a research institute to study market reforms, or a university to initiate a new school of public administration, or a trade union to enhance its bargaining ability, those grants may be for economic and social development, but they also have political consequences. By strengthening the capacity of independent actors in civil society, they broaden participation and enhance the prospects for democratic accountability and responsiveness.

Aid to challenging groups in civil society (including groups in exile) is often the most effective way of pressuring for democratic change in a country with an entrenched authoritarian regime. In a great many developing and post-Communist countries, organizations and especially broad coalitions in civil society have been at the forefront of pressure for democratic transitions. However, while aid to civil society can empower democratic groups, it usually cannot do so sufficiently to tip the balance toward a democratic transition without additional international pressures, fortuitous fractures in the regime, or other changes in society and politics (e.g., induced by economic development) that take place only gradually, over a long period of time.

International assistance to civil society can also contribute significantly to democratic consolidation, for which civil society may perform a number of crucial functions: scrutinizing and containing the power of the state; educating people about public affairs, political issues, and their civic rights and duties; increasing citizen participation, efficacy, and skill; developing a democratic culture of tolerance, moderation, and willingness to compromise; providing additional channels for interest representation; recruiting and training new political leaders; monitoring elections and government performance; and generating democratic constituencies for market reforms. Again, these functions do not merely involve watching and challenging the state; in the end they strengthen

342   *Larry Diamond*

it by enhancing its accountability and responsiveness (Diamond 1994b: 7–11). Many of the political assistance grants described earlier and illustrated in Table 15.1 serve these long-term goals of building a pluralistic, informed, participatory, and tolerant civil society.

However, democracy assistance organizations must be sensitive to the tensions they may generate by aiding civil society actors. In strengthening challenging and oppositional groups to the neglect of state institutions, they may undermine governability. In aiding numerous interest groups with particularistic demands, they may diminish political parties and risk generating a floodtide of spending appeals and interest conflicts that may overwhelm state capacities. Related to this is the potential to stimulate religious and cultural conflict by advancing Western notions of development, democracy, and the "good society" in societies with strong alternative notions of these values (Blair 1994: 24). None of this provides reason not to act in support of civil society development abroad, but it does counsel international donors to proceed with caution, weighing the long-term consequences of their assistance and the need for institutional balance and synergy between state and civil society.

Economic assistance

New democracies around the world have shown much greater capacity to launch bold economic reforms than many critics could have imagined (Remmer 1990, 1991; Geddes 1994). Nevertheless, history and logic suggest that economic crisis and decline cannot continue indefinitely without undermining the legitimacy of democracy and gravely damaging its quality. Already, significant erosion of democracy is apparent in Latin America, due in part to the strains of the prolonged economic crisis in countries like Peru, Venezuela, and Brazil (Diamond 1996).

New democracies, and international actors who wish them well, together confront a major dilemma. Democracy cannot be consolidated unless the regime lays the basis for (eventual) sustainable economic growth. Such economic dynamism, it is increasingly apparent, cannot be achieved without reforms (of a very radical nature in post-Communist and formerly very statist economies) to stabilize and liberalize the economy. Yet such policies are extremely painful in the short term, and therefore risk generating intense political opposition that may deter, dilute, or reverse their implementation. How can the tensions between democracy and economic reform be mitigated? There are many answers to this question, involving shrewd political strategies, the education and mobilization of key, potentially supportive domestic constitu-

Promoting democracy in the 1990s   343

encies, and the construction of social safety nets to ease the pain of adjustment (Diamond 1995a). But the success of these strategies depends in part, perhaps crucially, on the availability of international support, conditioned on the pursuit of economic reform policies.[34]

At the center of the new political economy of international aid has been an implicit bargain between the creditors and donors on the one hand and the (usually deeply indebted) reforming governments on the other: that if these Third World and post-Communist countries "successfully reform their economies in a neoclassical manner with the direction and help of the [IMF and the World Bank], then new voluntary bank loans and foreign investment will be available to underpin and sustain the reform efforts. This implicit bargain has failed in most places" (Callaghy 1992: 173–4). While capital flows did increase to Latin America in the late 1980s and early 1990s (mainly attracted by reform), foreign investment has been slow to enter much of the post-Communist world and Africa in particular. The massive levels of Africa's external debt (relative to GDP) present a particularly difficult problem, both because debt servicing eats up resources badly needed for investment in human and physical capital, and because the debt is held by the very international financial institutions (IFIs) that are pressing for reform. "To insist that African countries meet their debt repayments weakens reform, but not to enforce arrangements weakens the IFIs as creditor agencies" (Callaghy and Ravenhill 1993: 526).

Prospects for reform and democratic consolidation would clearly be advanced around the world by making the bargain real. A number of new democracies have received, as a reward for democratizing, at least a temporary aid bonus from the US and other donors. That is helpful but inadequate. In the poorest countries, particularly in Africa, debt relief must feature prominently, because the debt will never be repaid. A concrete bargain that could do much to facilitate renewed development and to strengthen domestic constituencies for reform would freeze debt service payments in these countries and then retire the debt at some fixed rate (e.g., 10 percent per year) for every year that a country remains committed to democracy and economic reform policies. Specific levels of new aid might also be incorporated into this ten-year commitment (Diamond 1994b). Long-term commitments of this nature offer hope of overcoming the two most serious problems with aid conditionality at present: the lack of adequate resource flows to assist adjustment, and the temporary, episodic nature of assistance from international donors. "A temporary reward is a recipe for temporary liberalisation" (Collier 1991: 161). By contrast, if an explicit longer-term agreement could help lock a country into economic reform policies

344   *Larry Diamond*

and democratic institutions for a decade or so, these policies and institutions would have the time to begin to yield concrete results, developing new constituencies of support and self-sustaining political momentum.

Among the most urgent needs for international assistance is to help fund safety net programs, which temporarily provide food, income, jobs, schools, health care, and infrastructure to the poor, ideally in response to decentralized initiatives from grassroots community organizations and local governments (Graham 1994). This is not mere charity to aid the poor abroad, but an investment in the economic reform of particular countries, therefore in their democracies, and therefore in their long-term political stability and responsibility on the international stage. The case for aiding countries (most of all Russia, but also Ukraine and Eastern Europe) that could impact the national security of the US, Europe, and Japan is especially compelling.

Yet curiously, for the country where the West has the biggest self-interest in the success of reform – Russia – international aid was notoriously slow to be delivered, despite lofty promises of first a $24 billion commitment from the G-7 in 1992, raised to $44 billion the following year.[35] In January 1993 Jeffrey Sachs proposed that the West boldly assist Russian reform with *"real* stabilization support" for the ruble, and a deep debt rescheduling; a support fund for small businesses: several billion dollars in funds to assist long-term industrial restructuring; and support for social programs, "mainly unemployment compensation and job retraining – both to serve as a political signal and to provide budgetary support, which is crucial to stabilization" (Sachs 1994b: 521).[36] This might have made a real difference. However, the failure of the West to support Russian economic reform with the tangible assistance pledged seriously undermined the agents of reform, led by Yegor Gaidar (McFaul 1994: 33). Compare this with the $1 billion stabilization fund Poland got in 1990 to help launch the Balcerowicz plan. As Sachs argues, the IMF's insistence on seeing demonstrated progress before aid is forthcoming may be poorly suited to the crisis pressures of "life in the economic emergency room." In fact, the IMF and World Bank do not seem to be the appropriate institutions for delivering assistance whose urgent imperatives rely more on political than technical economic calculations (McFaul 1994: 31).

At the same time, however, international advocates of reform must not lose sight of the important connections between economic and political reform. "It is naive to pour millions of dollars into promoting privatization when the legal framework and political support for protecting private property do not exist. Political reform in Russia has helped,

Promoting democracy in the 1990s

not impeded, economic reform (McFaul 1995: 98–99). Yet the overwhelming bulk of the US and international assistance that has been delivered to Russia has been for economic reform.

International support for reform also needs to maintain a low profile and some sense of humility and sensitivity to individual country circumstances and national pride. We have seen already, in the neo-Fascist Zhirinovsky's strong showing in the December 1993 elections, how tough times and personal hardships can generate acute resentment of foreign models and influences, which is readily exploitable by zealots, demagogues, and xenophobes. In assisting reform, international actors have to tread a careful path between firm conditionality and arrogant (and often ill-informed) imposition of detailed policy prescriptions (see Williamson and Haggard 1994: 566).

Diplomacy, aid conditionality, and sanctions

Diplomatic persuasion and pressure, and such tangible instruments of pressure as sanctions and aid conditionality, may induce a regime to do politically what it would not otherwise do: become more democratic. They do so by offering rewards and/or imposing costs greater than the costs the regime perceives from the conditions demanded: improving human rights, relaxing political restrictions, backing down from a military coup or an election annulment, implementing democracy. Thus, conditionality works best upon a regime that is sufficiently divided or ambivalent over the issue of political reform so that external pressure can help to tip the balance (Nelson and Eglington 1992: 48–49).[37]

Democratic aid conditionality may be imposed *ad hoc* on certain countries at pivotal moments of political stress and change, or it may be institutionalized in universal standing conditions. The latter is most effective, because it is more credible and can have a prophylactic effect in preventing democratic erosion or reversals. The growing institutional architecture of Europe, beginning with the EC, has been the most effective in using explicit, standing conditionality both to encourage countries to become democratic (in Eastern Europe) and to discourage member states from abandoning democracy. Increasingly, would-be autocrats have to ponder the heavy price their country would pay in loss of aid, capital, trade, investment, and symbolic status if they were to roll back democracy.

However, aid conditionality has its costs and risks as well. It may generate conflicting logics if it encompasses both economic and political dimensions, as some regimes will satisfy one dimension and not the other. Its democratic aims may conflict with other (strategic and

346   *Larry Diamond*

commercial) foreign policy goals, "pitting credibility against realistic flexibility" (Nelson and Eglington 1992: 38). It may provoke further repression by a regime that resents the violation of sovereignty and feels itself strong enough to resist the pressure. International sanctions may be welcomed by democratic forces within a country, but they may also enable the regime to marginalize a democratic movement, discredit them as unpatriotic, and rally national anger and frustration, particularly if the population suffers broadly from the imposition of sanctions. Alternatively, some have argued, democratic (and also economic) conditionality may work but only superficially, inducing ruling elites to make tactical concessions they will later hollow out, or "externalizing responsibility" for a country's political fate and thereby preempting "longer-run processes of learning and organization" crucial to enduring democratization (Nelson and Eglington 1992: 53).

Thus, several factors shape the potential utility of conditions and sanctions. The more they focus on specific, monitorable goals (such as human rights conditions, free and fair elections, a return to civilian constitutional rule), the more likely they will have a discernible effect. The more they can be targeted to hurt an offending regime without damaging the population – as with cut-offs of military and security assistance – the less the chance of a popular nationalist reaction. The more the regime's international Allies, donors, and partners can be rallied to support the sanctions or conditions, the less feasible it will be for the regime to resist them. And at best, aid conditionality can only be "a useful complement to other approaches encouraging political reforms – not a strategy in its own right" (Nelson and Eglington 1992: 4).

Beyond friendly dialogue to persuade a regime of "its own best interests" – what the Reagan Administration termed "constructive engagement" with respect to its South Africa policy – diplomatic pressure or aid conditionality requires real leverage to be successful. Even where that exists, as with the huge volume of US imports of Chinese goods, the target regime may judge the political cost of the conditions too great and the levers at its own disposal not insignificant. Thus did the Clinton Administration correctly judge in 1994 that China would not yield to US human rights conditions for "Most Favored Nation" trading status, which it had imposed unilaterally. One wonders whether the US and European democracies would not have more success in inducing Turkey to improve its deteriorating human rights record, and to give full citizenship rights to the Kurds, if they did not so much depend on Turkey as a strategic counterweight to the radical Islamic states and a conduit for assistance and outreach to the Central Asian republics of the former

Promoting democracy in the 1990s 347

Soviet Union; and if the EU were willing to commit itself to Turkey's admission in exchange for fundamental improvements in human rights.[38] This raises another problem with democratic conditionality – that the US historically has tended to satisfy itself with the civilian, electoral form of democracy rather than the substance, and has too little concerned itself with actual regime behavior after the transition. This is a problem the Western European democracies may increasingly confront as pressure grows for integration with Central and Eastern Europe.

During the "third wave," US and international diplomatic pressures have contributed to democratization and political liberalization, but only when they followed the above lessons and reinforced significant domestic pressures. One way diplomatic pressures have worked has been to narrow the domestic support of authoritarian regimes and aggravate the divisions within them. Carter Administration human rights pressure on Uruguay and especially Argentina, including cut-offs of military and economic aid and other sanctions, had this kind of effect, while bringing significant improvement in those human rights situations (Sikkink 1991).[39] Carter Administration human rights policies, along with specific diplomatic initiatives, also supported democratic transition in Peru, "prevented an authoritarian relapse" in Ecuador in 1978, and in that same year deterred vote fraud in the Dominican Republic's presidential election (Huntington 1991: 96–97). Although the Carter Administration marked a new departure in emphasizing and operationalizing human rights concerns in US policy, it was also torn by the same pull of conflicting interests, and thus the inconsistency, that has characterized every liberal internationalist presidency from Wilson to Clinton (Smith 1994).

Pressure from the Reagan Administration, the US Congress, and international public opinion, interacting with rising domestic mobilization and a loss of business confidence, led Philippine dictator Ferdinand Marcos to call the 1986 presidential "snap election" that independent election observers judged he lost to Corazon Aquino. In the tense days following the February 7 vote, a deliberate US policy to "accelerate the succession" helped to frustrate Marcos' effort to retain power through massive electoral fraud. The US warned Marcos against suppressing the independent pollwatching group, NAMFREL; vigorously challenged the election's credibility; threatened to cut off military aid if Marcos used military force against a pro-democratic army rebellion; and finally (with the prospect of mass bloodshed hanging in the balance) told Marcos it was time to go (Shultz 1993: 608–642). American pressure (both coercive and diplomatic) figured prominently, too, in the decision of the Sandinistas to hold early and free elections, as did a

348   *Larry Diamond*

mix of other domestic and international factors (including the promise of new Western aid after free elections) (Pastor 1990: 15). During the Reagan years, US diplomatic and economic pressure, and its symbolic support for human rights and peaceful democratic change, ultimately contributed to democratic transitions in Chile and South Korea as well, while preventing planned military coups in El Salvador, Honduras, and Bolivia in the early 1980s and in Peru in January 1989 (Huntington 1991: 95).[40] "In each case, however, international support for democracy *reinforced* domestic groups and sectors of the military opposed to military intervention" (Fitch 1993: 203 [emphasis in the original]). Moreover, throughout these years, the goals of democracy promotion and of fighting Communism struggled for policy dominance (and for Reagan's soul), and massive military assistance to El Salvador, Guatemala, and Honduras appear to have undermined the ability of embattled civilian, democratic forces to get control of abusive and powerful militaries.[41]

US diplomatic pressure (backed by the threat of severe sanctions) also played an important role in dissuading the Guatemalan military from throwing its weight behind the *autogolpe* of President Jorge Serrano in May 1993, thus leading to its unraveling. More important, however, "was the unanimity of purpose shown by the OAS member states and the unequivocal and immediate message conveyed to the Serrano administration and other forces that Guatemala would face political isolation and economic sanctions if constitutional rule remained disrupted" (León 1993: 124). Again, however, both OAS and international pressure worked as rapidly as they did only because of the massive mobilization of Guatemalan civil society.[42] Overall, Huntington concluded that (between 1974 and 1991) "US support was critical to democratization in the Dominican Republic, Grenada, El Salvador, Guatemala, Honduras, Uruguay, Peru, Ecuador, Panama, and the Philippines and that it was a contributing factor to democratization in Portugal, Chile, Poland, Korea, Bolivia and Taiwan" (Huntington 1991: 98). More difficult to assess but probably quite significant during the third wave – not only in encouraging democratic transitions but in discouraging reversals – has been the cumulative effect of the US and European policies in generating a global normative climate inhospitable to authoritarian rule.

Both governments and societies respond to international sanctions, and also to anticipated rewards. In Taiwan, "the political reform movement was initially triggered" in the early 1970s by the "forced severance of its formal ties with many Western countries and its loss of membership in the United Nations," which catalyzed a wave of new intellectual concern with domestic politics (Cheng 1989: 484). Sophisticated Taiwanese began to realize that democratization was the only way their country could become politically reintegrated into the world and ultimately accepted as a full partner among advanced, industrial nations. This factor also played an important, if intangible, role in the transition to democracy in South Korea (which feared losing the prestige of hosting the 1988 Olympics) and in Chile. In these contexts of economic dynamism, broad international criticism of authoritarian rule bred a sense of isolation and a desire to be regarded with respect by the industrialized democracies.[43]

Nowhere was the sense of isolation sharper and more dispiriting than in South Africa. Years of stiffening international sanctions and opprobrium, along with other dramatic changes in the international environment, were instrumental in inducing key elites in South Africa's business establishment and ruling National Party to abandon apartheid and opt for a negotiated transition to democracy. Economic sanctions and disinvestment by the Western powers – "as much a psychological as a financial blow" – merged with the decline in global gold prices and domestically generated debt and inflation to produce "protracted recession, capital flight, and a profound sense of isolation ... Whites began to realize that unless they came to terms with the political demands of the black population, the economic noose would not loosen" (Baker 1990: 8–9). The South African experience shows that country-specific sanctions can work when major powers cooperate and domestic pressures converge.

International diplomatic pressure and economic sanctions have played an important role in facilitating Africa's "second liberation," which began with the release of Nelson Mandela and unbanning of the ANC in February 1990, and the assumption of effective power by the national conference in Benin that same month. These two seminal developments coincided with a sharp turnabout in the aid and diplomatic policies of the principal Western powers, the US, Britain, and France. Each of them announced that year new initiatives to tie economic aid to political and economic liberalization. Other bilateral aid donors as well – the Netherlands, Norway, Sweden, Canada, and to some extent Germany and Japan – had been or would soon be moving toward some degree of conditionality or consideration for human rights and democracy conditions in the allocation of aid (Nelson and Eglington 1992: 16–17, 32). The French embrace of democratic conditionality was the most dramatic in its departure from past cynical and clientelistic behavior, and it quickly contributed to the downfall of the Kerekou regime in Benin (which, without French subsidies could not pay its civil

350   *Larry Diamond*

servants), initiation of democratic transitions (since successfully completed) in Mali, Niger, and Madagascar as well, and more limited and equivocal political openings in Chad, the Congo, Ivory Coast, Cameroon, and Gambia (Diamond 1995b).

The most decisive evidence of the new conditionality in Anglophone Africa came in Kenya, where US Ambassador Smith Hempstone had already become a controversial thorn in the side of the Moi regime with his open appeals for democratic reform and gestures of support for human rights causes. At the November 1991 meeting in Paris of the Consultative Group for Kenya, the country's international aid donors "established explicit political conditions for assistance, making Kenya a precedent for the rest of Africa" (Barkan 1993: 91). New aid was suspended for six months, pending "the early implementation of political reform" (quoted in Barkan 1993 from World Bank 1991). These international pressures forced the regime to repeal the ban on opposition parties one week after the Paris meeting (a fact which President Moi bitterly conceded two months later) (Muigai 1993: 29), and to hold multiparty elections a year later that could have led to a democratic transition if the political opposition (with Machiavellian help from the regime, to be sure) had not fractured along ethnic lines. A similar decision by international donors in May 1992 to freeze $74 million in aid to Malawi (following the first mass protest demonstrations in twenty-eight years) also compelled the iron-fisted regime of Hastings Banda in Malawi to liberalize, holding a national referendum on multiparty competition that it lost badly in June 1993, leading to multiparty elections in which it was similarly crushed the following year.

It would seem that the power of the democratic donors was nowhere greater than in Africa, and particularly during the 1990s, when one country after another experienced vigorous domestic mobilization for democratic change. Yet since 1990, only about a dozen of some four dozen non-democratic regimes in Africa had adopted multiparty, constitutional systems. A number of transitions, as in Nigeria and Zaire, have effectively been aborted, or hijacked by ruling elites through fraudulent elections (as in Cameroon, Kenya, Gabon, and the Ivory Coast). If international actors have so much relative power in Africa, and the moment is so propitious, why has there not been more democratic progress?

As the above examples demonstrate, the power of international donors to induce democratic change (or otherwise shape behavior) through aid conditionality is directly proportional to the dependence of the aid recipients (or debtors) upon them, and to the unity of the donor community in imposing conditions on individual authoritarian regimes

(Diamond 1979).[44] Disastrous divisions and miscalculations on the part of regime opponents (some of whom have questionable commitments to democracy themselves) heavily contributed to setbacks in most of these instances. But so did equivocation and division on the part of the international community. Although the US imposed serious sanctions on the Nigerian military regime following the annulment of the June 12, 1993 presidential election (including suspension of a very modest aid program, and, most seriously, a ban on individual travel to the US by regime members), other key actors such as France, Germany, and Japan held back, and Britain later backed away from its initial tough stance. British and World Bank pressure to resume aid to Kenya, and the arrival of a new American ambassador with a more economy-centered perspective, led to a limited resumption of assistance to Kenya, and a consequent weakening (at least for the time being) of democratizing pressure on the Moi regime.

Most damaging has been the rapid French retreat from its November 1990 embrace of democratic conditionality. At the subsequent Francophone conference a year later, President Mitterand considerably diluted the message he had given at La Baule; six days after announcing that more lax stance, troops loyal to Togolese dictator Eyadema launched a coup in Lome to derail the democratic transition (Heilbrunn 1993). Despite ample evidence of fraud in Cameroon's 1992 elections, France endorsed the results and proceeded two months later to grant Cameroon roughly $110 million in new loans (while the US suspended $14 million in aid following the election) (*Africa Report* 1993: 62).[45] This barely enabled Cameroon to reschedule its debts to the IMF and World Bank (failing which all international aid would have been halted) (*West Africa* 1993: 1146). The following May, "Mr Biya was welcomed in Paris by both Mr Mitterand and the new French prime Minister Edouard Balladur" (*The Economist* 1993: 46).

Before international actors can even have the possibility of promoting democracy, they must first have the collective will. In an increasingly multipolar world (with US dominance declining), divergent, mercantilist, and narrowly self-interested policies on the part of the principal established democracies considerably diminishes the prospects for democratic change in the short term. Aid conditionality can only work if the major donors coordinate their conditions, both in their treatment of specific countries and also on general principles.

The need for coherence is no less compelling *within* the US government. One of the greatest handicaps to the effective exercise of US diplomacy and aid for democracy promotion has been inconsistency across different policy centers and in the treatment of different regimes.

352   *Larry Diamond*

Increasingly, traditional policy rivalry between the White House and the Congress, and among the State and Defense Departments, National Security Council, and intelligence agencies, is compounded by the disparate policy interests and demands of the Treasury, Commerce, Agriculture and Justice Departments, the Drug Enforcement Agency, the Office of the Trade Representative, etc.[46] Two types of cleavages drive these increasingly complex conflicts. There are sharply differing perspectives and priorities, deriving from different conceptions of the national interest in the post-Cold War world; these not only pit "new" emphases on trade and economics against the "old" emphases on military security and political alliances, they also pit conventional conceptions of national security against new, more global and preventive orientations of the kind emphasized in this chapter. A second, related source of cleavage stems from concern to protect bureaucratic *raison d'êtres* and overseas client relationships. Reports that the CIA covered up information about political assassinations and human rights violations by one of its own paid agents in the Guatemalan military, even in these post-Cold War years, suggest how profound and contemporary are these clashing bureaucratic interests and conceptions of the national security.

The Clinton Administration's creation of an Interagency Working Group on Democracy, under the leadership of the Assistant Secretary of State for Democracy, Human Rights, and Labor, is a welcome step at improved coordination, but it is only a facilitating mechanism. If there is not the political will (and skill) at the top to back a unified, pro-democracy foreign policy, no amount of coordination can produce it. The US needs to craft a pro-democracy policy (indeed a foreign policy) that has the coherent backing of all foreign policy branches of the government and bipartisan support that can be sustained across administrations. This requires strong presidential leadership and clear preeminence for a forceful Secretary of State as the president's chief foreign policy advisor and spokesperson. Such leadership must then take care to provide "unambiguous and consistent signals" about the high priority it attaches to the maintenance of democracy and human rights (Lowenthal 1991: 263). The concern for human rights (codified in aid conditionality) must be pressed with formally democratic regimes as well as undemocratic ones, and with friendly countries as well as unfriendly ones.[47]

Yet this raises one of the most troubling issues confronting democracy promotion policy, especially for a great power such as the US: the conflict between promoting democracy and securing other, "harder" national interests. Globally, the expansion of democracy serves the national interests of the United States and other established democracies, by advancing peace, stability, legality, human dignity, property rights, and environmental protection in the international system. But it does not always do so immediately, and everywhere. Democratic powers thus cannot avoid facing the "Algeria problem": what to do when a free and fair election, or a process of democratic opening, risks bringing to power an authoritarian and actively hostile government, which might ally with similar regimes. There is no easy answer to this painful dilemma, which is not usefully wished away by dismissing that particular experience as an "experiment." Democracies are under no moral obligation to support the coming to power of anti-democratic forces through elections (which were, after all, the vehicle which the Nazis rode to power). To demand clear and unequivocal commitment to democratic standards and values by oppositional forces, in exchange for active support for their political rights, is not for the established democracies to engage in hypocrisy or double standards, so long as the test is evenly applied.

The only real resolution to the "Algeria problem" lies in earlier and more proactive engagement on behalf of democracy and human rights. Regime legitimacy deteriorates and extremist opposition develops in the face of sustained decadence, corruption, repression, and ineptitude on the part of ruling elites. If the democratic powers do not want to be faced with a choice between an existing and a future authoritarianism (as in Algeria) or between autocracy and anarchy (as may now be the case in Zaire), they must press friendly authoritarian regimes (like Egypt's) to reform, renew, liberalize, and open up before it is too late.

Issues and imperatives

If recent trends are any guide, the period of rapid and easy gains for democracy in the world is now over. At best, we have probably entered a long period of halting institutionalization, uneven marketization, and considerable regime instability, in which most new democracies that progress toward consolidation will do so incrementally, others will continue to deteriorate institutionally or perform very poorly, and some will break down altogether.

Skeptics question whether external assistance can do much to foster democracy in the face of historical traditions, value systems, class structures, and embedded power distributions that are profoundly hostile to democracy.[48] To be sure, socioeconomic development (especially at higher levels) does alter political culture, class structure, civil society, and patterns of participation in ways that make stable democracy more

354   *Larry Diamond*

likely (Lipset 1981; Diamond 1992a). Yet there are numerous grounds to resist an emphasis on societal preconditions. Democratization is triggered mainly by political factors. And many of the countries that are stably democratic today were dismissed as unready for democracy only shortly before they achieved it. Given the precarious balance of political and social forces in many newly democratic and transitional countries, international actors would appear to have real scope to influence the course of political development. Their ability to do so, however, will depend on the extent to which they can rally their will, improve their effectiveness, and extend their time horizons. Whether and how they can do so raises a few additional issues worth mentioning in conclusion.

As the number of donor organizations, programs, and potential recipients proliferates, improved communication and coordination among political assistance efforts looms as an ever more important challenge. Greater networking and coordination may help to avoid duplication and waste, pool resources for major projects and urgent priorities, and diffuse knowledge about what works. Within individual countries, coordination of donors in the field can improve the efficiency and political leverage of their efforts (Barkan 1993: 21–22). Indeed, the need to systematize and share learning, develop common norms and rules, and coordinate more closely among the donors was the overarching conclusion of the conference organized by the Swedish government in May 1994 to consider improved donor cooperation in electoral assistance (International Electoral Institute 1994).

In recent years, the official aid donors have made progress in coordinating their policies and programs for promoting democracy and good governance. Since 1990, the Development Assistance Committee (DAC) of the Organization for Economic Cooperation and Development (OECD) has become increasingly active in promoting common policy orientations and shared learning with respect to what it has termed "Participatory Development and Good Governance" (PDGG), a catchall term encompassing political democratization, human rights, the rule of law, public sector management, controlling corruption, reducing excessive military expenditures, strengthening civil society, and mobilizing broad-based participation in development (including of women and minorities, and especially at the local level). At its December 1993 High Level Meeting, the DAC adopted a remarkably comprehensive statement of common principles, approaches, and objectives for rendering assistance in these various areas, and established an *ad hoc* Working Group on PDGG (OECD 1993).[49] At the level of general principles and priorities, the donor countries appear increasingly united around the above PDGG aims. In practice, however, some powerful countries continue to chart divergent courses in the spirit of traditional, amoral "realism" in foreign affairs. French policy in Africa has heavily reverted to this pattern, and Japan has been the slowest of the major powers to break from it. This is perhaps not surprising, since Japan has also had the least democratic input into its foreign policy, and within the established democracies, the concern for promoting democracy, human rights, and good governance abroad has been heavily driven by pressure from the media, civil society, legislators, and the informed public in their own societies (Arase 1993).

Effective coordination must go beyond principles, to specific countries and programs. For more than two decades, that has been the province of the "consultative groups" (CGs) of aid donors for various specific countries, which are convened by the World Bank. During the 1990s, the CGs have become much more assertive in considering political issues of governance, democratization, and human rights, and even in conditioning aid on democratic progress, as was done for Kenya and Malawi. However, with a charter and organizational culture that constrains it from venturing beyond economic considerations, the World Bank has not been comfortable dealing with democracy and human rights issues. This underscores the importance of tapping a different (bilateral donor) member, perhaps on a rotating basis, to take leadership responsibility for democracy issues within each CG, not only in preparing and facilitating the meeting but in following up and monitoring compliance. Helpful also may be preparatory meetings within the recipient country to elicit broad commentary and open debate about the official aid relationship from civil society, opposition politicians, policy analysts, and the press in advance of the closed CG meetings in Paris.[50] Had such in-country meetings taken place in Kenya, and had there been rigorous monitoring of the regime's post-election assaults on democracy, it would have been much more difficult to justify the resumption of official economic assistance. PDGG principles and goals now appear firmly established on the agendas of the individual country CGs. But their consideration must become more institutionalized, with standard procedures for broad consultation, more active participation of civil society in the policy dialogue, and sustained monitoring and enforcement.

Greater sharing of information and approaches is also needed among non-governmental democracy assistance organizations. NED sought to initiate enhanced cooperation with a "democracy summit" in February 1993 that brought together representatives of NED and its four core institutes, the German *Stiftungen*, the Westminster Foundation, Canada's International Center for Human Rights and Democratic

356   *Larry Diamond*

Development, plus observers from the Japan Institute for International Affairs. Such exchanges and dialogues need to be, and are beginning to be, regularized. A useful instrument of communication may be the new NED International Forum for Democratic Studies, which is constructing an electronic data base of democracy promotion grants, a directory of democracy promotion organizations, and a global electronic information network among democracy promotion organizations and study centers, as well as conducting research and publishing on problems of democracy.

Another valuable point of coordination will be the International Institute for Democracy and Electoral Assistance (International IDEA), which was established in February 1995 at a founding conference of fourteen country sponsors, led by Sweden, whose government has contributed substantial resources to the effort. The result of a two-year planning effort, International IDEA aims to facilitate interaction between organizations, agencies, and individuals active in the field of democratic development and electoral assistance; to establish and promote common guidelines for electoral and democratic assistance; to create a user-friendly data bank and inventory of existing research on elections and democracy; to produce and disseminate new research; to link donors and recipients, and researchers and practitioners; and to offer advisory and capacity-building services for improving elections and other aspects of democratic functioning (International IDEA 1994, 1995a, 1995b; International Electoral Institute 1993).[51]

Other private efforts are also underway, some regional and some sectoral, to facilitate the regular (even instantaneous) exchange of information among democracy assistance organizations (and research and studies programs) through e-mail and other networks. Comprehensive coordination of the incredible profusion of efforts is beyond the capacity of any organization, and may even threaten pluralism. But overlapping networks of information exchange and collaboration are gradually emerging and will be broadly beneficial.

As we have seen, nowhere is coordination more needed, and could it make a quicker and more decisive difference, than in the area of diplomacy (including sanctions and conditionality). Sanctions and diplomatic pressure only succeed where they are backed cohesively by the countries with influence over the target regime. In most countries where democratic possibilities have been squandered, stalled, or diminished, the trail of big-power divisions is easy to locate. Beyond Africa, one could point to Cambodia, where France and Japan supported antidemocratic demands of the incumbent Cambodian People's Party (while Thailand treated with the Khmer Rouge in an exceptionally greedy pursuit of logging and gemstone profits); or Burma, where Thailand and Japan backed a brutally repressive regime (to which Europe is also now resigning itself); or Vietnam, where some major Western democracies abandoned any leverage they might have exercised for political liberalization in a headlong race to open Asia's next booming market; or Pakistan and Turkey, where, for strategic reasons, the US has reacted rather passively to human rights violations and covert military domination.

Major and middle powers are not going to surrender their freedom to act to secure their interests, but stronger democratic conditionality for aid, more closely coordinated among the major donors, would force ruling or military elites to think twice before desecrating democracy, "even if they know that the principle is not entirely consistently enforced" (Nelson and Eglington 1992: 42). More vigorous and creative diplomacy might mobilize pressure on dissenting donors, fashioning a more coherent stance of the democratic powers in a number of critical cases. That requires US leadership, however, the lack of which has facilitated drift and division in the Western democratic alliance.

Failure to hone and coordinate the big-power and multilateral diplomatic instruments of democracy promotion could exact a heavy price. Not only does it risk big, visible setbacks for democracy with potentially potent regional demonstration effects – as in Nigeria, Pakistan, and most of all Russia – but it also threatens to erase enormous investments of money and human resources in specific democracy promotion projects that come to naught. One of the most serious problems in the democracy promotion business today is the disarticulation between the hundreds of democracy assistance donors, seeking incremental gains in civic and institutional capacity at the micro level, and the foreign policy strategies and actions – or inactions – of the major powers, which, with early action at crucial moments, might prevent the macro-level blow-ups that level the democratic terrain. What democratic assistance impacts have survived the holocaust in Rwanda? Or the ruthless dictatorship in Sudan? What will survive in Nigeria if it descends into civil war? Or in Russia if an ultra-nationalist dictator takes power?

Both for individual organizations and governments, and for the international community of democracy promoting organizations and states, sharper strategic thinking is needed. The leading democracies, through their foreign policies and official aid commitments, must set priorities. Several criteria suggest themselves: the strategic importance of the country to their own security and to regional and global security more broadly; the degree to which democratic assistance is needed and could have a positive impact; and the capacity of a country to serve as a model,

358   *Larry Diamond*

a point of diffusion, a "beachhead" for democratic development (and even a stabilizing anchor) within a region. Small countries like Costa Rica and Botswana have been able to play that latter role, and this argues for a global strategy that seeks to advance and consolidate democracies in every region, while recognizing that some countries are more plausible and serious democratic prospects than others. Partly because of its own ethnic complexity, the US – and increasingly Europe, Canada, and Australia as well – cannot afford to write off any portion of the less developed world.

Among individual donor organizations, often too little thought is given to weighing resource constraints against desirable – and achievable – end goals, especially strategic objectives. NED, for one, has been criticized for the "scattershot nature" of its programming, trying to fund too many types of programs in too many countries with a limited budget (Carothers 1994: 135). Yet, for democracy promotion, strategic objectives must be large in scale and time horizon, involving prolonged (and often subtle) engagement. Such sustained engagement must aim for enduring improvements in institutional capacities, in the quality and stability of democracy in a country, and in structural variables, such as market development and civil society, whose democratic impact will be felt most over the long run. Even if the international community collectively can help to bring about changes of this magnitude, individual organizations, even with $35 million annual budgets, most certainly cannot.[52] Only if the principal governmental and non-governmental donors strategize with one another from time to time can they maximize their chances to tip truly uncertain but plausible democratizers – from Russia and Ukraine to South Africa and Benin – firmly into the democratic column. Similar farreaching coordination is needed to develop the democracy-building and conflict-regulating capacities of regional organizations, most urgently the OAU, at a time when global actors are increasingly exhausted with direct intervention and new patterns of dependency need to be broken.

Most strategically, the major democratic powers of the world need to think boldly and creatively about the kind of world order that can best nurture and sustain democracy and human rights. This involves many of the most controversial collective security issues of our time – when and how to intervene against genocide, civil war, human rights atrocities, and forcible overthrows of democracy; how to bring to *international* justice the perpetrators of these crimes; how to reconfigure and revitalize alliance structures and multinational organizations toward these ends. It may demand hard choices, for example, between the desire of arms industries, defense ministries, and trade bureaucrats for ever-expanding

Promoting democracy in the 1990s

weapons exports, on the one hand, and the urgent need, on the other – for democracy, development, and peace – to reduce military expenditures in less developed countries. And it raises issues of world order that have not even entered serious international discussion, such as the construction of a truly global rule of law to confront the increasingly global threats of terrorism, narcotics trafficking, financial fraud, political bribery, money laundering, weapons smuggling, and other organized crimes.

Particularly needed is an international mechanism for imposing biting and specifically targeted sanctions (as the US did belatedly in Haiti) on the ruling elites directly responsible for violating international laws and accords and quashing popular aspirations for democracy, so that pain and pressure can be pinpointed on them and not wantonly inflicted on innocent and long-suffering people.[53] The international community, ideally acting through the UN, must have the ability to freeze the personal assets of these elites worldwide and to deny them and all their family members visas to enter any law-abiding country. This will require intensive new efforts to gather international financial and political intelligence, radical changes in international banking practice, and probably a new international covenant.

Finally, and not less importantly, the established democracies – and not least the United States – must "heal themselves." The post-Cold War ideological hegemony of democracy in the world has been brief, indeed – if it ever really existed. Today, new ideological challengers scorn democracy, and scoff at the social decay, economic stagnation, political corruption, and general sclerosis of the most powerful practitioners and promoters of democracy in Europe and North America. The most sophisticated challenge in this regard comes not from the Islamic fundamentalists or East European and post-Soviet ultranationalists, though they are vigorous and passionate enough. Rather, it emanates from the more economically dynamic East Asian countries (such as Singapore, Malaysia, China, and Indonesia), whose governments (and pro-government intellectuals) claim they have found – in the convergence (in varying degrees) of economic liberalism, limited societal pluralism, and centralized political hegemony – a truly superior political system. Democracy will only expand and triumph in the twenty-first century if comparative development proves them wrong.

NOTES

This paper has benefited from the cooperation, assistance, and insights of a number of people in and out of government. I have chosen to leave them

360   *Larry Diamond*

unnamed so as not to allow inference of any responsibility on their part for the views expressed here (or for any errors of fact or interpretation that may remain). Nevertheless, I am indebted to them, and to Svetlana Tsalik for her skillful research assistance on the revised draft of this chapter.

1 For a conceptualization of the third wave, see Huntington (1991).
2 Although there are 24 more independent countries in the world today (191), the increase is due mainly to a dramatic rise in the percentage of countries with the formal institutional arrangements of democracy: from 38 percent in 1984 to 60 percent in 1994, by the count of Freedom House.
3 The focus here on US government agencies is in no way intended to disparage the increasingly significant efforts of a number of European and Scandinavian overseas development agencies. For some further consideration of their efforts, see Joel Barkan's chapter in this volume.
4 Something around this figure appears to be the most reasonable estimate.
5 For a detailed critical assessment of these AID democracy assistance programs in Latin America during the 1980s, see Carothers (1991: 206–226). Actually, the earliest AID involvement in explicitly political assistance began in the early 1960s, when AID and the Ford Foundation supported the development of law faculties in a number of Latin American, Asian, and African countries. Premised in modernization theory, the "Law and Development" program expected that cadres of lawyers schooled in Western law "would spearhead the process of political and economic modernization." This program gave way in the mid-1970s to a focus on making legal services available to the poor, as part of AID's new emphasis on poverty alleviation and basic needs. Women's rights and human rights assumed a larger focus in the late 1970s, but it was not until the Reagan Administration that a third generation, "Administration of Justice," program began, focused initially on Central America. The current "Rule of Law" program, much broader geographically and conceptually, represents a fourth generation of AID programs in this area. However, the comprehensive democracy promotion endeavor of which it is a part is without precedent in the Agency.
6 For example, in 1988 about half of their total of $170 million in income from the German government was spent on these democracy-promoting activities ($85 million), exceeding by a factor of more than five the NED budget and nearly equaling estimated total US democracy-promotion spending in 1989 of $100 million. Pinto-Duschinsky (1991). My estimate of $85 million is derived from applying the percentages on the first four types of foreign activities he lists in Table 4 to the total funding amounts he lists in Table 1. The US figure is drawn from his essay but is consistent with what US administration figures estimated to me in 1989. Pinto-Duschinsky (1991: 47) judged at the time "that overall US government spending on political aid (excluding CIA activities) is about half West German spending on the party foundation's foreign operations."
7 These totals were obtained by adding the figures for Asia and the Pacific, Africa, and Latin America and the Caribbean, and do not include a number of projects the Ebert Foundation was then initiating in Russia and several East European countries. Friedrich Ebert Foundation (1992).

Promoting democracy in the 1990s 361

8 On the origins of NED, see Carothers (1991: 202–205).
9 In addition to the *Annual Reports* of NED and its core grantees, see Diamond (1992b) and Carothers (1994). In recent years, the parent organization has spent about 20 percent of the total funding on its own discretionary programs, while roughly 31.5 percent has been allocated to FTUI, 14 percent to CIPE, and 12.25 percent each to the two party institutes (with 10 percent going to administrative expenses). Carothers (1994: 126).
10 The other regional labor institutes, which have been functioning for several decades and were important instruments of political and ideological competition with Communist forces during the Cold War, are the African-American Labor Center, the Asian-American Free Labor Institute, and (for Latin America) the American Institute for Free Labor Development. FTUI, established in 1977, is both a regional institute (for Central and Eastern Europe and the former Soviet Union) and an administrative center through which NED funding for the other three AFL–CIO institutes flows.
11 Annual congressional funding ranged from $15 to 18 million from 1984 to 1990, and from $25 to 30 million from 1991 to 1993. The Clinton Administration's request to raise its funding for FY 1994 to $50 million sparked intense congressional debate that almost killed the Endowment altogether. Total funding of the Endowment family of organizations is larger because of grants from AID, which now exceed for the two party institutes what they receive from the NED appropriation, and because of occasional grants of up to $10 million earmarked by Congress for programs in particular countries (e.g., Poland, Nicaragua, and Haiti). Carothers (1994: 126).
12 See NED (1993, 1994), covering the relevant fiscal years (October 1–September 30). On the Mexican Civic Alliance, see Aguayo (1995).
13 For a summary of CIPE programs, see CIPE (1993).
14 IRI has similar (though less extensive) programs, but is more inclined to focus party assistance on one or more conservative parties. Carothers (1994: 127).
15 About 40 percent of this budget ($16 million in FY94) derives from its annual congressional appropriation through the State Department, but its total government funding is much larger because, like the two party institutes, it receives substantial annual, project-specific grants from AID ($23.1 million in FY94). The two party institutes and FTUI also operate field offices abroad, but many of these service regions rather than individual countries.
16 The thirteen countries in which the Centre now works are: El Salvador, Guatemala, Haiti, Mexico, Peru, Eritrea, Kenya, Rwanda, Tanzania, Togo, Burma, Pakistan, and Thailand.
17 By contrast, the Canadian Centre has three representatives from developing countries on its thirteen-member international board of directors, including former Costa Rican President Oscar Arias.
18 With membership from some 2,000 leading editors, publishers, broadcasting executives, and journalists, in over eighty countries, IPI holds conferences and seminars on a wide range of topics relating to press freedom and the journalistic profession. It also runs regular training programs in developing

362 Larry Diamond

and post-Communist countries and publishes both a monthly magazine and an annual report that monitor country developments with respect to press freedom. See Feinstein (1995). The annual survey of the CPJ, *Attacks on the Press*, is a particularly detailed account of violations of press freedom, and that organization also publishes a monthly *Update*.

19 When the US House of Representatives voted in mid-1993 to eliminate funding for NED (a vote that was soon reversed), more than 100 US NGOs and study centers joined in a statement of support for the Endowment.

20 Carothers concludes that AID "does not like to do political development work and is not good at it," in part because its officers lack expertise (1991: 221). This longstanding and widely shared criticism was more or less true in the 1980s but appears increasingly invalid, however, as AID experience with democracy assistance projects cumulates over time and as commitment to the goal becomes entrenched at the top, as it has during the Bush and Clinton Administrations. Moreover, AID has utilized a growing array of consultants and specialists (many on leave from academia) with real expertise in democracy, and it is now developing a multiyear program to train specialized career officers in democracy promotion.

21 Carothers in particular points to its cumbersome and risk-averse nature (1991: 221–222).

22 NDI, which has a network of some 500 *pro bono* consultants, estimates that from February 1993 to January 1994 it saved more than $2 million in consulting fees for more about 7,600 days of expert assistance rendered *pro bono*. NDI (1994b: 12).

23 In FY94, the Asia Foundation received about 55 percent ($23 million) of its entire budget in project-specific funding from AID; NDI received four-fifths ($14 million) and IRI also got most ($11 million) of its budget from AID. The Eurasia Foundation obtains virtually all its funding from AID.

24 Leading NGOs like NED, NDI, and the Asia Foundation have all raised these concerns in recent years. See also Carothers (1994: 134).

25 Problems of auditing and accountability are among the most frequently cited objections by critics of NED and its core institutes. In response to these criticisms, and to a critical evaluation by the US General Accounting Office (GAO), NED implemented in FY94 a new audit strategy with more formal, comprehensive procedures, more frequent audits (twice as many during fiscal years 1993 and 1994 as during the previous two years), and more on-site visits to evaluate and improve grantee accounting systems (NED 1994: 8). It must be remembered, however, that as audit procedures become more rigorous and comprehensive, cost-effectiveness in a different sense may diminish, partly because auditing involves certain minimum fixed costs that are difficult to justify for small grants. Congressionally funded donor organizations like NED are publicly accountable in that they are subject to Congressional oversight and are periodically audited by the GAO, AID, and the USIA Inspector General.

26 Membership in the European Bank for Reconstruction and Development (EBRD), established in 1990, has similar democracy and market conditionality.

Promoting democracy in the 1990s 363

27 The Group of 24 industrialized countries came together in mid-1989 to coordinate aid to Poland and Hungary, and then later agreed to extend aid to other Eastern European countries that pursued democracy and free markets.

28 PHARE stands for "Poland/Hungary Aid for Restructuring of Economies," which was launched for those two countries in July 1989 but soon expanded to other Central and Eastern European countries.

29 A reform of the OAS Charter adopted in December 1992 (the Washington protocol) provides for the suspension of a member state whose democratic government has been overthrown by force.

30 These insights derive from an AID draft assessment (December 1993) of approaches to donor supported rule of law programs which had not yet been cleared for formal citation.

31 Election observing is the term used to describe the work of international visitors who watch and assess the electoral process, typically for periods of no more than a few weeks in the country (though this may be spread out over a few periodic visits during preparation for the election and then the campaign). Election monitoring denotes the work of a much larger number of indigenous observers, organized and deployed by non-partisan NGOs as well as the various political parties. A comprehensive monitoring effort will place at least one non-partisan observer (usually from a broad umbrella organization in civil society) at every polling site in the country.

32 The South African case was entirely unique in the scale of international involvement, which included over 1,000 UN-organized international observers (augmenting thousands of domestic monitors) and millions of dollars in public and private assistance for voter education and electoral administration.

33 This was no doubt in part because the organization's unmatched experience in election observing, and its early warning of serious flaws in preparations for the December 1992 voting, made it too great a risk to the Kenyan government. See NDI (1993: 8).

34 An eleven-country study shows that many of the most prominent success stories of economic reform in the developing and post-communist worlds (Korea in the 1960s, Indonesia from the late 1960s, Chile, Mexico, Turkey, and Poland) received very generous financial aid and debt rescheduling, whereas the successful cases of reform without substantial aid were the already rich countries of Australia and New Zealand, as well as Spain and Poland with the implicit aid of imminent entry into the European Union. Williamson and Haggard (1994: 566–567).

35 As of early 1994, Sachs estimates, the West had transferred only about one seventh of the resources pledged (1994a: 14).

36 This paper was delivered at a January 1993 conference. For a similar and more recent perspective, emphasizing the funding of social safety net programs based in major regional cities throughout Russia (with parallel transfers of Russian subsidies for state enterprises into the safety net programs), see McFaul (1994: 34–35).

37 As they note, when reform elements are too weak, external pressure fails; when reformers predominate, pressure is not needed. Yet, some states, par-

364   *Larry Diamond*

ticularly in Africa, are so weak that even a militantly authoritarian regime may have little choice but to capitulate to coherent external pressure, or face collapse. Still, Nelson and Eglington (1992) provide a very thoughtful and balanced treatment of the issues which has heavily influenced the discussion that follows.

38 Although Turkey remains a constitutional democracy in form, the deterioration of its empirical democratic standards is reflected in its declining freedom rating from Freedom House and in the harsh assessments of international human rights groups. See for example Freedom House (1993–1994: 551–554) and Human Rights Watch (1994: 243–246).

39 Uruguay's first post-transition democratic president, Julio Sanguinetti, declared shortly after taking office in 1984, "The vigorous policies of the Carter Administration were the most important outside influence on Uruguay's democratization process." Quoted in Huntington (1991: 96).

40 On the US efforts to induce and support democratic transition in Chile, see Carothers (1991: 150–163). As far back as 1983, and repeatedly thereafter, President Reagan and Secretary of State Shultz had emphasized to Chun Doo Hwan the importance of his commitment to transfer power to an elected successor at the end of his presidential term in 1988. Shultz (1993: 976–980).

41 Reagan struggled throughout his presidency between his passionate commitment to freedom and democracy and his strong emotional attachment to Cold War authoritarian Allies like Marcos, Chilean General Augusto Pinochet, and the Angolan insurgent Jonas Savimbi. Moreover, the first year and a half of Reagan's Presidency, with Alexander Haig as Secretary of State, charted a very different course, seeking to reverse Carter's human rights emphasis and refurbish relations with anti-Communist authoritarian regimes in the Third World. See Smith (1994: 286–290) and Carothers (1991: 118–127). Carothers provides a largely critical perspective of what the Reagan Administration ultimately accomplished for democracy in Latin America; Smith, taking a global view, offers a more sympathetic assessment (pp. 297–307).

42 However, Sikkink concludes that US human rights pressure over the years has not been particularly effective in Guatemala, and cautions that even superpower pressure for democratization may be ineffective unless it is applied in a comprehensive and forceful manner, clearly conveyed through multiple channels and utilizing a wide range of policy instruments; and unless there exists a moderate faction within the authoritarian regime prepared to be receptive to such pressure. Sikkink (1991: 32–38).

43 On this effect in Chile late in Pinochet's rule, see Shultz (1993: 972, 974).

44 These principles are also emphasized by Nelson and Eglington (1992), who also stress the importance of a reform element within the regime (pp. 48–49). However, if aid dependence is extreme enough, as it is in much of Africa, and the donor community is sufficiently united (as with Kenya initially and Malawi), even a regime in which hardliners predominate may have little choice but to concede to the pressure (or face financial collapse).

45 Worse still, reports the defeated opposition candidate Fru Ndi, "The French government's ministry to Cameroon openly accused the U.S. government"

Promoting democracy in the 1990s 365

of supporting his party, the Social Democratic Front (SDF), in charges that were repeated by the government-controlled press.
46 Divergent bureaucratic goals and agendas have also been evident in other countries, such as France and Germany (though probably not to the same degree). Nelson and Eglington (1992: 23).
47 Fitch proposes that military aid be conditional not only on decent human rights performance (as evaluated by independent organizations like Amnesty International and the OAS) but also on "certified progress toward greater democratic control" over the military. Fitch (1993: 205).
48 Carothers, a cautious supporter of democracy promotion, nevertheless takes this view. Carothers (1991: 224, 257, and *passim*).
49 The first meeting of the Working Group was held in May 1994. A subsequent, November 1994, meeting was preceded by a seminar on the role of the Consultative Group process in addressing PDGG issues at the level of individual countries. A seminar on aid to civil society was planned for 1995.
50 These procedural directions appeared to enjoy general consensus at the November 1994 meeting, but the DAC PDGG Working Group is not a policy-making body, and it remains to be seen if the DAC itself will formally adopt them.
51 The fourteen sponsoring countries are: Australia, Barbados, Belgium, Chile, Costa Rica, Denmark, Finland, India, the Netherlands, Norway, Portugal, South Africa, Spain, and Sweden.
52 Moreover, an argument can be made for *some* organizations taking a global approach, rather than ruling out certain countries, so that (with modest investments in a small country like Sierra Leone) democratic aspirations and ideals can at least be kept alive everywhere, even against great odds.
53 By this principle, the US should also rethink its current broad requirement to cut off all aid to gross human violators or military regimes. It is fine to punish those regimes, but why not leave open the possibility of assisting NGOs (with both economic development and political aid) where possible?

REFERENCES

Africa Report. 1993. March/April.
Aguayo, Sergio. 1995. "A Mexican milestone," *Journal of Democracy* 6 no. 2: 157–167.
Arase, David. 1993. "Japanese policy toward democracy and human rights in Asia," *Asian Survey* 33 no. 10: 935–952.
Baker, Pauline H. 1990. "South Africa's future: a turbulent transition," *Journal of Democracy* 1 no. 4: 8–24.
Barkan, Joel D. 1993. "Kenya: lessons from a flawed election," *Journal of Democracy* 4 no. 3: 85–99.
Bjornlund, Eric, Michael Bratton, and Clark Gibson. 1992. "Observing multiparty elections in Africa: lessons from Zambia," *African Affairs* 91: 405–431.
Blair, Harry. 1994. "Civil society, democratic development, and international donors: a case study from Bangladesh." Paper presented to the American

366　　*Larry Diamond*

Political Science Association Annual Meeting, New York, September 1–4.

Callaghy, Thomas R. 1992. "Vision and politics in the transformation of the global economy," in Robert O. Slater, Barry M. Schutz, and Steven R. Dorr, eds., *Global Transformation and the Third World*. Boulder, Colo.: Lynne Rienner Publishers.

Callaghy, Thomas M., and John Ravenhill. 1993. "How hemmed in? Lessons and prospects of Africa's responses to decline," in Callaghy and Ravenhill, eds., *Hemmed In: Responses to Africa's Economic Decline*. New York: Columbia University Press.

Carnegie Corporation. 1992. *Annual Report*. New York.

Carothers, Thomas. 1991. *In the Name of Democracy: U.S. Policy toward Latin America in the Reagan Years*. Berkeley: University of California Press.

1994. "The NED at 10," *Foreign Policy* no. 95: 123–138.

Cheng, Tun-jen. 1989. "Democratizing the quasi-Leninist regime in Taiwan," *World Politics* 41 no. 4: 471–499.

CIPE. 1993. *1983 to 1993: A Decade in Review*. Washington, DC: CIPE.

Collier, Paul. 1991. "Africa's external economic relations, 1960–1990," in Douglas Rimmer, ed., *Africa 20 Years on: The Record and Outlook after Thirty Years of Independence*. London: James Curry Ltd.

Dahl, Robert A. 1971. *Polyarchy: Participation and Opposition*. New Haven: Yale University Press.

Diamond, Larry. 1979. "Power-dependence relationships in the world system," in Louis Kriesberg, ed., *Social Movements, Conflicts, and Change*, vol. II. Greenwich, Conn.: JAI Press.

1991. "Political corruption: Nigeria's perennial struggle," *Journal of Democracy* 2 no. 4: 73–85.

1992a. "Economic development and democracy reconsidered," in Gary Marks and Larry Diamond, eds., *Reexamining Democracy: Essays in Honor of Seymour Martin Lipset*. Newbury Park, Calif.: Sage.

1992b. "Promoting democracy," *Foreign Policy* no. 87: 25–46.

1994a. "Democracy: the new wind," *Africa Report* 39 no. 5: 50–54.

1994b. "Rethinking civil society: toward democratic consolidation," *Journal of Democracy* 5 no. 3: 4–17.

1995a. "Democracy and economic reform: tensions, compatibilities, and strategies of reconciliation," in Edward Lazear, ed., *Economic Transition in Russia and Eastern Europe: Realities of Reform*. Stanford, Calif.: Hoover Institution Press.

1995b. "Promoting democracy in Africa," in John Harbeson and Donald Rothchild, eds., *Africa in World Politics*, 2nd edn. Boulder: Westview Press.

1996. "Democracy in Latin America: degrees, illusions, and directions for consolidation," in Tom Farer, ed., *Beyond Sovereignty: Collectively Defending Democracy in the Americas*. Baltimore: Johns Hopkins University Press.

Diamond, Larry, Juan J. Linz, and Seymour Martin Lipset, 1995. "Introduction: comparing experiences with democracy," in Diamond, Linz, and Lipset, *Politics in Developing Countries: Comparing Experiences with Democracy*, 2nd edn. Boulder, Colo.: Lynne Rienner Publishers.

Economist, The. 1993. May 29.

Eurasia Foundation. 1994. Summary of Grants Awarded during May.

Farer, Tom J. 1989. A "multilateral arrangement to secure democracy," in Robert A. Pastor, ed., *Democracy in the Americas: Stopping the Pendulum*. New York: Holmes and Meier.

Feinstein, Adam. 1995. "Fighting for press freedom," *Journal of Democracy* 6 no. 1: 159–168.

Fitch, J. Samuel. 1993. "Democracy, human rights and the armed forces in Latin America," in Jonathan Hartlyn, Lars Schoultz, and Augusto Varas, eds., *The United States and Latin America in the 1990s: Beyond the Cold War*. Chapel Hill, N.C.: University of North Carolina Press.

Franck, Thomas. 1992. "The emerging right to democratic governance," *The American Journal of International Law* 86 no. 1: 46–91.

Freedom House. 1993–1994. *Freedom in the World*. New York.

Friedrich Ebert Foundation. 1992. Handout, February.

Garber, Larry. 1993. "The OAU and elections," *Journal of Democracy* 4 no. 3: 55–59.

Garber, Larry, and Eric Bjornlund. 1993. "Election monitoring in Africa," in Festus Eribo, Oyeleye Oyediran, Mulatu Wubneh, and Leo Zonn, eds., *Window on Africa: Democratization and Media Exposure*. Greenville, N.C.: East Carolina University Center for International Programs.

Garber, Larry, and Cowan, Glenn. 1993. "The virtues of parallel vote tabulations," *Journal of Democracy* 4 no. 2: 95–107.

Geddes, Barbara. 1994. "Challenging the conventional wisdom," *Journal of Democracy* 5 no. 4: 104–118.

Gershman, Carl. 1993. "The United Nations and the new world order," *Journal of Democracy* 4 no. 3: 5–16.

Graham, Carol. 1994. *Safety Nets, Politics and the Poor: Transitions to Market Economies*. Washington, DC: The Brookings Institution.

Guie, Honoré Koffi. 1993. "Organizing Africa's democrats," *Journal of Democracy* 4 no. 2: 119–129.

Hakim, Peter. 1993. "The OAS: putting principles into practice," *Journal of Democracy* 4 no. 3: 39–49.

Halperin, Morton H. 1993. "Guaranteeing democracy," *Foreign Policy* Summer: 105–122.

Halperin, Morton H., and Kristen Lomasney. 1993. "Toward a global 'guarantee clause'," *Journal of Democracy* 4 no. 3: 60–69.

Heilbrunn, John R. 1993. "The social origins of national conferences: a comparison of Benin and Togo," *Journal of Modern African Studies* 31 no. 2: 277–300.

Human Rights Watch. 1994. *Annual Report 1993*. New York.

Huntington, Samuel P. 1968. *Political Order in Changing Societies*. New Haven: Yale University Press.

1991. *The Third Wave: Democratization in the Late Twentieth Century*. Norman, Okla.: University of Oklahoma Press.

IDEE. 1995. *Newsletter* no. 7.

International Centre for Human Rights and Democratic Development. 1993–1994. *Annual Report*.

1994. Brochure.

368   Larry Diamond

International Electoral Institute. 1993. *Report of the Ministry of Foreign Affairs of the Swedish Government on the Working Group for an International Electoral Institute (IEI)*. Stockholm, October.

1994. "Free and fair elections and beyond. Summary and conclusions from the Conference on the International Electoral Commission." Stockholm, May 18–19.

International IDEA. 1994. *Conclusions and Suggestions for the Mandate of the Proposed Institute for Democracy and Electoral Assistance*. Stockholm, October.

1995a. *Declaration of the Founding Conference for the International Institute for Democracy and Electoral Assistance*. Stockholm, February 27–28.

1995b. *Newsletter* 1. Stockholm, March 8.

IRI. 1994. "IRI: a decade of democracy, 1984–1994." Washington, DC.

Jeldres, Julio. 1993. "The UN and the Cambodian transition," *Journal of Democracy* 4 no. 4: 104–116.

Karatnycky, Adrian. 1995. "The comparative survey of freedom 1994: democracies on the rise, democracies at risk," *Freedom Review* 26 no. 1: 5–10.

Klitgaard, Robert. 1991. "Political corruption: strategies for reform," *Journal of Democracy* 2 no. 4: 86–101.

Kritz, Neil J. 1993. "The CSCE in the new era," *Journal of Democracy* 4 no. 3: 17–28.

León, Francisco Villagrán de. 1993. "Thwarting the Guatemalan coup," *Journal of Democracy* 4 no. 4: 11–124.

Lipset, Seymour Martin. 1981. "Economic development and democracy," in Seymour Martin Lipset, *Political Man*. Baltimore: Johns Hopkins University Press.

Lowenthal, Abraham. 1991. "The United States and Latin American democracy: learning from history," in Abraham Lowenthal, ed., *Exporting Democracy: The United States and Latin America*. Baltimore: Johns Hopkins University Press.

MacArthur Foundation. 1992. *Annual Report*. Chicago.

McCoy, Jennifer, Larry Garber, and Robert A. Pastor. 1991. "Making peace by observing and mediating elections," *Journal of Democracy* 2 no. 4: 102–114.

McFaul, Michael. 1994. "Causes and consequences of the 'end of market romanticism' in Russia." Paper presented to the Council on Foreign Relations, Washington, DC, March 31.

1995. "Why Russia's politics matter," *Foreign Affairs* 74 no 1: 87–99.

Muigai, Githu. 1993. "Kenya's opposition and the crisis of governance," *Issue* ("A Journal of Opinion" of the US African Studies Association) 21 no. 1/2.

Muñoz, Heraldo. 1993. "The OAS and democratic governance," *Journal of Democracy* 4 no. 3: 29–38.

Muravchik, Joshua. 1991. *Exporting Democracy: Fulfilling America's Destiny*. Washington, DC: AEI Press.

NDI. 1993. "1992: a year in review." Washington, DC.

1994a. "1993: a year in review." Washington, DC.

Promoting democracy in the 1990s

1994b. "Submission of NDI to the congressionally authorized study on US government-funded democracy programs." Washington, DC.

NED. 1993. *Annual Report*. Washington, DC.

1994. *Annual Report*. Washington, DC.

Nelson, Joan M., and Stephanie J. Eglington. 1992. *Encouraging Democracy: What Role for Conditioned Aid?* Washington, DC: Overseas Development Council.

New York Times. 1990. October 15.

Nwankwo, Clement. 1993. "The OAU and human rights," *Journal of Democracy* 4 no. 3: 50–54.

OECD. 1993. "DAC orientations on participatory development and good governance." Paris.

Pastor, Robert A. 1990. "Nicaragua's choice: the making of a free election," *Journal of Democracy* 1 no. 3: 13–25.

Pinder, John. 1994. "The European Community and democracy in Central and Eastern Europe," in Geoffrey Pridham, Eric Herring, and George Sanford, eds, *Building Democracy? The International Dimension of Democratisation in Eastern Europe*. New York: St. Martin's Press.

Pinto-Duschinsky, Michael. 1991 "Foreign political aid: the German political foundations and their US counterparts," *International Affairs* 67 no. 1: 33–63.

Putnam, Robert D., with Robert Leonardi and Raffaella Y. Nanetti. 1993. *Making Democracy Work: Civic Traditions in Italy*. Princeton: Princeton University Press.

Remmer, Karen L. 1990. "Democracy and economic crisis: the Latin American experience," *World Politics* 42 no. 3: 315–335.

1991. "The political impact of economic crisis in Latin America in the 1980s," *American Political Science Review* 85 no. 3: 777–800.

Rose, Richard. 1994. "Rethinking civil society: postcommunism and the problem of trust," *Journal of Democracy* 5 no. 2: 18–30.

Sachs, Jeffrey. 1994a. "Betrayal," *The New Republic* 211: 14–18.

1994b. "Life in the economic emergency room," in John Williamson, ed., *The Political Economy of Policy Reform*. Washington, DC: Institute for International Economics.

Shultz, George P. 1993. *Turmoil and Triumph: My Years as Secretary of State*. New York: Charles Scribner's Sons.

Sikkink, Kathryn. 1991. "The effectiveness of US human rights policy: Argentina, Guatemala, and Uruguay." Paper presented to the World Congress of the International Political Science Association, Buenos Aires, July 21–25.

Smith, Tony. 1994. *America's Mission: The United States and the Worldwide Struggle for Democracy in the Twentieth Century*. Princeton: Princeton University Press.

Somogyi, Paul. 1995. "Assisting independent trade unions in post-communist countries," *Problems of Post-Communism* 42 no. 2: 3–7.

Soros, George. 1994. "The Soros Foundations network." February. New York: The Soros Foundations.

Stayden, Rozann M. 1994. "Democratization: legal transformation – the

370   Larry Diamond

necessity of strong legal systems and institutions in emerging African democracies." Discussion Paper from a Seminar on Democratization in Africa, the Carter Center of Emory University, May 13–14.

Sullivan, John D. 1994. "Democratization and business interests," *Journal of Democracy* 5 no. 4: 146–160.

TransAtlantic Perspectives. 1994. Autumn, no. 30 (published by the German Marshall Fund of the United States).

Tvedten, Inge. 1993. "The Angolan debacle," *Journal of Democracy* 4 no. 2: 108–118.

USAID. 1994. "Building democracy: USAID's strategy," in *Strategies for Sustainable Development.* Washington, DC: USAID.

US Information Agency. n.d. Africa Bureau, "Summary of AF democracy programming in FY 95 AF country plans."

West Africa. 1993. July 5–11.

Westminster Foundation for Democracy. 1994. *Annual Report 1993–94.* London.

Whitehead, Laurence. 1986. "International aspects of democratization," in Guillermo O'Donnell, Philippe C. Schmitter, and Laurence Whitehead, eds., *Transitions from Authoritarian Rule: Comparative Perspectives.* Baltimore: Johns Hopkins University Press.

Williamson, John, and Stephan Haggard. 1994. "The political conditions for economic reform," in John Williamson, ed., *The Political Economy of Policy Reform.* Washington, DC: Institute for International Economics.

World Bank. 1991. Press release of the meeting of the Consultative Group for Kenya, November 26. Paris.

16 Can established democracies nurture democracy abroad? Lessons from Africa

Joel D. Barkan

Can established democracies nurture the establishment of democracies abroad? Should they do so? What issues – ethical, strategic, theoretical, operational, and diplomatic – accompany this exercise? What are the prospects for success? This chapter seeks to sketch out some tentative answers to these questions based mainly on the author's participation in, and observation of, the process by which established democracies – acting as nation-states or via surrogate organizations – currently seek to nurture democratic transitions worldwide, particularly in Africa.[1] It is a process informed by social science, but not, on the whole, designed or implemented by scholars of democracy or transitions to democratic rule. It is also an exercise in which those responsible for arranging such assistance are "learning on the job" but have sought the advice of the social science community. In some cases, it has afforded a few individuals the opportunity to straddle, and in some instances join, two realms – the realm of the academic political scientist informed by the literature and one's own research in several countries emerging from authoritarian rule, and the realm of the policy maker, bureaucrat, and provider of assistance to support this process. As those who have previously straddled these realms know well, the interface between these two cultures is not always smooth nor does it necessarily result in more effective policy. Putting theory into practice is rarely automatic.

Between foreign policy and social science research

Although current programs by established democracies to nurture democratization date their existence from the end of the Cold War, the promotion of transitions to democracy and the consolidation of democracy worldwide has been a foreign policy objective of the Western democracies, especially the United States, since the end of World War II. While the exigencies of the Cold War often led Western democracies to cooperate with non-democratic regimes to advance the policy of containment, the policy itself was driven by the objective of defending the

372   *Joel D. Barkan*

Western variant of democracy against its non-democratic adversaries, and replicating its manifestation wherever possible. Promoting democracy as a foreign policy objective, in short, is not new. What is new is the higher priority now accorded to this objective and the provision of more systematic and sustained forms of technical and financial assistance to nurture democratic transitions and/or the strengthening of democratic institutions. Even now, some elements of current bilateral portfolios to support democratization are replications or partial replications of earlier efforts in selected countries (e.g., in Germany and Japan after World War II, in Vietnam and Latin America during the 1960s and again in the 1980s).[2]

What is different today is the scale and explicitness of these initiatives, and the fact that they are being pursued simultaneously, in varying degrees of sophistication, expenditure and coordination, by at least eight "like-minded" established democracies: Canada, Denmark, Germany, the Netherlands, Norway, Sweden, the United Kingdom, and the United States.[3] Each currently devotes a small but significant portion of its foreign assistance budget to nurturing democracy. Since 1991, most have established units within their foreign assistance agencies and/ or semi-autonomous entities funded by these agencies to design and mount programs that support the process of democratization abroad. In addition to these bilateral efforts, multilateral organizations including the World Bank, the UN, the Commonwealth as well as regional organizations such as the European Community and the Organization for African Unity, have begun to incorporate a concern for political reform – especially guarantees of human rights as well as improved governmental accountability, transparency, and a reduction of corruption (what these organizations usually label as "good governance"[4]) – into their agendas. Bilateral and multilateral assistance to nurture democracy and improved governance has been complemented – and in several instances predated – by an expanding array of programs mounted by foundations and non-governmental organizations (NGOs), some of which work closely with or are directly or indirectly funded by one or more of the "like-minded." These include (but are not limited to) Amnesty International, the Carter Center, the Ford Foundation, the Friedrich Ebert Foundation, the Friedrich Naumann Foundation, the Human Rights and Development Center, Human Rights Watch, the Konrad Adenauer Foundation, the National Democratic Institute (NDI), the International Republican Institute (IRI), the International Foundation for Election Systems (IFES), the National Endowment for Democracy (NED), Transparency International, the Westminster Foundation, and the International Institute for Democracy and

Electoral Assistance (IDEA). Finally, an array of foundations and NGOs is also emerging in countries which have recently experienced democratic transitions – in Chile, in the Philippines, in Benin – to support democratic transitions in neighboring countries and consolidate their own.

Virtually none of this programmatic activity existed five years ago. Indeed, the promotion of democracy has become something of a "growth industry" – within established democracies and within countries emerging from authoritarian rule. New organizations have sprung up in the former to assist democratic transitions or prospective transitions in the latter where a diversity of organizations, both public and private, have stepped forward to request and receive donor support. The fact that the established democracies are now the only providers of conventional development assistance has not only led them to establish these programs, but to require progress towards democratization and/or "good governance" as a condition for aid. Whereas during the Cold War, bilateral donors were hesitant to condition development assistance on the fulfillment of political criteria, today they are not. This is particularly true in respect to the provision of so-called "quick-disbursing" aid or non-project assistance (NPA) – cash disbursements to cover balance of payments and budget deficits in the world's poorest countries. Regimes that require NPA, including many in sub-Saharan Africa, are especially dependent on the international donor community for their survival and thus vulnerable to donor pressure for political reform. While multilateral institutions such as the Bank and the International Monetary Fund (IMF) remain reluctant to invoke political criteria, some democratic member states are beginning – at least informally – to push the international financial institutions (IFIs) in this direction.[5] Invoking political conditionality, however, remains a hotly debated and controversial policy as some thoughtful observers doubt its effectiveness (Nelson and Eglinton 1992, 1993).

The current initiatives by established democracies to promote democratization and their willingness to condition aid, together with support for these policies from within countries in the midst of democratic transitions, reflect a second factor that distinguishes these efforts from the past. During the Cold War and the heyday of alternative socialist strategies for development (e.g., Cuba, Ghana, Nicaragua, Tanzania, Vietnam), Western notions of democracy were frequently challenged as "false" or "bourgeoisie" conceptions that did not result in systems that were responsive to the needs of their peoples. Any efforts by the established (i.e., Western) democracies to support democratic transitions in non-democratic societies were invariably viewed as a direct interference

374   *Joel D. Barkan*

in the internal affairs of these countries. Today the Western conception of democracy is more or less accepted throughout the world, while Western programs to support democratization are welcomed by all save those who would be dislodged by the process. The Western conception of democracy, with its emphasis on individual rights, limited and accountable government, and the periodic opportunity of the governed to replace their current rulers via free and fair elections, has become the universal standard – albeit in various permutations – of what democracy entails.[6]

A series of parallel caveats can be made with respect to social science research on the conditions under which transitions to democracy and the consolidation of democracy occur. Notwithstanding the recent proliferation of research literature and the emergence of journals such as the *Journal of Democracy* and *Democratization*, the study of comparative politics as a subfield of political science has been long dominated by inquiries into the conditions under which democracy is most likely to flourish. The same can be said of the related fields of comparative political sociology and political economy. Following World War II and throughout the 1950s, students of comparative politics and related fields were preoccupied with identifying the conditions under which democracy flourished as well as the conditions which led to its breakdown. The desire to avoid a repetition of the collapse of European democracy that characterized the interwar period, coupled with the specter of the Soviet Union and its East European Allies, resulted in a literature that sought to explain why some democracies had failed, why others had remained robust, and how some could be strengthened. Some students of this period such as Carl Friedrich (1950) focused on the constitutional requisites for sustaining democracy. Some, most notably Maurice Duverger (1954), examined electoral procedures and political parties to determine what type of an electoral system would best facilitate the stability of democracies. Others such as Seymour Lipset (1960) and Barrington Moore (1966) focused on the economic requisites and the requisites of class. Still others, including Edward Banfield (1958), and later Gabriel Almond and Sidney Verba (1963), subsequently examined the requisite dimensions of political culture.

The second historical impetus for identifying the conditions supportive of democracy during the postwar period, was the decline and eventual demise of the European colonial empires, and the emergence of the "new states" of the "Third World." Beginning with David Apter (1958), Gabriel Almond and James Coleman (1960) and the members of the SSRC's Committee on Comparative Politics, and continuing throughout the 1960s, many of the leading social scientists of the period

Can established democracies nurture democracy abroad? 375

sought to determine how these emergent polities would develop and modernize into viable systems. Notwithstanding the politically neutral terminology employed by these scholars,[7] their perspective was fundamentally Westerncentric and developmental – how to transfer Western democratic institutions to non-Western soil and make them work.[8] They assumed that responsive, authoritative, and legitimate government was democratic government. The scholarship of the 1950s and 1960s on the conditions for democracy paralleled and to some extent reflected Western foreign policy objectives of the times, but rarely informed the policy-making process. Apart from Lipset's finding that democracy was most likely to occur in countries that had achieved economic development, a correlation which may have influenced US policy towards Latin America during the Kennedy Administration (e.g., the Alliance for Progress), and perhaps the writings of Walt Rostow (1959), few attempts were made to translate the insights of social science research on the requisites for democracy into programs of technical assistance which promoted democracy abroad. Similarly, in the 1970s and early 1980s, the United States Agency for International Development (USAID) made a series of research grants to support research on selected democratic institutions and aspects of the democratic process in developing countries, but the Agency rarely mounted programs abroad to strengthen democracy or programs based on this research.[9] Indeed, the prevailing view at USAID was that programs to support democratization, let alone research on the subject, were inappropriate for an agency whose principal mission was economic development.[10]

Current scholarship on democratization is thus a continuation of an exercise that dates back at least fifty years. What is different, is that today's scholarship is concerned not only with determining the conditions for democracy, but also the nature and sequencing of events that make up democratic transitions and how new democracies are consolidated. The explosion of contemporary research on these and related topics since the mid-1980s is a reflection of the times. More than sixty countries have made or nominally made transitions from authoritarian to democratic rule since 1974 – a series of regime changes worldwide that Huntington (1991) has deemed the "third wave" of democratization. For the first time, more than half of the world's 180 countries can be classified as "democratic" (McColm 1993). Many of these emergent democracies, however, are fragile systems whose futures are in doubt. Indeed, a large proportion of the most recent transitions to democracy have occurred in poor and in ethnically plural societies where, according to conventional wisdom, the prospects for democratization – especially the consolidation of democracy – are low.

376   *Joel D. Barkan*

This rapid yet fragile spread of democracy has raised a host of new questions and reframed old ones for contemporary students of the process. As in the past, issues of constitutional engineering and the structure of the electoral process loom large for many scholars such as Lijphart (1984, 1994), Grofman (1986), and Horowitz (1991). A second topic is the process of the transition as exemplified by the studies of O'Donnell *et al.* (1986). The concern here is with the sequence of changes within and outside authoritarian regimes that lead them to embark upon democratic transitions. A related topic is the significance of regime type for the outcomes of the process, for example, the different outcomes of transitions initiated by bureaucratic-authoritarian regimes compared to those initiated by neo-patrimonial ones (Bratton and van de Walle 1994; Linz and Stepan 1996). As with the earlier literature, the relationship between class formations and democracy (Rueschemeyer, Stephens, and Stephens 1992) and the relationship between economic development and democratization (Lipset, Seong, and Torres 1993; Burkhardt and Lewis-Beck 1994; Przeworski and Limongi in this volume) continues to be a major focus of investigation, but at a higher level of methodological sophistication and with more comprehensive data (especially for developing countries) than the earlier studies. A fifth topic that has drawn the attention of contemporary scholars is the function and composition of civil society. This is particularly true for students of democratization in agrarian societies where associational life is limited in the rural areas or where it may articulate communal interests of an ethnic or fundamentalist religious nature (Bratton 1989; Harbeson *et al.*, 1994). A sixth and increasingly important topic about which little is known is the institutionalization and consolidation of democratic practice over long periods of time (Putnam 1993). Finally, there is the impact of the changing international environment as a result of the end of the Cold War coupled with the willingness of the United States and other donors to withhold foreign assistance from authoritarian regimes that do not democratize (Nelson and Eglinton 1992, 1993).

The concerns underlying today's research are as much operational and normative as they are theoretical – what actions can and should be taken to facilitate democratization given our explanations of the process? Bureaucrats charged with mounting programs to support democratic transitions also appear to be more receptive and interested in what social scientists have to say, because they need answers to the same questions. To a much greater extent than in the past, the current exercise to promote democratization falls between the realm of the policy maker and the realm of social science research. How has this fact structured the enterprise, and what are its likely outcomes?

The initiation of donor programs to promote democratization

Notwithstanding the abundance of recent research on transitions from authoritarian to democratic rule, the main impetus for donor programs that support these transitions came not from the social science community but from the political realm, particularly the makers of Western foreign policy. While the end of the Cold War was the principal catalyst, the collapse or weakening of authoritarian regimes in Southern Europe, Latin America and Southeast Asia, and the prospect of an end to minority rule in Southern Africa combined to move several key policy makers, most notably former US Secretary of State James Baker, to include democratization as a key element in their conception of an evolving "New World Order." Apart from the usual diplomatic pressures in support of democratization, Baker asked what the United States and other established democracies could do to directly facilitate democratic transitions and the consolidation of democracy in countries where a regime change had already occurred. Other countries, especially the Scandinavian countries (whose foreign policies had been less driven by Cold War imperatives than those of the United States, and whose support for fledgling democratic movements and a concern for human rights had long been cornerstones of their policies) became increasingly interested mounting programs to support democratic transitions.

The initial programs were limited and reflected an oversimplification of what was required. These efforts also reflected the limited capacity on the part of the bilateral assistance agencies of established democracies to mount such programs. To a greater extent than their counterparts in other established democracies, American policy makers have long regarded the holding of "free and fair" multiparty elections as the litmus test of democratic transitions. According to this view, a respect for human rights, the establishment of the rule of law, a vibrant civil society, a free press, and increased transparency and accountability of government, etc. – all critical ingredients of any democracy – are not as important as the opportunity for the governed to choose between alternative groups of leaders to serve as their rulers. As a result, initial American efforts to promote democratic transitions on an official bilateral basis consisted mainly of support for transitional elections. This took two forms: the provision of technical assistance and supplies to facilitate the administration of these elections, and the recruitment, training, and deployment of international observers, and in some instances domestic observers, to monitor them.

American emphasis on the holding of multiparty elections was the result of at least five considerations. First, the belief that one-party

378   *Joel D. Barkan*

regimes were inherently non-democratic, notwithstanding the fact that in some countries (e.g., Kenya during the Kenyatta period, and the United States[11]) meaningful electoral competition that affords citizens the opportunity to choose between alternative representatives (if not between alternative regimes), occurs within parties as often as between. American fixation on the need for interparty competition is no doubt a result of the absence of such competition in the former Soviet Union and other states ruled by Communist parties as well as the experience in most African one-party states. Second, the significance of free and fair multiparty elections in countries that had recently made the transition from authoritarian to democratic rule seemed to confirm to American policy makers that such elections were the bottom line of any transition. The Aquino election in the Philippines, as well as the transitional elections in Argentina, Brazil, Nicaragua, South Korea, and Zambia, all suggested that elections were the single most important component of transition.

Third, external assistance to support transitional elections was usually welcomed in these countries, and particularly by the democratic challengers to incumbent regimes. One of the ironies surrounding this assistance is that the very individuals and groups which have been most eager for external involvement are those which were once among the severest critics of the Western democracies for supporting the status quo. As the number of transitional elections increased from the late 1980s onward, the challengers to authoritarian rule realized that these "first-time" events could be manipulated and hijacked by those in power.[12] This specter of election fraud gave rise to one of the more interesting accouterments of democratic transitions worldwide: the international election observer. As those pressing for multiparty elections became sensitive to the potential for election fraud, they sought assistance from sympathetic organizations and governments in the established democracies to guarantee that these events would be "free and fair." Whereas in an earlier period, the provision of technical assistance and involvement by foreign observers might have been construed as interference in the internal affairs of a sovereign state, in the context of transition this involvement was eagerly sought, or at least tolerated.[13] Indeed, the demand for such involvement was at times so strong that the contestants of transitional elections became overly dependent on these "international referees."

Fourth, assisting elections was feasible within the existing capacity for supporting democratization. Because the provision of support for democratic transitions is a new and unfamiliar exercise for the principal donor agencies of the established democracies (i.e., USAID, CIDA,

DANIDA, GTZ, ODA, NORAD, SIDA, etc.[14]), many have reached outside their bureaucracies for assistance to mount these programs – to a small number of NGOs which had become involved in this type of work during the mid-1980s, and to academic specialists knowledgeable about the political process in countries in the midst of transition. Such expertise, and especially the existence of organizations with which the donor agencies could work, has tended to be concentrated in the area of election assistance. By the early 1990s, several NGOs including IFES, the Carter Center, and NDI, had already provided various forms of support to transitional elections around the world. The Commonwealth Secretariat had also assisted several elections of its member states. The provision of technical assistance in the form of consultants experienced in election administration and/or the provision of critical supplies (e.g., ballots, ballot boxes, indelible ink, etc.) could be quickly accomplished via organizations like IFES and the Commonwealth. Others, such as NDI, developed a wealth of expertise in mounting, deploying, and coordinating delegations of international observers, and in recruiting and training cadres of local volunteers to serve as independent poll watchers (monitors) in their own countries. These organizations had become involved in supporting multiparty elections before the bilateral development agencies of the established democracies started to provide electoral support on a direct and programmatic basis. Some, such as the Carter Center, occasionally mounted programs with their own funds. Others, such as NDI, were indirectly funded by the US government via NED, and/or became involved in providing electoral support via the United Nations (e.g., the 1989 elections in Namibia, and the 1992 elections in Angola). Once the US and other established democracies put the promotion of democratization on the agendas of their development assistance agencies, it is not surprising to whom they first turned. Indeed, these organizations had developed more than a passing interest in the emergence of the "democracy industry."

A fifth and related reason why initial efforts to promote democratization was concentrated in the area of election assistance was that such assistance was relatively short term. Stated simply, a donor could get in and out with minimal entanglement in the political life of the recipient country. Because programs to nurture democratization require a direct intervention in the political system of the recipient country, many administrators of conventional development assistance programs have not shared the enthusiasm of the architects of Western foreign policy when it comes to the design and implementation of such programs. Indeed, many have been either indifferent or hostile. This is particularly true of the directors of bilateral missions in the field. To them,

380   *Joel D. Barkan*

democracy and governance (DG) programs are high risk and open-ended compared to conventional programs, and thus programs to be approached with extreme caution. In this context, support for elections may be fraught with risk, but it does have an end date. And, as noted in the previous paragraph, support can be quickly provided by simply drawing on one of the extant organizations that has a track record in this area.

Not all of the established democracies have emphasized support for transitional elections to the extent of the United States, but most – as well as some multilateral organizations such as the Commonwealth and the UN – are periodically swept up by the process.[15] This is particularly true in respect to "high profile" elections which attract the attention of the world community, and are fueled by the international media. While the NGOs which specialize in electoral assistance are mostly American, all of the established democracies have provided and continue to provide support for transitional elections. International participation in the recent South African elections (for which all of the "like-minded" democracies provided financial support and/or international observers) is a case in point. Many countries are also beginning to provide support for "consolidating elections," the second and third rounds of the electoral process that is already following the initial multiparty contests.

While elections have been the principal focus of official American efforts to date, other donors, particularly Denmark, Norway, Sweden, and Germany via its party foundations, have placed greater emphasis on strengthening civil society in countries undergoing democratic transitions as well as those in the process of consolidating democratic rule.[16] While these countries have provided support for transitional elections, they have found that they can make a greater contribution to the process of democratization by establishing portfolios of very small- to medium-size grants ($10,000 to $300,000) which they make to nurture the development of local NGOs. These include associations that monitor various aspects of public policy, trade unions, groups which provide legal assistance to poor, human rights organizations, journalist associations, or trusts to accelerate the growth of a free press, women's associations, civic education groups, election monitoring organizations, and, on rare occasions, political parties. These donors often supplement such grants with short-term technical assistance appropriate for the recipient group. For example, Denmark has funded and provided instructors for workshops designed to improve the skills of journalists in countries where it has provided grants to press associations, independent periodicals, etc. These donors have also provided grants and technical assistance to selected governmental agencies where it is clear that such support is

Can established democracies nurture democracy abroad?

likely to increase the accountability and accessibility of the state to its citizens. For example, the provision of grants to the Justice Training Centre in Namibia for the purpose of improving the skills of local magistrates, or support to the Office of the Attorney General in Tanzania to update the legal code of that country, and support for improving decentralized planning and budgeting at the district level in Kenya.

Compared to support for transitional elections, these programs to strengthen civil society are "low profile," indeed so low that they are largely unknown to all except the recipient organizations and the regimes challenged by these organizations. Their impact may also be more enduring, because they strengthen the capacity of *local* organizations – especially in the private sphere – to carry out a wide range of vital activities over relatively long periods, both before and after elections. Put differently, these programs are more likely than electoral assistance to nurture institutions of countervailing power, institutions which in turn increase the level of state accountability to the governed. Compared to support for transitional elections, these programs are also of longer duration, and personnel intensive. They are also personnel intensive compared to conventional development assistance programs; that is to say, the proportion of a program's budget spent on administrative and advisory personnel is high relative to its overall cost. European bilateral assistance agencies which have mounted these programs appear to have accepted these costs by assigning (on average) a half- or full-time program officer or advisor to administer their democracy and governance portfolios in each country where such assistance is provided. Such officers are also normally individuals of middle to senior diplomatic rank.

The contrast between American and European approaches to promoting democracy and governance should not be overdrawn. Although the United States has devoted the largest proportion of its resources to supporting multiparty elections, its efforts to assist democratic transitions have not been limited to election support. Since 1979, beginning in the Carter Administration, the United States has mounted a modest program of small grants known as Human Rights Development Grants (HRDG) under section 116e of the Foreign Assistance Act. This program, which is jointly implemented by the Department of State and USAID, has facilitated grants of the type that characterize the country portfolios of the European donors. Unlike the latter, however, the HRDG is limited to one or two, sometimes three, grants per country per year for a maximum of one year's support. The HRDG cannot be used to nurture the development of a given organization or program over several years. As a result, the program has never realized its

382   *Joel D. Barkan*

potential in terms of assisting the building of democratic institutions.[17] NED, an independent foundation funded by Congress, also makes small grants to organizations and publications that defend human rights and promote democratic transitions. The Endowment has made grants of this type since the mid-1980s under its discretionary grants program, but its budget for this program ($7 million for approximately 300 grants worldwide in FY1994) pales compared to what USAID spends on its democracy and governance programs. In FY1994, USAID spent $152 million on its democracy and governance programs worldwide of which $85 million were devoted to Africa.[18]

American and European approaches to the promotion of democracy may also be converging. The United States is moving rapidly, and in some countries, more comprehensively towards the type of programming heretofore associated with European assistance. At the same time, some European donors – most notably Sweden and the Netherlands through their sponsorship of the International IDEA – appear to be moving towards providing greater and more systematic support for transitional and consolidating elections.[19]

In 1991, the United States, via USAID, moved to significantly expand its DG programs, and to devote an increasing proportion of these efforts to the establishment and strengthening of democratic institutions over the medium (if not the long) term. While US support for transitional elections continued, and indeed expanded during the early 1990s, the US commenced a series of bilateral programs which resembled those of the European democracies, but which were often more ambitious in scope. In a small number of African countries in the midst of democratic transitions, the US began to design and implement multiyear programs of institutional support that, depending on the size of the country, provided assistance in three to five related areas of activity. For example, a three-year $5 million program was initiated in Ethiopia in 1992 to both support and encourage the Transitional Government of Ethiopia (TGE) to move forward with its stated program of establishing a multiethnic federal and democratic state in that country. Consistent with initial US thinking, this effort devoted roughly a third of its program budget to supporting the establishment of an electoral commission and the observation of Ethiopia's first nationwide multiparty elections which were held in June 1992. The elections, which were seriously flawed and compromised by government intimidation of the principal opposition party, the Oromo Liberation Front, raised questions about the wisdom of concentrating so much effort on the electoral process.[20] Other components of this program which have continued since the elections are assistance to the Constitutional Commission charged with writing a new

Ethiopian constitution; funding for the Ministry of Justice to proceed expeditiously and fairly with its prosecution of former officials of the Mengistu regime accused of war crimes; support for the development of an independent press; and funds to design a future program of assistance to strengthen the thirteen regional governments specified in the transitional constitution. Because it remains unclear whether President Meles Zanawi and other key leaders of the TGE[21] are truly committed to establishing a democratic system in Ethiopia, progress in that country has been mixed yet instructive in respect to how programs intended to support democratic transitions are likely to unfold.

A second example of this multiyear multifaceted approach to supporting democratic transitions in Africa is USAID's democracy and governance project in Zambia. More ambitious than its Ethiopian counterpart and launched late in 1992, this project is intended to operate for five years with a budget of up to $15 million. As in Ethiopia, programmatic support has consisted of a combination of technical assistance and grants in several discrete yet related areas of activity. These include the Constitutional Commission charged with drafting a new Zambian constitution consistent with the return to multiparty politics; the Zambian National Assembly for the purpose of improving its internal procedures, strengthening its committee system and its professional staff; a media institute to train Zambian journalists and to facilitate the emergence of new periodicals and broadcast media independent of state control; the organization which recruited and trained domestic monitors for Zambia's return to multiparty elections in October 1991, and which is now engaged in campaigns of civic education; and a team of American and Zambian political scientists who are conducting a series of public opinion and related studies over the life of the project to determine its impact on the Zambian public.[22]

A third example of US bilateral assistance is Kenya where a four-year project to be funded at approximately $5 million will provide support to the National Assembly (for staff training and improvement of the Assembly's library); the Ministry of Finance to extend a computerized system of budget monitoring down to the district level; and a newly created and private Institute for Policy Analysis and Research (IPAR). In addition, the Kenya project will support a rolling portfolio of small-to medium-size grants to strengthen civil society in Kenya via a series of grants to local NGOs including one that monitors the country's record on human rights, another engaged in civic and voter education that is the successor to an organization which monitored the 1992 multiparty elections, several organizations that provide legal assistance including the local chapter of the International Federation of Women Attorneys

384   *Joel D. Barkan*

(FIDA), and an NGO that seeks to advance the principal of judicial review by litigating potentially precedent setting cases. Grants to support civil society in Kenya are also likely to be made to the secretariat of an association of businesspeople and professionals which is attempting to improve the quality of municipal government in Nairobi, and a press association. Many of the groups to be supported by these grants, as well as IPAR, will be assisted in close coordination and on the basis of co-financing with other donors. More about the utility of such arrangements will be said below.

Finally, no description of US initiatives in this area would be complete without mention of USAID's program in South Africa. Space does not permit an extensive discussion. Suffice to say, this program predated the current array of programs in support of democracy and governance in the rest of Africa, and was one thrust on the Agency by the enactment (over President Reagan's veto) of the Comprehensive Anti-Apartheid Act (CAAA) in 1985. Under the CAAA, USAID was charged to provide assistance to the majority population and hasten the end of apartheid without providing funds to any entity of the South African government or other public institution (e.g., universities and other educational institutions). The result was a major effort to strengthen civil society although it was never termed as such. Most assistance was provided to local NGOs. While much of this support was "conventional" insofar as it financed education and other training programs for black South Africans, a significant proportion of the aid went towards strengthening "the civics" in the townships, community-based organizations which were part of the ANC-allied United Democratic Front. Support was also given to groups providing legal defense to those charged under the security acts, human rights organizations, and organizations such as the Institute for Multi-Party Democracy and the Institute for a Democratic South Africa which laid the basis for the first all-race elections held in April, 1994. Like other donors, the US became heavily involved in the transitional elections, including funding for the South African Election Support Project, the provision of grants for campaign consultants to any party which eschewed violence, and a delegation of international observers.[23] Ultimately, the US spent $35 million on the election.[24]

To design and launch these extended projects of bilateral assistance, USAID has found it necessary to recruit short- and medium-term (two to three years) expertise from outside the Agency. Following the example of the principal European donors, the Agency has recognized the necessity of a full-time resident staff person in the field, that these programs cannot be run from Washington, and that they are relatively personnel intensive compared to conventional programs of developmen-

Can established democracies nurture democracy abroad? 385

tal assistance. However, in marked contrast to the procedures of other donors, the Agency has established the position of a resident "democracy and governance advisor" for each bilateral project, and (with one exception) recruited political scientists drawn mainly from the academic community to fill these posts. USAID has also appointed academics to serve as regional DG advisors for East and West Africa. Approximately sixteen additional social scientists and/or lawyers will be recruited in 1995 to serve as "democracy fellows" at USAID's new Center for Democracy in Washington. Thus, while the European donors (the Scandinavian countries, the Netherlands, the UK, and the EEC) have relied on career foreign service officers to run their democracy programs, the US has consciously employed academics with significant field experience and/or established records of social science research in the country or regions to which they are posted.[25]

These differences in staffing practice should also not be overdrawn and are already undergoing modification. As its portfolio of DG grants has expanded, Sweden has begun to draw on members of its own social science community to serve as advisors to refine its assistance. Likewise, the United Kingdom appointed its first group of four academics in late 1994 to serve as "Commonwealth and Foreign Office Fellows" in the Foreign Office. The fellows will serve as DG advisors for Asia, the Middle East, East and Southern Africa, and the Balkans with duties similar to their counterparts at USAID. These moves on recruitment, however limited, reflect a growing measure of coordination and mutual learning among the representatives of the "like-minded" democracies working in this field. I shall return to the process of coordination below.

Though it was not possible to obtain budgetary data for the DG programs of the eight principal donors, it would appear that the magnitude of these programs has increased significantly since 1992. At a time when most donors are reducing the overall size of their foreign assistance programs, the emergence and growth of donor efforts in this area represents a significant change in priorities as well as a reallocation of funds. This is especially true when one remembers that conventional bilateral aid is becoming increasingly tied to progress towards democratization, or at a minimum, political liberalization and improved governance. While the proportion of donor assistance spent on nurturing democracy remains modest – indeed probably no more than 5 to 12 percent of total aid budgets are spent on programs explicitly defined as DG – considerations of support for democracy are clearly more prominent now than ever before. More systematic thought and specialized expertise is also being brought to bear on the implementation of these programs as the

386   *Joel D. Barkan*

"like-minded" learn what type of interventions work and which do not, and as they scrutinize each other's approach.

American policy is illustrative of these trends which other donors manifest to varying degrees. Following the election of Bill Clinton, the new administration decided to elevate democratization to become one of five strategic objectives of US assistance policy in the post-Cold War era.[26] The administration also moved to reorganize USAID and rewrite the Foreign Assistance Act to facilitate implementation of the new policy. This policy is basically an expansion and refinement of the policy initially articulated by James Baker at the end of the Bush Administration. Perhaps most significant was Clinton's appointment of J. Brian Atwood to be the new administrator of USAID. Prior to heading USAID, Atwood was president of NDI, and the person most responsible for NDI's emergence as a major non-governmental provider of technical assistance to transitional elections around the world. Atwood and his colleagues have made slow but steady progress towards establishing support for democratization as a cornerstone of US developmental assistance. Under Atwood, the United States has begun to concentrate its conventional development assistance programs as well as its DG programs in those countries which have made a genuine commitment to both economic (i.e., structural adjustment) and political reform. As such, these programs focus increasingly on the consolidation of democracy than on the initial phases of transition including elections.

Countries to which the US currently provides assistance have been divided into three categories: (1) "sustainable development countries" or countries where there is a clear commitment on the part of the host government to democratization and economic reform (i.e., to structural adjustment for those countries that are in economic trouble; to the expansion of a market economy by those which are not); (2) "transitional countries," or countries that have recently experienced a national crisis and where timely assistance is needed to reinforce institutions and national order; and (3) countries "where USAID's presence is limited, but where aid to non-governmental sectors may facilitate the emergence of a civic society, help alleviate repression, meet basic humanitarian needs, enhance food security, or influence a problem with regional or global implications" (USAID 1994: 5). Notwithstanding the open-ended caveat for the last category, the major bilateral programs are being reserved for the first. Based on these criteria, the number of countries with bilateral programs is being reduced from over eighty-five to between sixty and sixty-five,[27] and the Agency will probably fund DG programs in roughly half to two-thirds of these. In respect to Africa, the United States began to reduce the number of its missions in FY1994 from thirty to twenty-one. Another six to eight closures are expected next year. Support for these missions totaled approximately $760 million in FY1995 of which $85 million or 11 percent is reserved explicitly for the promotion of democracy. USAID has also established a new Center for Democracy in Washington to provide expertise to all of its missions abroad with democratization programs.

This reorientation of policy, however, poses several policy dilemmas and numerous operational problems. Some are obvious, but bear restating; others are not. I now turn to a discussion of the most salient of these dilemmas as well as to a discussion of the principal lessons learned from the donor experience at promoting democracy since mid-1991 when the "like-minded" democracies began to formalize their democracy programs. While this discussion is based mainly on observations from sub-Saharan Africa most of the lessons learned are generic and should be applicable, in varying degrees, to DG programs pursued elsewhere.

Dilemmas and Lessons Learned

The promotion of democracy requires a consistent foreign policy, but such a policy is usually impossible to pursue

If the promotion of democracy is to be a cornerstone of a nation's development assistance program, it must also be a cornerstone of a nation's overall foreign policy. Support for democratic transitions, particularly contested transitions where established democracies weigh in on the side of insurgent reformers, involve donors in the political life of the recipient state. While it is possible to maintain the figment of an "apolitical" program in respect to conventional forms of development assistance (even though they produce clear "winners" and "losers"), it is impossible here. Programs to nurture democratization often become highly controversial precisely because they are intended to alter the current rules of the game, and may place donor countries in a confrontational position vis-à-vis the host government. Even where this is not true, those charged with implementing these programs in the field cannot proceed with their assignment unless they can count on appropriate political backing – from their embassy, and from their foreign ministry at home. Assistance programs in support of democratization blur the traditional distinctions between the roles of the diplomat and foreign ministry on the one hand, and the aid officer and development assistance agency on the other. In this exercise they are, or are perceived to be, one and the same.

388   *Joel D. Barkan*

Given this reality, it is highly desirable that countries seeking to nurture democracy articulate a clear and consistent standard of what democracy entails lest the purpose of these programs be either misunderstood or lose credibility. States which press hard – diplomatically and/or programmatically – for progress towards democratization (e.g., for an end to human rights abuses, for a free press, for "free and fair" multiparty elections, etc.) must do so on a consistent basis worldwide, or at a minimum be consistent vis-à-vis categories of polities with similar characteristics,[28] lest the policy cease to be viable.

It is very difficult, however, for any nation – especially for the world's remaining superpower – to articulate and apply a single and consistent standard of what democracy entails to every country with which it does business. This is not because there is no single institutional configuration of democracy – we all know that democracy takes many forms; but we also "all know a democracy when we see one." Rather, it is because support for democratization is just one of several objectives that form the basis of the foreign policies of the established democracies that now share this concern. Maintaining peace and security, halting the spread of nuclear weapons, promoting and protecting a nation's share of world trade, protecting investments in a country that was once part of one's former colonial empire, controlling drugs, conserving the environment, providing humanitarian relief (e.g., to Somalia and Rwanda) – all compete to varying degrees and depending on the locale, with democratization as a foreign policy objective. The particular ranking accorded to the promotion of democratization by each of the "like-minded" also varies from one country to another, a situation which sometimes complicates the prospect for donor coordination. To the extent that a nation's commitment to democratization varies as a result of other foreign policy objectives, the prospects for effective political backing for programs to nurture the process is reduced.

This situation begs the question of whether it is possible for each established democracy to formulate a viable set of decision rules so that all will know – the other established democracies as well as countries in the midst of transition or resisting reform – when and where each principal donor will be most supportive and/or aggressive in pursuing democratization and where it will not. If there is a "rule" it would appear to be as follows: that the "like-minded" will be most supportive of those countries where there is a genuine commitment on the part of the government to respect human rights, increase political liberalization, and accommodate competitive politics. However, the converse of this rule – that donors will apply substantial pressure and condition aid where these commitments are not present will *not* be invoked automati-

Can established democracies nurture democracy abroad? 389

cally but on a case-by-case basis. This in turn suggests that countries seeking to promote democracy will need to distinguish between programs and forms of assistance that are possible in countries that have demonstrated a commitment to democratization and those which have not. As described above, the United States is beginning to make such distinctions as are other established democracies, particularly the Scandinavian countries and the Netherlands.

> *Democratization is fundamentally a process of institution-building and political socialization, and not the occurrence or non-occurrence of single events*

When established democracies mount initiatives in support of democratization, whether as part of their bilateral assistance programs or via NGOs, they must not become overly preoccupied with single events or activities, but remain sensitive to the fact that democratization requires the building of appropriate institutions of countervailing power and the establishment of a supportive political culture. Both are processes that occur over relatively long periods. The holding of a single multiparty election, even if free and fair, does not a democracy make – witness the aftermath of elections in Angola, Ethiopia, Kenya, Russia, and probably South Africa. Indeed, in the last case, one can argue that although the elections were essential for the future evolution of democracy, they would not have been held in the first place if a more basic precondition had not been established, namely the willingness on the part of the principal protagonists to bargain and accommodate each other on a new set of rules under which South Africa will operate during an extended transition.[29]

Elections are not unimportant, but it is the periodic holding of elections over many years – the institutionalization of the process – that establishes one foundation for an enduring democratic system. Programs to support the electoral process must be conceived accordingly. The same perspective must be maintained in designing programs to strengthen other institutional arenas – legislatures, the judiciary, civil society, a free press, etc. The observation of a transitional election, a study tour to Westminster by a group of MPs, the holding of a single workshop on human rights, or short-term support for a single magazine that thoughtfully considers economic policy in a country faced with structural adjustment – all activities recently funded by one or more of the established democracies – do not go very far in providing sustained support for the desired institution. Those responsible for nurturing democracy abroad must begin to question whether their agencies should

390   *Joel D. Barkan*

continue funding such activities, and if not, what forms of assistance can be designed to address the fundamental needs of the process.

A few examples suggest that at least on a conceptual level, support for institution-building is possible. (1) A multiyear grant and the provision of technical assistance to nurture the development of a local NGO for the purpose of monitoring elections and conducting campaigns of civic education is more likely to make a lasting contribution to the electoral process (and be much less expensive) than flying in fifty to sixty international observers the week before an election. (2) The funding of a comprehensive program to provide supplemental and sustained training for selected members of the judiciary, staff support (e.g., prosecutors and court reporters), and needed reference materials (e.g., the updating, publication, and dissemination of a country's legal code to its local courts) will do far more than a two- to three-day workshop on human rights, or even a series of such exercises. (3) A program to design, establish, and staff an appropriate system of revenue generation for local government will do more to enable these bodies to function on an autonomous basis than a single grant to a municipality to build some needed facility. (4) Assistance in the area of curriculum development in social studies at the primary school level, including the writing of textbooks, is likely to have a more lasting impact on young citizens than occasional programs in civic education. Put simply, programs to nurture democratization must be more sustained and broader in scope than most current initiatives even if limited to the strengthening of a single institution.

Nurturing democracy will take time; progress will be uneven and uncertain

Given the inherent nature of the process of democratization, nurturing democracy will take time. The time horizons for measuring progress in this area are decades and half-decades – as long or longer than the duration of the average presidential administration or premiership in the established democracies, and much more than the period of service of an ambassador or an aid director in a country in the midst of transition. Progress, especially when measured at the country level, will also be halting with many ups and downs. In some instances, the transition to democracy will be stalled. These realities are sure to test whether the established democracies are truly serious about assisting the process. If they are, the "like-minded" must get into the game for the long-haul, design programs accordingly, commit appropriate personnel to the field, and, above all, be patient.

Can established democracies nurture democracy abroad? 391

Having recently spent two years observing the culture of one of the world's largest development assistance agencies, and mindful of the political pressures such agencies are subjected to back home, I am not overly sanguine that these implementing bodies will be able to do what is required. Nor, for the same reasons, am I overly confident that such agencies can bear the risks associated with this approach. If these conclusions are valid, then policy makers in the established democracies should ask whether this form of foreign assistance is best left to foundations and NGOs – entities that are not under as much pressure to perform in the short term. Germany, which channels most of its funding for democratization, via its party foundations, appears to have answered this question in the affirmative. The United Kingdom via the Westminster Foundation has taken the same stance, while the United States has taken a two-track approach. Although all major programs are now initiated by USAID, NED also operates as a foundation in the field. Compared to the programs of the major bilateral agencies, however, the budgets of all these foundations are relatively small with the result that although they can accept risk, they do not have the capacity to support programs of institution-building over long time periods.[30]

Most donor agencies will need to change the ways they do business if they are to make a significant impact in this new area of development assistance

In addition to taking a long-term/institution-building perspective and a willingness to accept risk, the principal bilateral and multilateral agencies need to make several additional adjustments in the way they conduct their day-to-day operations to be effective in this new area of development assistance. The first is to recognize that these programs are inherently personnel intensive. Because most DG programs are multifaceted in content, a typical program requires continuous or near continuous oversight and adjustment by an appropriately trained program officer. A related reason is that most forms of assistance are small and non-replicable compared to conventional programs of development assistance. For example, a program to establish a cadre of appropriate staff for the Namibia National Assembly and National Council will require a sequencing of different types of training for different types of personnel (clerks, budgetary analysts, committee staff, librarians, etc.) that are appropriate for that legislature. While programs that have succeeded in strengthening the legislature in other countries might serve as a guide, the particular configuration of assistance is country specific. Moreover, unlike conventional development assistance programs, for

392   *Joel D. Barkan*

example in family planning or agriculture, there are no economies of scale. Successful programs are not those which expand and repeat initial interventions after a period of testing and refinement of a single package of assistance. Rather they are programs that simply proceed on to the next unique stage of implementation. As a result, a typical DG program requires that many small amounts of money be obligated on a continuous basis. This too raises personnel costs relative to the overall cost of these projects, a fact which troubles most bureaucrats for whom the nurturing of democracy is a new and unfamiliar exercise. It should not and must not. Indeed, the bilateral agencies and foundations which are most effective in nurturing democratization in the African context are those which appreciate the personnel intensive nature of the work.[31]

Second, bigger is not better. Although programs to nurture democratization are personnel intensive, their overall costs are not expensive compared to conventional development programs – and need not be. The average annual costs of the major bilateral democracy programs described earlier in this chapter (excluding South Africa) is roughly $2 million per year, a level of funding that is adequate for the types of assistance provided. This is particularly true in respect to the level of funding to strengthen civil society. Most organizations worthy of support in a typical African country are small and incapable of utilizing grants larger than $25,000 to $100,000 per year. Indeed, larger grants particularly at the early stages of these organizations' development are not only wasteful, they undermine the donors' purpose of nurturing the emergence of autonomous organizations. Organizations which obtain excessive donor support before raising funds on their own have little incentive to become self-supporting. Agencies which mount democracy and governance programs, must therefore exercise restraint, and to provide funds on a matching grant basis. Put differently, doing less often increases the prospects of giving rise to a sustainable institution.

Third, there is the need to recruit appropriate personnel to design and implement this new form of assistance. I have already discussed USAID's tendency to draw on political scientists and academic specialists from outside the Agency to establish its initial DG programs, and that other bilateral agencies may also be moving in this direction. For the most part, the IFIs have not. A basic problem in all these agencies is that they are staffed mainly by generalists or economists, few of which are particularly sensitive to the institutional variables that structure the developmental process, particularly political institutions. But as suggested throughout this chapter, the nurturing of democracy is inherently an exercise in "getting the political institutions right."[32] Virtually none of these officers are students of neo-patrimonial politics, state–society

Can established democracies nurture democracy abroad? 393

relations, regime change, voting behavior, etc., all of which determine the prospects for democratization and the interventions required to nurture it. While it would be a gross oversimplification to argue that these programs will succeed as soon as the established democracies recruit a cadre of political scientists to run them, it is also likely that they will fail if knowledgeable personnel and the literature of the discipline are not brought to bear on the exercise.

In sum, the first place to begin a program to support DG abroad, may be in altering the internal systems of governance of the agencies charged with mounting this initiative.

It is desirable that the "like-minded" democracies increase coordination between themselves, and with the IMF and the World Bank

There are several reasons why increased coordination, if only on an informal basis, is desirable among the "like-minded." The first and most important is that democratization is a universal value. Initiatives taken by the established democracies to promote democracy are likely to be more persuasive and possibly less threatening in countries in the midst of a transition when they are conducted in concert, and even on a joint basis via parallel programs mounted by multiple donors. Authoritarian regimes which drag their feet on liberalizing their systems find it more difficult to do so when confronted by a united front of like-minded donors. For the same reason, political reformers in these countries who seek the support of the established democracies, enjoy a greater measure of political cover when more than one donor supports their efforts.

Second, no one donor can do it all. Depending on the type of institution to be strengthened and the country, some donors have a comparative advantage over others in which case it is useful to arrive at a division of labor that capitalizes on their respective strengths. Coordination is also desirable in the few instances where it is necessary to fund large and relatively expensive interventions (e.g., the establishment of IPAR in Kenya which is expected to cost $4 million over a five-year period).

Third, coordination avoids duplication as well as smothering recipient organizations with excessive support.

Fourth, coordination is desirable simply to share information about "what works and what does not" in this still infant area of foreign assistance. One must remember again that most administrators of such programs in the field – and certainly their heads of mission – are learning on the job. As a result, coordination is most effective when it occurs in

394   *Joel D. Barkan*

the field; that is to say, between the relevant staff of the "like-minded" missions. A successful example of such information exchange has been the "Donors Democracy and Governance Group" in Kenya formed in early 1992 during the run-up to the country's first multiparty elections in twenty-six years. The group, which includes representatives of the eight "like-minded" as well as the European Community, the German foundations and the Ford Foundation initially formed as a defense against the duplicate funding proposals that all had received from various Kenyan groups seeking to participate in the anticipated transition. Over time, the individual members of the group, some of whom had served in Zambia at the time of that country's transitional election in October 1991, realized that the sharing of information about the nature of such exercises around the world, the literature on African elections, where to obtain needed expertise, etc., was beneficial to all. The group, which sometimes met as often as twice a week, became the principal policy forum of the "like-minded" with respect to the elections and eventually drew in the UN and other diplomatic and development assistance missions. The group still functions to coordinate assistance in the post-election period, and has been replicated, albeit on a much smaller scale, in Uganda.

However valuable, coordination in the field should be complemented by greater sharing of information between the headquarters of the agencies pursuing these programs. The principal reason is to enhance the institutional memories of a diverse number of agencies, memories that ebb and flow with the movement of individuals between overseas assignments and assignments back home. High turnover of key personnel, as has occurred in Kenya since 1995, weakens the donor effort in the field, while a weak institutional memory at home means that field officers are often reinventing the wheel in respect to program design.

Finally, and perhaps most important, coordination between the "like-minded" is becoming increasingly necessary to arrive at a common position on how to deal with the IFIs on the one hand, and selected recipient countries on the other on questions of political conditionality. An appropriate discussion of the issue of political conditionality is beyond the scope of this chapter. Since 1991, however, most if not all of the "like-minded" as well as Japan have suspended quick-disbursing aid, and in some instances conventional assistance, to the Cameroon, Kenya, Malawi, Nigeria, and Zaire pending progress towards political liberalization and multiparty democracy. Such suspensions are normally effected at the annual meetings of the Consultative Group of donors that take place in Paris under the aegis of the World Bank. As previously noted, the IFIs are the major providers of quick-disbursing aid, but have

Can established democracies nurture democracy abroad? 395

historically been reluctant to enter the thicket of political conditionality. In this context, the bilateral donors of the "like-minded" must hang together if they are to persuade the IFIs to follow their lead. Coordination is also important when it comes to the resumption of assistance. The exercise of conditionality is a very blunt instrument, and aid flows cannot be turned on and off like a faucet. If conditionality with respect to political reform is to be employed in a nuanced manner, the donors must speak with one voice.

Even when they are well designed and well executed, donor initiatives in support of democratization operate at the margin

The final observation is one that perhaps should have been made at the outset of this section, or even at the outset of this chapter. It is also an observation that should be obvious, but is sometimes forgotten: *regardless of whether all of the aforementioned considerations are applied to the exercise of nurturing democracy, it is important to appreciate that these programs are at best programs that operate at the margin of the process* – as facilitators of transitions that are driven mainly by the internal dynamics of the societies in which they occur and/or by the internal dynamics of the regimes that govern these societies. In other words, progress towards democratization or the lack of it is a home-grown phenomena. While "like-minded" donors can provide useful support to accelerate or consolidate the process, they cannot do so without indigenous democrats. Indeed, one of the principal tests for any potential donor intervention is the quality of the local leaderships and their commitment to the exercise over the long pull. Not every country should have a democracy program supported by one or more of the "like-minded." Some are not ready to absorb this type of assistance, while those that are should not become so dependent on the donors to achieve what in the final analysis they must achieve for themselves.

Conclusions

What impact? What likely impact?

So what is the proverbial bottom line? Can the established democracies nurture democracy abroad? Probably, but in a limited and nuanced manner and only if they refine their operations. Should they do so? As discussed above, the issue is all but moot; democracy's "victory" may not be an accomplished fact, but democratization has become a near universal value among those who participate in the political process. As

396   *Joel D. Barkan*

for actual accomplishments, it is too early to make any definitive judgments. While there have clearly been many major successes in terms of an initial transition to democratic governance, and while the donor community can justifiably claim some credit in facilitating these transitions – in Malawi, in Namibia, in South Africa, in Zambia, and possibly in Tanzania and Uganda. International presence, if not donor programs, also made a difference in Korea, the Philippines, and Thailand. The consolidation of democracy, however, is a more problematical exercise, one that is even more dependent on internal conditions than the first stages of transition. Again, the "like-minded" are at best facilitators at the margin. Their programs can assist and nurture, but they are no substitute for local commitment and political will. Does this mean that the established democracies should simply sit back and let events unfold? The answer is obviously a judgment call made on a case-by-case basis, but for those of us who have witnessed successful or even partial transitions in countries that previously experienced political repression, the choice is not difficult.

What role for social science?

Finally, is there a role for social science, particularly political science, in this exercise? Is the accumulated literature of the last fifty years and the recent literature of the past decade simply the stuff of academics, or can some portion of it be distilled and put to use at an operational level? Here I return to observations from recent experience as a long-time practitioner of field research turned short-term policy advisor. There is much in the literature, especially that grounded in empirical research, that speaks to the exercise of nurturing democracy. If nothing else, it suggests "the dos and don'ts" – the broad parameters of what to attempt and what to avoid, as well as what is essential for democratization to occur. As the literature becomes increasingly refined, we become more cognizant of the particular configurations of conditions that are necessary for democratization in one context as distinct from another. This knowledge alone may assist those who implement programs that promote democratization to avoid serious mistakes in what is an inherently uncertain enterprise *provided* it can be easily consumed.

The extent to which social scientists will actually inform the process of assisting democratic transitions, however, is unclear. Although donor assistance agencies and NGOs around the world are probably more receptive today than ever before to input from the social sciences, it must be recognized that the realm of the development assistance program officer and the realm of the academic social scientist researcher

Can established democracies nurture democracy abroad? 397

are fundamentally different and separate from each other. The results that the student of democratization and the promoter of the process seek to achieve interact only on an intermittent basis. Bureaucrats in large development assistance agencies as well as staff members of NGOs seeking to nurture democratization are absorbed with the operational problem of the moment. Their immediate task is to mount a credible series of interventions that will not go wrong within the shortest possible time. While they acknowledge the need to understand the explanatory theories of the processes they seek to shape, few have the time or patience to read the research-based literature. They are consequently "satisficers" rather than optimizers when it comes to evaluating the merits and limitations of alternative theories or the costs and benefits of the particular interventions they choose to pursue. Most want to make intelligent programmatic decisions, but most also believe that if they wait until all the answers are in, their programs will never be launched. Moreover, in as politically sensitive an area as DG, a typical bureaucrat will hedge his bets by pursuing a variety of actions, some of which he or she knows may be less than optimal or even potential failures but which will facilitate the overall success of the program.[33]

This, as well as the other constraints discussed in this chapter, is the frustrating reality of putting theory into practice in what is nevertheless an exciting new area of development assistance. If social science is to seriously inform this exercise beyond its contributions to the literature, a portion of the social science community will need to immerse itself periodically in the day-to-day operations of one of the bilateral assistance agencies, international organizations, or NGOs seeking to nurture democratization abroad. Contributing to the literature alone or explicating recent major findings in the literature through the occasional paper or presentation for key personnel in such organizations will not provide them with an ongoing guidance for their work. Put simply, if social science is to have a significant impact on the exercise, some social scientists with an active research agenda must work inside these organizations on a fixed-term basis. This is quite different from the permanent recruitment of recently trained students of democracy into these organizations. While such recruitment will no doubt inform the exercise in the short term, long-term tenure will ultimately transform these individuals into the bureaucrats and program officers they are supposed to inform. Indeed, the nature of the work and of the organization demand that this be so – that they cease being research social scientists. The suggestion here is that agencies committed to infusing the promotion of democracy with an understanding of recent social science research on democratization do so by rotating researchers into the organization on a regular

398   *Joel D. Barkan*

basis for periods of service of up to three years or four years and/or by sending their own personnel out for extended periods of residence at research institutions. It is equally important that those selected for such rotations have the temperament to "fit in" at their respective temporary realms for they are "outsiders" in each. Only through such exercises are the two cultures likely to be bridged, and the richness of what has been learned about democratization be incorporated into programs that nurture it.

NOTES

1 From 1992 through 1993 the author served as the first regional democracy and governance advisor for Eastern and Southern Africa to the United States Agency for International Development.
2 Though they are not bilateral assistance agencies, Western trade unions have long promoted democratization, particularly in Eastern and Southern Europe with both financial and official support from the governments of their own countries.
3 The most active members of this group in terms of programmatic assistance are the US, Canada, Germany, the Netherlands, and the Scandinavian countries. In addition to the eight "like-minded" democracies, Austria, Australia, Belgium, Finland, and Japan periodically join the enterprise, especially when it comes to providing international observers for transitional elections.
4 It is noteworthy that the multilateral organizations, whose member states include several still under authoritarian rule or others which are not enthusiastic about the promotion of democracy, have limited their official policies to the promotion of "good governance." However, these organizations are also beginning to take up the challenge of nurturing democratization.
5 The IFIs have historically limited their conditions to economic criteria for two reasons. First, as economic institutions, the IFIs have not been particularly concerned with the need for political reform, especially when the experience of several high growth countries (e.g., the Southeast Asian "tigers") suggested that economic growth could occur first, and indeed might require, a period of authoritarian rule. Under this scenario, political liberalization and democratization follow rather than precede or accompany initial periods of economic growth. Second, multilateral organizations such as the IFIs are composed of a diversity of political systems, including many under authoritarian rule. Invoking political criteria for economic assistance has been customarily regarded as an infringement of the sovereignty of a member state. The African experience, however, challenges this reasoning. Here, authoritarian rule or at least its neo-patrimonial variation, has crippled the economies of virtually every country on the continent leading many to conclude that economic improvement will only occur when regimes become more accountable to the governed. It is in this context that the new pressures for political conditionality have emerged. The established democracies – which also happen to be the major financial underwriters of the IFIs – increasingly realize that their bilateral programs have the potential of being

Can established democracies nurture democracy abroad? 399

undercut by these organizations. Indeed, when it comes to "quick-disbursing" aid, the Bank and the Funds provide more than half to two-thirds of what is currently being provided.

6 Even regimes that reject the Western definition of democracy rarely speak of "people's democracy" or some other variation of democratic rule; rather they simply argue that democracy is not appropriate for their society (e.g., Daniel arap Moi in Kenya, the military regimes in Burma and Haiti).

7 I refer particularly to the language of "structural functionalism," i.e., "interest articulation," "interest aggregation," "outputs," etc. See Gabriel Almond introductory chapter, "A functional approach to comparative politics" in Almond and Coleman (1960) and Almond and Powell (1966).

8 See, for example, Apter's introduction to his landmark study (1958).

9 For example, the Agency supported an extensive research program on the functions and operations of legislatures which was carried out at Duke University, the University of Hawaii, the University of Iowa, and the State University of New York (Albany). USAID also supported a large research program on the nature of political participation implemented by Cornell and the University of California at Berkeley, and on various aspects of public administration. However, to the knowledge of this writer, no grants were made which focused explicitly on the process of democratic transitions – their causes, and the conditions under which they were most likely to succeed. Nor, with one or two exceptions, were the scholars who participated in these exercises ever brought back to design and/or implement a program of assistance in a country in which USAID maintained a mission.

10 USAID did mount a small number of programs in the 1980s to support democratization in Central America, most notably in El Salvador, and in South Africa but these efforts appear to be unconnected to any of the research sponsored by the Agency and isolated from the mainstream work of the Agency as a whole.

11 Americans need to be reminded that roughly 75 percent of their congressional districts are one-party districts and that their only opportunity for replacing their representatives is the primary election of the dominant party; in short, via intra-party competition.

12 The 1986 transitional election in the Philippines which brought Cory Aquino to power was probably the most significant in this regard, and set the standard for other transitional elections which followed. International observers and media poured into the country to put the elections in the international spotlight. Local groups organized thousands of independent poll watchers to ensure that the elections were "free and fair." The methodology of observation was perfected to a new level via the procedure of parallel vote counts. These procedures set a precedent that was later replicated in other countries.

13 While never eager for external observers, incumbent regimes realized that unless they let observers in, the international community would assume they had something to hide.

14 For those not conversant with the acronyms of these agencies they are the USAID, the Canadian International Development Agency, the Danish International Development Agency, the German Agency for Technical

400 *Joel D. Barkan*

Cooperation, the Overseas Development Authority (United Kingdom), the Norwegian Agency for Development, and the Swedish International Development Agency).

15 In response to increasing demand from member states, the UN has established the Electoral Assistance Division within the Department of Peace-Keeping Operations of the Secretariat. The unit serves as a conduit for providing consultants to electoral commissions charged with administering elections as well as a coordinating body for delegations of observers from member states that go out to monitor these elections. The unit sometimes recruits international observers directly when they operate solely under UN flag (e.g., Angola, Cambodia). The configuration of international observer delegations varies widely. For example, for the Kenyan elections in December 1992 the US, Commonwealth, and UN all mounted their own independent delegations with the last composed of approximately a dozen mini delegations from UN member states. At the same time the UN served as the point of coordination between itself, the Commonwealth and the US. Such arrangements are often *ad hoc* and thus vary considerably from one election to the next.

16 A notable exception to this generalization about American assistance are the programs in human rights and governance of the Ford Foundation and the programs of the NED.

17 The HRDG has been a relatively modest effort. From 1979 through 1990 the program had a budget of only $500,000 per year for Africa, with similar amounts for Asia and Latin America. As a reflection of the times, the annual budget for Africa was increased to $2 million in FY1992, and raised again to $3 million in FY1993.

18 As Diamond also notes in his own contribution to this volume (n. 6) the precise amount that USAID spends on democracy promotion is a function of what programs are included when estimating the total and any figure cited must be treated with caution. The figures cited here are for those development assistance projects that are explicitly devoted to the promotion of democracy. These include projects mounted by USAID's individual country missions plus centrally funded efforts directed from Washington such as the Africa Regional Election Assistance Fund. I do not include that portion of non-project assistance or "quick disbursing aid" which USAID has set aside to support economic and political reform. My estimate of USAID's expenditures in Africa is also somewhat lower than Diamond's. Assuming that USAID's spent $152 million worldwide and $85 million in Africa on democratization projects, this represents only 5.6 percent and 10.6 percent respectively of the Agency's total budget for development assistance and of the Development Fund for Africa.

19 The Institute, which is also sponsored by ten other countries including the remaining Scandinavian states and Spain, commenced operations in 1995.

20 For a comprehensive report of the events surrounding the election as well as the election itself, see NDI and the African American Institute (1993).

21 The TGE consists of a broad coalition of ethnic-based guerrilla movements which overthrew the Soviet-backed Marxist regime of Mengistu Haile

Can established democracies nurture democracy abroad? 401

Mariam in May 1991. The dominant member of the coalition was and continues to be the Tigrayan Peoples Liberation Front (TPLF) headed by Meles Zanawi.

22 This research exercise is very atypical of most DG projects funded by USAID, but reflects a recognition on the part of the Agency that it has embarked on a new form of assistance which must itself be carefully monitored. This is also consistent with the Agency's new policy of pursuing programs that yield "measurable results."

23 The South African Election Support Project was a joint effort of NDI, International Republican Institute, and the Joint Center for Economic and Political Studies which was principally concerned with mounting voter education efforts to insure a high turnout for the elections.

24 Statement by US Vice-President Albert Gore to the White House Conference on Africa, Washington, DC, June 26, 1994. Notwithstanding the Vice-President's statement, this figure seems high in terms of direct assistance to the election. It is probably valid in terms of total US assistance since 1990 to South African organizations and political parties concerned with the election as well as funds used to support US NGOs involved with various aspects of the elections.

25 It is quite likely, however, that in the future budgetary constraints will force USAID to employ relatively junior social scientists compared to those initially engaged to serve as governance advisors. The Democracy Fellows Program at the Center for Democracy is likely to be an example.

26 The others are protecting the environment, stabilizing world population growth and protecting human health, encouraging broad-based economic growth, and providing humanitarian assistance and aiding post-crisis transitions. For the complete statement of these objectives see (USAID 1994).

27 The exact numbers vary with the definition of what is a "bilateral program." At the end of 1993, USAID maintained a presence of some type in 108 countries, but supported a resident in country missions in only 86.

28 Under this decision rule, the policy might best be described as "picking on the weak"; that is to say, the policy is pursued aggressively vis-à-vis countries that are either most dependent on the donor community such as the African states, or vis-à-vis countries where competing interests weigh less heavily – again, the poorest countries.

29 Proponents of electoral assistance often make the same point in reverse: that it is precisely because the outcomes of elections depend on a host of other considerations that elections are a critical event in the passage of any country from authoritarian to democratic rule. Without elections to serve as a catalyst, many of the "prerequisite" type issues would never be addressed.

30 The Ford Foundation, a wholly private entity, may be the one exception to this generalization. However, the Foundation operates in a comparatively small number of countries.

31 Here again, the Ford Foundation as well as the Friedrich Ebert Foundation provide useful examples. Program officers at Ford are responsible for grant portfolios that disburse approximately $1 million per annum. The typical project manager at USAID normally moves five to ten times this amount.

402   *Joel D. Barkan*

32 This may become the new mantra of political adjustment, and corollary of the mantra of economic adjustment, i.e., "getting the prices right."
33 For example, in a country where the government desires that a donor agency fund an item that the agency regards as a low priority, the bureaucrat may support such action if he concludes that it is "the price" of pursuing other initiatives of higher priority. By contrast, these actions are usually regarded as "wasteful" by social scientists advising the agency.

REFERENCES

Almond, Gabriel, and James S. Coleman, eds. 1960. *The Politics of Developing Areas*. Princeton: Princeton University Press.

Almond, Gabriel, and G. Bingham Powell. 1966. *Comparative Politics: A Developmental Approach; Systems, Process and Policy*. Boston: Little Brown, 1966.

Almond, Gabriel, and Sidney Verba. 1963. *The Civic Culture*. Princeton: Princeton University Press.

Apter, David E. 1958. *The Gold Coast in Transition*. Princeton: Princeton University Press.

Banfield, Edward C. 1958. *The Moral Basis of a Backward Society*. Glencoe: The Free Press.

Bratton, Michael. 1989. "Beyond the state: civil society and associational life in Africa," *World Politics* 51, 3: 407–430.

Bratton, Michael, and Nicholas van de Walle. 1994. "Neopatrimonial regimes and political transitions in Africa," *World Politics* 46, 4: 453–489.

Burkhart, Ross, and Michael S. Lewis-Beck. 1994. "Comparative democracy: the economic development thesis," *American Political Science Review* 88, 4: 903–910.

Duverger, Maurice. 1954. *Political Parties: Their Organization and Activity in the Modern State*. London: Methuen.

Friedrich, Carl J. 1950. *Constitutional Government and Democracy*. Boston: Ginn and Company.

Grofman, Bernard, and Arend Lijphart, eds. 1986. *Electoral Laws and their Consequences*. New York: Agathon Press.

Harbeson, John *et al.*, eds. 1994. *Civil Society and the State in Africa*. Boulder: Lynne Rienner Publishers.

Horowitz, Donald. 1991. *A Democratic South Africa? Constitutional Engineering in a Divided Society*. Berkeley: University of California Press.

Huntington, Samuel P. 1991. *The Third Wave: Democratization in the Late Twentieth Century*. Norman: University of Oklahoma Press.

Lijphart, Arend. 1984. *Democracies: Patterns of Majoritarian and Consensus Government in Twenty-One Countries*. New Haven: Yale University Press.

1994. *Electoral Systems and Party Systems*. Oxford: Oxford University Press.

Linz, Juan J., and Alfred Stepan. 1996. *Problems of Democratic Transition and Consolidation: Southern Europe, South America and Post-Communist Europe*. Baltimore: Johns Hopkins University Press.

Lipset, Seymour Martin. 1960. *Political Man*. New York: Doubleday.

Lipset, Seymour Martin, Kyoung-Ryung Seong, and John Charles, Torres.

Can established democracies nurture democracy abroad? 403

1993. "A comparative analysis of the social requisites of democracy," *International Social Science Journal* 45: 155–75.

McColm, R. Bruce. 1993. "The comparative survey of freedom, 1993," *Freedom Review* 24 no. 1: 3–10.

Moore, Barrington. 1966. *The Social Origins of Dictatorship and Democracy.* Boston: Beacon Press.

NDI and African American Institute. 1993. *An Evaluation of the June 21, 1992 Elections in Ethiopia.*

Nelson, Joan, and Stephanie J. Eglinton. 1992. *Encouraging Democracy: What Role for Conditioned Aid?.* Washington: Overseas Development Council.

1993. *Global Goals, Contentious Means: Issues of Multiple Aid Conditionality.* Washington: Overseas Development Council.

O'Donnell, Guillermo *et al.*, eds. 1986. *Transitions from Authoritarian Rule.* Baltimore: Johns Hopkins University Press.

Putnam, Robert D. 1993. *Making Democracy Work: Civic Traditions in Modern Italy.* Princeton: Princeton University Press.

Rostow, Walt W. 1960. *The Stages of Economic Growth: A Non-Communist Manifesto.* New York: Cambridge University Press.

Rueschmeyer, Evelyne, Huber Stephens, and John D. Stephens. 1992. *Capitalist Development and Democracy.* Cambridge: Polity Press.

USAID. 1994. *Strategies for Sustainable Development.* Washington: US Agency for International Development.

17 Some thoughts on the victory and future of democracy

Juan J. Linz

Introduction

The title of the Symposium Victory and Crisis reflects very well the mood of scholars in the mid-1990s. The wave of transitions from non-democratic rule to democracy since the mid-1970s to around 1990 led to that feeling of victory of democracy. The work with Alfred Stepan on a book on *Problems of Democratic Transition and Consolidation* (Linz and Stepan 1996), leads me to introduce a caveat on both victory and crisis. When we think of the victory of democracy since 1974, we tend to forget the failures of democratic transitions and the fact that democracy in many parts of the world, including two large countries, China and Indonesia, has not yet been victorious. When we speak about crisis, it is unclear if we mean by that the "desencanto," the "Entzauberung" of democracy that, with greater or lesser intensity, has followed practically all the transitions since the Spanish in 1977, where the term was coined.[1] Or if we are referring to some deeper questioning by the intellectuals and sectors of the public, perhaps influenced by them, about the functioning of democracies. In addition, there is the question of the consolidation of democratic institutions and processes in some societies in which formal transitions from authoritarianism have taken place.

What do we mean by victory of democracy? First of all, the fact that in many countries authoritarian and post-totalitarian rulers have been replaced by elected governments in an overwhelming number of cases without much bloodshed. Secondly, most importantly, is the fact that after the fall of the Berlin wall no anti-democratic ideology appeals to politicians, intellectuals, religious leaders (with the possible exception of Islamic countries) as an alternative to political democracy in the way that Bolshevik revolutionary dictatorship, Fascism, traditional authoritarianism, authoritarian corporativism or even the military as guarantors of the social order or revolutionary change did for much of the twentieth century. Ideologically developed alternatives have discredited themselves and are exhausted leaving the field free for the democrats. Even

Some thoughts on the victory and future of democracy 405

if we were to accept the caveats of Huntington (1993) about the undemocratic, if not anti-democratic, values of certain cultures, great civilizations, and religious traditions, they do not offer an alternative form of political institutionalization like the ideologies just mentioned. At the most, those values provide a ground in which non-democratic polities might take root if someone attempts to establish them or might, as in the case of some Islamic countries, even use democratic institutions and processes to fill them with an illiberal content claiming to be democratic since they are based on the will of the majority of the people. The radical Islamists in addition want to constitutionalize Islamic principles beyond the reach of changing democratic majorities.

These facts should not lead us to ignore that the Communist Chinese leadership has yet to commit itself to a transition to democracy and that it might have reasons not to do so in view of the events in the former USSR. The incertitudes of democratization may be too great. In that case, it is more important than ever to keep the processes of liberalization distinct from democratization. There is little doubt that the economic changes taking place in China might lead to certain forms of liberalization but I am not yet certain that they will lead to democratization, and that in fact the transition to democracy in China, after the totalitarian Communist rule and considering the cultural traditions, might not be traumatic. In my view, future developments in Indonesia, probably after the death of Suharto, will tell us much more about how victorious democracy really is.

We should not forget either the number of failed or extremely difficult transitions after the demise of regimes that fit the category that I have labeled "sultanistic", beginning with Cuba after Batista, the Dominican Republic after Trujillo, Nicaragua after the Somozas, Iran after the Shah, Haiti after Baby Doc Duvalier and even Romania after Ceauçescu (Chehabi and Linz n.d.). This experience creates a caveat on a number of transitions to democracy in Black Africa. The difficulty of establishing or maintaining non-democratic rule after the delegitimation of such rule does not always assure a transition to democracy. In fact, in a number of countries it has led to political disintegration leading to a regression to chaos. Civil war and political fractionalization makes a transition to democracy particularly difficult. Countries like Afghanistan, Ethiopia, Somalia, Liberia, come to mind, to which many observers would quickly add in the future Zaire and others Bosnia and Herzegovina. Some of the successor states of the former USSR in the southern tier might not be far from such a situation.

These pessimistic considerations are, however, compensated by the hopeful process initiated in the Union of South Africa (Friedman 1995).

406   *Juan J. Linz*

That process shows the enormous importance of leadership or, to use the language of the social science jargon, agency, when structure seems to lead to deterministic, pessimistic predictions.

In some countries with incomplete transitions, with non-consolidated democracies, and where – like in Central America – we had authoritarian regimes with pseudo- or semi-democratic forms we can expect what we might call "distorted" democracies. Such regimes hold competitive elections, but sometimes some parties are excluded and the "democratically" elected leaders do not have full authority in the whole country or in some policy areas in which the military exercise decisive control under martial law, or those elected are unable to stop "private" political violence linked with political parties or the security services. Strictly speaking, to call such regimes democracies is a misnomer (Di Palma 1986; Karl 1995; *Panorama Centroamericano, Reporte Político* – a regular newsletter that gives an excellent account of the difficulties of building democracies in Central America). In fact, such a type of rule is likely to contribute to the alienation from democracy.

An analysis of the transitions to democracy and the ongoing consolidation of many of the new democracies leads us to a cautiously optimistic conclusion. It is almost totally unlikely that any of the democracies consolidated before the third wave of Huntington will experience a breakdown and almost none will undergo serious crisis (Huntington 1991: 14–15). Those which have been established in Southern Europe, the Southern Cone of South America and more recently in Central Europe are most likely on the way to full consolidation if not already consolidated. In these two groups of democracies the relevant question, particularly for the second one, is the quality of democracy not its persistence or stability and the possibility of a breakdown. It should be noted however that *no* democracy, even a consolidated one, is forever guaranteed to be crisis-free and even stable. Democracies in other parts of Latin America, in the Balkans, and even paradoxically in Poland face serious problems in their consolidation and some of them may experience difficult crises. Those crises might result in making their democratic quality questionable but even so the likelihood of the establishment of authoritarian rule is not high.

The case of Peru is mentioned as an example of backsliding and even as a breakdown of democracy (Ferrero Costa 1992a and 1992b; Cotler 1994; McClintock 1993). Before reaching that conclusion, it would be important to note that a democratically elected President acted in an anti-constitutional way closing the Congress, the other democratically elected body. As I have noted elsewhere, there is no democratic principle by which one can resolve the conflict in the case of dual legitimacy

Some thoughts on the victory and future of democracy 407

as we find it in presidential systems. It can even be argued that the decision of President Fujimori involved a reequilibration of a political system in deep trouble and that many citizens of Peru felt that way about his actions. Fujimori's anti-constitutional actions and authoritarian way of governing aroused an international reaction that obliged him to convene a constituent assembly and to obtain the approval of a new constitution in a referendum. The fragmentation of the opposition and the success of capturing the leader of the terrorist Sendero Luminoso allowed him to win reelection. The Peruvian crisis indirectly shows that even a ruler with authoritarian proclivities cannot dispense with democratic legitimacy. The recent so-called transition from the first to the second republic in Italy, although worrisome, again shows that a discredited political class was not, as many thought years back, displaced by extremists of the left or the right and their violent actions against the system, but by the electorate choosing a new political class. Those pessimistic about the new democracies like to point to the electoral success of the more or less reformed Communist parties in Lithuania, Poland, and Hungary, forgetting that they did not come into power committed to change the regime as the Nazis did explicitly in the early 1930s before assuming power, and that they have not pursued systematically a change in the political institutions or limited the freedoms of the citizens. In the context of the 1990s, they felt and feel obliged to conform with democratic rules.

It is more questionable if the new states in the former Soviet Union which have given themselves democratic institutions and have held elections fit the definition of a democracy, particularly when their leader is the same party Secretary General that exercised power as a Communist now identifying himself as a nationalist. In a number of those new states the question is not whether there will be a reversal of democracy but if democracy has really been established and is now on the way to consolidation (*The Economist* 1995; Olcott 1993). The case of Russia is the most complex and important and it seems reasonable to withhold judgment about the ultimate outcome. It is even more difficult to argue that new democracies in Black Africa are on the way to consolidation.

This quick overview of the crises of democratization and consolidation of democracies suggests that it would be very dangerous to predict a third reverse wave, although it would be foolhardy to argue that there will be no reversals in the process of democratization. What any analysis of the new democracies will tell us is that many of them will be far from satisfying ideal criteria of democratic political processes and quality of democratic politics. It should, however, be clear that even bad

408   *Juan J. Linz*

democracies are better than authoritarian rule or chaos since we can assume that they may undergo processes of reequilibration, and with improved conditions and leadership might become fully consolidated. Although as Claus Offe puts it there is a "tunnel at the end of the light" I would add there is light at the end of the tunnel that may be long and dark.[2]

In the future we will have to distinguish if a country satisfies the basic conditions to be a democracy and how liberal the state and the society will be. Certainly every democracy has to guarantee basic freedoms to be a democracy, but the extent of freedoms and rights to be enjoyed by citizens are likely to vary considerably. Liberal democrats will have to fight for their expansion.

Structural problems in the new democracies

Alfred Stepan and I as well as other students of transitions have rightly been accused of emphasizing the role of agency, leadership, and conjecture in the study of transitions. There is little doubt that structural factors, political, economic, social, and cultural, are of particular relevance in understanding the processes of consolidation and the tasks of democrats in that process. Since many of those structural conditions cannot be changed in the short run, we have to focus more on those amenable to political engineering (Sartori 1994). We have to pay particular attention to the ways in which the diversity of democratic institutions affect the quality of democracy: presidentialism, parliamentarianism, federalism, electoral laws, rules regulating political parties, etc. The renewed attention paid to the social economic conditions, favorable or unfavorable to democracy, on which our knowledge is quite solid is not without significance. However, we cannot exclude the possibility of transcending those conditioning factors by political leadership and political engineering. There is also a renewed emphasis on the role of political culture and values, although there is considerable evidence (and there could be in my view much more) that some of the values shared by most of mankind favor liberal, democratic institutions and that on that count there is less reason for pessimism.

In any discussion of the importance of a democratic political culture it should not be forgotten that many new democracies were not made by democrats but by people who had more or less passively supported non-democratic regimes. Non-democrats of yesterday can become democrats, even convinced democrats (Di Palma 1990: 210; Linz 1981: 142–144 tables 9 and 10). A different question is if any transition to democracy, and, even more, the consolidation of new democracies,

Some thoughts on the victory and future of democracy 409

requires leaders committed to democracy, and basic liberal values sustaining it. This means readiness to abide by the rules of the democratic political game even when it means losing power.

There is also need to gain greater clarity about what democracy can and cannot accomplish in different contexts since many of the reasons for disenchantment are a result of false, magical, conceptions of democracy. The problems linked with the consolidation of democracy in many parts of the world should lead to a much more thoughtful analysis of democratic institutions and their enormous variety, and to solid research on the implications of alternative institutions. There can be no question that democracies have been successful in capitalist economic systems, systems based on market and private property of means of production. But the mixture of non-market practices and public property in capitalist societies that are and have been democratic is much more complex than a vulgar-neoliberalism would lead us to expect. A hopeful sign is that in practically all the new democracies (perhaps with the exception of the former USSR, leaving aside the Baltic republics) people consider the new political institutions more positive than those existing before, and that in practically all the countries the expectations five years hence are more positive. The fact that the evaluation of the economic change, not only the reality of that change but the institutions of the new market economy, is in those countries (as it was in the older democracies) less positive and in some cases negative, should not obscure this other fact, that the expectations for the future seem to be positive (Rose 1994: 12 table 2, on evaluating political regimes past, present, and future, and 15 table 4, on increased perceptions of gains in freedom; Rose 1995). That difference between the evaluations of the political institutions and the economic institutions should give thought to those who believe that the legitimation of new political systems is dependent on the rapid success of the establishment of the market economy. It is misleading to believe that the efficacy of the economic system is the basis for the legitimation of the new political institutions; there is sufficient evidence to argue that only the legitimation, the belief in those institutions and their success as institutions, will make possible the economic and social changes needed in many countries.[3]

It is interesting to note that there is a certain discrepancy between the many writings about the crisis of democracy and the data we have from public opinion research about how the people feel about democratic institutions. It is now even more important than ever to distinguish in the democracies the response of people to the institutions and the response to the incumbents of office, to distinguish between the awareness of the need for political parties and the critique of the existing

410   *Juan J. Linz*

parties, to give one example. I hope that the talk of "desencanto" does not become a self-fulfilling prophecy. Undoubtedly, there is a "tunnel at the end of the light" to use the metaphor of Offe which can also be hopeful because at the end of any tunnel whose construction is finished there is also light.

The sociological theory of democracy has focused very much on the socioeconomic structure of societies, the level of economic and social development and to some extent although much less explicitly, on class conflict and democracy (Lipset 1959; Diamond 1992; Maravall 1995). Class conflict has been in the twentieth century one of the critical issues in the stability of democratic polities. The Marxist theory of Fascism interpreted that complex phenomenon fundamentally in terms of social classes and the turn toward authoritarian solutions as a response to class conflict. Undoubtedly, in some societies class warfare was a major cause of the breakdown of democracy. That approach, however, neglected the cumulation of conflicts in the economic sphere, between classes, and all the more cultural and ideological tensions like the fusion between leftist movements and anti-clericalism and even anti-religious sentiments. In fact if we look at European and Commonwealth democracies in the twentieth century, the most striking fact is that they were able to find solutions to the conflicts between capitalists, entrepreneurs, and the workers and the trade unions and that in many of them very stable patterns of negotiation, conflict resolution, and even cooperation developed within democratic politics. This is perhaps not surprising when we consider that to a large extent the conflicts were about divisible resources in which there was no need for a zero-sum conflict, which was not the case when the issues were more symbolic like the nature of the political institutions, the place of religion in society, language policies, and national identity. It was the accumulation of such conflicts with those derived from class interests that contributed decisively to the instability of some democracies. Even in those countries where the world economic crisis in the late 1920s and 1930s contributed to the breakdown of democracy, the issues derived from a lack of consensus on the legitimacy of the political institutions made those conflicts so damaging, while in other countries like those of Scandinavia and the Benelux as well as the United States the dominant commitment to the democratic institutions allowed solutions to the class-based conflicts (Berg-Schlosser and Mitchell forthcoming; Zimmermann 1985; Zimmermann and Saalfeld 1988; Zimmermann 1993).

In the post-1989 world, conflicts about the distribution of resources, the demands for greater equality and social justice, are likely to produce crises but the failure of the Marxist revolutionary utopia, that was so important for the labor movement up to the 1960s, has made those

Some thoughts on the victory and future of democracy 411

interest conflicts more manageable. In addition, it is difficult to articulate a conflict of social classes in the post-totalitarian, ex-Communist societies. In fact, it could be argued that the absence of structured social classes makes it difficult to articulate a party system homologous to the West until economic development would generate them.

The focus on economic interest conflicts has led sociologists studying the conditions for stable democracy to pay considerably less attention to other conflicts, those derived from clashes of identity, language policies, and the role of religion. Democratic theory has basically worked with a model of the nation-state and of a largely secularized society in which religion was pushed into the area of the private or at the most was one more element in the social pluralism.

The expansion of democracy to multinational, multiethnic, multilingual, multiculture societies and those in which there is a dominant religious tradition and only a secularized minority has to be built into a theory of the conditions for democracy. From that perspective, the question of who constitutes the demos, the underlying sense of community that makes possible democratic decision making, has to be considered anew. The assumptions of a nation-state (let us not forget that very often the expression national sovereignty was used as equivalent to democracy) and the American and French revolutionary model of separation of church and state have to be reexamined. The traditional conception of nation-building as a basis of state-building and constituting the demos that would make decisions democratically, in many parts of the world has to be questioned.

Efforts of the nationality controlling the state to use it in the nation-building incompatible with the existence of any other national identity within its territory are now and in the future the major difficulty for the consolidation of many democracies. How multinational democratic states can be constructed is a major task for political engineering including constitutional engineering. The same can be said about how the democratic state can recognize the religious identification and the role of religious institutions of the majority of citizens while protecting religious freedom or freedom of non-religion of minorities. To these two problems one has to add those derived from the demand for equality between the sexes, when the culture and/or the religion are not favorable to gender equality.

State, nation, and democracy

A number of new democracies are also new states – the fifteen former Soviet republics and the five emerging from the disintegration of Yugoslavia – and several of them are simultaneously confronting the tasks of

412   *Juan J. Linz*

state-building and democratization. Many of them are also multi-national states, whose leaders, identified with what in the Soviet language was called a titular nationality, are also committed to nation-building. There is, however, a serious tension and often a conflict between those three goals. In multinational states the logic of nationalism and the logic of democracy are not always compatible. Several of those states have opted for "nation-building," sacrificing to that goal democracy and even endangering in the process "state-building" (Linz 1993 and 1995).

The state-builders in new states can pursue different policies toward ethnic, linguistic, cultural, national minorities: exclusionary policies, that is not to consider them to be citizens or not citizens with equal political rights, or inclusionary policies, that is granting to all those in the territory full citizenship, except foreigners coming to the country knowing that they cannot expect automatic citizenship. They can also opt for a nation-building policy aiming at making the demos identical with the nation – either by exclusion or assimilation – or accept the differentiation as a fact – a plural society – or recognizing that fact as more or less valuable and aiming at creating a pluralistic society, even a multinational society and state.[4]

The combination of the two dimensions leads to four different types of polity, two of which can be democratic. In Type I, the identification of the demos with the nation and an exclusionary strategy toward citizenship of those defined as alien leads to expulsion, encouragement of emigration, if not more serious violation of human rights. It is difficult to conceive the building of democracy under such conditions.

In Type II, the acceptance of a differentiation between the demos and the nation and the exclusionary strategy towards citizenship leads to a policy that residents who are not part of the nation will be extended civil rights as resident aliens but not political rights. The result will be an ethnic democracy, that is democratic politics for the members of the dominant national or ethnic group.

In Type III, an inclusionary strategy toward citizenship, combined with an identification in principle between demos and nation, will allow the minority or minorities to participate politically only if they assimilate into the dominant culture. In the absence of a positive value attached to diversity the result will be a plural but not a pluralistic society. The assimilation strategy might involve considerable discrimination, sometimes second-class citizenship of those unable or unwilling to assimilate and the denial of group rights. Only the small size of the minority, its lack of pride in its culture, or its sharing the dominant language and culture, its incapacity or unwillingness to protest against the assimi-

Some thoughts on the victory and future of democracy   413

Table 17.1. *A typology of state, nation, and democracy-building strategies in multinational polities*

Nation-building strategies: ideology toward demos/ nation relationship	State-building strategies: policies toward non-national minority or minorities	
	Exclusionary strategy	Inclusionary strategy
Demos and nation should be the same	Type I Expel or at least systematically encourage the "exit" option	Type III Make major effort to assimilate minorities into national culture and give no special recognition to minority political or cultural rights
Demos and nation can be different	Type II Isolate from political process by granting civil liberties but no political rights and thus discouraging "voice" option	Type IV Make major effort to accommodate minorities by crafting a series of political and civil arrangements which recognize minority rights

lationist policy, would make compatible simultaneous state- and nation-building and democracy.

In Type IV there is an inclusionary conception of citizenship and varying degrees of recognition of group rights to the minority or minorities: the acceptance of a pluralistic society in which diversity is not considered negative. There are many ways in which group and individual rights, bilingualism in education and the public sector, and rights of religious communities might be recognized. In some cases patterns of consociational democracy and federalism might make possible a democratic multinational state based on a loyalty to the state without integration into a nation: a state-nation rather than a nation-state.

Types III and IV represent very different conceptions of democracy and their respective success depends on many factors. In the nineteenth century, Type III was a successful option; today it is, for reasons we cannot develop here, less likely to be so. In that case, the option might be to turn to strategies associated with Type II, which might endanger democracy (or at least affect its quality) or turn to policies of Type IV.

To understand the problems of democracy in many countries and to predict the consolidation or crisis of democracy in many states we need to know much more about the conditions in which these different polity

414   *Juan J. Linz*

options are likely to succeed or fail. Here we can only call attention to this problem area without developing it further.

Religion, the secular state, and democracy

In Western Europe and Latin America we are confronted with largely secularized societies in which religion and the role of the churches are not anymore a highly conflictual issue. Both democrats and religious leaders, at one point or another, believed that democracy and religion were incompatible. The conflict between anti-clericalism and clericalism in a number of Catholic countries contributed to destabilize democracies and exacerbate social conflicts, although early on in countries like Belgium, the Netherlands, Imperial and Weimar Germany, the Catholics came to accept and support democracy. The same was true for the United States and the countries of the British Commonwealth. The memory of those conflicts, the totalitarian experience or the costs of politicized religion in authoritarian regimes like Spain, and the United States model of friendly separation of church and state, ultimately led to religious peace (the *paix scolaire* in that difficult issue) and more friendly patterns of separation and even cooperation of church and state (Weigel 1990: 33). Certainly, contemporary democracies range widely in the patterns of church and state relations: from established churches in the Protestant monarchies, to the cooperative arrangements in the constitutions of the German Federal Republic and Spain, to the pro-religion separation based on religious pluralism (rather than secularism) of the United States, or the granting to religion a privileged position in Ireland and Israel. All these alternatives have been supported or accepted by democratic electorates. Obviously there is room for conflict about specific issues and the interpretation of the constitutional principles, but the churches, including the Catholic Church and the Papacy, as well as most secularists, have concluded that democracy is compatible with religion. A publicly recognized role for religion and the churches is not perceived as incompatible with democracy.

Therefore, the problem of a conflict between religion and democracy has not arisen in the newly democratized Southern European and Latin American countries. In Eastern Europe the profound and massive secularization under Communism (with the significant exceptions of Poland and Lithuania), the national Orthodox churches and the traditions of Caesaro-papism have largely eliminated religion as a political factor. In fact, this has been, and continues being in most of them, another factor in the weakness of "civil society," even though in some of them the link

Some thoughts on the victory and future of democracy 415

between a national church and national identity has come to reinforce the upsurge of nationalism.

In this respect, the situation in many countries in Asia and the Islamic world is different: the masses are often still strongly attached to their religious traditions, which serve to provide a cultural identity in relation to an encroaching West (that often does not export the best of its culture and values). In addition, the secularized segment is often thin, socially and economically privileged, and sometimes alienated from the native culture. We can thus expect the question of the place of religion to be important in any process of democratization. Although the Turkish Ataturk secularizing revolution sometimes seems an ideal model, the specific character of Turkey as an emerging nation-state should not be forgotten, as well as the fact that the *laicité* reforms took place in an authoritarian context. A similar attempt by the Pahlevi Shahs ultimately failed.

Therefore, we have to think of alternatives involving a constructive cooperation between religion and democracy, religious leaders and democratic leaders, at the same time that religious freedom for minorities and rights of the non-religious are protected. Those issues probably have to be dealt with up-front in the constitutional debates, and many of the solutions will not be acceptable to members of the American Civil Liberties Union or Americans for Separation of Church and State, or to French proponents of *laicité*. They will, however, fit with those who, like Lijphart, defend consociational or consensus democracy rather than majoritarian democracy. Democratic electorates may be willing to allocate a special place to religion, to devote resources to religion (which the secularist will feel could be better spent on public welfare activities) but this is neither anti-democratic nor ademocratic. The democratic state might in the tradition of the Buddhist or Hindu kings and the raj – and even the liberal Mogul shahs – assume the role of protector of religion and use that position to modernize discreetly the religious institutions. It might even enlist them in some of the modernization efforts like the Thai Dhammathud program. There is always the risk of fundamentalist extremism, of religious demagogues, using the democratic freedoms to limit the freedom of others and ignite communal conflict, but that risk is not absent even in our Western societies. To prevent it, the strengthening of constitutional restraints and the role of the courts is the only hope. An authoritarian alternative probably is not a long-term solution.

Democrats in the first half of the century developed institutions and policies channeling, bridging, and moderating class conflict; democrats

416   *Juan J. Linz*

today would have to think about institutions and policies to deal with those other conflicts within a democratic and liberal framework. Just as the utopia of a classless society based on the socialization of the means of production became an obstacle to solving class conflicts in the context of democratic liberal politics, equally simple and utopian ideas, like the indiscriminate invocation of the principle of national self-determination or the ideal of the nation-state can be obstacles to democratization and the consolidation of democracy. The same would be true for the identification of democracy with a rigid separation of church and state and the secularization of society.

The new democracies are different

When we think of new democracies we should not expect them to be like the old-established democracies. They are appearing in a different historical, social, and cultural context. To mention just one difference, of no little importance, they are being established in societies in which a large proportion of the population has access to television. In most of them, the industrial blue collar working class will be a smaller part of the population, and more of their citizens have considerable education. As a result of some of those changes, the new political parties are not likely to be mass membership parties, parties anchored in homogeneous and socially distinct electorates. They will be "catch-all parties," parties less committed to integrate their supporters into a variety of mass organizations, and even less into an encapsulated subculture, as some socialist and Christian democratic parties did in the past. There will be fewer voters with a strong party identification, and more of them will be "floating voters."

This undoubtedly poses problems for democratic politicians and leads some scholars, nostalgic about the structured and stable parties and party systems of the past, to worry about the future of democracy. However, it could be argued that the freedom from a socially structured constraining political climate will allow people to respond more readily to changing conditions and issues, to make politicians more accountable and to moderate the antagonism between social groups and their political representatives. In a sense, voters might be freer to choose, to reward and punish politicians, have more "exits" and "voice" and weaker loyalties (to use Albert Hirschman's terms), and that is far from less democratic. The question is the degree of "loyalty" needed so that parties can have sufficient continuity to go on competing, to assure some permanency to elites with experience in politics and governing. We should be on guard about confusing change in the way democracies work and

Some thoughts on the victory and future of democracy 417

parties are organized and compete, with a lack of democratic consolidation or quality of democracy.

It can, however, also be argued that the greater freedom of the voters, the lesser loyalty to parties will affect politics negatively. Candidates with ambition, financial resources, or popularity gained outside of politics, combined with television (particularly in presidential systems [Linz 1994: 26–29]) will be able to appeal to the voters without any experience in politics and government, as outsiders on anti-party "anti-politics" platforms like Timinski, Fujimori, Ross Perot. In a presidential system they will not need to organize a party and have the support of politicians with experience. This can open the door to demagogues using plebiscitarian appeals. The weakening of parties as organizations, channeling political ambitions and serving as a selection mechanism from lower office, local, regional, national, up to the top, although facilitating lateral entry, will have considerable impact on the process of recruitment of political elites.

There is an open question in democracies: to what extent do we want professional politicians, devoted to a career in public office and with experience in different aspects of the role of politician, or amateurs with a passing interest, maybe involved in single issues. Do we want legislators or officials who may serve for one or two terms, as proponents of term limits (so popular in the United States) advocate? Is it possible for the latter to acquire the knowledge of the issues and the capacity to articulate them? Would they be capable of working closely with others, learning to convince them, making compromises, accepting, and supporting leadership?

We need to know more about who goes into politics and who does not – or who leaves politics – in different democracies. Some of the questions raised by Max Weber on "dispensability" for politics are still relevant. Are some of the rules we are establishing, like the incompatibility of politics with any other professional or business activity, not forcing people to become full-time politicians dependent on the parties, party or interest group functionaries, and therefore with limited autonomy?

The quality of democracy

The quality of democracy is a complex problem that in coming years will demand both theoretical and systematic comparative analysis. We will have to specify standards – on which agreement will not always be easy – some weighting of different dimensions and ranges of tolerance of imperfection. We will also have to compare the by-now large number

418   *Juan J. Linz*

of democracies, both as objective outsider scholarly observers, and by taking into account subjective perceptions of the citizens. In fact, both objective and subjective indicators do not always coincide. For example, objective observers do not rate present Rumanian democracy very high but the citizens in different surveys express a surprisingly positive response, particularly considering the much more critical opinions about democracy in a number of Central European countries. The task ahead therefore is gigantic and efforts like the Freedom House reports, those of Amnesty International, and a few cross-national surveys are far from sufficient for our needs.

It has been noted that with the collapse of Communism and the transition from terrible authoritarian regimes to democracy, the arguments in favor of democracy by comparison have lost strength and that a more positive justification becomes imperative, that the performance of democracies on a variety of dimensions will have to serve to legitimize them. This is in part a fallacy. The positive aspects, stressed in the comparison with dictatorships, continue being important and deserve to be emphasized, particularly since they are inherent to any democratic regime. Many other positive aspects may be expected from democracy but they are more dependent on other aspects of their democratic societies as well as on the choices the democrats might or might not make, and therefore possible, probable, but not inherent to political democracy.

Although it might appear to belabor on the obvious, let us note again the unique contributions of political democracy to a better society. Foremost is a consensus and certain guarantees that violence – revolutionary or military coups – are not the method to attain power, irrespective of the desirability of the goals to be achieved by those gaining power. Democracy substitutes ballots for bullets. Democracy also prevents any attempt to stay in power beyond the time at which the voters should make again a choice of who shall govern. We often tend to take this for granted but in many parts of the world for the majority of the people this is a real gain.

Democracy in societies with inequality, even great inequalities, introduces an element of fundamental equality, equality of citizenship in which the preferences of individuals can be expressed, and – unless electoral laws and political institutions are greatly distorted – the sum of those preferences can have some consequence. It also provides in principle some opportunity for all citizens to compete for some share in power. It is an old tradition of ademocratic and anti-democratic thought to stress the actual inequalities that affect the democratic process, ignoring the importance of a recognition of the principle of equality of

Some thoughts on the victory and future of democracy 419

citizens, irrespective of a whole range of inequalities, particularly adscriptive ones.

Democracy – the free competition for power – implies a whole list of freedoms and rights (which we are not going to enumerate here) which citizens do not enjoy in other political systems and that are in themselves valuable (and from all we know valued by people unless they are abused grievously).

Democracy creates and legitimates power but also limits power as government *pro tempore*, for a limited time between elections; it does not allow (except by free consent) the perpetuation in power. It allows those defeated the hope of gaining power the next time (this is the problem for permanent adscriptive minorities like ethnic, religious, linguistic minorities that have little hope of becoming majorities by convincing the majority to support them). It also assures, unless power is used to destroy freedom and thereby democracy, the possibility of making those governing accountable for bad government and ousting them peacefully from power at the end of their mandate. Perhaps democracy is not government by the people or for the people, but it is government accountable at regular intervals to the people.

The characteristic of being government *pro tempore* (with the possibility of continuously consolidated support) is essential to democracy and cannot be democratically abolished since such a decision would deprive future voters (and those not agreeing with the decision to do so) of the right to be part of the demos. It is a defining characteristic often forgotten, but an absolutely essential one (Linz 1986: 34–43). It is also the one that makes failures of democratic government tolerable and gives democracies a breathing space in bad times by at least allowing two successive governments of different parties (normally for eight years) to fail, before one could question the desirability of democratic institutions. This might be one of the explanations for the fact that low efficacy of democracies – incapacity to solve important problems – does not immediately affect the legitimacy of democratic institutions and lead to their breakdown.

Civil peace, reduction of political violence, basic civil liberties, temporal limits to power, possibility of accountability, a margin of tolerance for government failure, are positive contributions to a better society (not without some elements of ambiguity). There are many other positive gains, some almost inevitable, others probable, others possible, and they will allow us to analyze qualitative differences between democracies.

Some of these are even basic criteria to consider a country a democracy, and among those enumerated by Robert Dahl in *Polyarchy* (1971:

420   *Juan J. Linz*

2–3). Other criteria, like those discussed by Juan J. Linz and Alfred Stepan, are necessary to consider a new democracy consolidated. In fact, some authors would include many more conditions for consolidation. On any of those criteria there can be a range beyond which we might question whether a country is a democracy even if there has been a transfer of power to freely elected representatives and leaders. Within the positive range very different ratings of particular states would be possible.

When we start exploring more the problem of the quality of democratic leadership we have to ask ourselves to what extent are the failings due to the way in which institutions structure the political process and the recruitment of political elites. I have tried to do so in the comparison between presidential and parliamentary democracies. The populism in Latin American democracies is not unrelated to the style of politics made possible, even necessary, by presidentialism as the fractionalization and often irresponsibility of parties in Congress in such systems. The impact of electoral laws on party systems, the type of parliamentary leaders, etc., has often been noted while the impact of unenforceable and perhaps ill-advised laws about party financing in generating corruption remains to be analyzed. The consequences of democratization of many institutions – from saving banks to university trustees, from the judiciary to the boards of public enterprises – in creating what the Italians call "partitocrazia," the patronage of parties and with it opportunities for corruption, is another example. The laws about incompatibility of office and private activities on the quality of recruitment, would be worth further analysis. The burdens we are ready to impose on politicians, including the strains on their private and family life, cannot be ignored when we ask about the quality of politicians.

Beyond those basic institutional dimensions and their behavioral manifestations we want to focus on several others, some more easy to define, operationalize, and even observe and measure, and some more intangible.

Foremost we want to mention the quality of political personnel and leadership, not so much the quality of particular office holders (prime ministers and presidents) but what is sometimes called – with a term taken from Gaetano Mosca and Italian political discourse – the "political class." We mean the great majority of those who at different levels, both in government and opposition, aspire to gain the support of the voters. Already Joseph A. Schumpeter (1947: 290–291), among his five requirements for the functioning of democracy stressed this factor when he wrote:

Some thoughts on the victory and future of democracy   421

The conditions which I hold must be fulfilled for the democratic method to be a success ... The first condition is the human material of politics – the people who man the party machines, are elected to serve in parliament, rise to cabinet office – should be of sufficient high quality. This means more than that individuals of adequate ability and moral character must exist in sufficient numbers.

Indicators of the quality of the "political class" would be:

1. The proportion for whom politics is "a vocation" rather than just a way of making a living.
2. The commitment to some (obviously different for different parties) values or goals relevant for the collectivity, without, however, pursuing them irrespective of consequences. This means some mixture between being guided by a *Gesinnungsethik* and a *Verantwortungsethik*.
3. The amount of political corruption, relatively narrowly defined, as the use of power for private-personal ends, specifically enrichment, or to favor particular organizations or groups illegally.
4. The use or tolerance of illegal violence even against enemies of the state and democracy, even when a majority of citizens are ready to condone it.
5. Willingness to play with or use the disloyal opposition, revolutionary extremists or putchists, against other democratic forces or the institutions, to blackmail them or gain power. Semi-loyal oppositions in my view have been more crucial in the breakdown of democracy than the openly disloyal oppositions (Linz 1978: 32–34, 75–76).

The style of political discourse in the competition for power is also likely to affect the quality of democracy. There are forms of political behavior which, although undesirable, are relatively "normal" in some democracies. However, when carried to extremes and displacing other forms of political debate, they contribute to destroy the trust in politicians, the confidence in parties (not just a particular party), and even weaken the legitimacy of the democratic process. Those patterns might lead to the withdrawal from politics of qualified and potentially motivated persons, reducing the overall quality of the political class. I am thinking of levels of aggressiveness, unjustifiable lack of respect for opponents and their motivations, making cooperation and compromise impossible, even in the case of threats to democracy; appeals to the baser sentiments of the electorate, to prejudices and hatred, activating memories of past conflicts and bloodshed, ethnic hatred; demagoguery and outbidding, attempting to deceive the voters rather than disagreement on policies or interests; some forms of populism, defining the

422   *Juan J. Linz*

issues as between the "people" and "them" as part of a conspiracy or traitors of the national interest. It is obviously difficult to define and measure tolerable rather than destructive adversary politics and even more difficult to devise mechanisms to prevent the sliding into such patterns. Responsible, independent, and quick action by the courts and constructive actions of the media are the obvious responses. However, even more important is the effort of the moderate and prestigious leaders to dissociate themselves from such actions.

Even in the absence of such anti-democratic or destructive patterns of political competition there are in modern democracies sufficient reasons for criticism or ambivalence of citizens about political parties and politicians. Some arise out of contradictory conceptions and expectations in principle compatible with democracy, often held simultaneously by the voters. I just want to mention a few. People want parties to be united and support the policies of a government distrusting intra-party debates and conflict, but at the same time complain that politicians are obedient party loyalists without personality. Citizens want experienced leaders but at the same time reject the idea of professional politicians, even advocating the principle of no reelection. The voters complain about the fact that their representatives do not represent their specific interests sacrificing them to broader policy considerations, the government policy, but also criticize them for representing special interests (obviously other than their own). People feel that politicians lose touch with society, live in a world of their own, dependent on the party or office for their living, but at the same time advocate the incompatibility between running for office, representative mandates, and any other professional activity. We need to know more about how those contradictory images and expectations affect the perception of the quality of democracy.

Some of the quality of the political class will be determined by the "quality of the electorate," the readiness of the voters to support leaders with clearly negative characteristics on the one hand and on the other a public opinion disinterested in the quality of leaders. We could make a parallel list of negative characteristics of electorates in democracies. It is not always clear if undesirable leaders have "corrupted" the electorate, they often do, or if the voters for a variety of motives condone actions detrimental to the quality of democracy, not minding who would represent and govern them.

The political culture approach touches on some of these problems but having been developed in advanced stable democracies has focused more on citizen participation, on the sense of political efficacy, and on the rights of citizens than on the willingness to respond to, accept, or condone freely bad leadership.

Some thoughts on the victory and future of democracy 423

Considering participation and contestation the two basic dimensions of a democratic policy, the quality of democracy should be related to both. A democracy in which the right to participate in politics, from voting to other forms of legal participation, is limited unduly or subject to pressure or control by those in power or with power resources like employers (beyond the legitimate efforts to influence the voters) is deficient. Extremely high rates of participation *and* extraordinary majorities for one party or candidate (in presidential systems) are to be suspected. While the freedom not to participate, not to vote, or to vote blank should be respected, extremely low turnouts and many void votes can be indicators of a low level of support for democratic processes. Indeed, the two extremes of very high and very low participation can be signs of a crisis of democracy. Extreme levels of political mobilization may indicate that too much is at stake in an election, and very low levels indicate that leaders are not able to articulate the interests and preferences of citizens or a passive rejection of the whole democratic process.

The distinction between loyal and disloyal opposition is central, to which semi-loyal should be added as an important category. The style of democratic politics is largely determined by the style of opposition. There are better forms of democratic contestation than existential conflict, the "friend–foe" distinction of Carl Schmitt; the me-too-ism in which parties become indistinguishable; party competition that becomes disaggregated into competition between individual candidates (making parties incoherent and undisciplined and representatives of a congery of local or special interests); or a party system based on fractions following personalities with few distinct policy positions. Without advocating "a responsible two-party system" as an ideal, certainly between systems producing either a hegemonic party or an extremely fractionalized party system, there is a middle ground of a limited, moderate multiparty system with responsible parties offering real choices to the voters.

One of the great questions we will face as students of contemporary democracies is how to combine a critical analysis of their performance with a sense of proportion that would prevent us from delegitimizing them *in toto* in view of blatant and grievous failures. *Tout comprendre* is not *tout pardonner*, but the alternative is not to condemn everything. We should also be cautious not to be skeptical about the possible working of self-corrective mechanisms already in place or that can be introduced, including some constitutional changes, rather than looking for new utopian alternatives (after so much hope wasted over this century we should be more than cautious) or quick fixes. Our task as scholars and democrats is far from easy.

424   *Juan J. Linz*

NOTES

1 The complexity and psychology underlying "desencanto" is beautifully explored in Hirschman's chapter "On disappointment" (1982: 9–21).
2 I am taking on the title of the excellent book by Claus Offe (1994). See chapter 5: "Die 'Demokratische Revolution' in Osteuropa – eine neue Bewährungsprobe der Demokratietheorie . . ."
3 There is evidence analyzed in detail in Linz and Stepan (1996: particularly in chapter 21) that there is no "tight coupling" between economic performance (and the perception of that performance) and the legitimacy of democracy and democratic institutions in Eastern Europe. The data from the Latinobarometro directed by Marta Lagos for the four Southern Cone democracies that have just become available show the same pattern. The success of the Chilean economy and the many positive aspects of democracy in that country paradoxically have not resulted in a stronger commitment to democracy than in Uruguay, where people perceive the poorer performance of the economy and the weak prospects for the country.
4 This section is taken from the forthcoming book by Linz and Stepan 1996, where the argument is further developed.

REFERENCES

Berg-Schlosser, Dirk, and Mitchell, Jeremy, eds. forthcoming. *Conditions of Democracy in Europe 1919–1939. Systematic Case Studies.* London: MacMillan.
Chehabi, Houchang, and Linz, Juan J., eds. n.d. *Sultanistic Regimes,* chapter 1, "Sultanism: a type of non-democratic regime." Unpublished MS.
Cotler, Julio. 1994. *Política y sociedad en el Perú. Cambios y continuidades.* Lima: Instituto de Estudios Peruanos.
Dahl, Robert A. 1971. *Polyarchy, Participation and Opposition.* New Haven: Yale University Press.
Diamond, Larry. 1992. "Economic development and democracy reconsidered," in Gary Marks and Larry Diamond, eds., *Reexamining Democracy.* Newbury Park: Sage.
Di Palma, Giuseppe. 1990. *To Craft Democracies. An Essay on Democratic Transitions.* Berkeley: Berkeley University of California Press.
Di Palma, Giuseppe. 1986. "The European and the Central American experience," in Giuseppe DiPalma and Laurence Whitehead, eds., *The Central American Impasse.* London: Croom Helm.
Economist, The. 1995. Review of "Less poor, less democratic," April 22–28.
Ferrero Costa, Eduardo. 1992a. "Peru's presidential coup," *Journal of Democracy* 3: 28–40.
   ed. 1992b. *Proceso de retorno a la institucionalidad democrática en el Perú.* Lima: Centro Peruano de Estudios Internacionales (CEPEI).
Friedman, Steven. 1995. "South Africa, divided in a special way," in Larry Diamond, Juan J. Linz, and Seymour Martin Lipset, eds., *Politics in Developing Countries, Comparing Experiences with Democracy,* 2nd edn. Boulder: Lynn Rienner.

Some thoughts on the victory and future of democracy 425

Hirschman, Albert O. 1982. *Shifting Involvements. Private Interest and Public Action.* Princeton: Princeton University Press.

Huntington, Samuel P. 1991. *The Third Wave. Democratization in the Late Twentieth Century.* Norman: University of Oklahoma Press.

——— 1993. "The clash of civilizations?," *Foreign Affairs* 72 no. 3: 22–49.

Karl, Terry Lynn "The hybrid regimes of Central America," *Journal of Democracy* 6, 3: 72–86.

Linz, J. 1978. "Crisis, breakdown and reequilibration," vol. I of J. Linz and Alfred Stepan, eds., *The Breakdown of Democratic Regimes.* Baltimore: Johns Hopkins University Press.

——— 1981. "The legacy of Franco and Democracy," in Horst Baier, Hans Mathias Kepplinger and Kurt Reumann, eds., *Öffentliche Meinung und sozialer Wandel. Public Opinion and Social Change.* Opladen: Westdeutscher Verlag.

——— 1986. "Il fattore tempo nei mutamenti di regime," *Teoria Politica* 2.1: 3–47.

——— 1993. "State building and nation building," *European Review* 1, 4: 355–369.

——— 1994. "Presidential or parliamentary democracy: does it make a difference?," in J. Linz and Arturo Valenzuela, eds., *The Failure of Presidential Democracy.* Baltimore: Johns Hopkins University Press.

——— 1995. "Plurinazionalismo e Democrazia," *Rivista Italiana di Scienza Politica* 24, 1: 21–50.

Linz, Juan J., and Stepan, Alfred. 1996. *Problems of Democratic Transition and Consolidation. Southern Europe, South America and Post-Communist Europe.* Baltimore: Johns Hopkins University Press.

Lipset, Seymour M. 1959. "Some social requisites of democracy: economic development and political legitimacy," *American Political Science Review* 53: 69–105.

McClintock, Cynthia. 1993. "Peru's Fujimori: a caudillo derails democracy," *Current History* 92, no. 572: 112–119.

Maravall, José María. 1995. *Los resultados de la democracia.* Madrid: Alianza Editorial.

Offe, Claus. 1994. *Der Tunnel am Ende des Lichts. Erkundungen der Politischen Transformation im Neuen Osten.* Frankfurt/Main: Campus.

Olcott, Martha Brill. 1993. "Central Asia on its own," *Journal of Democracy* 4, 1: 92–103.

Panorama Centroamericano, Reporte Político. Guatemala: Instituto Centroamericano de Estudios Políticos (INCEP).

Rose, Richard. 1994. "What's in the change for democracy in Central and Eastern Europe? Testing the Churchill hypothesis," *Studies in Public Policy* no. 236. Centre for the Study of Public Policy. Glasgow: University of Strathclyde.

——— 1995. "Freedom as a fundamental value," *Studies in Public Policy* no. 242. Centre for the Study of Public Policy. Glasgow: University of Strathclyde.

Sartori, Giovanni. 1994. *Comparative Constitutional Engineering. An Inquiry into Structures. Incentives and Outcomes.* New York: New York University Press.

Schumpeter, Joseph A. 1947. *Capitalism, Socialism and Democracy.* New York: Harper & Brothers.

Weigel, George. 1990. "Catholicism and democracy: the other twentieth cen-

426   *Juan J. Linz*

tury revolution," in Brad Roberts, ed., *The New Democracies: Global Change and US Policy*. Cambridge: MIT Press.

Zimmermann, Ekkart. 1985. "The 1930s world economic crisis in six European countries: a first report on causes of political instability and reactions to crisis," in Paul M. Johnson and William R. Thompson, eds., *Rhythms in Politics and Economics*. New York: Praeger Special Studies.

1993. "Political breakdown and the process of national consensus formation: on the collapse of the Weimar Republic in comparative perspective," in *Research on Democracy and Society*, vol. I. Greenwich, Conn.: JAI Press.

Zimmermann, Ekkart, and Saalfeld, Thomas. 1988. "Economic and political reactions to the world economic crisis of the 1930s in six European countries", *International Studies Quarterly* 32: 305–34.

Index

Addi, Lahouari 5–6
Afghanistan 405
Africa 1, 8, 79, 196, 214–230, 242–257, 316–320, 333–334, 343–356, 377–392
aid foundations 48, 314–326, 328–332, 354, 372, 391, 394
Ake, Claude 9
Alesina, Alberto 198
Algeria 1, 105–119, 294, 353
   the army 105–108
   democratization of 115–118
   ideological limits 112–114
   the Islamist movement 108–112
Almond, Gabriel 374
Angola 330, 389
Apter, David 374
Arendt, Hannah 107, 112
Argentina 106, 347, 378
Aristotle 17, 126, 282–283
Asia 1, 79, 196–197, 228, 246, 271, 316–319, 346, 385
Atwood, Brian J. 386
Australia 144, 151, 358
Austria 17, 144–157

Bagehot, Walter 19
Baker, James 377, 386
Balkans 385, 406
Banda, Hastings 350
Banfield, Edward 374
Barkan, Joel 10
Barro, Robert J. 220, 225
Baudrillard, Jean 289
Beard, Charles 132
Becker, Gary 84
Belgium 150, 414
Belhadj, Ali 109
Bendjedid, Chadli 109
Benelux 410
Benin 349, 358, 373
Berlusconi, Silvio 2

Bhagwati, Jagdish 9
Bhalla, Surjit 7, 8, 198, 200
Biya, Paul 284
Bodin, J. 112
Bolivia 348
Bolshevism 10–21
Bosnia 294, 316, 405
Botswana 206, 214, 358
Brazil 74, 204, 335, 342, 378
British colonialism 72–73, 204
British Commonwealth 339, 372, 414
Buchanan, James 131
Bulgaria 128, 135, 331–332, 339
Burkina Faso 284
Burma 316, 325, 357
Burundi 206, 227, 294

Cambodia 318, 330, 339, 356
Cameroon 284, 339, 350–351
Canada 2, 130, 144, 150–153, 304, 313, 319, 328, 349, 358, 372
Cardoso, Fernando Henrique 74, 270
Carter, Jimmy 324, 347, 381
Case, Anne 29
Central America 325, 406
centralism 71–79, 243–247
Chad 350
Chile 167–168, 316, 339, 348–349, 373
China 1, 197, 209, 212–214, 316, 346, 359, 404–405
citizenship
   deliberative competence 5, 11, 81–104
   ideal of 100–104
   left-liberal republican position 82–83, 88–100
   libertarian position 82–88
   role of 81–83
Clermont-Tonerre 134
Clinton, Bill 305, 313, 346, 352, 386
Cohen, Joshua 97, 101
Cold War 178, 248, 282, 284, 287, 290, 314, 329, 352, 371, 373, 376–377

428   *Index*

Coleman, James 28, 374
Colombia 74, 311
colonialism 72–73
Comer, James 29
Conant, James B. 21, 22
Condorcet Jury Theorem 165
Confucian dummy 111–222, 208–211
Congo 350
constitution
    definition of 123–125
    models of 125–126
    Napoleonic constitution 126
    normative study of 137–138
    psychology of 131–137
Costa Rica 207, 227, 358
Cuba 304, 316, 373, 405
Czechoslovakia 286
Czech Republic 125, 132, 331

Dahl Robert 157, 311, 419
democracy
    autonomy 300
    cleavages 410–416
    closed model of 72
    consensus form of 147–149
    consociational form of 130, 144
    definition of 311
    distribution of power 78
    empirical criteria of 177–179
    established liberal democracies (ELD)
        297–301
    failure of 15–22
    fragile neo-democracies (FND) 297–
        306
    history of 282–285
    majoritarian form of 145–147
    national liberation 295–301
    political economy 78
    political institutions 73–75
    political leadership 71–79
    promotion of 335–359, 372–396
    quality of 10–11, 417–420
    reciprocal representation 303–307
    victory of 404–408
Denmark 149, 153, 154, 157, 313, 372,
    380
Diamond, Larry 9–10
Dobb, Maurice 264
Dominguez, Jorge I. 178
Dominican Republic 347, 348, 405
Dresang, Dennis 247
Drèze, Jean 166
Dubey, Ashutosh 225
Dunn, John 19, 276
Duverger, Maurice 374
Dworkin, Ronald 85

East Asia 164, 197–215, 227, 265, 359,
    377
East Europe 1, 22, 133–135, 202, 228,
    249–250, 314–359, 414
East Germany 213
economic growth
    democracy 161–169
    dictatorship 161–169
    empirical criteria of 178, 225
    model of 200–205, 214–228
Ecuador 347, 348
Egypt 204, 316
Eisenstadt, S.N. 243, 246
electoral rules
    majority rule 145–158
    proportional representation 145–158
El Salvador 311, 330, 333, 335, 339,
    348
Elster, Jon 6, 165
Enzensberger, Hans 289
Estonia 332
Ethiopia 286, 324, 382, 383, 389, 405
Europe 10, 15–17, 77, 196, 243–244,
    257, 271–272, 299, 345, 358, 374,
    381

Fascism 20–21, 143, 410
Finland 150, 152
Fishkin, James S. 86
France 4, 17–21, 117, 125–127, 133–
    135, 145, 150–154, 244–247, 269,
    312, 328, 339, 349–356
Franklin, Mark 151
Freedom House 205, 206, 311, 320,
    418
freedoms
    economic 200–210
    political 200–207
French Revolution 108, 243, 283,
    411
Friedrich, Carl 374
Fujimori, Alberto 333, 407

Gabon 350
Gaidar, Yegor 344
Galbraith, John Kenneth 263
Galenson, Walter 163, 178
Gallagher, Michael 154
Gambia 350
Gastil, Raymond D. 206, 214, 227
de Gaulle, Charles 20, 21, 127
General Social Survey (GSS) 38, 49, 51
    52
Germany 17–21, 94, 99, 128, 138, 148,
    244, 304, 305, 313, 349, 372, 380,
    391, 414

Index

Ghana 250, 373
globalization
  demise of the social 287–290
  democracy 278, 285
  High Standards' countries 267
  impact of 268–272, 290–294
  Low Standards' countries 267
  nation-state 285–287
  sovereignty 273–277
Great Britain 15, 73, 124, 128, 148–153, 244, 269, 312, 328, 349–351, 372, 385, 391
Great Depression 18, 250
Greece 272–273, 300, 331
Grenada 348
Grofman, Bernard 376
Grossman, Herschel I. 164, 165
Guatemala 311, 348
Gurr, Ted Robert 143

Habermas, Jürgen 289
Haiti 207, 316, 330, 333, 335, 359, 405
Hakim, Peter 333
Hamilton, Alexander 145, 283
Harris Alienation Index 36
Harrod–Domar model 264
Harsanyi, John C. 86
Havel, Václav 22
Hayek, Friedrich August von 199, 210
Hegel, Friedrich 288
Helliwell, John F. 198, 199
Herbst, Jeffrey 250
Heston, Alan 224–225
Hitler, Adolf 18
Hobbes, Thomas 107
Honduras 348
Hong Kong 197, 209–212, 265
Hopkins, Gerald Manley 266
Horowitz, Donald 376
Hungary 125, 325, 331, 407
Huntington, Samuel P. 163, 178, 247, 250, 335, 348, 375, 405–406
Huxley, Aldous 263
Hydén, Göran 8

Iceland 154
India 73–74, 117, 128, 131, 196–197, 200–201, 204, 227, 265, 276–277, 311
Indonesia 1, 359, 404–405
intergovernmental organizations (IGOs) 46, 58, 74, 249, 264–268, 269–271, 274–278, 186, 301–306, 319, 329–334, 336, 343–345, 347–348, 351, 354–355, 359, 372, 385, 394
interwar period 17–22

Iran 405
Iraq 316
Ireland 153, 154
Islam 5–6, 72, 105–116, 346, 405
Israel 124, 144, 148, 157
Italy 2, 20, 30, 131, 150, 340, 407, 420
Ivory Coast 350

Japan 2, 127, 144, 153, 209–212, 265, 269, 272, 278, 304, 312, 328, 344, 349–357, 372
Jillson, Calvin 131

Katz, Lawrence 29
Kennedy, John F. 375
Kenya 206, 252–253, 284, 316, 339, 350–354, 378, 383–384, 389, 393–394
Khaldun, Ibu 4
Khattab, Omar Ibn 110
Kingsley, Donald J. 246–247
Kohli, Atul 4–5, 10, 264
Korea 212, 348, 396
Kuznet's curve 223
Kydland–Prescott variety 165
Kymlicka, Will 89

Labor Department's Current Population Survey (CPS) 46
La Palombara, Joseph 178
Latin America 1, 79, 196, 225–228, 248–249, 270–271, 313–317, 325, 340, 343, 327–377, 406, 414, 420
Le Pen, Jean Marie 2
League of Nations 17
Lee, Jong-Wha 220, 225
Levine, Ross 221
Lewis, Sir Arthur 144
Liberia 204, 316, 324, 405
Lijphart, Arend 6, 376, 415
Limongi, Fernando 7, 135, 198
Lindsay, A. D. 15, 22
Linz, Juan 10–11, 420
Lipset, Seymour M. 178, 203, 374–375
Lithuania 407, 414
de Long, Bradford J. 221, 223
Luxembourg 152–157
Lycurgus 126

Macaulay, Thomas 165, 283
Madagascar 350
Madison, James 136, 283–284
Magna Carta 129
Malawi 339, 350, 355, 394–396
Malaysia 212, 359
Mali 350

430   *Index*

Mandela, Nelson 349
Mankiw, G. 202
Mann, Thomas 16
Marx, Karl 72, 165, 242, 264, 410
Masaryk, T. G. 19
Mason, George 131
Mauritius 206
Mead, Walter Russell 267
Medani, Abbassi 109
Meles, Zanawi 383
Merghani, Hamza 247
Mexico 268–269, 274–277, 304, 316
Middle East 1, 316
Mill, John Stuart 6, 10, 16, 89, 144–148,
    151–154, 157, 158
Mitterand, François 351
Moi, Arap 284, 340
Moldovia 332
Moore, Barrington 374

Namibia 316, 329–330, 381, 391, 396
Nash equilibrium 267
Nehru, Vikram 225
Nelson, Joan M. 178
Netherlands, The 313, 349, 372, 382,
    385, 389, 414
New Deal 20, 41
new democracies 408–423
New Zealand 2, 124, 144, 150, 153
Nicaragua 316, 324, 330, 339, 373, 378,
    405
Niebuhr, Reinhold 21
Niemi, Richard 151
Niger 350
Nigeria 1, 73, 106, 206, 316, 335, 350–
    351, 357, 394
Noh, Suk Jae 164, 165
non-governmental organizations (NGOs)
    41, 46–47, 51–52, 58, 275–278, 302,
    312–339, 356, 358, 372–397, 415,
    418
North, Douglass 3
North Korea 213
Norway 152–154,157, 313, 349, 372,
    380

Offe, Claus 5, 11, 410
Olson, Mancur 61, 165
Orwell, George 263
Osiatynski, Wiktor 129

Pakistan 131, 311, 357
Panama 204, 339, 348
Paraguay 333
patrimonialism 248–257

Perot, Ross 151, 417
Peru 333, 342, 348, 406–407
Philippines 204, 311, 339, 347–348, 373
    378, 396
Pilsudski, Marshal 20
Poland 19–20, 125, 129, 133–134, 316,
    325, 332, 344–348, 406–407, 414
political parties 75–76, 418–420
populism 71–79
Portugal 74, 348
Prussia 16, 126, 244
Przeworski, Adam 7–8, 135, 163, 198
public administration
    accessibility 253–256
    rise of 242–251
    transparency 251–253
Putnam, Robert 5, 340

Reagan, Ronald 315, 347–348
Renelt, David 221
Ricardo, David 283
Riggs, Fred 246
Riker, William H. 147
Robespierre, Maximilien de 134
Roman empire 243
Romania 128, 134, 331–332, 405, 418
Romer, D. 202
Roosevelt, Franklin 20
Roosevelt, Theodore 17
Rostow, Walt, 375
Rousseau, Jean-Jacques 4
Russia 304, 317, 324–325, 344–345,
    357–358, 389, 407
Russian Revolution 16, 108
Rwanda 294, 357, 388

Sachs, Jeffrey 344
Sah, Raj 165, 214
Scandinavia 157, 377, 385
Schaffer, Bernard 247
Schmitt, Carl 21, 423
Schmitter, Philippe 9
Schumpeter, Joseph A. 21, 420
de Schweinitz, Karl, Jr. 163, 178
Sen, Amartaya 166
Serbia 316
Serrano, Jorge 348
Shils, Edward 245
Singapore 196–197, 209, 265, 359
Slovakia 331
Smith, Adam 266
social capital
    definition 31
    erosion of 56–63
    role of 28–31
    trends in participation 31–56

Index

Solon 126
Solow model 198, 202
Somalia 286, 294, 388, 405
Soros, George 325
South Africa 1, 316–318, 325, 339, 346–349, 358, 380, 384, 389–396, 405
South Europe 133, 143
South Korea 164, 197, 204, 209, 213, 265, 339, 348–349, 378
sovereign national states 298
Soviet Union 1, 20, 166, 178, 249–251, 286, 316–319, 324–325, 331–332, 374, 378, 405, 409
Spain 1, 133, 138, 268, 404, 414
Sparta 126
Sri Lanka 200, 201, 227
state aid agencies 10, 313–315, 319, 325–329, 337, 372–377, 381–387, 391–392
Stepan, Alfred 404, 408, 420
Stern, Fritz 4, 15
Stiglitz, Joseph E. 165
Sudan 294, 316, 357
Summers, Lawrence H. 221, 223
Summers, Robert 224–225
Sunstein, Cass 88, 90, 95–99, 135
Surinam 333
Swanson, Eric 225
Sweden 153–157, 313, 328, 349, 354–356, 372
Switzerland 150–158

Taiwan 208–212, 265, 348–349
Tanzania 204, 373, 381, 396
Thailand 204, 276, 277, 357, 396
Thompson, Victor 247
Tibet 316
Tingsten, Herbert 3
Tocqueville, Alexis de 2, 4–5, 16–17, 27–28, 31, 56, 62–63, 89, 102
Togo 351
Turkey 311, 331, 346–347, 357, 415

Uganda 394, 396
Ukraine 358
United Nations 269, 286, 329–334, 348, 359, 372, 380, 394
United States 4, 10, 16–17, 17–63, 99, 102, 117, 123, 127, 132–133, 144, 150–153, 178, 212, 227, 269–277, 302–304, 312–320, 326–334, 339–352, 357–359, 371–382, 386–391, 410, 414, 417
Uruguay 347, 348
Uslaner, Eric 55

Vanberg, Viktor 131
Venezuela 74, 311, 342
Verba, Sidney 374
Versailles, Treaty of 18, 137
Vietnam 316, 357, 372–373

Wallerstein, Michael 165
Walzer, Michael 62–63
Washington consensus 273
Weber, Max 17, 93, 242–243, 257, 417
Weil, D. 202
Weimar Republic 4, 17–19, 414
Weizsäcker, Richard von 21
West Europe 1, 144, 249, 301, 347, 414
West Germany 213
Westphalia, Treaty of 276–277
Whitten, Guy 151
Wilson, William Julius 29
Wilson, Woodrow 16, 17
World Values Survey 55
World War I 15–17
Wuthnow, Robert 41, 48–49

Yugoslavia 286, 411

Zaire 316, 350, 353, 394, 405
Zambia 247, 311, 316, 334, 339–340, 378, 383, 394
Zeroual, Liamin 109

For EU product safety concerns, contact us at Calle de José Abascal, 56–1°,
28003 Madrid, Spain or eugpsr@cambridge.org.

www.ingramcontent.com/pod-product-compliance
Ingram Content Group UK Ltd.
Pitfield, Milton Keynes, MK11 3LW, UK
UKHW020349060825
461487UK00008B/594